THE DAILIES AND SUNDAYS

1973

THE WIZARD OF ID: DAILIES AND SUNDAYS 1973

ISBN: 9781848566859

Published by Titan Books, a division of Titan Publishing Group Ltd., 144 Southwark St, London, SE1 0UP

A CIP catalogue record for this title is available from the British Library.

Special thanks to Annalisa Califano and Beatrice Doti at Panini, Brian Crane, and Patti Pomeroy.

First published: September 2013

1 3 5 7 9 10 8 6 4 2

Printed in China

What do you think of this book? We love to hear from our readers. Please email us at readerfeedback@titanemail.com, or write to us at the above address.

To receive advance information, news, competitions, and exclusive offers online, please sign up for the titan newsletter on our website: www.titanbooks.com

THE DAILIES AND SUNDAYS

1973

Brant Parker & Johnny Hart

Titan Books

FOREWORD BY BRIAN CRANE

A couple of weeks ago I was taking a walk in the desert near my home and I happened to notice a large, flat rock that I thought would look perfect atop the water feature in my back yard. So I hurried home, got my pickup truck and drove back to the rock. I realized, in the sensible, logical part of my brain, that I should probably wait until I could get a friend to help me lift the rock into the truck. But, in the self-delusional, egotistical part of my brain, which is very large, by the way, I was sure I could handle it by myself. So I bent over, grasped the rock in a firm, manly grip, and with a mighty heave, threw my back into blinding paroxysms of pain. Thankfully, the agony has gradually subsided a bit since then, but even now, as I am writing this, I have to be careful how I sit, in order to avoid a recurrence of the pain. I guess I deserved it, though. To quote the great philosopher, John Wayne, "Life is tough, but it's even tougher when you're stupid."

What, you may ask, does any of this have to do with this new collection of the complete Wizard of Id comic strips from 1973? The answer is, absolutely nothing.

Except that I have found that laughing out loud really makes the pain in my back get a lot worse! And reading Wizard of Id strips does tend to make one laugh out loud. So, after a few painful attempts, I have had to force myself not to read any Wizard of Id comics in preparing for this assignment. However, assuming that you have a healthy spinal column, I have no hesitation in heartily recommending them to you.

I must confess that, in addition to the aching back, I have another disadvantage in writing this foreword. And that is that I never had the opportunity of actually meeting the creators, Johnny Hart and Brant Parker. And sadly, since they are both now gone, the chances of ever getting that opportunity are looking less and less likely.

A few years after my own comic strip, "Pickles," was syndicated, I sent a fan letter to Johnny Hart. This was a very non-typical thing for me to do. I am not one to write fan letters. And even if I were to write one, I would most likely think better of it before I got to the mail box and would quickly feed it into the shredder. But I somehow felt a connection to Johnny Hart. And so I penned a few lines of admiration to him. Since I didn't have his address, I sent the letter to him in care of his syndicator.

Sadly, I never received a reply to that letter. I knew that he probably received a huge amount of fan letters, and so I did not think any the less of him for not responding to mine. I just assumed he was way too busy to answer every fawning fan letter he got. I mentioned this recently to Johnny's daughter Patti, and she told me that she was sure he had never received my letter, because he was a big fan of "Pickles" and he surely would have answered it if it had made its way into his hands.

Of course I didn't believe her. Having grown up around cartoonists,

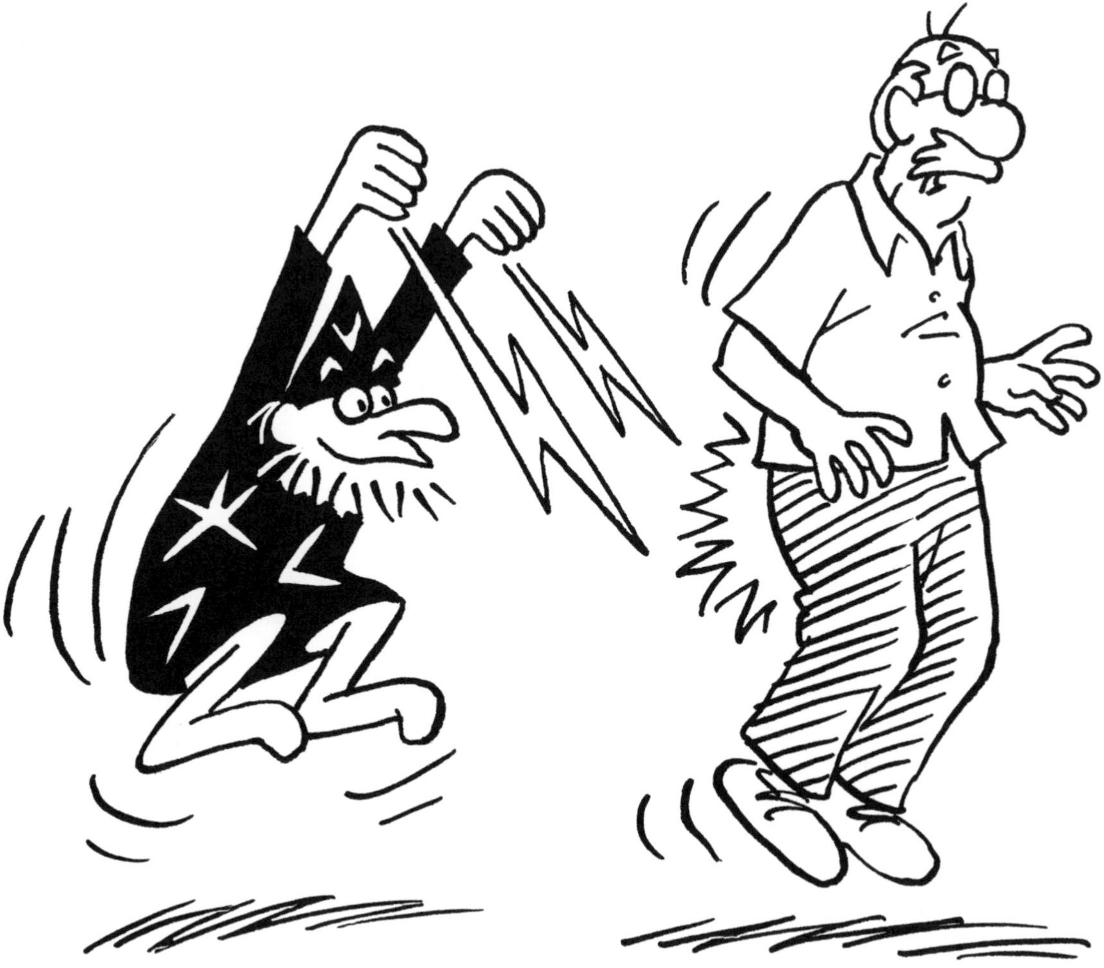

The Wizard & Earl by Brian Crane

Blanche & Opal by Brian Crane

she undoubtedly knew what enormous egos we all have, so I figured she was just being kind, and sparing my insecure cartoonist feelings. However, later on, Patti's sons, Mason and Mick Mastroianni both verified that what she had said was true. Johnny Hart was a true "Pickles" fan.

Wow. This was monumentally gratifying news to me! As a twelve year old paper boy, I used to read "B.C." and later on "Wizard of Id" as I folded my papers in the early morning hours, and I would dream the impossible dream that someday I might be a comic strip artist just like Johnny Hart and Brant Parker.

But then it dawned on me that Mason and Mick are cartoonists themselves, working on Wizard of Id. And you can never believe what other cartoonists tell you about your work. They always lie and tell you how much they love your work, no matter how lousy they really think it is. So now I don't know what to believe.

But in the end, it doesn't really matter. What really matters is that my back start feeling better soon, so I can get back to reading Wizard of Id and getting some laughs.

CAST OF CHARACTERS

WIZARD OF ID
A sincere if only sporadically successful magician.

RODNEY
A cowardly knight.

THE KING
The pint-sized despot who rules the land of Id. A tyrant's tyrant.

CAST OF CHARACTERS

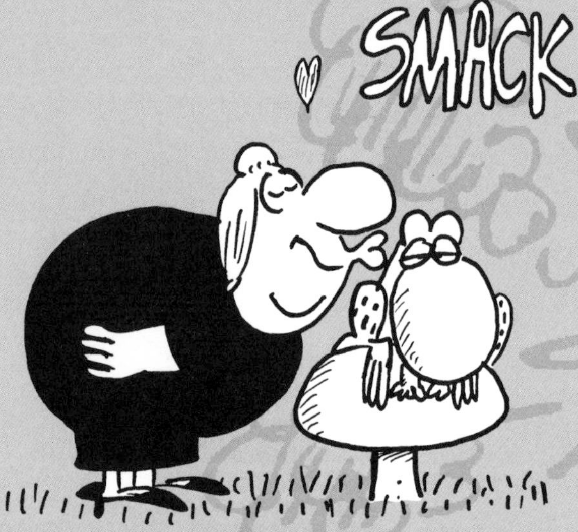
SMACK

BLANCHE
The Wizard's worse half.

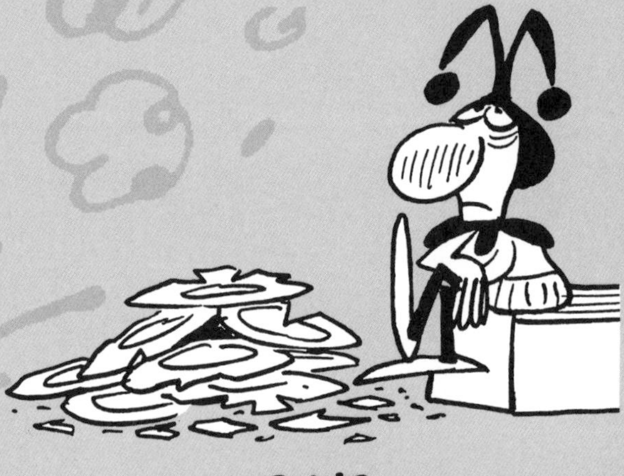

BUNG
A court jester, full of spirit…
liters of spirit!

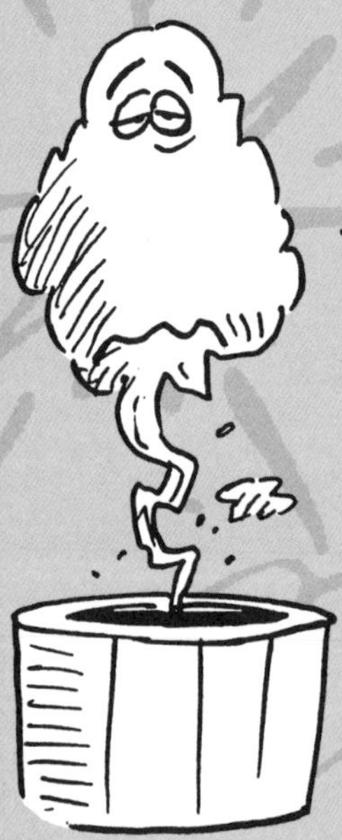

THE EVIL SPIRIT
A magical creature wished into being.

CAST OF CHARACTERS

SPOOK
A filthy hairball, held against his will.

THE PEASANTS
A seething mass of humanity and the focus of the king's seething rage.

LARSON E. PETTIFOGGER
An unscrupulous shyster.

GWEN
A sweet flower, whose love buds only for Rodney.

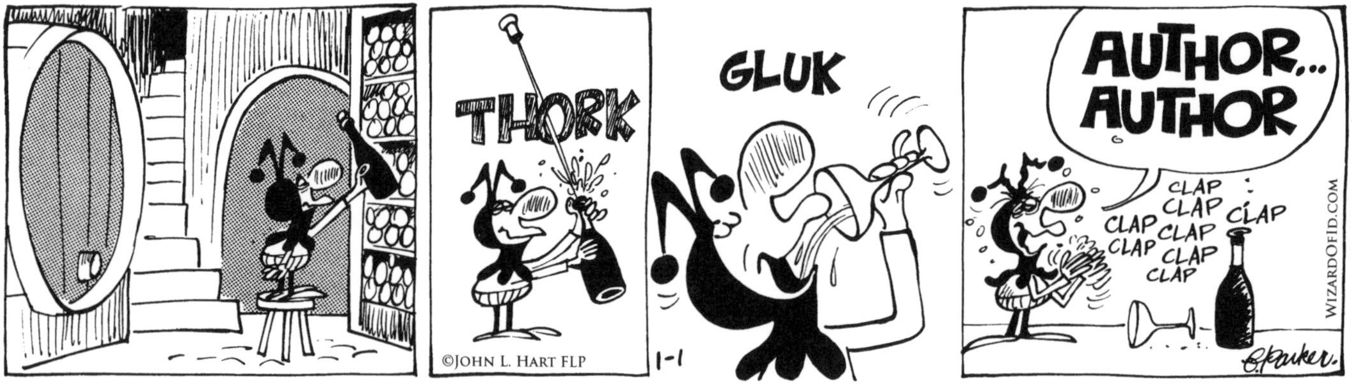

THORK
©JOHN L. HART FLP
GLUK
1-1
AUTHOR... AUTHOR
CLAP CLAP CLAP CLAP CLAP CLAP CLAP CLAP
WIZARDOFID.COM

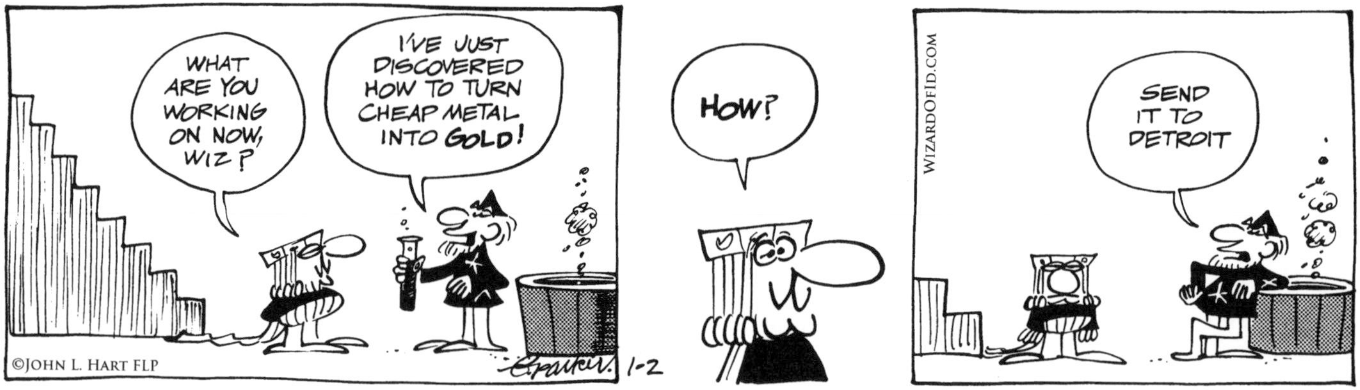

WHAT ARE YOU WORKING ON NOW, WIZ?
I'VE JUST DISCOVERED HOW TO TURN CHEAP METAL INTO GOLD!
©JOHN L. HART FLP
1-2
HOW?
WIZARDOFID.COM
SEND IT TO DETROIT

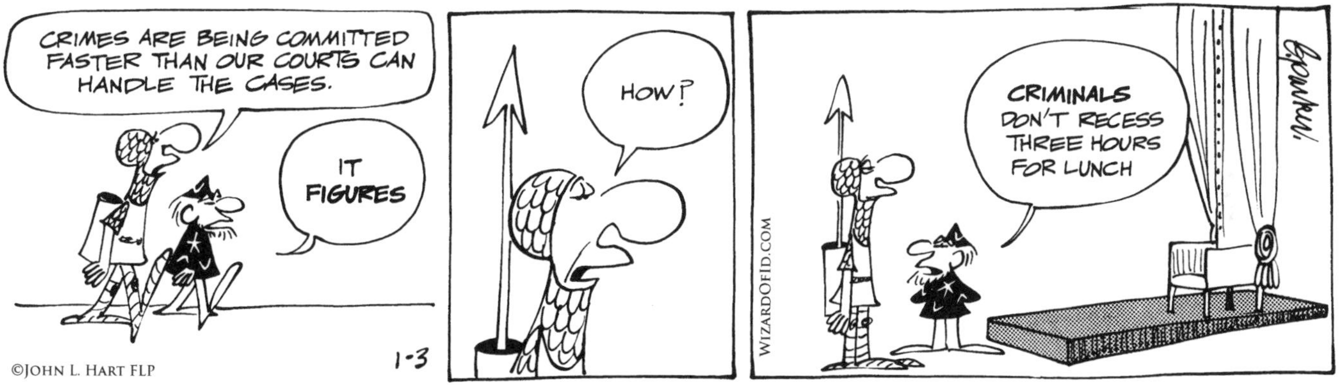
CRIMES ARE BEING COMMITTED FASTER THAN OUR COURTS CAN HANDLE THE CASES.
IT FIGURES
HOW?
CRIMINALS DON'T RECESS THREE HOURS FOR LUNCH
©JOHN L. HART FLP
1-3
WIZARDOFID.COM

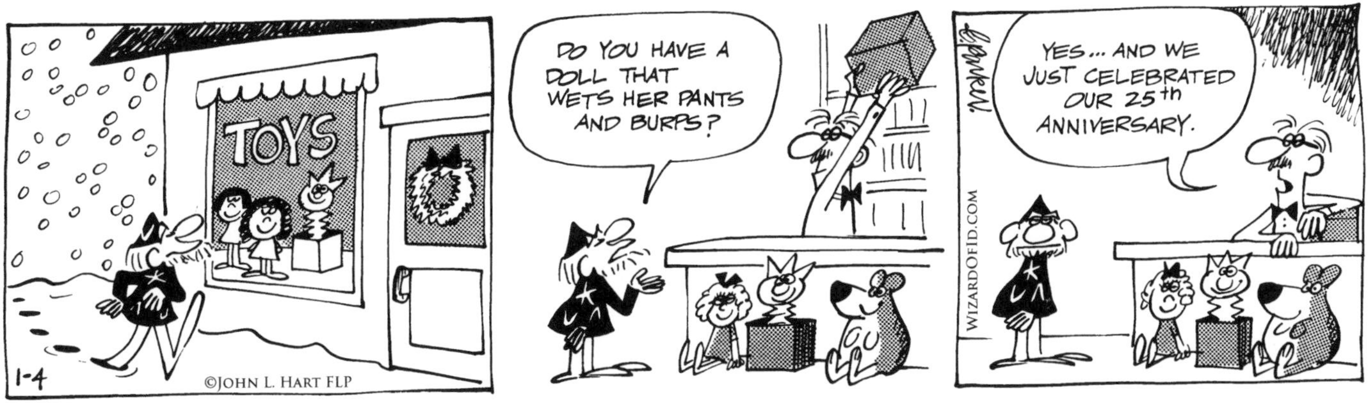
TOYS
DO YOU HAVE A DOLL THAT WETS HER PANTS AND BURPS?
YES... AND WE JUST CELEBRATED OUR 25th ANNIVERSARY.
1-4
©JOHN L. HART FLP
WIZARDOFID.COM

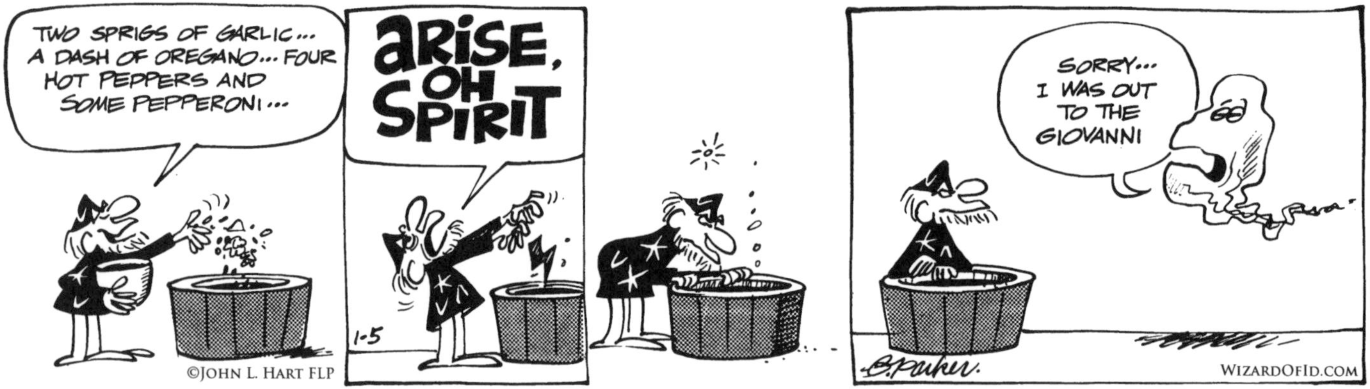
TWO SPRIGS OF GARLIC... A DASH OF OREGANO... FOUR HOT PEPPERS AND SOME PEPPERONI...
ARISE, OH SPIRIT
SORRY... I WAS OUT TO THE GIOVANNI
1-5
©JOHN L. HART FLP
WIZARDOFID.COM

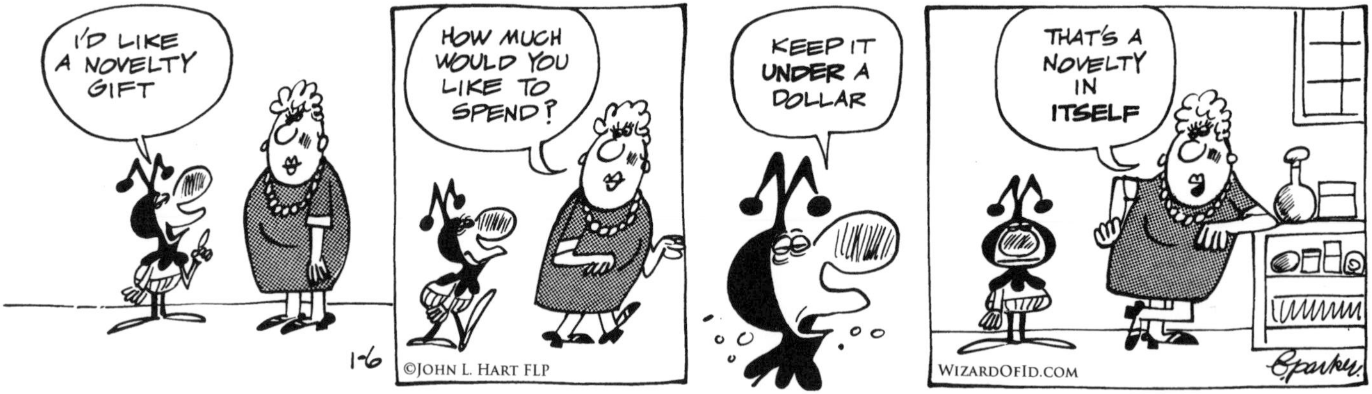
I'D LIKE A NOVELTY GIFT
HOW MUCH WOULD YOU LIKE TO SPEND?
KEEP IT **UNDER** A DOLLAR
THAT'S A NOVELTY IN **ITSELF**
1-6
©JOHN L. HART FLP
WIZARDOFID.COM

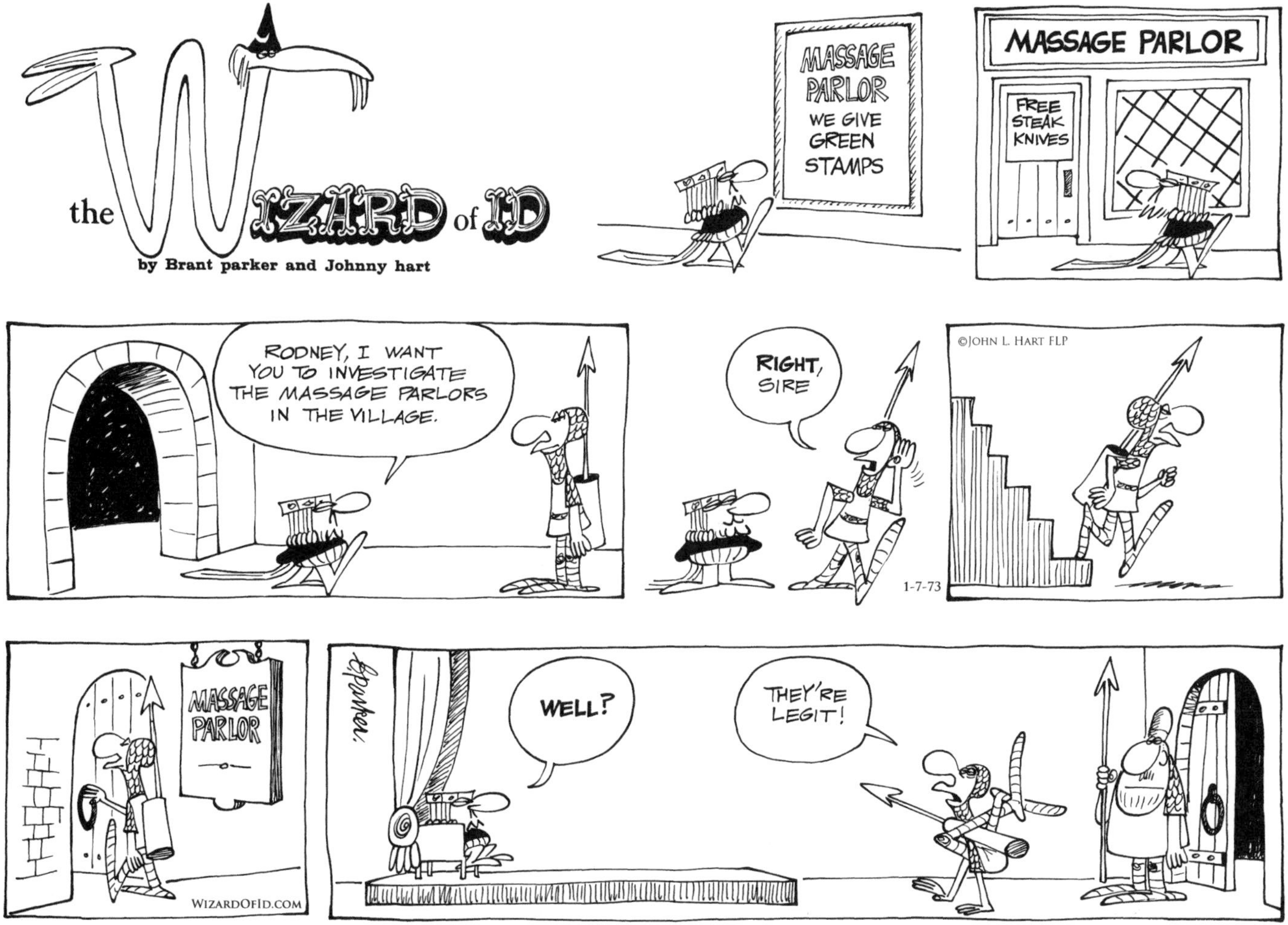
the WIZARD of ID
by Brant parker and Johnny hart
MASSAGE PARLOR
WE GIVE GREEN STAMPS
MASSAGE PARLOR
FREE STEAK KNIVES
RODNEY, I WANT YOU TO INVESTIGATE THE MASSAGE PARLORS IN THE VILLAGE.
RIGHT, SIRE
1-7-73
©JOHN L. HART FLP
MASSAGE PARLOR
WIZARDOFID.COM
WELL?
THEY'RE LEGIT!

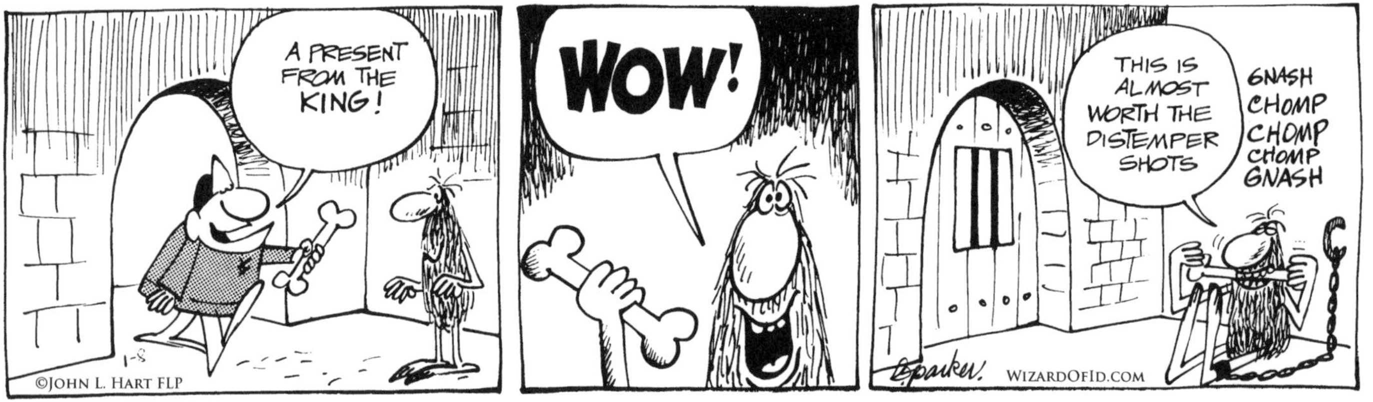
A PRESENT FROM THE KING!
1-8
©JOHN L. HART FLP
WOW!
THIS IS ALMOST WORTH THE DISTEMPER SHOTS
GNASH CHOMP CHOMP CHOMP GNASH
WIZARDOFID.COM

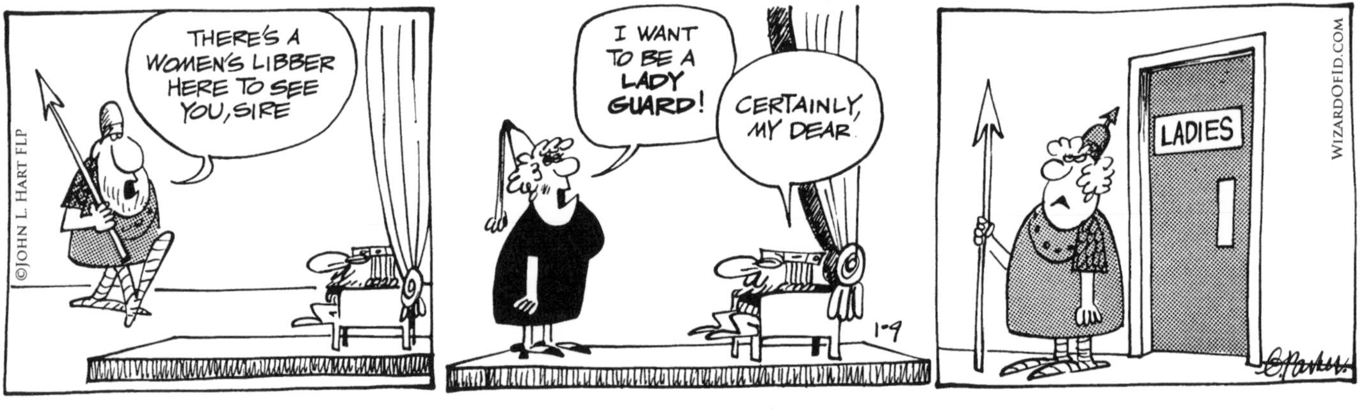
©JOHN L. HART FLP
THERE'S A WOMEN'S LIBBER HERE TO SEE YOU, SIRE
I WANT TO BE A LADY GUARD!
CERTAINLY, MY DEAR
1-9
LADIES
WIZARDOFID.COM

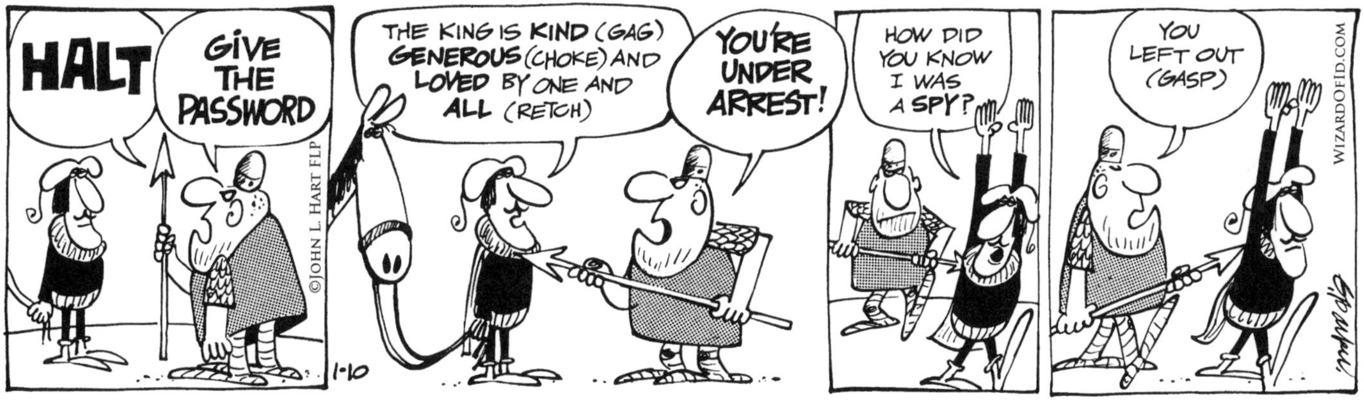
HALT
GIVE THE PASSWORD
©JOHN L. HART FLP
THE KING IS KIND (GAG) GENEROUS (CHOKE) AND LOVED BY ONE AND ALL (RETCH)
YOU'RE UNDER ARREST!
1-10
HOW DID YOU KNOW I WAS A SPY?
YOU LEFT OUT (GASP)
WIZARDOFID.COM

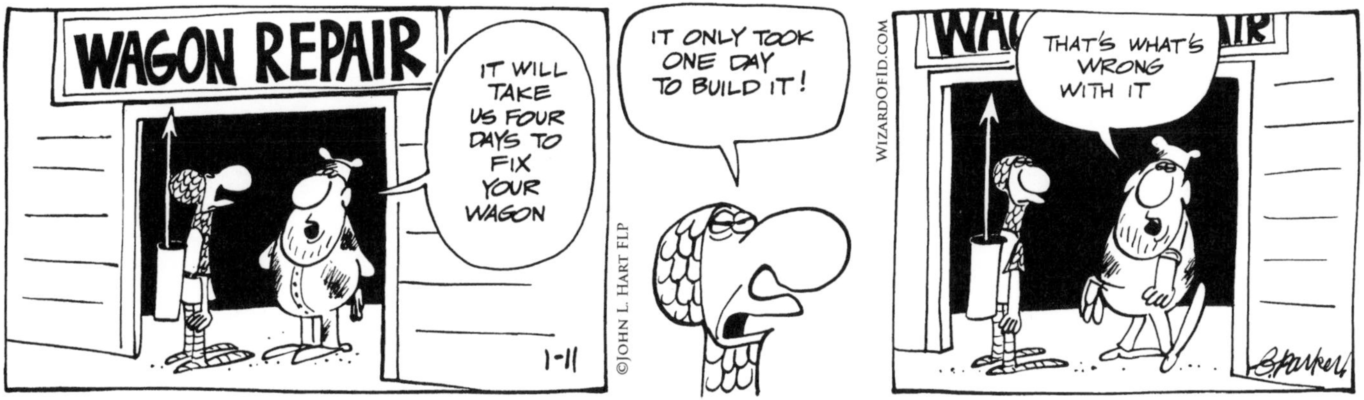
WAGON REPAIR
IT WILL TAKE US FOUR DAYS TO FIX YOUR WAGON
1-11
©JOHN L. HART FLP
IT ONLY TOOK ONE DAY TO BUILD IT!
WIZARDOFID.COM
THAT'S WHAT'S WRONG WITH IT

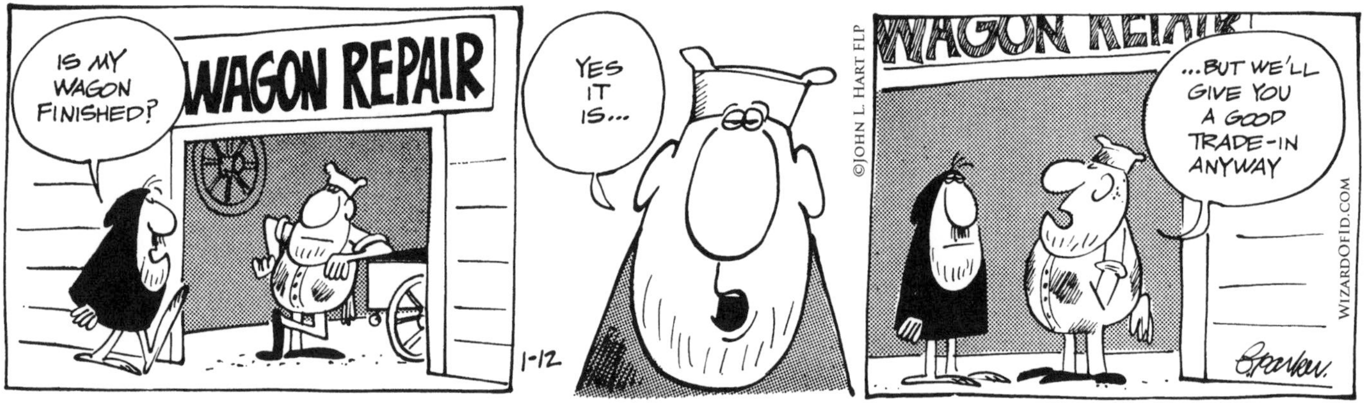

IS MY WAGON FINISHED?
WAGON REPAIR
1-12
YES IT IS...
©JOHN L. HART FLP
...BUT WE'LL GIVE YOU A GOOD TRADE-IN ANYWAY
WIZARDOFID.COM

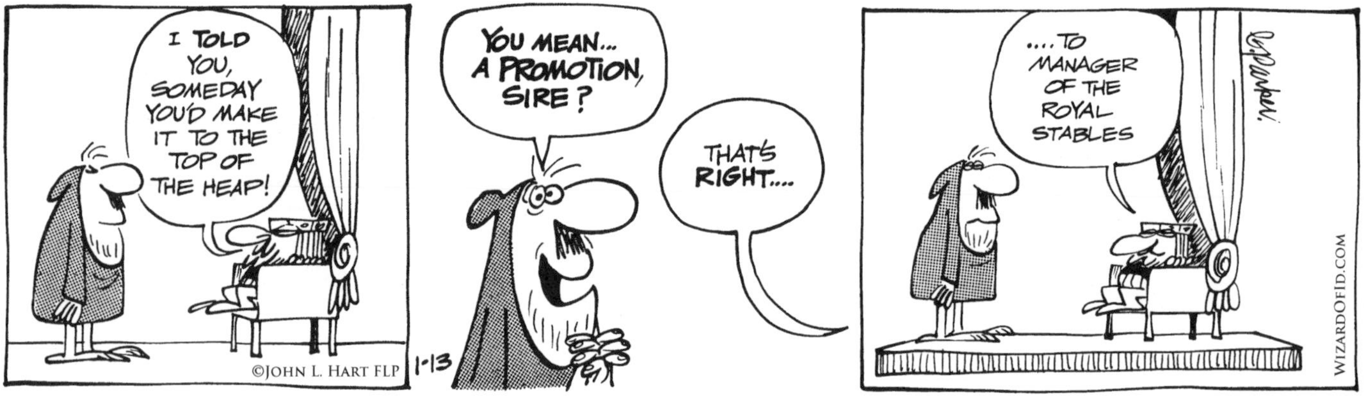

I TOLD YOU, SOMEDAY YOU'D MAKE IT TO THE TOP OF THE HEAP!
©JOHN L. HART FLP
1-13
YOU MEAN... A PROMOTION, SIRE?
THAT'S RIGHT....
....TO MANAGER OF THE ROYAL STABLES
WIZARDOFID.COM

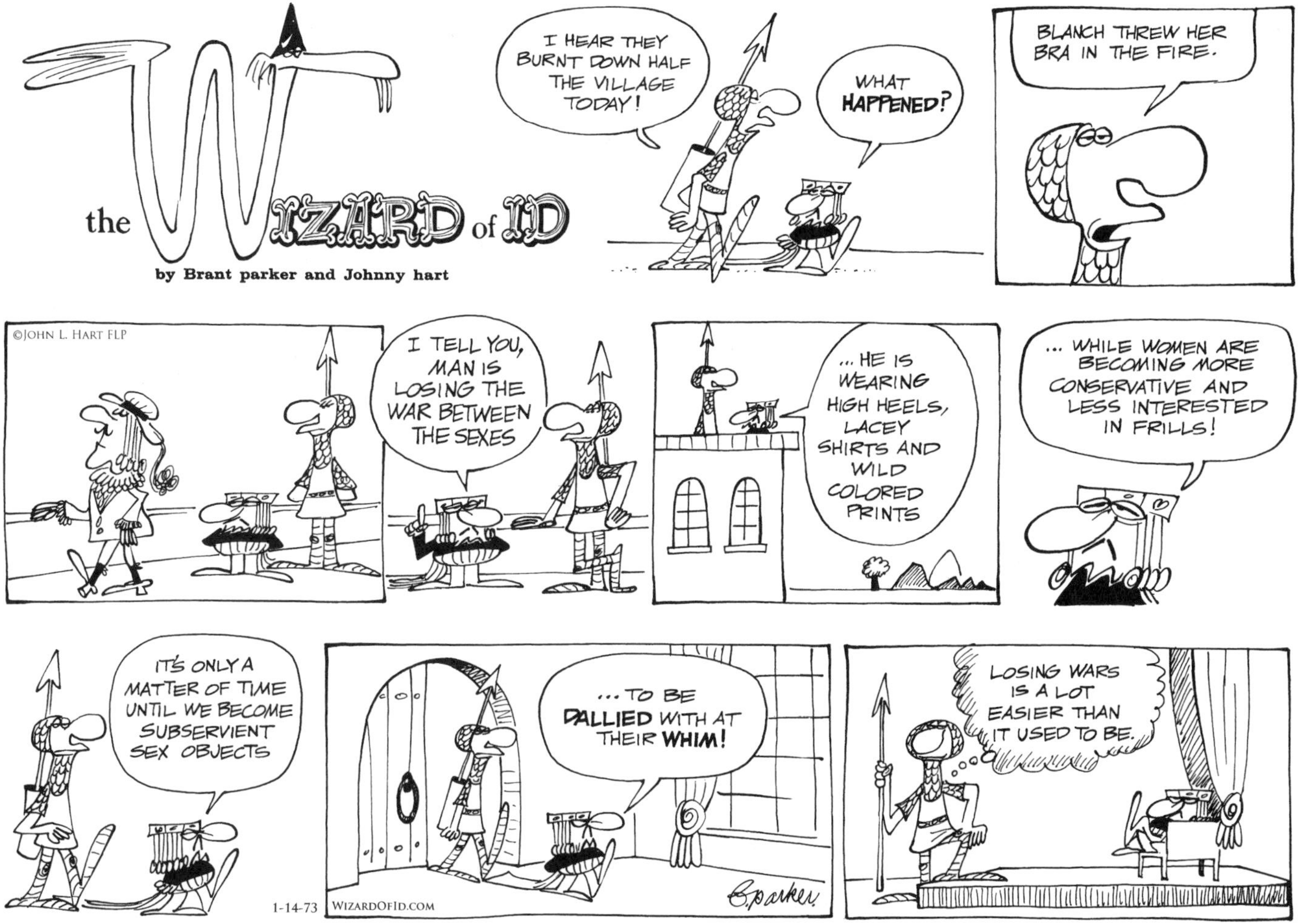
the WIZARD of ID
by Brant parker and Johnny hart
I HEAR THEY BURNT DOWN HALF THE VILLAGE TODAY!
WHAT HAPPENED?
BLANCH THREW HER BRA IN THE FIRE.
©JOHN L. HART FLP
I TELL YOU, MAN IS LOSING THE WAR BETWEEN THE SEXES
... HE IS WEARING HIGH HEELS, LACEY SHIRTS AND WILD COLORED PRINTS
... WHILE WOMEN ARE BECOMING MORE CONSERVATIVE AND LESS INTERESTED IN FRILLS!
IT'S ONLY A MATTER OF TIME UNTIL WE BECOME SUBSERVIENT SEX OBJECTS
... TO BE DALLIED WITH AT THEIR WHIM!
LOSING WARS IS A LOT EASIER THAN IT USED TO BE.
1-14-73
WIZARDOFID.COM
B. parker

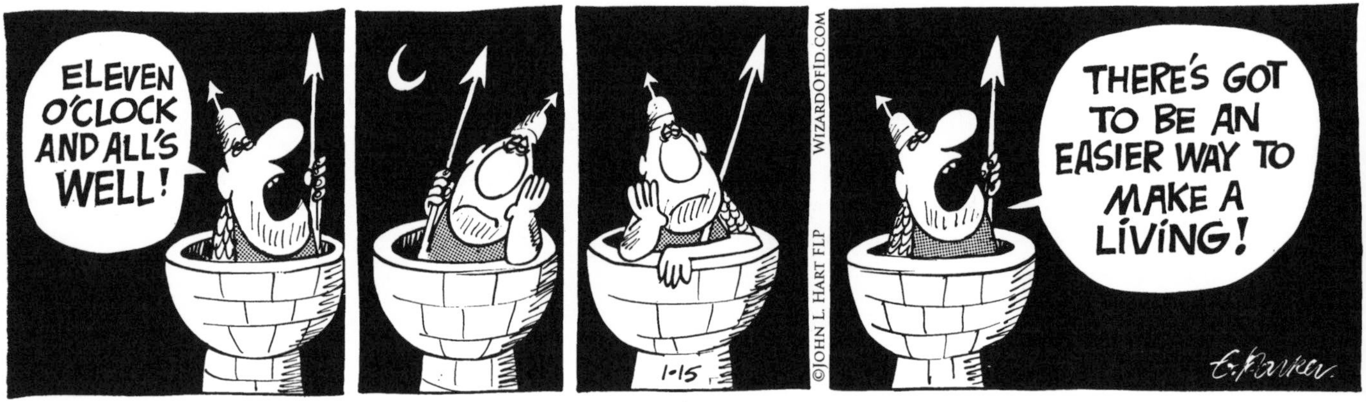
ELEVEN O'CLOCK AND ALL'S WELL!
1-15
©JOHN L. HART FLP
WIZARDOFID.COM
THERE'S GOT TO BE AN EASIER WAY TO MAKE A LIVING!

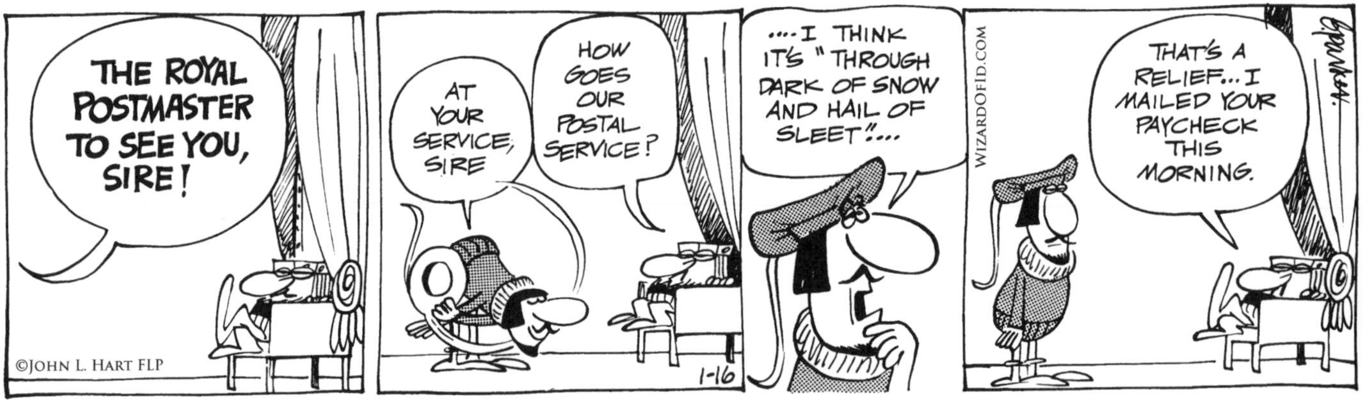
THE ROYAL POSTMASTER TO SEE YOU, SIRE!
©JOHN L. HART FLP
AT YOUR SERVICE, SIRE
HOW GOES OUR POSTAL SERVICE?
1-16
....I THINK IT'S "THROUGH DARK OF SNOW AND HAIL OF SLEET"....
WIZARDOFID.COM
THAT'S A RELIEF... I MAILED YOUR PAYCHECK THIS MORNING.

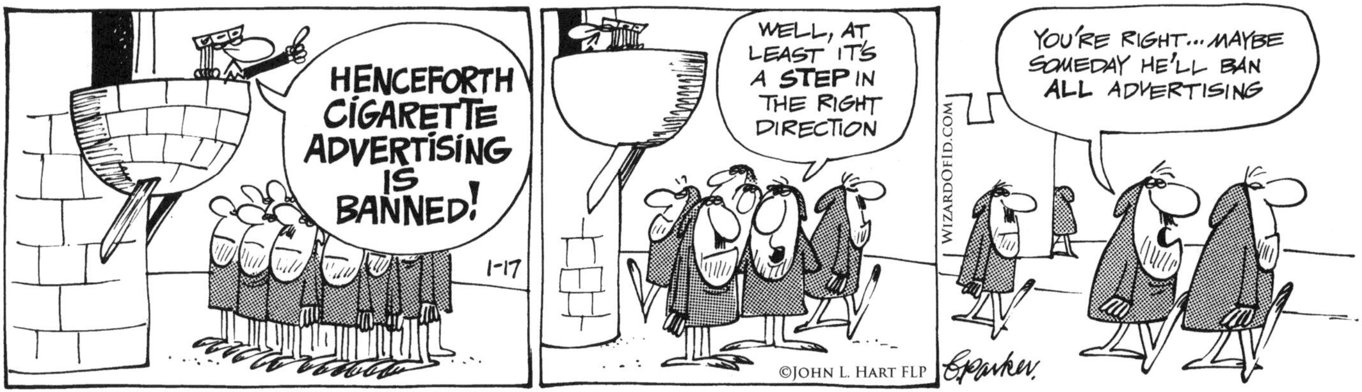
HENCEFORTH CIGARETTE ADVERTISING IS BANNED!
1-17
WELL, AT LEAST IT'S A STEP IN THE RIGHT DIRECTION
©JOHN L. HART FLP
WIZARDOFID.COM
YOU'RE RIGHT... MAYBE SOMEDAY HE'LL BAN ALL ADVERTISING

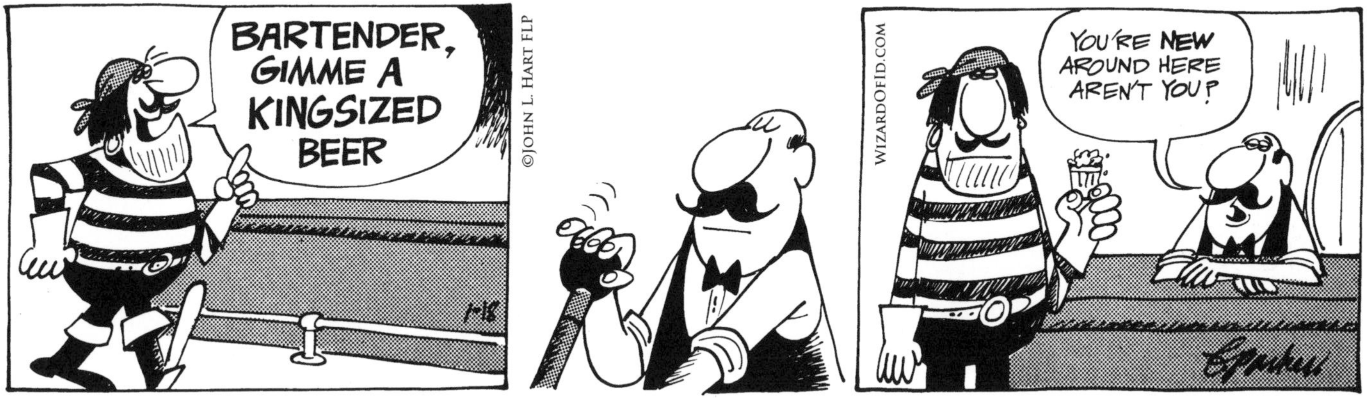
BARTENDER, GIMME A KINGSIZED BEER
1-18
©JOHN L. HART FLP
WIZARDOFID.COM
YOU'RE NEW AROUND HERE AREN'T YOU?

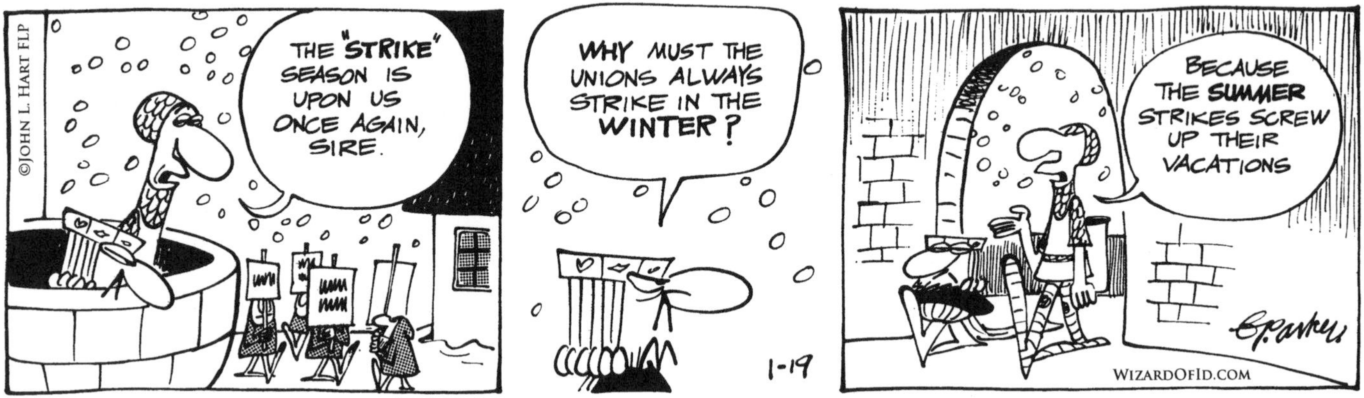
©JOHN L. HART FLP
THE "STRIKE" SEASON IS UPON US ONCE AGAIN, SIRE.
WHY MUST THE UNIONS ALWAYS STRIKE IN THE WINTER?
1-19
BECAUSE THE SUMMER STRIKES SCREW UP THEIR VACATIONS
Parker
WIZARDOFID.COM

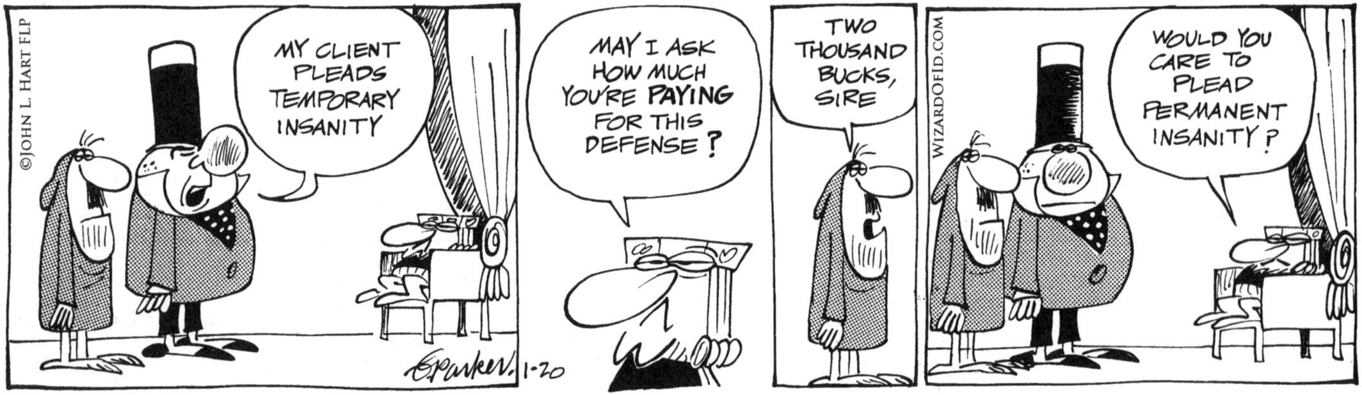
©JOHN L. HART FLP
MY CLIENT PLEADS TEMPORARY INSANITY
Parker 1-20
MAY I ASK HOW MUCH YOU'RE PAYING FOR THIS DEFENSE?
TWO THOUSAND BUCKS, SIRE
WIZARDOFID.COM
WOULD YOU CARE TO PLEAD PERMANENT INSANITY?

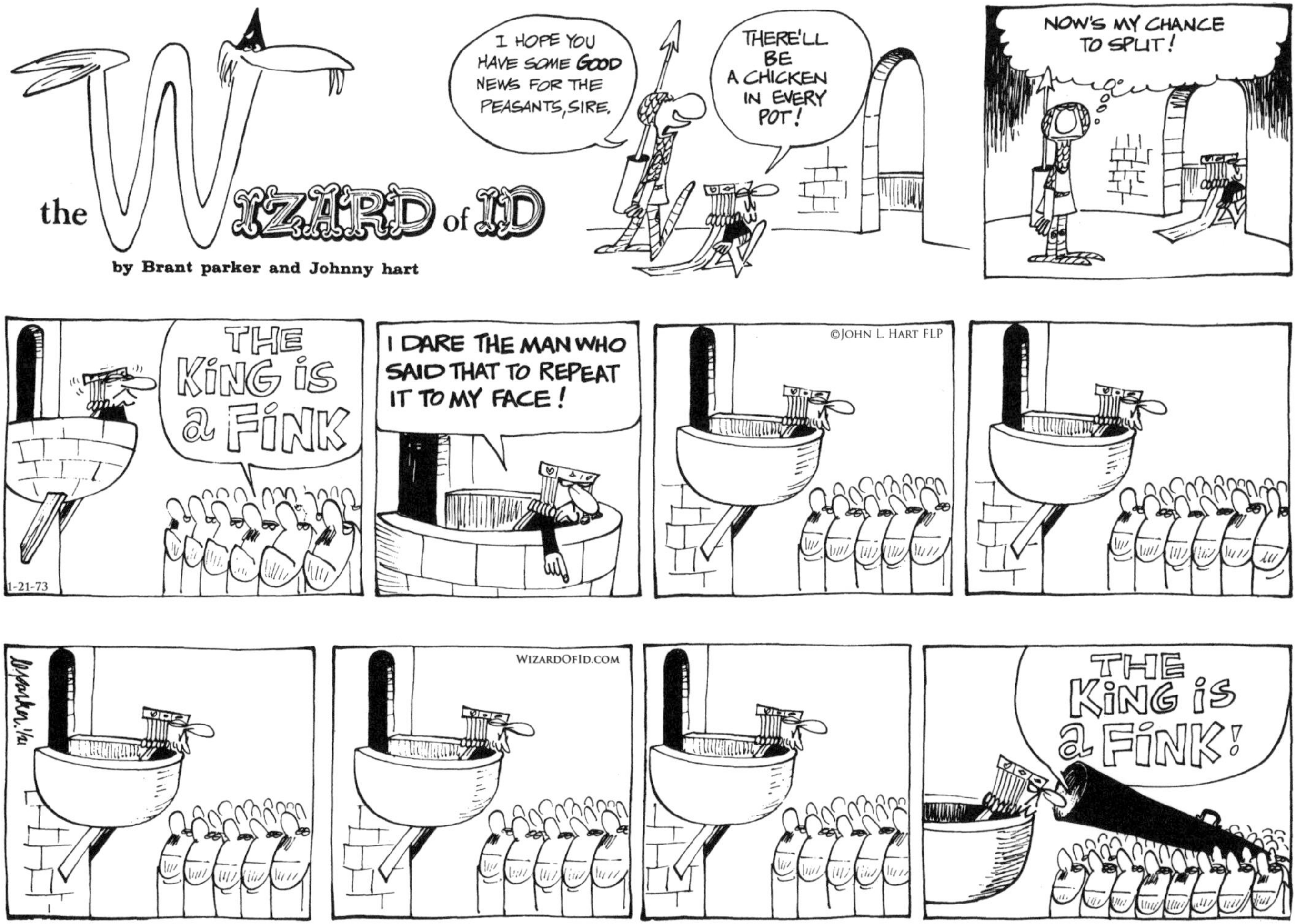
the WIZARD of ID
by Brant parker and Johnny hart
I HOPE YOU HAVE SOME GOOD NEWS FOR THE PEASANTS, SIRE.
THERE'LL BE A CHICKEN IN EVERY POT!
NOW'S MY CHANCE TO SPLIT!
THE KING IS a FINK
1-21-73
I DARE THE MAN WHO SAID THAT TO REPEAT IT TO MY FACE!
©JOHN L. HART FLP
WIZARDOFID.COM
THE KING IS a FINK!

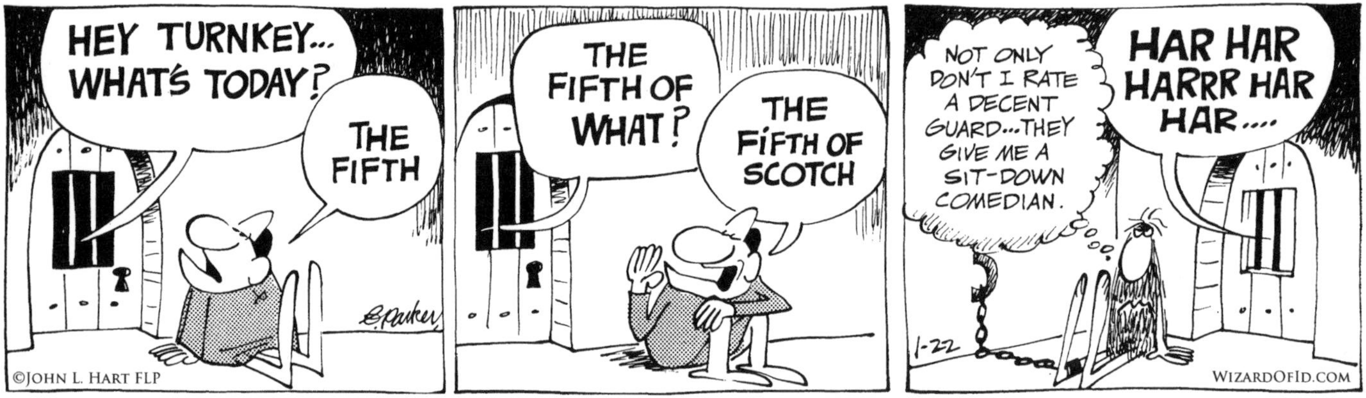

HEY TURNKEY... WHAT'S TODAY?
THE FIFTH
THE FIFTH OF WHAT?
THE FIFTH OF SCOTCH
NOT ONLY DON'T I RATE A DECENT GUARD...THEY GIVE ME A SIT-DOWN COMEDIAN.
HAR HAR HARRR HAR HAR....
1-22
©JOHN L. HART FLP
WIZARDOFID.COM

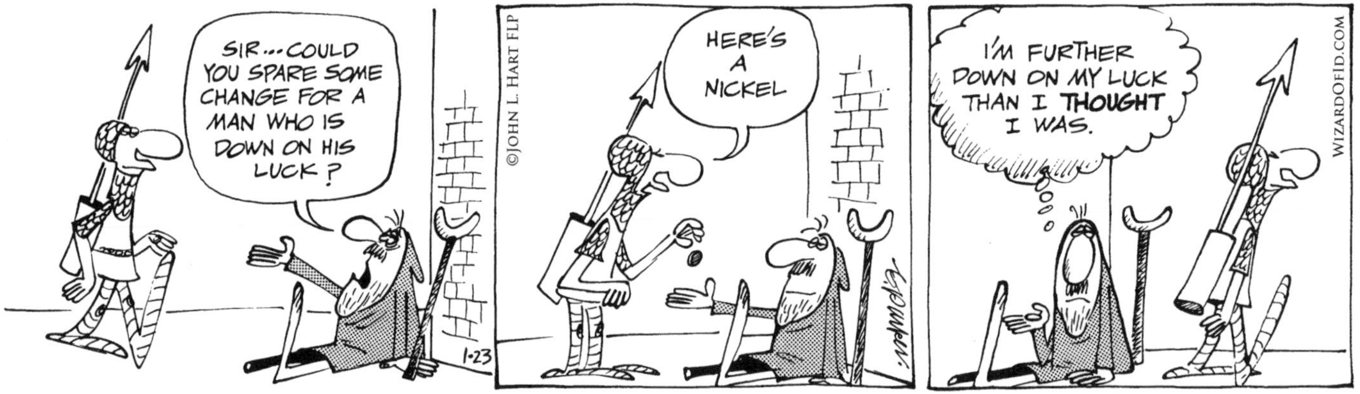

SIR...COULD YOU SPARE SOME CHANGE FOR A MAN WHO IS DOWN ON HIS LUCK?
1-23
HERE'S A NICKEL
I'M FURTHER DOWN ON MY LUCK THAN I THOUGHT I WAS.
©JOHN L. HART FLP
WIZARDOFID.COM

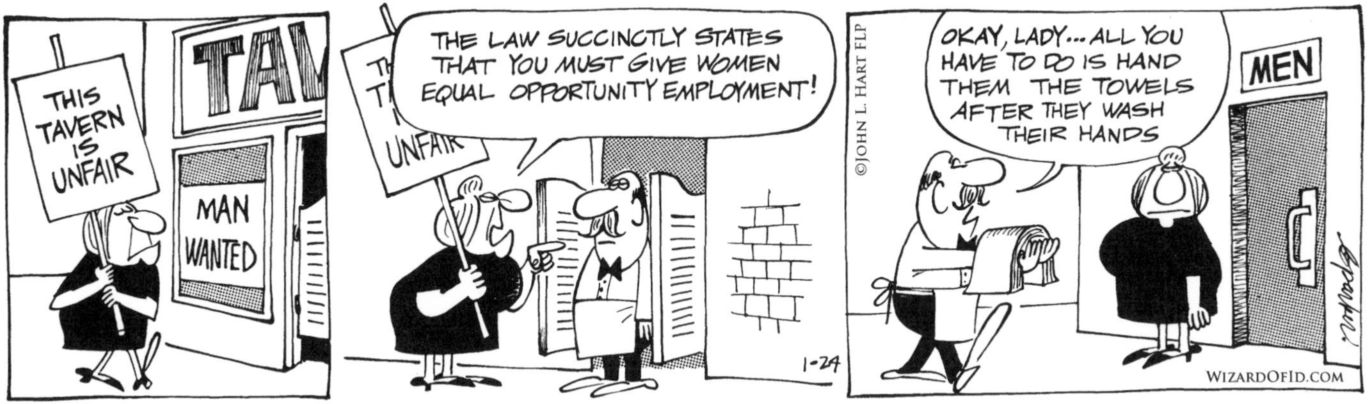
THIS TAVERN IS UNFAIR
TAV
MAN WANTED
THE LAW SUCCINCTLY STATES THAT YOU MUST GIVE WOMEN EQUAL OPPORTUNITY EMPLOYMENT!
1-24
©JOHN L. HART FLP
OKAY, LADY... ALL YOU HAVE TO DO IS HAND THEM THE TOWELS AFTER THEY WASH THEIR HANDS
MEN
WIZARDOFID.COM

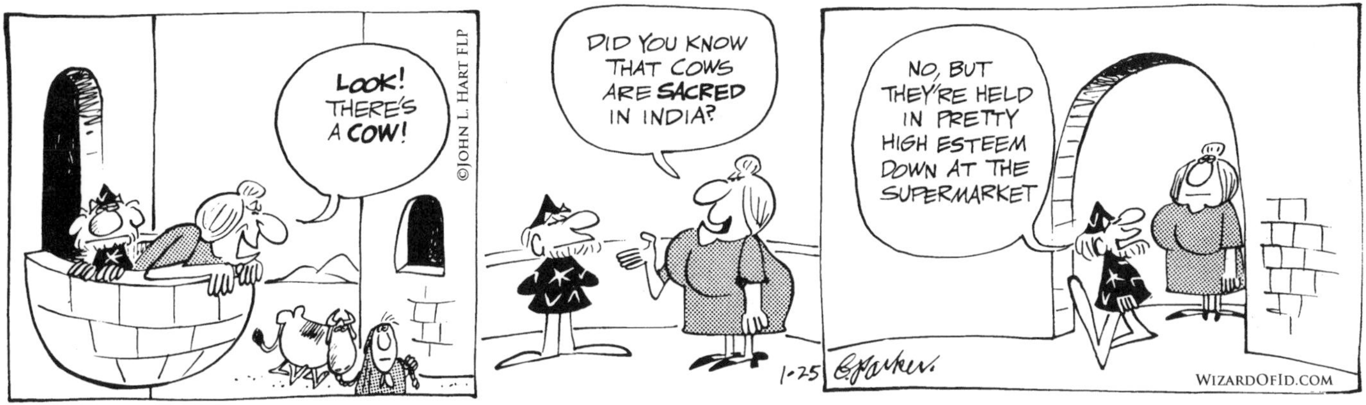
LOOK! THERE'S A COW!
©JOHN L. HART FLP
DID YOU KNOW THAT COWS ARE SACRED IN INDIA?
1-25
NO, BUT THEY'RE HELD IN PRETTY HIGH ESTEEM DOWN AT THE SUPERMARKET
WIZARDOFID.COM

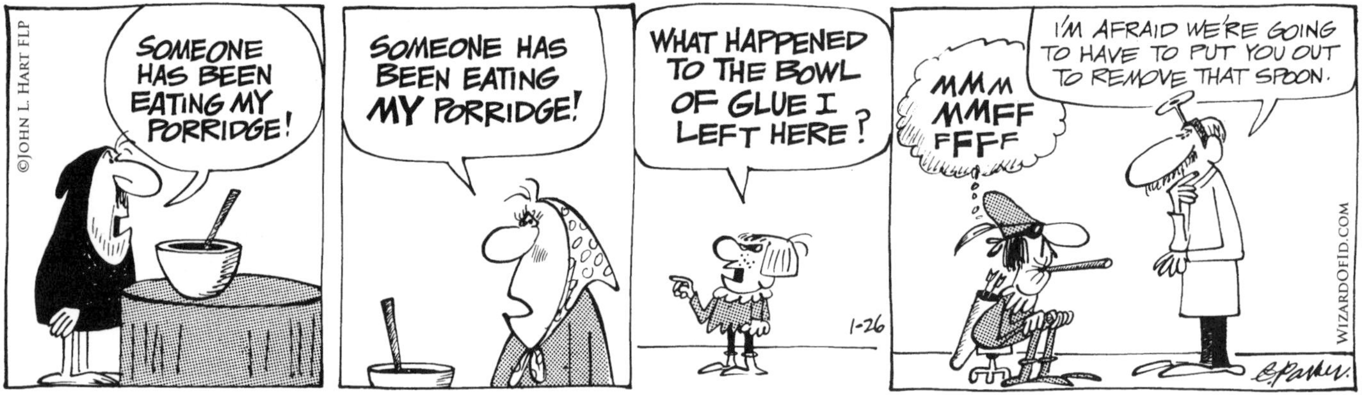
©JOHN L. HART FLP
SOMEONE HAS BEEN EATING MY PORRIDGE!
SOMEONE HAS BEEN EATING MY PORRIDGE!
WHAT HAPPENED TO THE BOWL OF GLUE I LEFT HERE?
1-26
MMM MMFF FFFF
I'M AFRAID WE'RE GOING TO HAVE TO PUT YOU OUT TO REMOVE THAT SPOON.
WIZARDOFID.COM

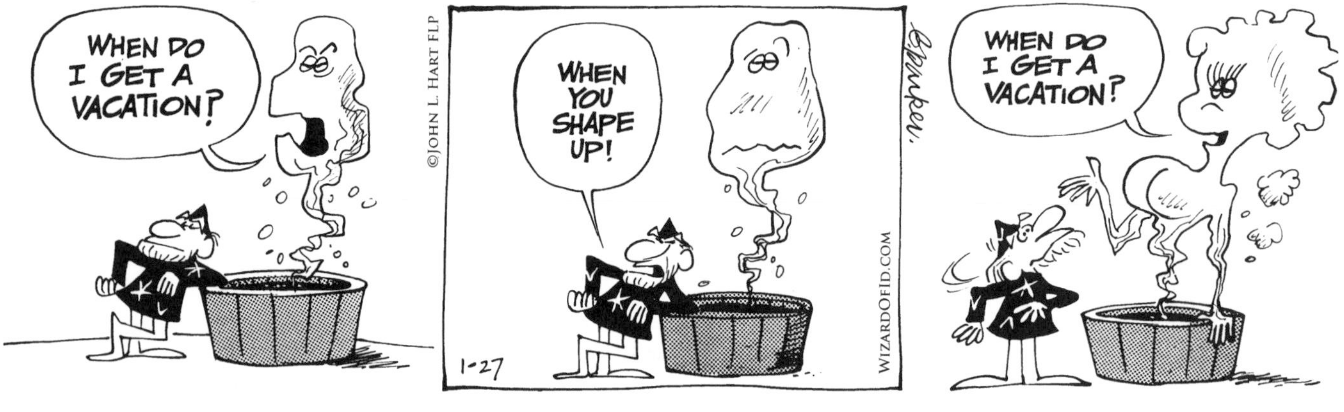
WHEN DO I GET A VACATION?
©JOHN L. HART FLP
WHEN YOU SHAPE UP!
1-27
WIZARDOFID.COM
WHEN DO I GET A VACATION?

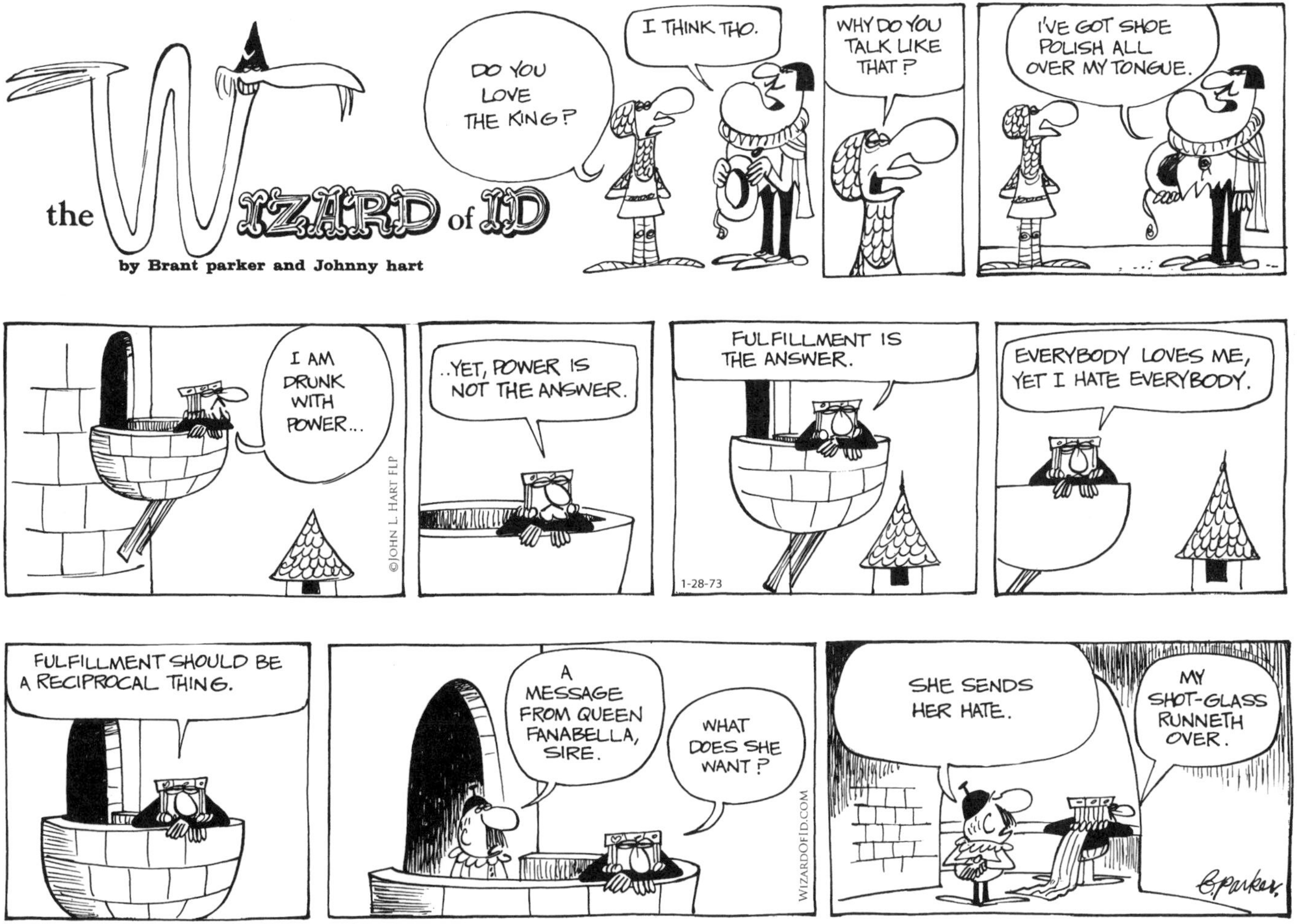
the WIZARD of ID
by Brant parker and Johnny hart
DO YOU LOVE THE KING?
I THINK THO.
WHY DO YOU TALK LIKE THAT?
I'VE GOT SHOE POLISH ALL OVER MY TONGUE.
I AM DRUNK WITH POWER...
©JOHN L. HART FLP
..YET, POWER IS NOT THE ANSWER.
FULFILLMENT IS THE ANSWER.
1-28-73
EVERYBODY LOVES ME, YET I HATE EVERYBODY.
FULFILLMENT SHOULD BE A RECIPROCAL THING.
A MESSAGE FROM QUEEN FANABELLA, SIRE.
WHAT DOES SHE WANT?
WIZARDOFID.COM
SHE SENDS HER HATE.
MY SHOT-GLASS RUNNETH OVER.
B.parker.

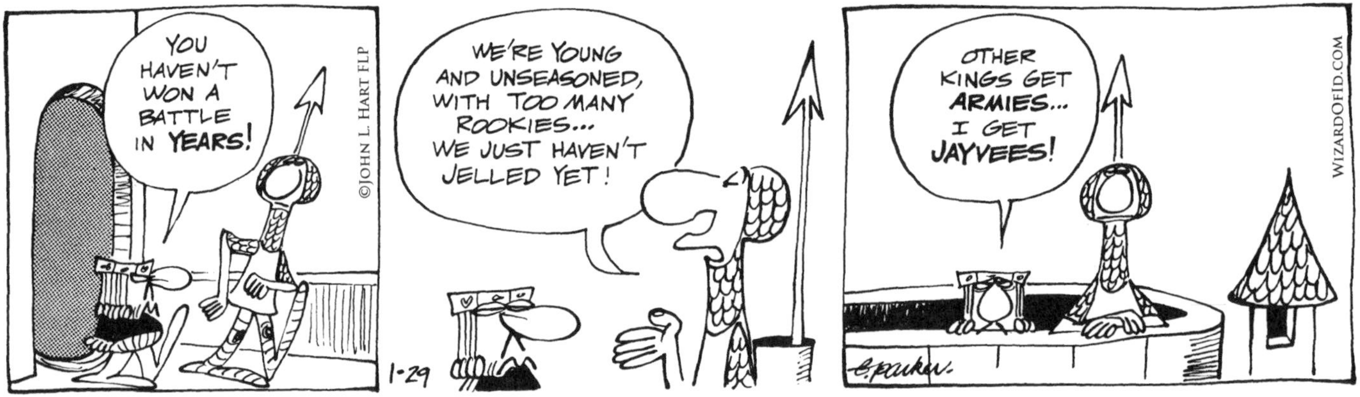
YOU HAVEN'T WON A BATTLE IN YEARS!
©JOHN L. HART FLP
WE'RE YOUNG AND UNSEASONED, WITH TOO MANY ROOKIES... WE JUST HAVEN'T JELLED YET!
1-29
OTHER KINGS GET ARMIES... I GET JAYVEES!
WIZARDOFID.COM
B. PARKER

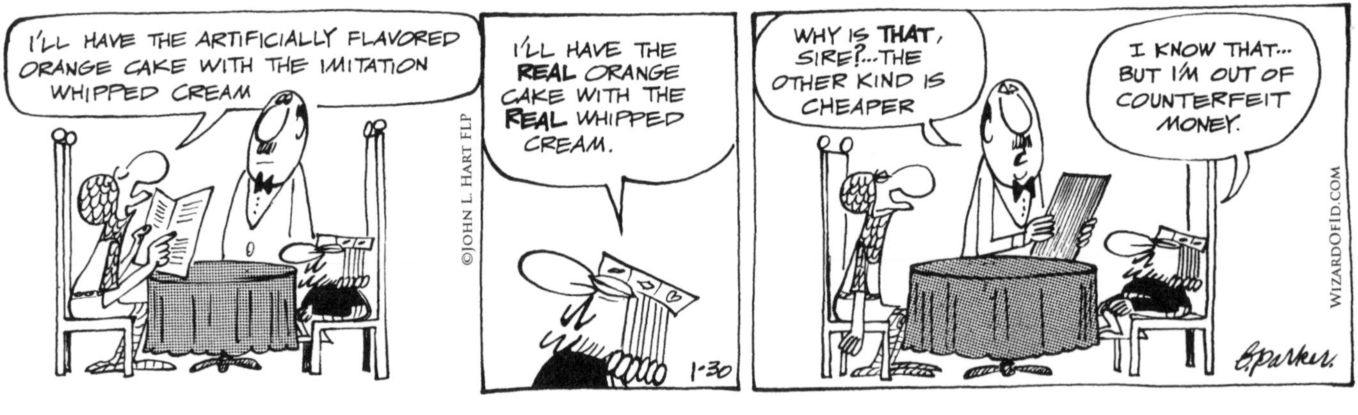
I'LL HAVE THE ARTIFICIALLY FLAVORED ORANGE CAKE WITH THE IMITATION WHIPPED CREAM
©JOHN L. HART FLP
I'LL HAVE THE REAL ORANGE CAKE WITH THE REAL WHIPPED CREAM.
1-30
WHY IS THAT, SIRE?... THE OTHER KIND IS CHEAPER
I KNOW THAT... BUT I'M OUT OF COUNTERFEIT MONEY.
WIZARDOFID.COM
B. PARKER

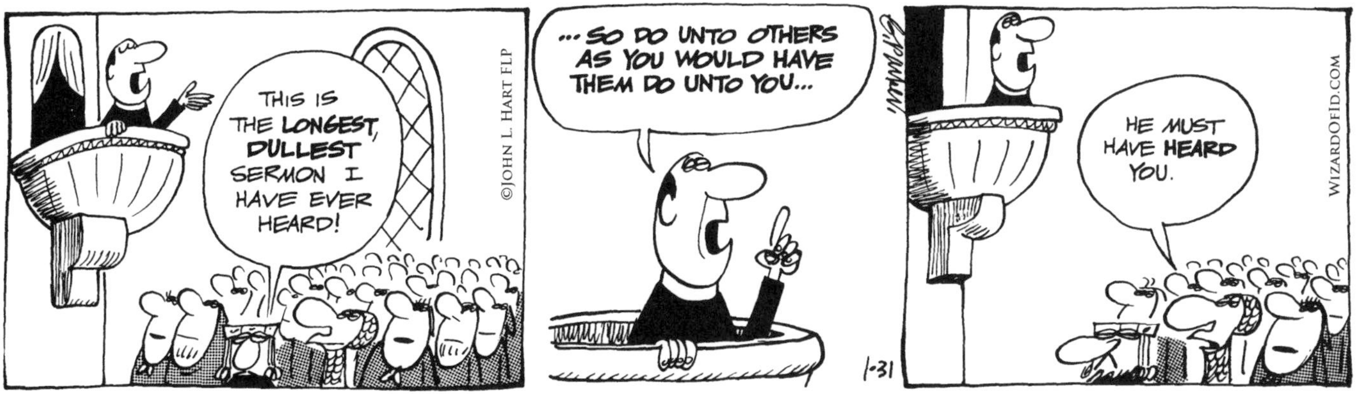
THIS IS THE LONGEST, DULLEST SERMON I HAVE EVER HEARD!
©JOHN L. HART FLP
...SO DO UNTO OTHERS AS YOU WOULD HAVE THEM DO UNTO YOU...
1-31
HE MUST HAVE HEARD YOU.
WIZARDOFID.COM

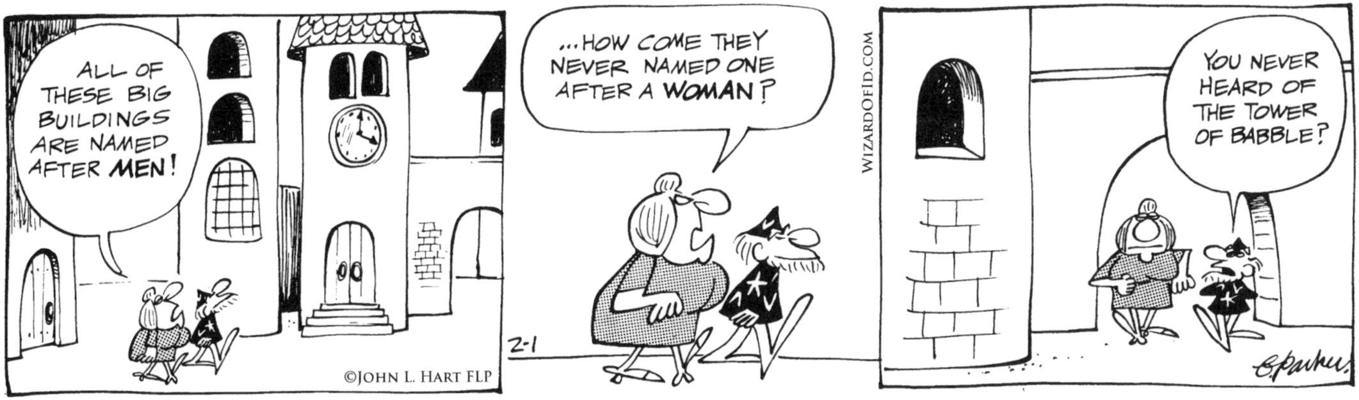
ALL OF THESE BIG BUILDINGS ARE NAMED AFTER MEN!
©JOHN L. HART FLP
2-1
...HOW COME THEY NEVER NAMED ONE AFTER A WOMAN?
WIZARDOFID.COM
YOU NEVER HEARD OF THE TOWER OF BABBLE?

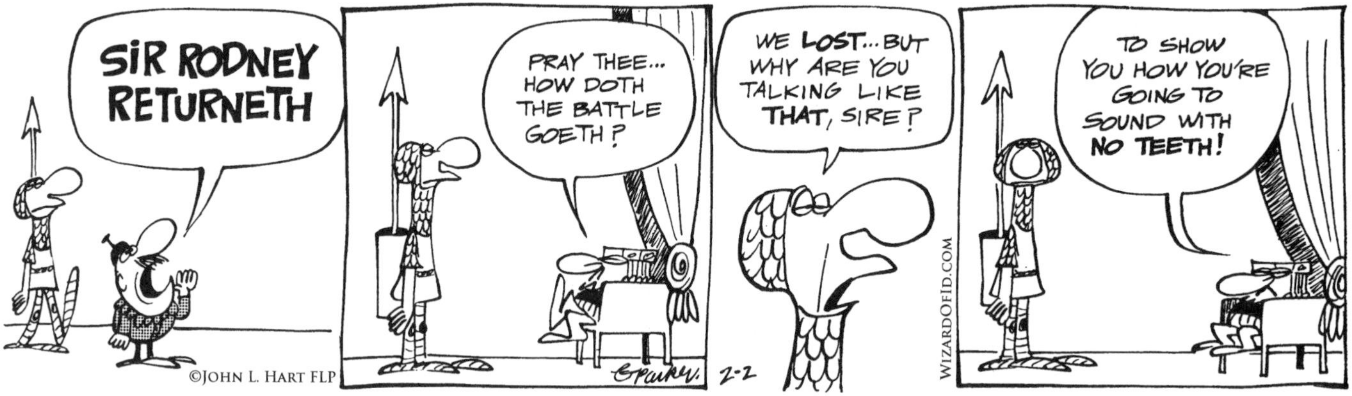
SIR RODNEY RETURNETH
PRAY THEE... HOW DOTH THE BATTLE GOETH?
WE LOST... BUT WHY ARE YOU TALKING LIKE THAT, SIRE?
TO SHOW YOU HOW YOU'RE GOING TO SOUND WITH NO TEETH!
©JOHN L. HART FLP
2-2
WIZARDOFID.COM

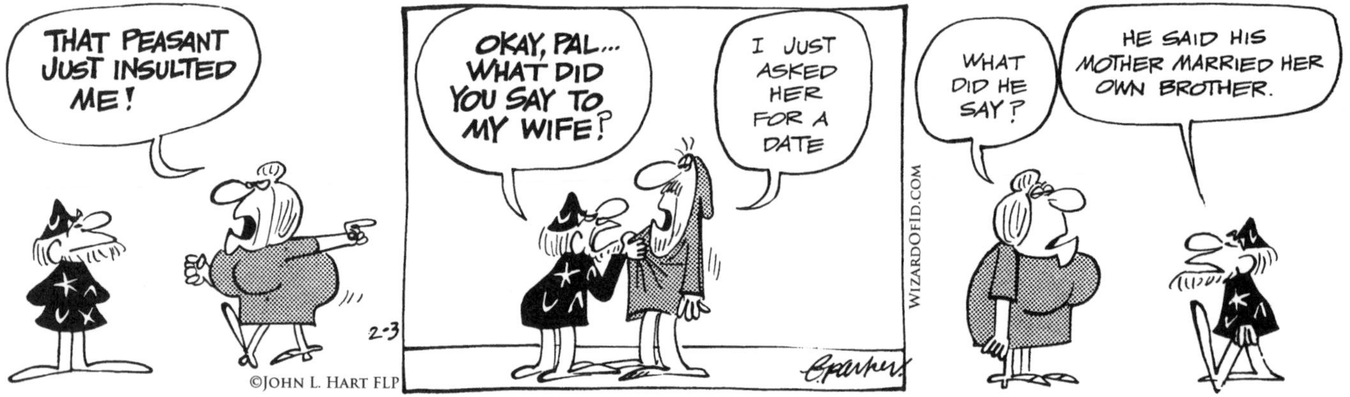
THAT PEASANT JUST INSULTED ME!
OKAY, PAL... WHAT DID YOU SAY TO MY WIFE?
I JUST ASKED HER FOR A DATE
WHAT DID HE SAY?
HE SAID HIS MOTHER MARRIED HER OWN BROTHER.
©JOHN L. HART FLP
2-3
WIZARDOFID.COM

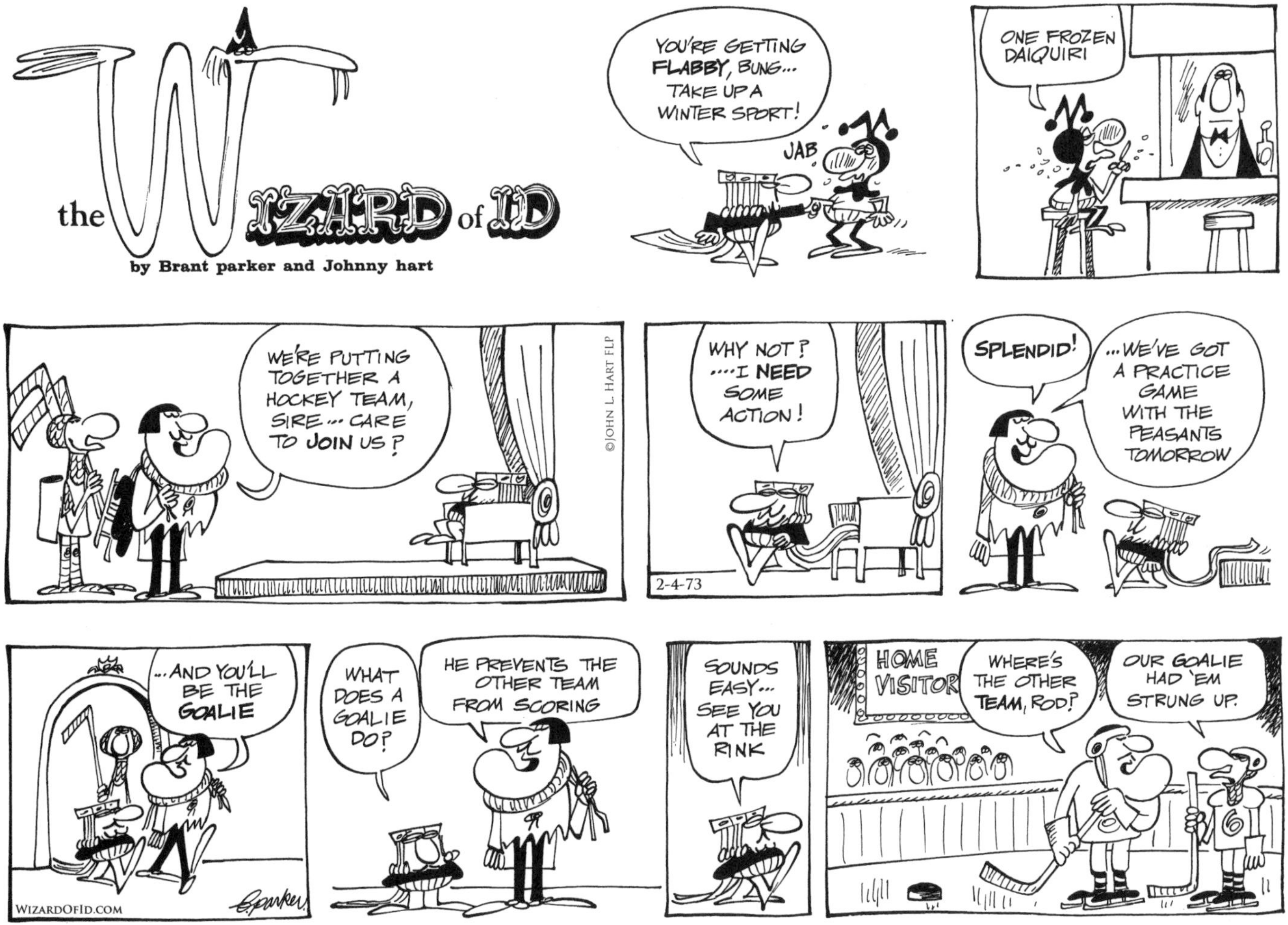

the WIZARD of ID
by Brant parker and Johnny hart
YOU'RE GETTING FLABBY, BUNG... TAKE UP A WINTER SPORT!
JAB
ONE FROZEN DAIQUIRI
WE'RE PUTTING TOGETHER A HOCKEY TEAM, SIRE... CARE TO JOIN US?
©JOHN L. HART FLP
WHY NOT? ....I NEED SOME ACTION!
2-4-73
SPLENDID!
...WE'VE GOT A PRACTICE GAME WITH THE PEASANTS TOMORROW
...AND YOU'LL BE THE GOALIE
WIZARDOFID.COM
B. parker
WHAT DOES A GOALIE DO?
HE PREVENTS THE OTHER TEAM FROM SCORING
SOUNDS EASY... SEE YOU AT THE RINK
HOME
VISITOR
WHERE'S THE OTHER TEAM, ROD?
OUR GOALIE HAD 'EM STRUNG UP.

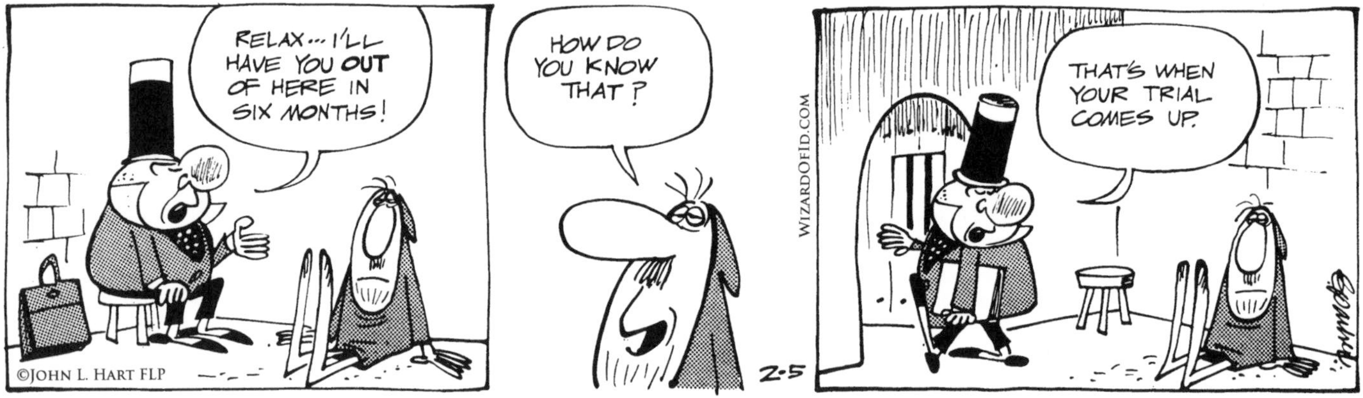
RELAX... I'LL HAVE YOU OUT OF HERE IN SIX MONTHS!
HOW DO YOU KNOW THAT?
THAT'S WHEN YOUR TRIAL COMES UP.
2·5
©JOHN L. HART FLP
WIZARDOFID.COM

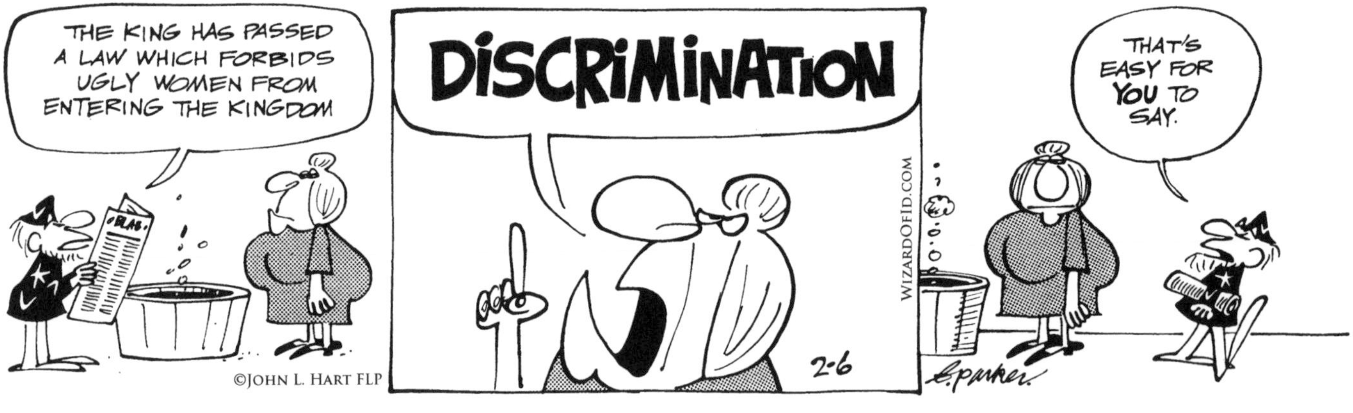
THE KING HAS PASSED A LAW WHICH FORBIDS UGLY WOMEN FROM ENTERING THE KINGDOM
DISCRIMINATION
THAT'S EASY FOR YOU TO SAY.
2·6
©JOHN L. HART FLP
WIZARDOFID.COM

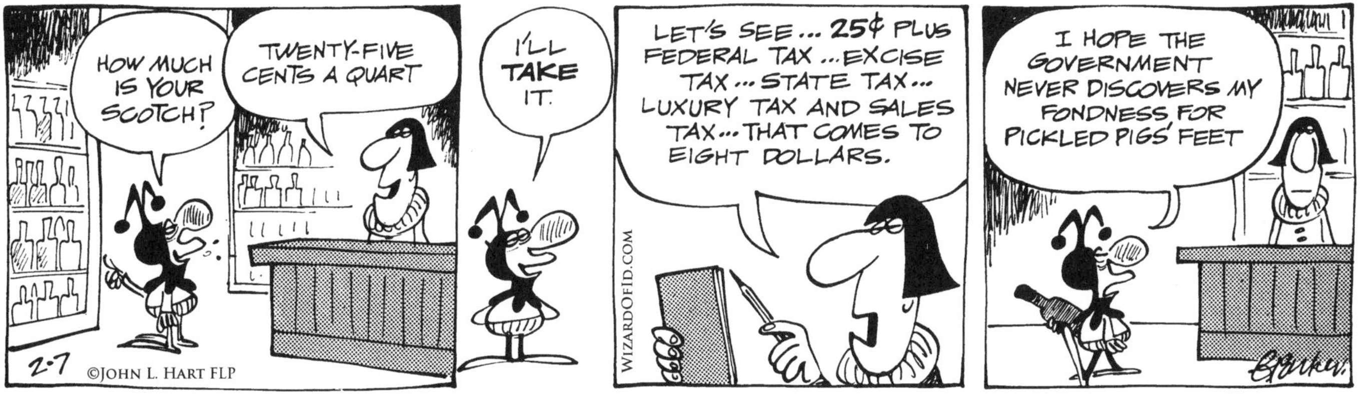
HOW MUCH IS YOUR SCOTCH?
TWENTY-FIVE CENTS A QUART
I'LL TAKE IT.
LET'S SEE... 25¢ PLUS FEDERAL TAX ...EXCISE TAX... STATE TAX... LUXURY TAX AND SALES TAX... THAT COMES TO EIGHT DOLLARS.
I HOPE THE GOVERNMENT NEVER DISCOVERS MY FONDNESS FOR PICKLED PIGS' FEET
2-7
©JOHN L. HART FLP
WIZARDOFID.COM

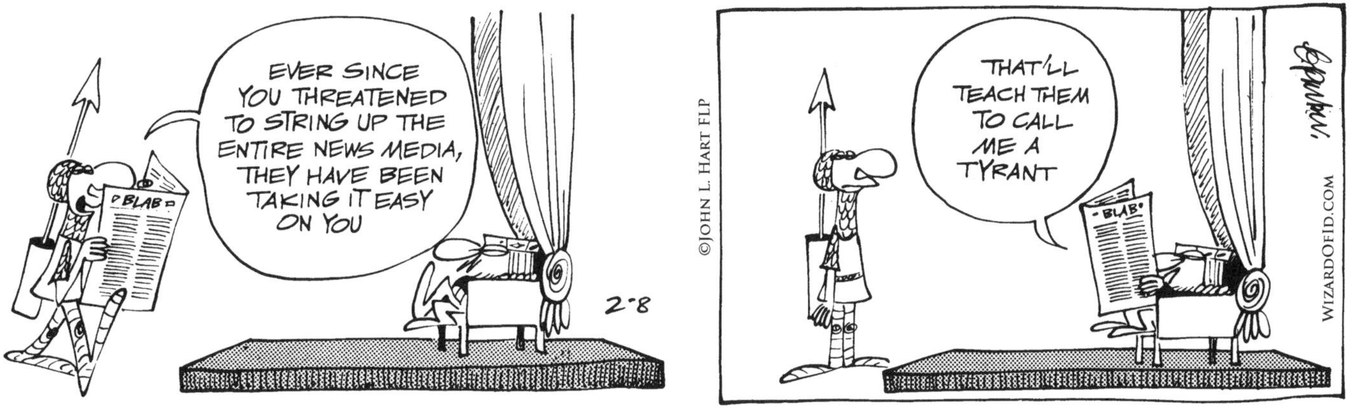
BLAB
EVER SINCE YOU THREATENED TO STRING UP THE ENTIRE NEWS MEDIA, THEY HAVE BEEN TAKING IT EASY ON YOU
2-8
©JOHN L. HART FLP
THAT'LL TEACH THEM TO CALL ME A TYRANT
BLAB
WIZARDOFID.COM

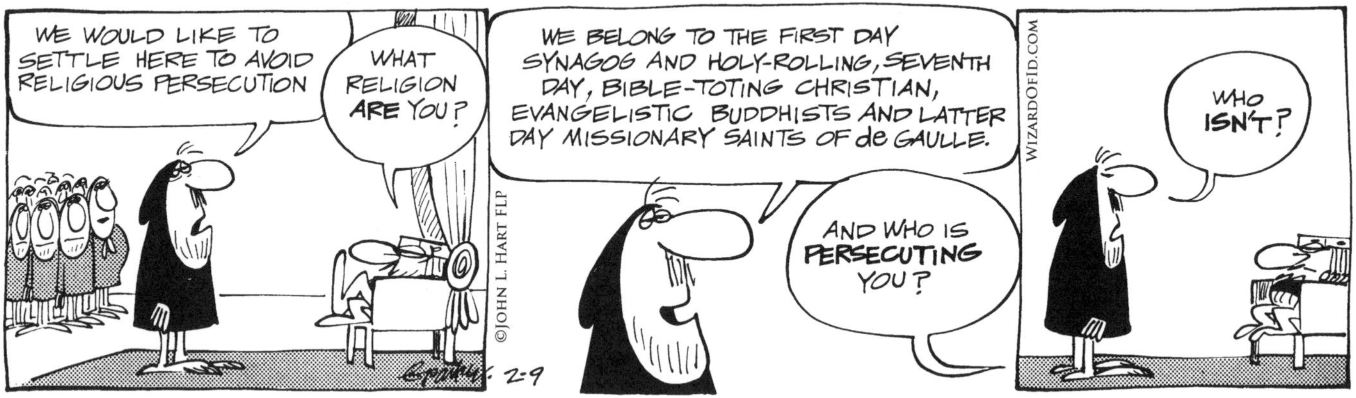
WE WOULD LIKE TO SETTLE HERE TO AVOID RELIGIOUS PERSECUTION
WHAT RELIGION ARE YOU?
WE BELONG TO THE FIRST DAY SYNAGOG AND HOLY-ROLLING, SEVENTH DAY, BIBLE-TOTING CHRISTIAN, EVANGELISTIC BUDDHISTS AND LATTER DAY MISSIONARY SAINTS OF de GAULLE.
AND WHO IS PERSECUTING YOU?
WHO ISN'T?
©JOHN L. HART FLP
WIZARDOFID.COM
2-9

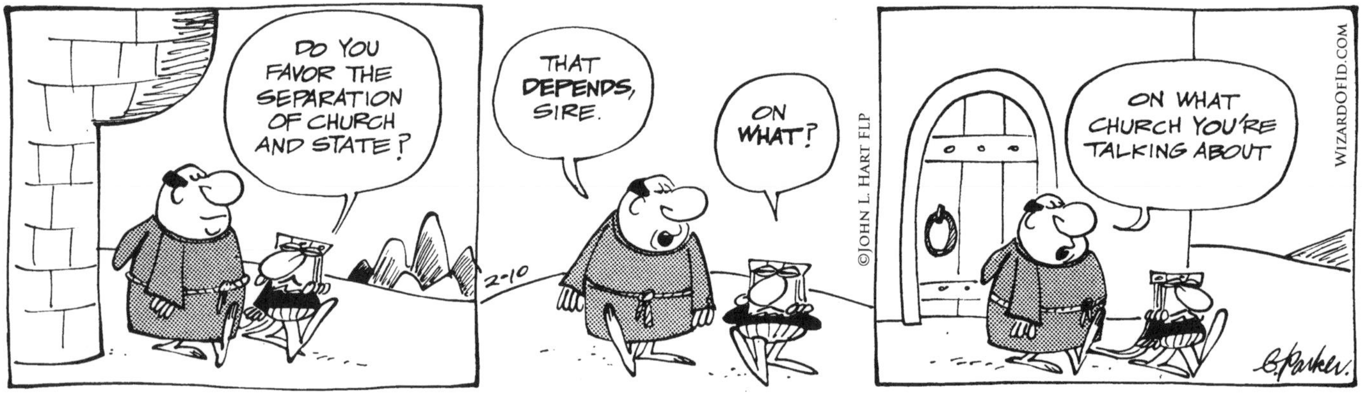
DO YOU FAVOR THE SEPARATION OF CHURCH AND STATE?
THAT DEPENDS, SIRE.
ON WHAT?
ON WHAT CHURCH YOU'RE TALKING ABOUT
©JOHN L. HART FLP
WIZARDOFID.COM
2-10
B. Parker.

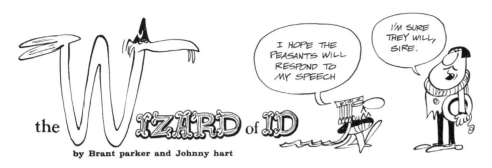

the WIZARD of ID

by Brant parker and Johnny hart

I HOPE THE PEASANTS WILL RESPOND TO MY SPEECH

I'M SURE THEY WILL, SIRE.

...THE GARDENER IS OUT OF VEGETABLES.

WHAT THE HECK IS THAT?

IT'S A BALLOON, MADE TO LOOK LIKE YOU, SIRE

...WE SET IT ON THE BALCONY AND YOU SPEAK FROM INSIDE, WHERE IT'S SAFE

HMMMM.... GOOD IDEA, ROD!

2-11-73

OKAY... ANNOUNCE ME

HIS MAJESTY, THE KING!

FELLOW PEASANTS...

HISSSSS-SSSSSS

IT WAS BOUND TO HAPPEN.

© JOHN L. HART FLP

WIZARDOFID.COM

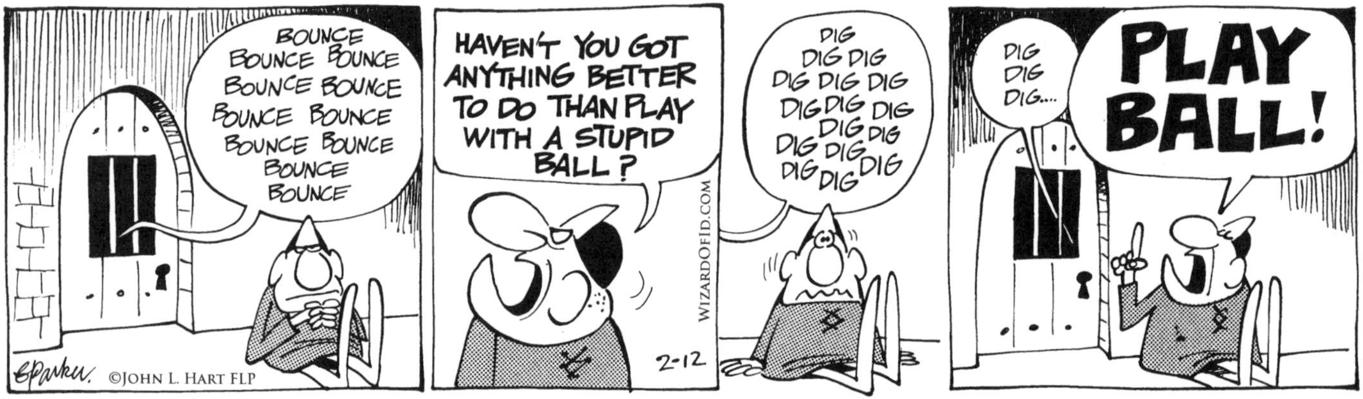
BOUNCE BOUNCE BOUNCE BOUNCE BOUNCE BOUNCE BOUNCE BOUNCE BOUNCE BOUNCE BOUNCE
©JOHN L. HART FLP
HAVEN'T YOU GOT ANYTHING BETTER TO DO THAN PLAY WITH A STUPID BALL ?
WIZARDOFID.COM
2-12
DIG DIG DIG DIG DIG DIG DIG DIG DIG DIG DIG DIG DIG DIG DIG DIG
DIG DIG DIG...
PLAY BALL!

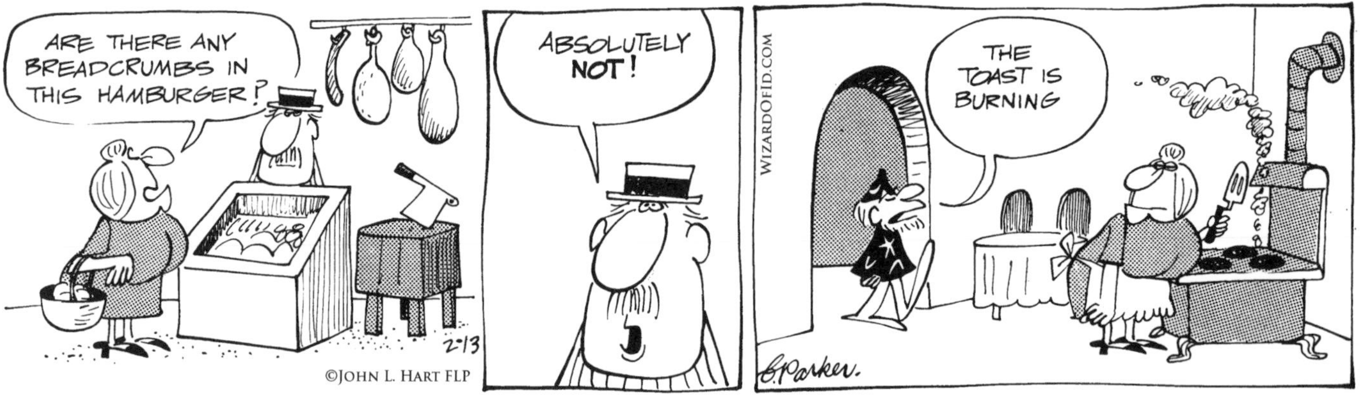
ARE THERE ANY BREADCRUMBS IN THIS HAMBURGER?
2-13
©JOHN L. HART FLP
ABSOLUTELY NOT!
WIZARDOFID.COM
THE TOAST IS BURNING

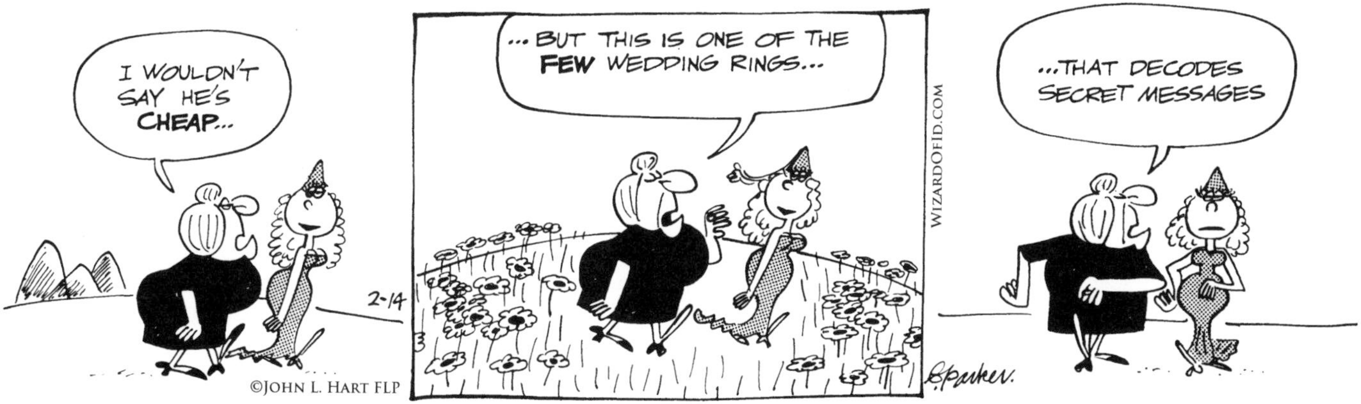
I WOULDN'T SAY HE'S CHEAP...
... BUT THIS IS ONE OF THE FEW WEDDING RINGS...
...THAT DECODES SECRET MESSAGES
2-14
©JOHN L. HART FLP
WIZARDOFID.COM

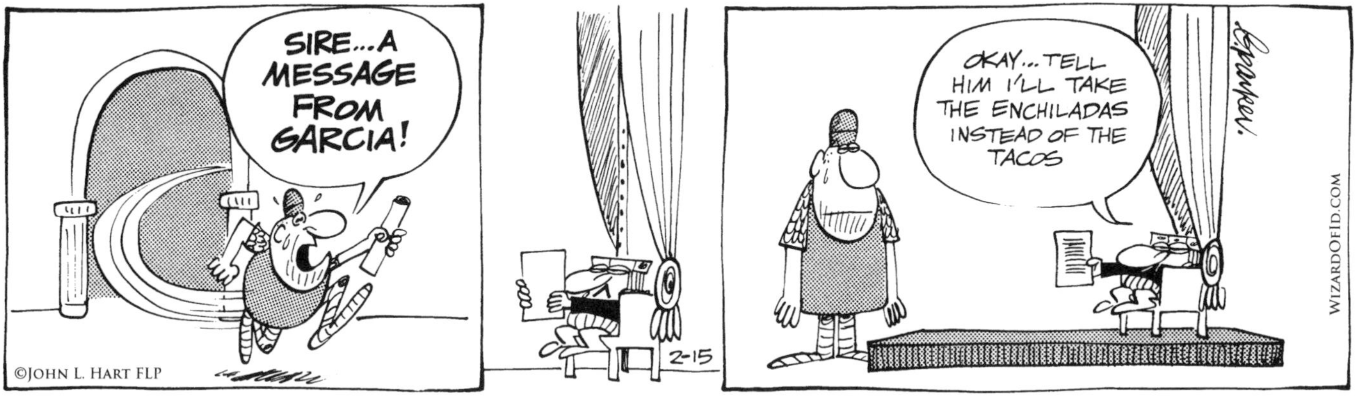
SIRE...A MESSAGE FROM GARCIA!
OKAY... TELL HIM I'LL TAKE THE ENCHILADAS INSTEAD OF THE TACOS
2-15
©JOHN L. HART FLP
WIZARDOFID.COM

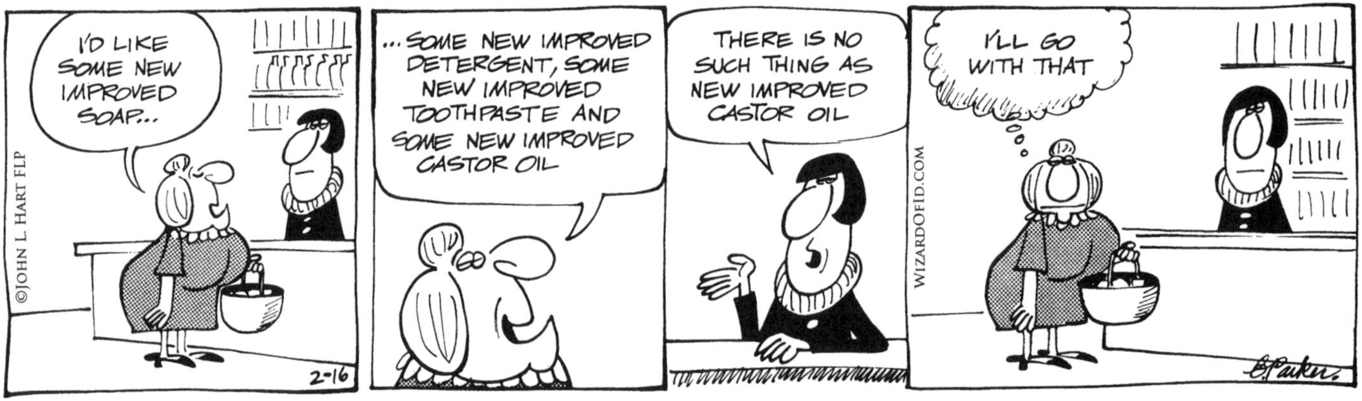
I'D LIKE SOME NEW IMPROVED SOAP...
...SOME NEW IMPROVED DETERGENT, SOME NEW IMPROVED TOOTHPASTE AND SOME NEW IMPROVED CASTOR OIL
THERE IS NO SUCH THING AS NEW IMPROVED CASTOR OIL
I'LL GO WITH THAT
©JOHN L. HART FLP
WIZARDOFID.COM
2-16

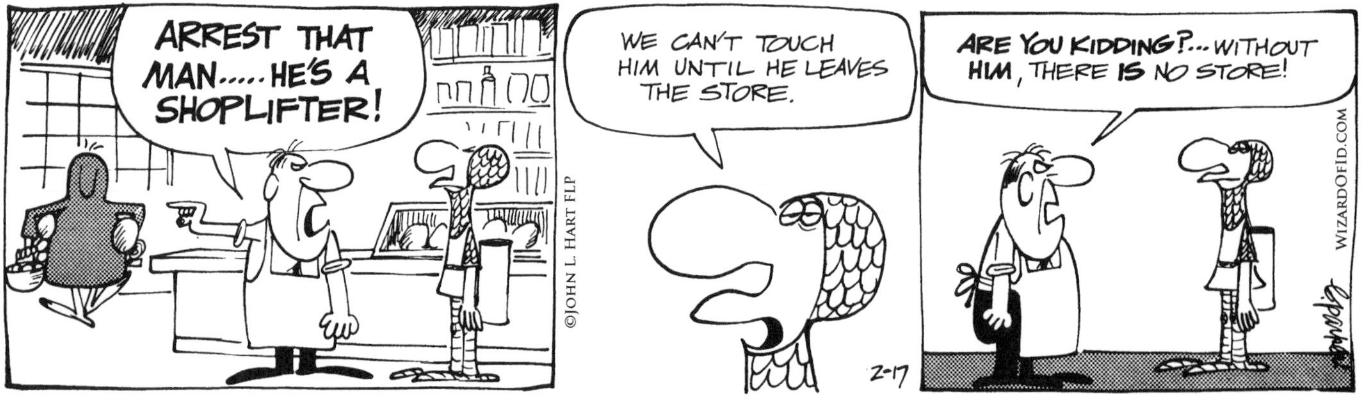
ARREST THAT MAN..... HE'S A SHOPLIFTER!
WE CAN'T TOUCH HIM UNTIL HE LEAVES THE STORE.
ARE YOU KIDDING?... WITHOUT HIM, THERE IS NO STORE!
©JOHN L. HART FLP
WIZARDOFID.COM
2-17

the WIZARD of ID

by Brant parker and Johnny hart

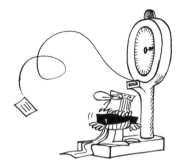

You weigh 72 lbs. and will meet a short, light stranger

...I HEREBY PROCLAIM THIS WEEK AS "BE KIND TO SHORT PEOPLE" WEEK

ALL DOOR KNOBS AND TROLLEY STRAPS WILL BE LOWERED...

©JOHN L. HART FLP

...ALL PEOPLE OVER THREE FEET HIGH WILL WALK IN A CROUCH AND ONLY SHORT BEERS WILL BE SERVED IN THE LOCAL PUBS

2-18-73

MEDIUM AND LONG SUITS SHALL BE REMOVED FROM ALL RACKS

C. PARKER

LONG STEMMED ROSES WILL BE NIPPED IN THE BUD ...

...AND THE WORDS RUNT... SHORTY AND PEEWEE WILL BE STRICKEN FROM THE LANGUAGE !

WIZARDOFID.COM

THE KING IS A DIMINUTIVE FINK

GET ME A LIST OF EVERYBODY WHO GOT PAST THE THIRD GRADE !

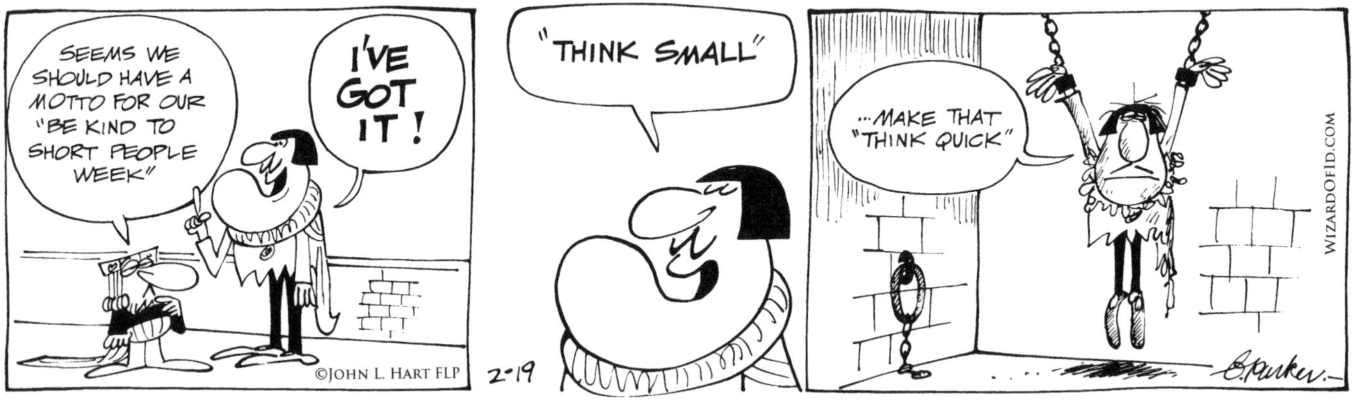
SEEMS WE SHOULD HAVE A MOTTO FOR OUR "BE KIND TO SHORT PEOPLE WEEK"
I'VE GOT IT!
©JOHN L. HART FLP
2-19
"THINK SMALL"
...MAKE THAT "THINK QUICK"
WIZARDOFID.COM

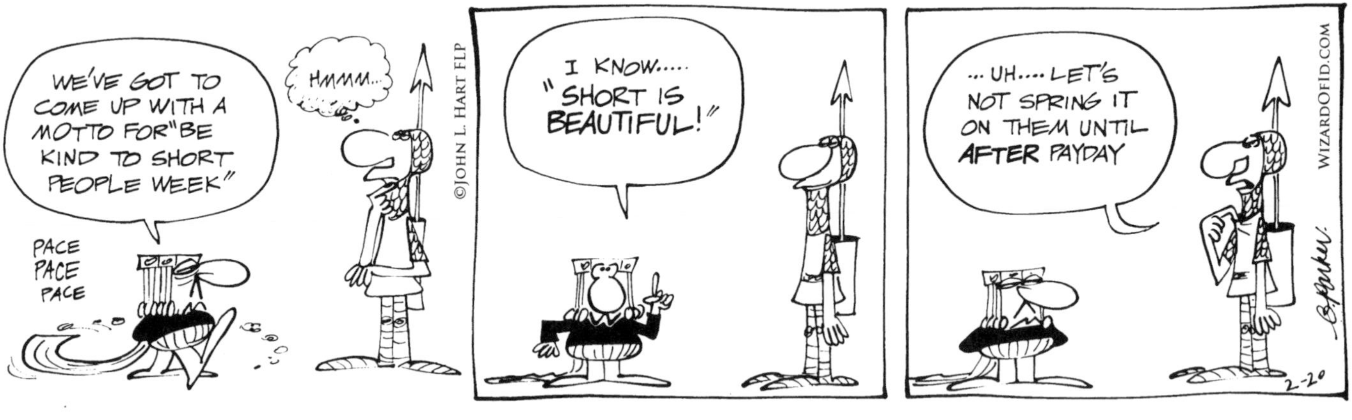
WE'VE GOT TO COME UP WITH A MOTTO FOR "BE KIND TO SHORT PEOPLE WEEK"
PACE PACE PACE
HMMM...
©JOHN L. HART FLP
I KNOW..... "SHORT IS BEAUTIFUL!"
... UH.... LET'S NOT SPRING IT ON THEM UNTIL AFTER PAYDAY
WIZARDOFID.COM
2-20

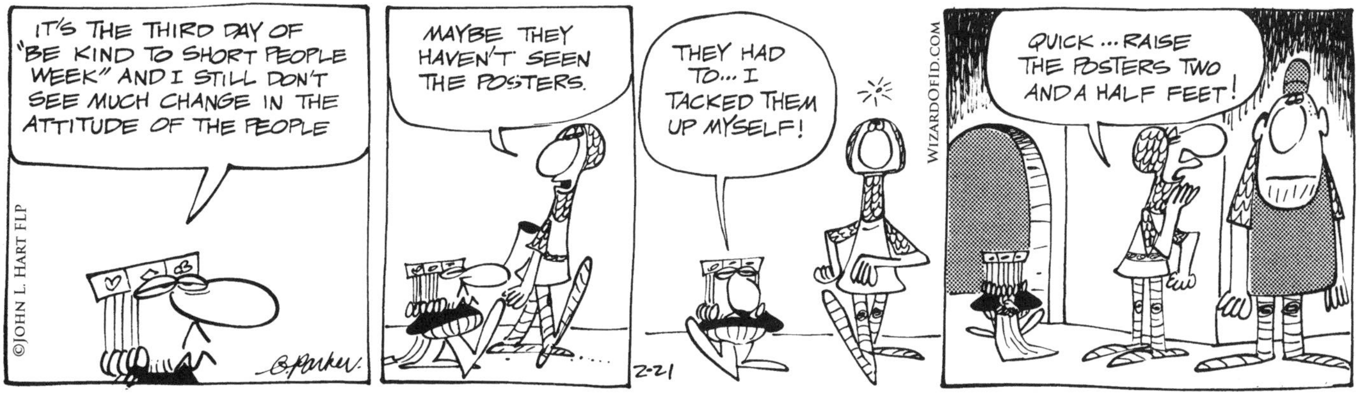
IT'S THE THIRD DAY OF "BE KIND TO SHORT PEOPLE WEEK" AND I STILL DON'T SEE MUCH CHANGE IN THE ATTITUDE OF THE PEOPLE
MAYBE THEY HAVEN'T SEEN THE POSTERS.
THEY HAD TO... I TACKED THEM UP MYSELF!
QUICK ... RAISE THE POSTERS TWO AND A HALF FEET!
2-21
©JOHN L. HART FLP
WIZARDOFID.COM

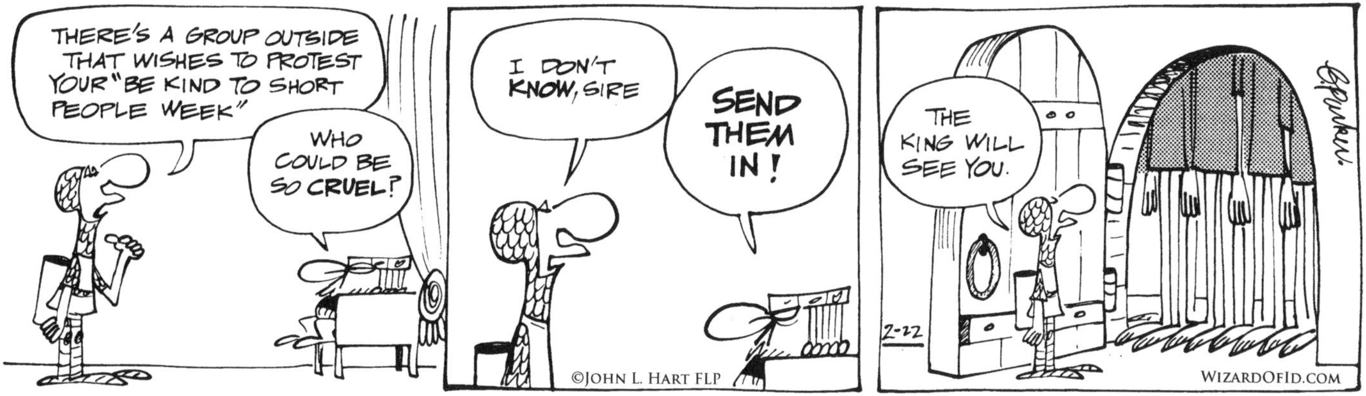
THERE'S A GROUP OUTSIDE THAT WISHES TO PROTEST YOUR "BE KIND TO SHORT PEOPLE WEEK"
WHO COULD BE SO **CRUEL**?
I DON'T **KNOW**, SIRE
SEND THEM IN!
THE KING WILL SEE YOU.
2-22
©JOHN L. HART FLP
WIZARDOFID.COM

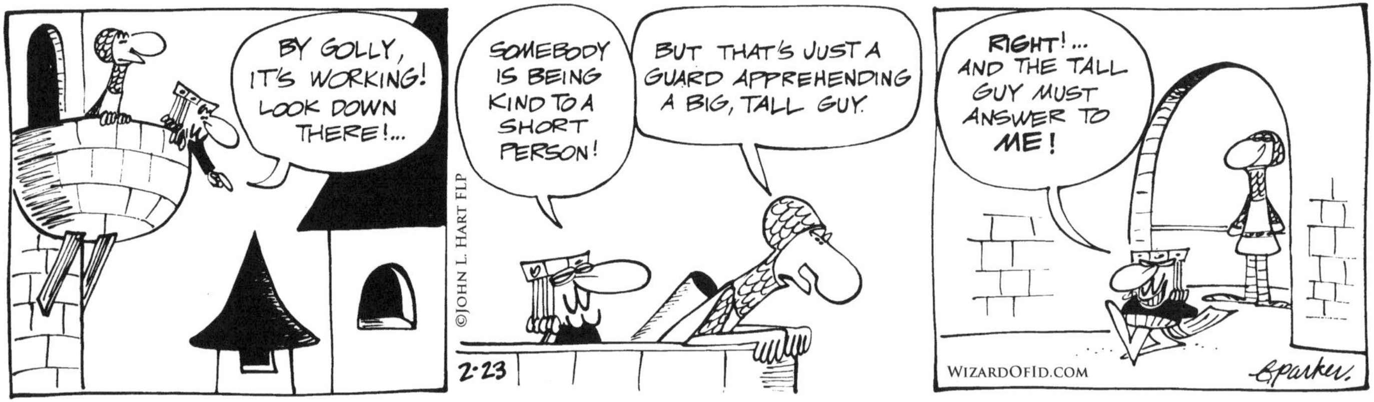
BY GOLLY, IT'S WORKING! LOOK DOWN THERE!...
SOMEBODY IS BEING KIND TO A SHORT PERSON!
BUT THAT'S JUST A GUARD APPREHENDING A BIG, TALL GUY.
RIGHT!... AND THE TALL GUY MUST ANSWER TO ME!
©JOHN L. HART FLP
2-23
WIZARDOFID.COM
B parker

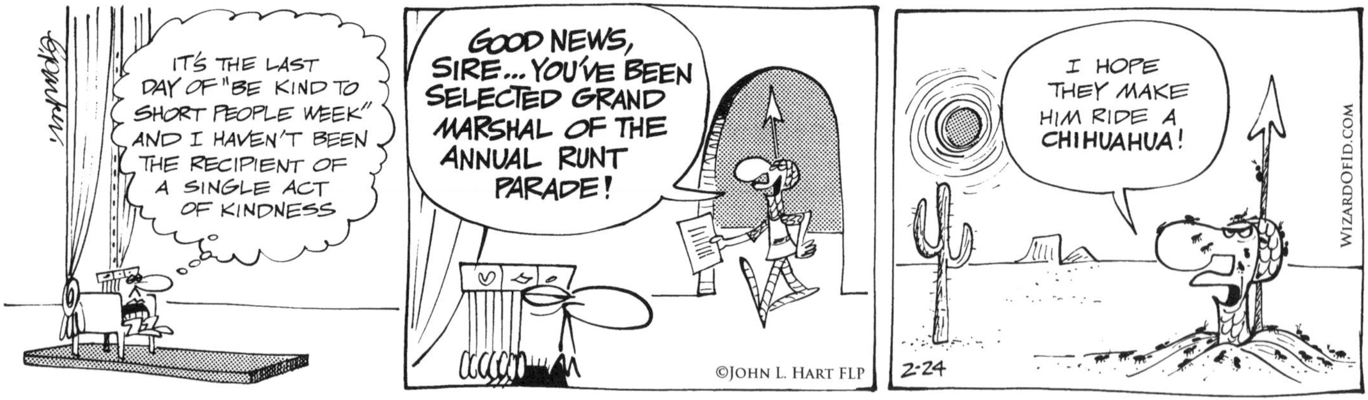
IT'S THE LAST DAY OF "BE KIND TO SHORT PEOPLE WEEK" AND I HAVEN'T BEEN THE RECIPIENT OF A SINGLE ACT OF KINDNESS
GOOD NEWS, SIRE... YOU'VE BEEN SELECTED GRAND MARSHAL OF THE ANNUAL RUNT PARADE!
I HOPE THEY MAKE HIM RIDE A CHIHUAHUA!
©JOHN L. HART FLP
2-24
WIZARDOFID.COM

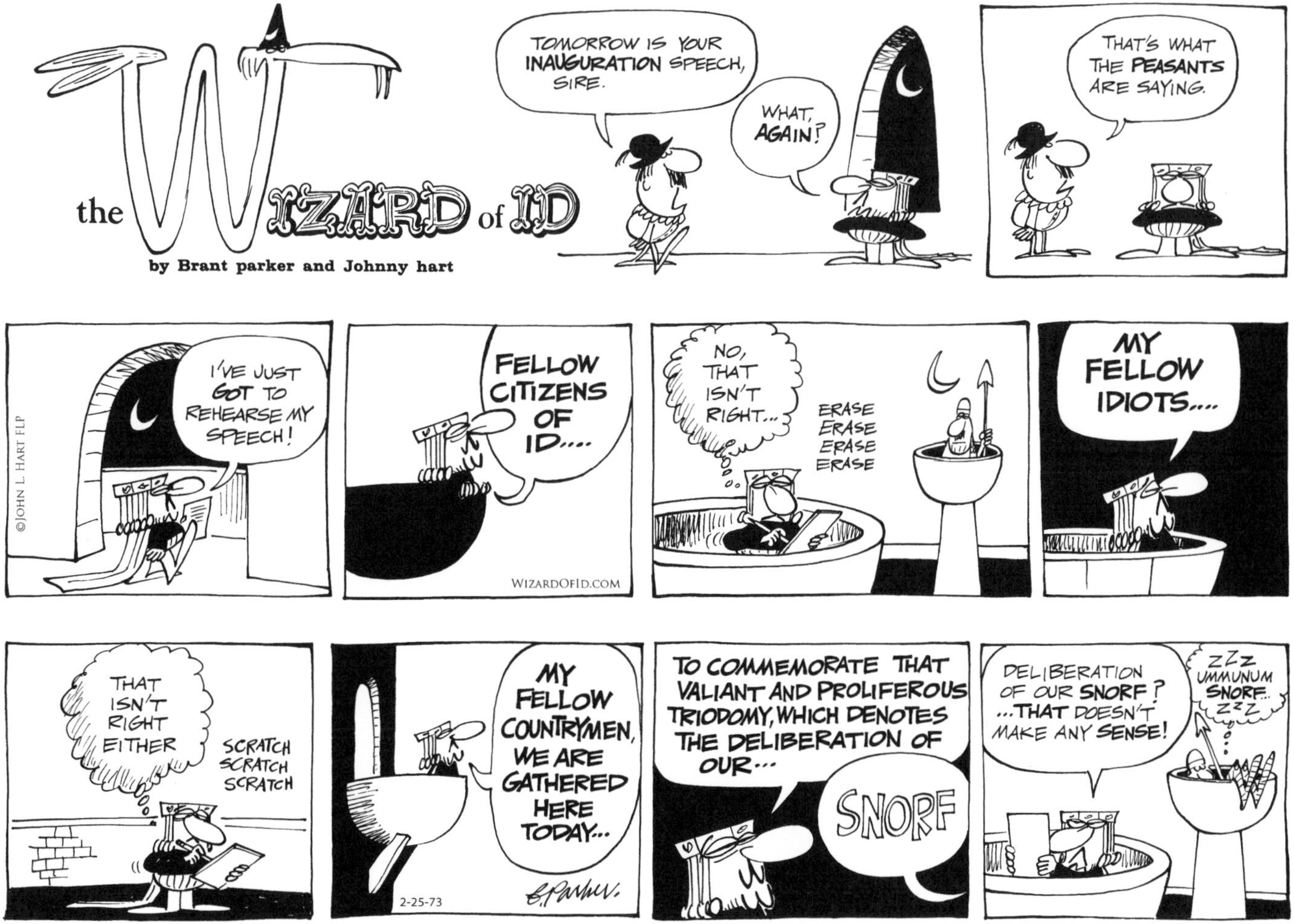
the WIZARD of ID
by Brant parker and Johnny hart
TOMORROW IS YOUR INAUGURATION SPEECH, SIRE.
WHAT, AGAIN?
THAT'S WHAT THE PEASANTS ARE SAYING.
©JOHN L. HART FLP
I'VE JUST GOT TO REHEARSE MY SPEECH!
FELLOW CITIZENS OF ID....
WIZARDOFID.COM
NO, THAT ISN'T RIGHT...
ERASE ERASE ERASE ERASE
MY FELLOW IDIOTS....
THAT ISN'T RIGHT EITHER
SCRATCH SCRATCH SCRATCH
MY FELLOW COUNTRYMEN, WE ARE GATHERED HERE TODAY...
2-25-73
B. Parker
TO COMMEMORATE THAT VALIANT AND PROLIFEROUS TRIODOMY, WHICH DENOTES THE DELIBERATION OF OUR...
SNORF
DELIBERATION OF OUR SNORF? ...THAT DOESN'T MAKE ANY SENSE!
ZZZ UMMUNUM SNORF... ZZZ

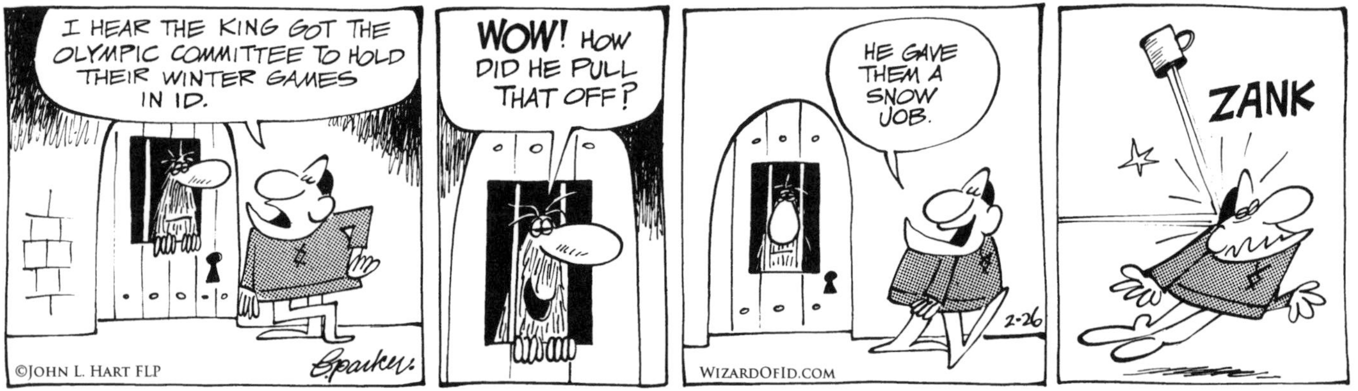
I HEAR THE KING GOT THE OLYMPIC COMMITTEE TO HOLD THEIR WINTER GAMES IN ID.
WOW! HOW DID HE PULL THAT OFF?
HE GAVE THEM A SNOW JOB.
ZANK
2-26
©JOHN L. HART FLP
WIZARDOFID.COM

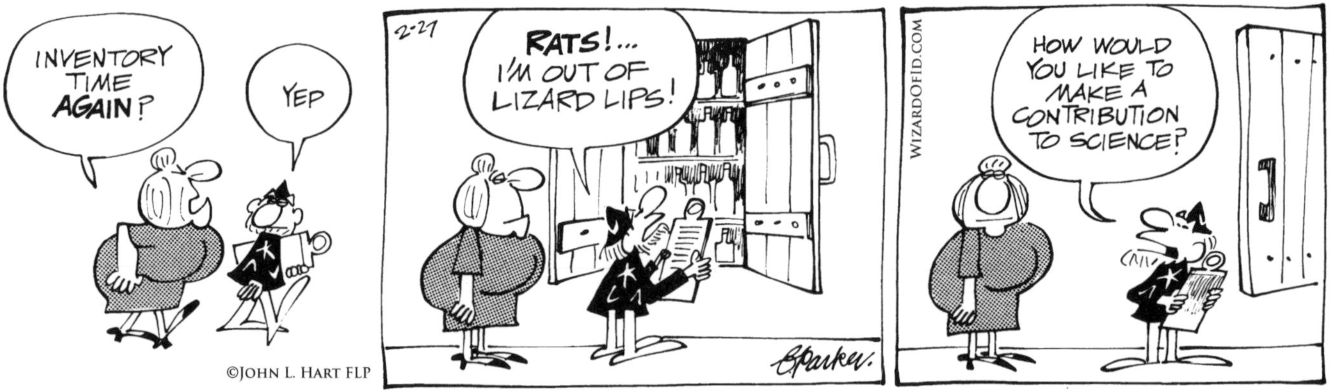
INVENTORY TIME AGAIN?
YEP
2-27
RATS!... I'M OUT OF LIZARD LIPS!
HOW WOULD YOU LIKE TO MAKE A CONTRIBUTION TO SCIENCE?
©JOHN L. HART FLP
WIZARDOFID.COM

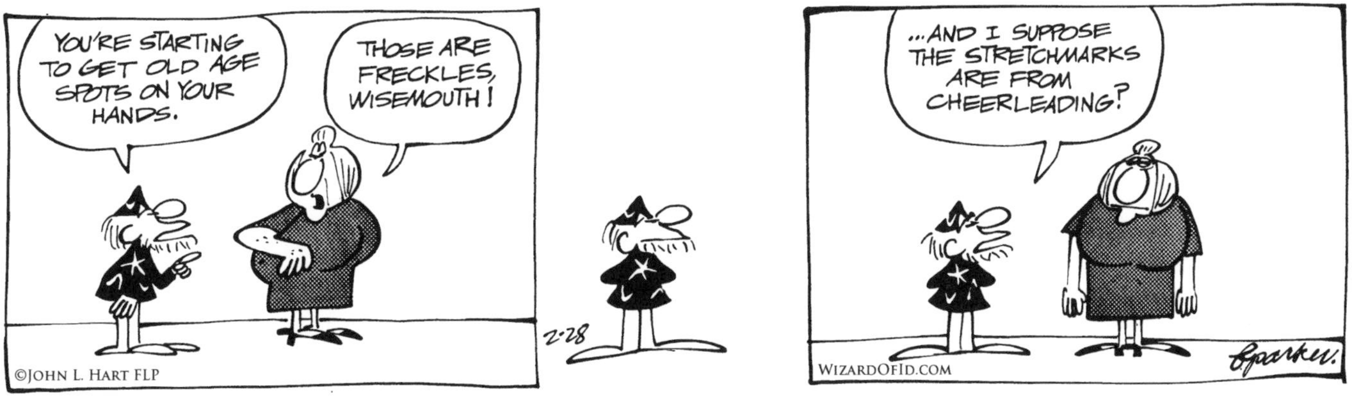
YOU'RE STARTING TO GET OLD AGE SPOTS ON YOUR HANDS.
THOSE ARE FRECKLES, WISEMOUTH!
...AND I SUPPOSE THE STRETCHMARKS ARE FROM CHEERLEADING?
2-28
©JOHN L. HART FLP
WIZARDOFID.COM

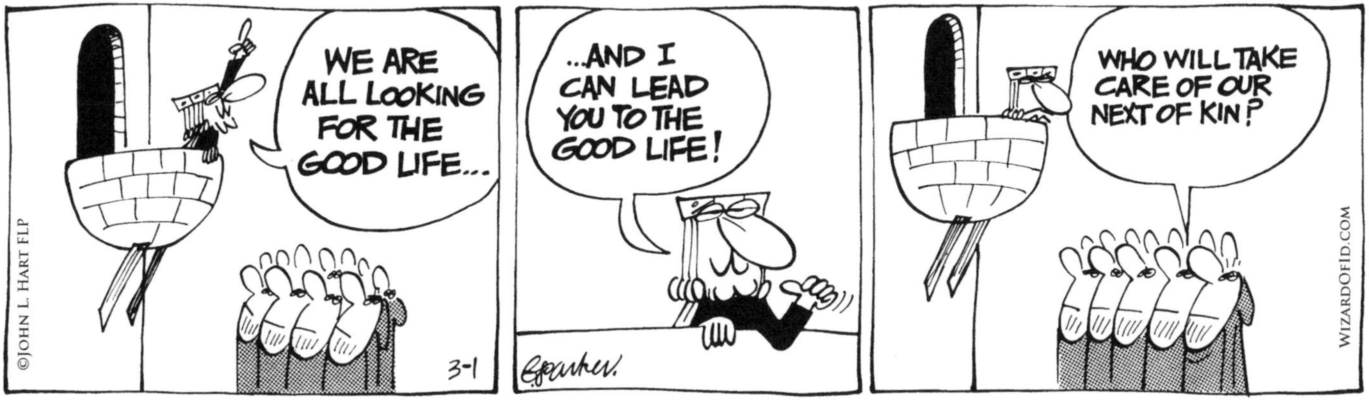
WE ARE ALL LOOKING FOR THE GOOD LIFE...
...AND I CAN LEAD YOU TO THE GOOD LIFE!
WHO WILL TAKE CARE OF OUR NEXT OF KIN?
3-1
©JOHN L. HART FLP
WIZARDOFID.COM

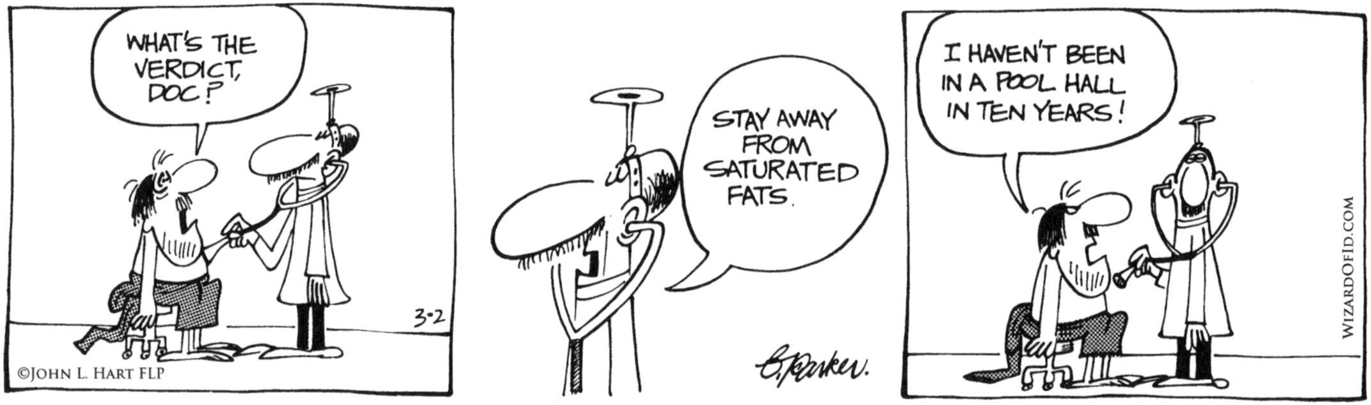
WHAT'S THE VERDICT, DOC?
3-2
©JOHN L. HART FLP
STAY AWAY FROM SATURATED FATS.
I HAVEN'T BEEN IN A POOL HALL IN TEN YEARS!
WIZARDOFID.COM

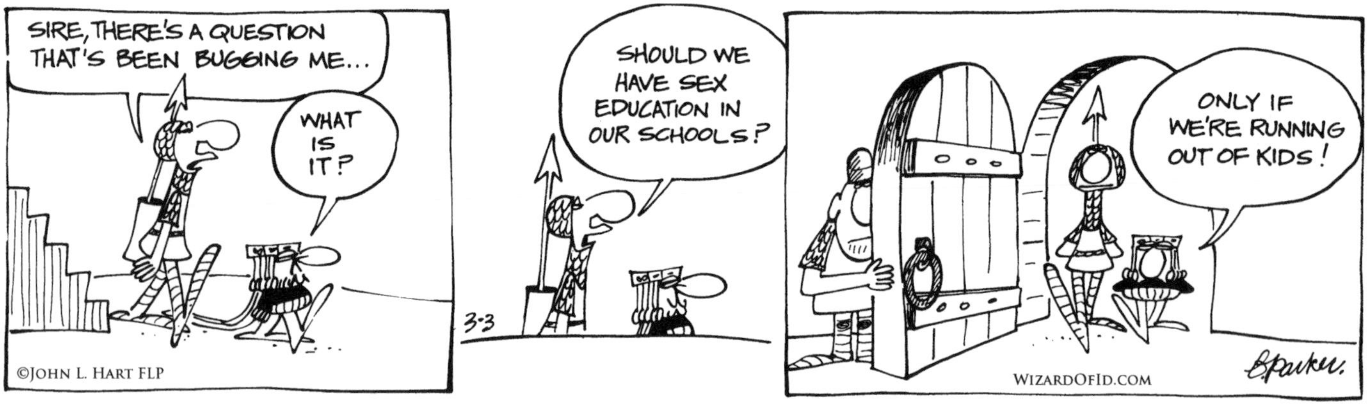
SIRE, THERE'S A QUESTION THAT'S BEEN BUGGING ME...
WHAT IS IT?
©JOHN L. HART FLP
SHOULD WE HAVE SEX EDUCATION IN OUR SCHOOLS?
3-3
ONLY IF WE'RE RUNNING OUT OF KIDS!
WIZARDOFID.COM

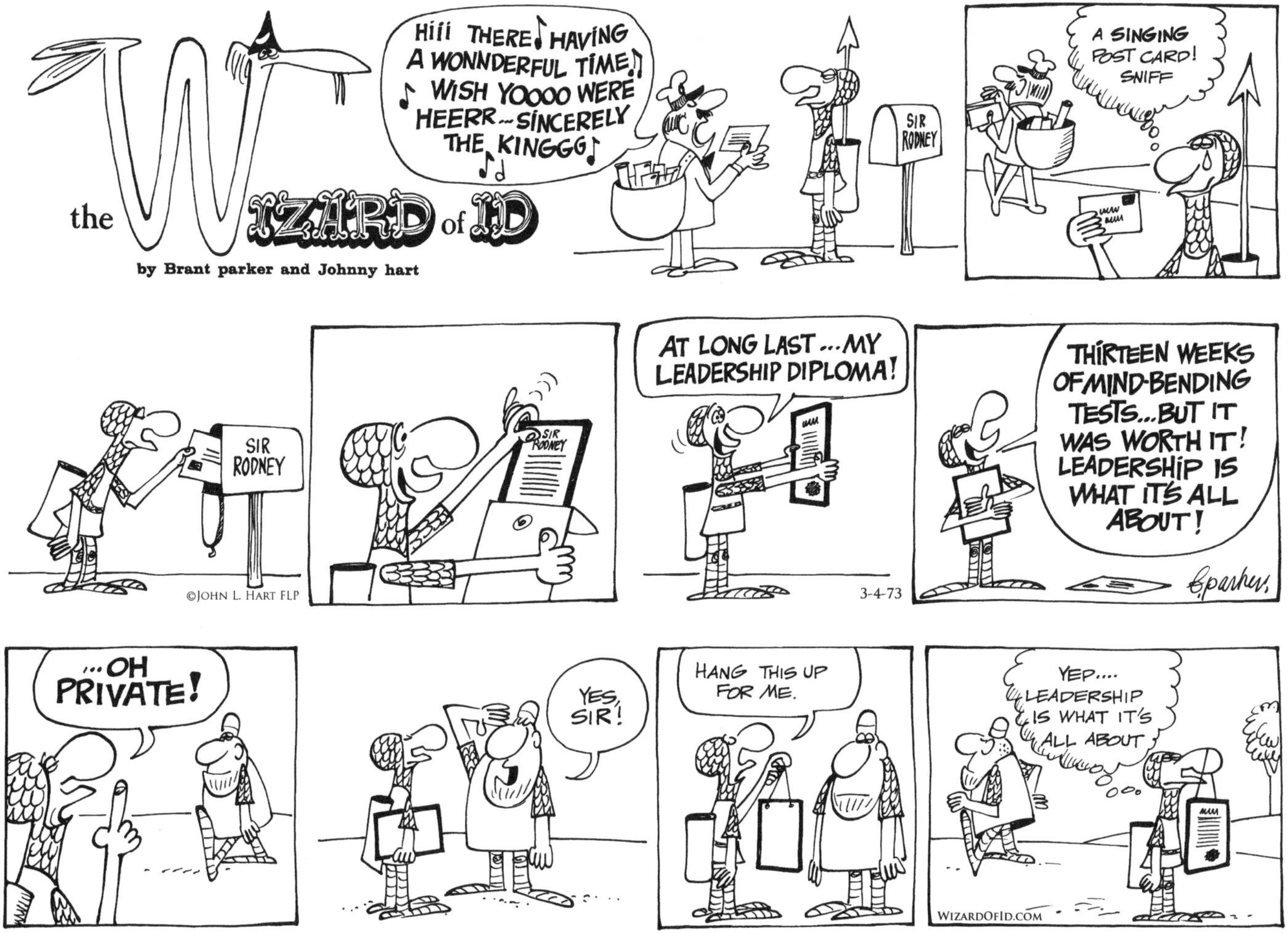
the WIZARD of ID
by Brant parker and Johnny hart
HIII THERE HAVING A WONNDERFUL TIME WISH YOOOO WERE HEERR... SINCERELY THE KINGGG
SIR RODNEY
A SINGING POST CARD! SNIFF
SIR RODNEY
SIR RODNEY
©JOHN L. HART FLP
AT LONG LAST ... MY LEADERSHIP DIPLOMA!
3-4-73
THIRTEEN WEEKS OF MIND-BENDING TESTS... BUT IT WAS WORTH IT! LEADERSHIP IS WHAT IT'S ALL ABOUT!
B. parker
...OH PRIVATE!
YES, SIR!
HANG THIS UP FOR ME.
YEP.... LEADERSHIP IS WHAT IT'S ALL ABOUT
WIZARDOFID.COM

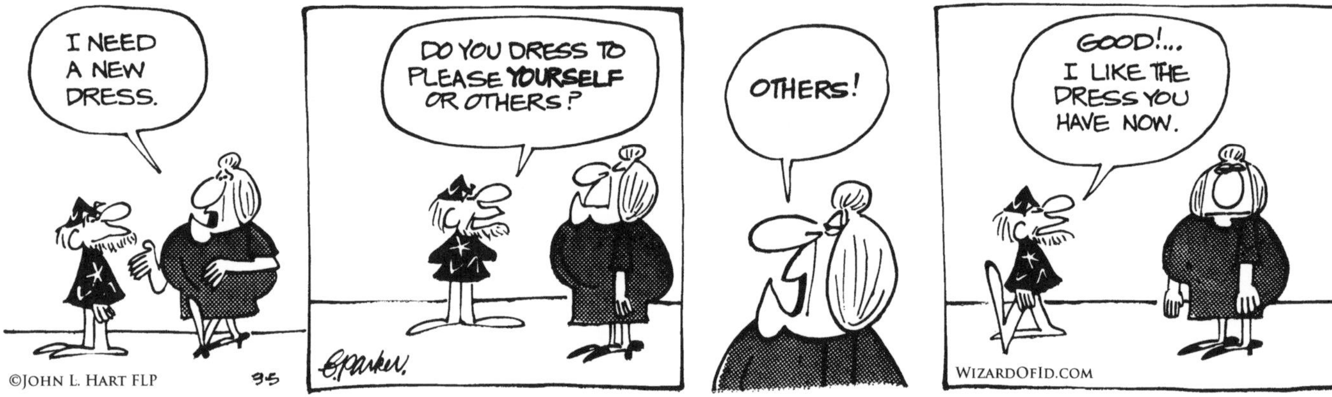
I NEED A NEW DRESS.
DO YOU DRESS TO PLEASE **YOURSELF** OR OTHERS?
OTHERS!
GOOD!... I LIKE THE DRESS YOU HAVE NOW.
©JOHN L. HART FLP
3-5
WIZARDOFID.COM

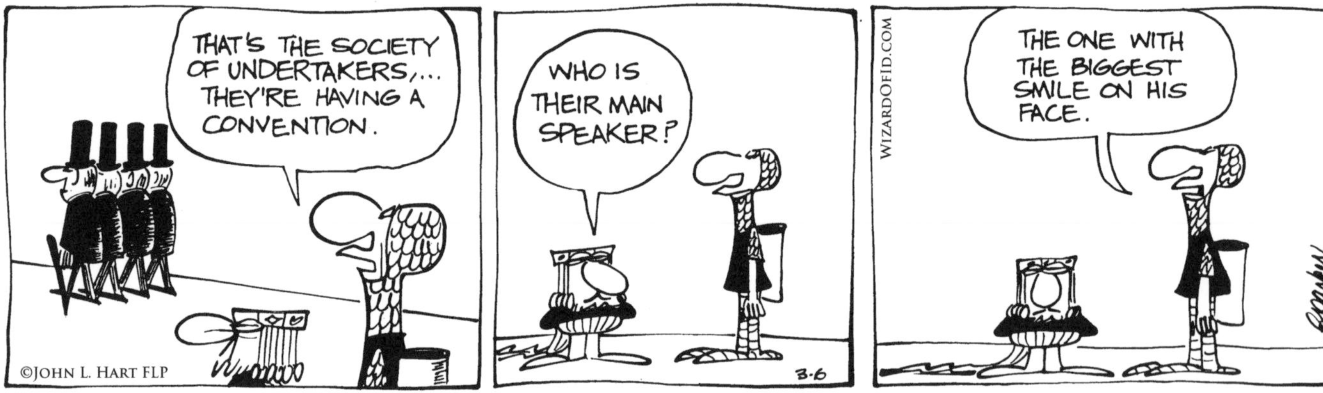
THAT'S THE SOCIETY OF UNDERTAKERS,... THEY'RE HAVING A CONVENTION.
WHO IS THEIR MAIN SPEAKER?
THE ONE WITH THE BIGGEST SMILE ON HIS FACE.
©JOHN L. HART FLP
3-6
WIZARDOFID.COM

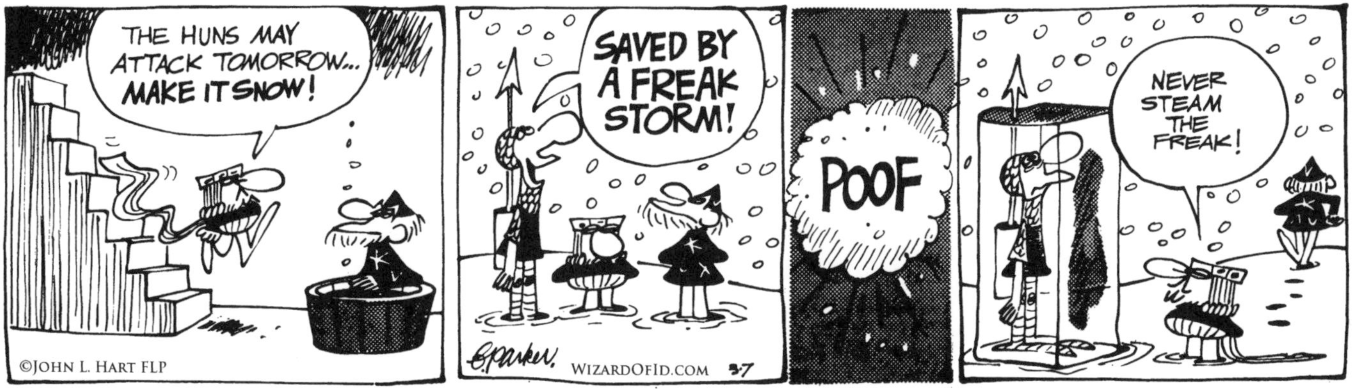
THE HUNS MAY ATTACK TOMORROW... MAKE IT SNOW!
©JOHN L. HART FLP
SAVED BY A FREAK STORM!
WIZARDOFID.COM
3·7
POOF
NEVER STEAM THE FREAK!

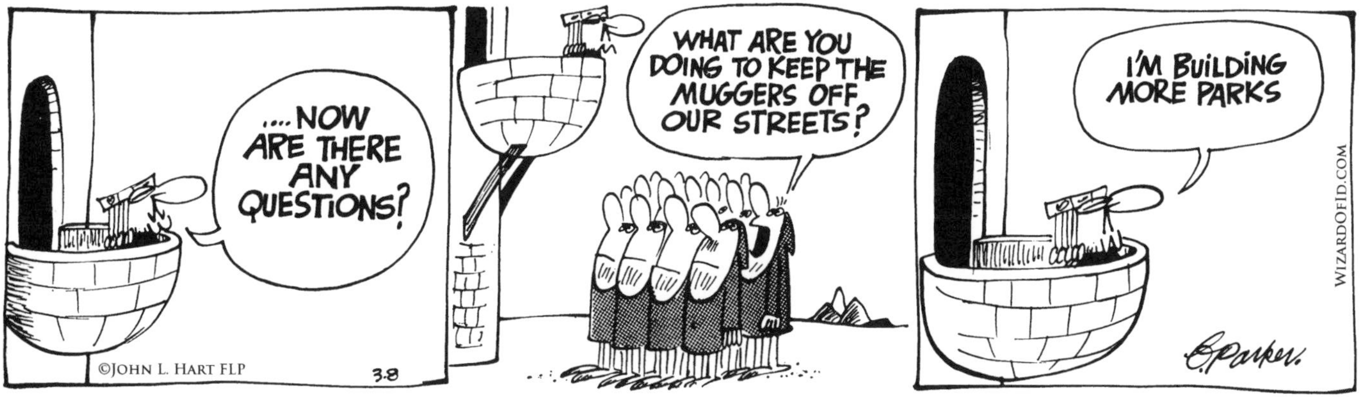
....NOW ARE THERE ANY QUESTIONS?
©JOHN L. HART FLP
3·8
WHAT ARE YOU DOING TO KEEP THE MUGGERS OFF OUR STREETS?
I'M BUILDING MORE PARKS
WIZARDOFID.COM

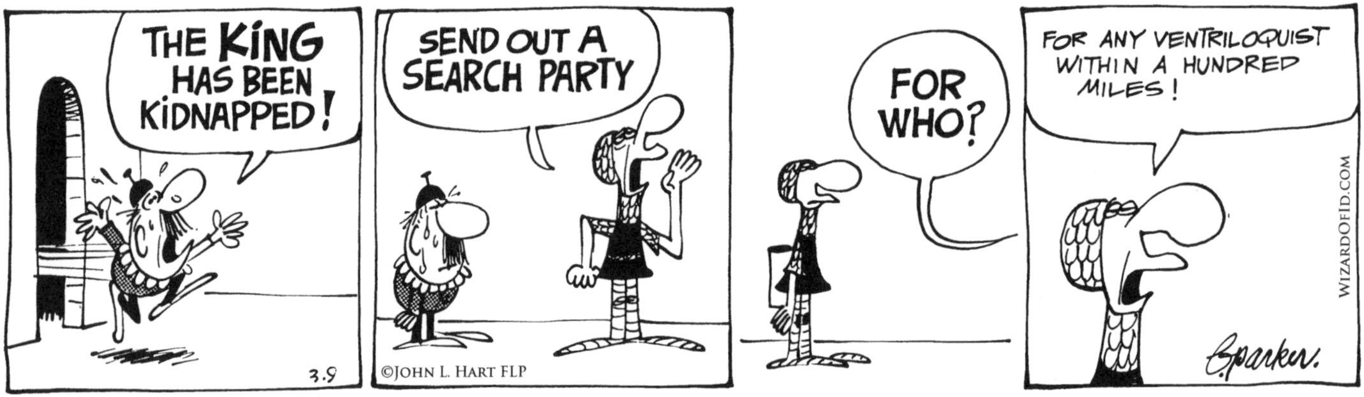
THE KING HAS BEEN KIDNAPPED!
SEND OUT A SEARCH PARTY
FOR WHO?
FOR ANY VENTRILOQUIST WITHIN A HUNDRED MILES!
3.9
©JOHN L. HART FLP
WIZARDOFID.COM
Parker.

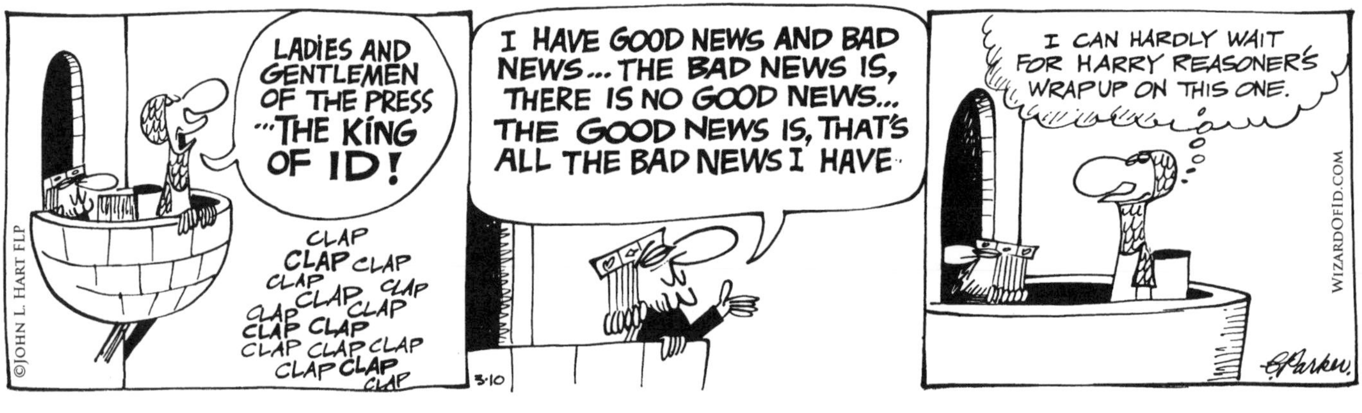
LADIES AND GENTLEMEN OF THE PRESS ...THE KING OF ID!
CLAP CLAP CLAP CLAP CLAP CLAP CLAP CLAP CLAP CLAP CLAP CLAP CLAP CLAP CLAP CLAP
I HAVE GOOD NEWS AND BAD NEWS... THE BAD NEWS IS, THERE IS NO GOOD NEWS... THE GOOD NEWS IS, THAT'S ALL THE BAD NEWS I HAVE..
I CAN HARDLY WAIT FOR HARRY REASONER'S WRAPUP ON THIS ONE.
3.10
©JOHN L. HART FLP
WIZARDOFID.COM
Parker.

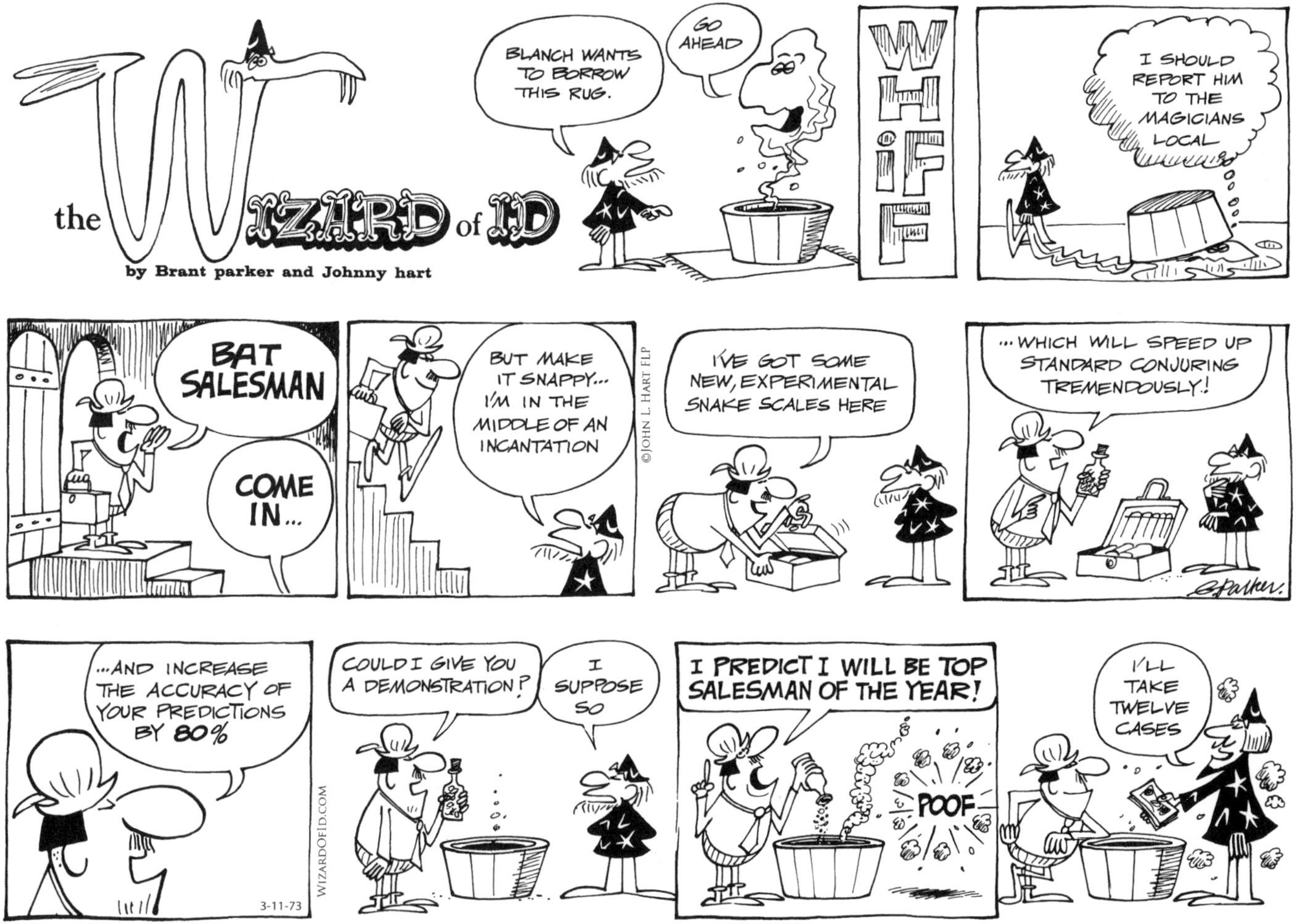
the WIZARD of ID
by Brant parker and Johnny hart
BLANCH WANTS TO BORROW THIS RUG.
GO AHEAD
WHIFF
I SHOULD REPORT HIM TO THE MAGICIANS LOCAL
BAT SALESMAN
COME IN...
BUT MAKE IT SNAPPY... I'M IN THE MIDDLE OF AN INCANTATION
©JOHN L. HART FLP
I'VE GOT SOME NEW, EXPERIMENTAL SNAKE SCALES HERE
...WHICH WILL SPEED UP STANDARD CONJURING TREMENDOUSLY!
B.Parker.
...AND INCREASE THE ACCURACY OF YOUR PREDICTIONS BY 80%
3-11-73
WIZARDOFID.COM
COULD I GIVE YOU A DEMONSTRATION?
I SUPPOSE SO
I PREDICT I WILL BE TOP SALESMAN OF THE YEAR!
POOF
I'LL TAKE TWELVE CASES

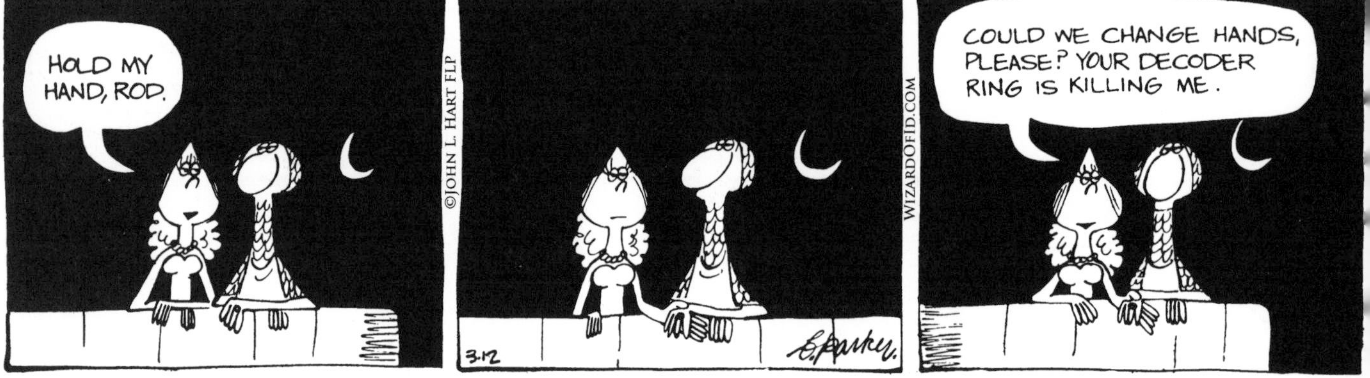
HOLD MY HAND, ROD.
©JOHN L. HART FLP
3.12
COULD WE CHANGE HANDS, PLEASE? YOUR DECODER RING IS KILLING ME.
WIZARDOFID.COM

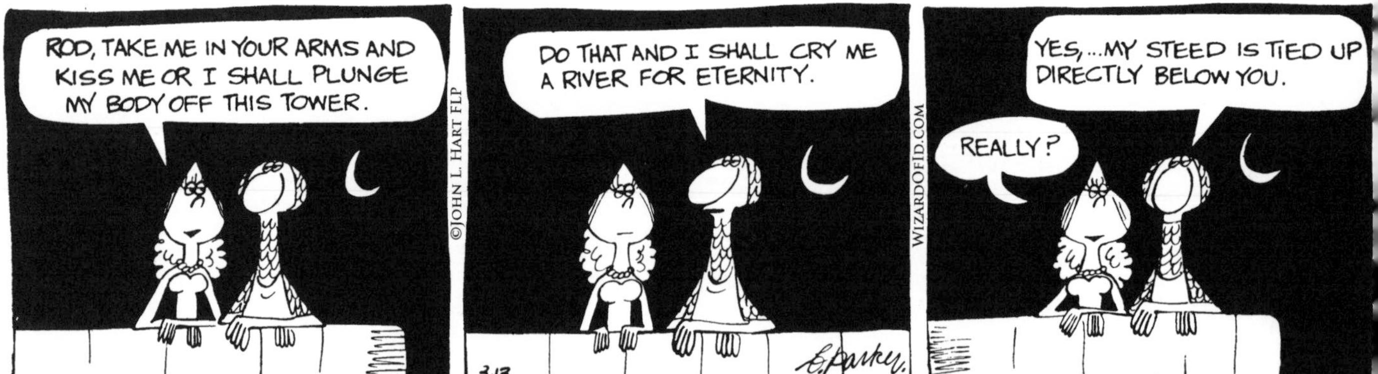
ROD, TAKE ME IN YOUR ARMS AND KISS ME OR I SHALL PLUNGE MY BODY OFF THIS TOWER.
©JOHN L. HART FLP
DO THAT AND I SHALL CRY ME A RIVER FOR ETERNITY.
3.13
YES, ...MY STEED IS TIED UP DIRECTLY BELOW YOU.
REALLY?
WIZARDOFID.COM

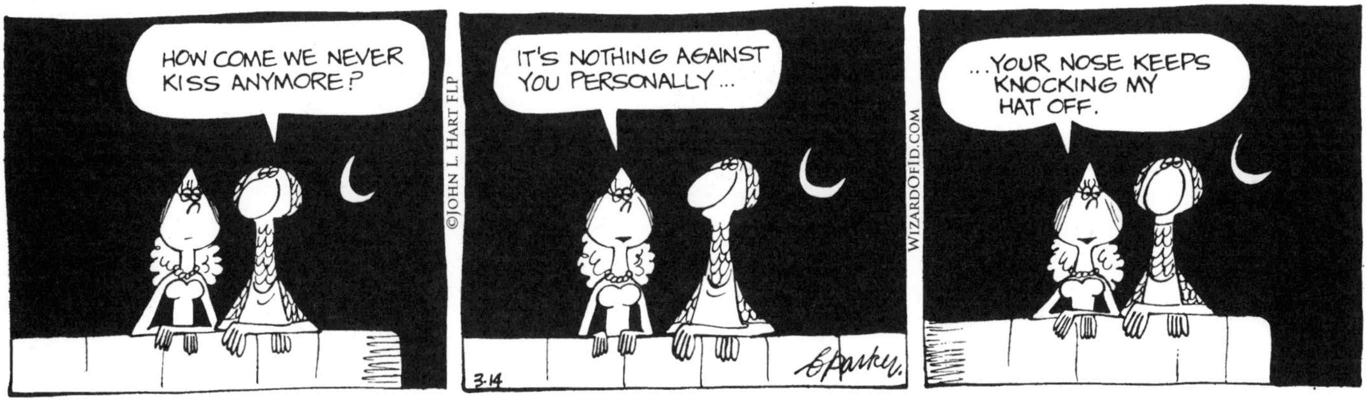
HOW COME WE NEVER KISS ANYMORE?
IT'S NOTHING AGAINST YOU PERSONALLY...
...YOUR NOSE KEEPS KNOCKING MY HAT OFF.
©JOHN L. HART FLP
WIZARDOFID.COM
3·14

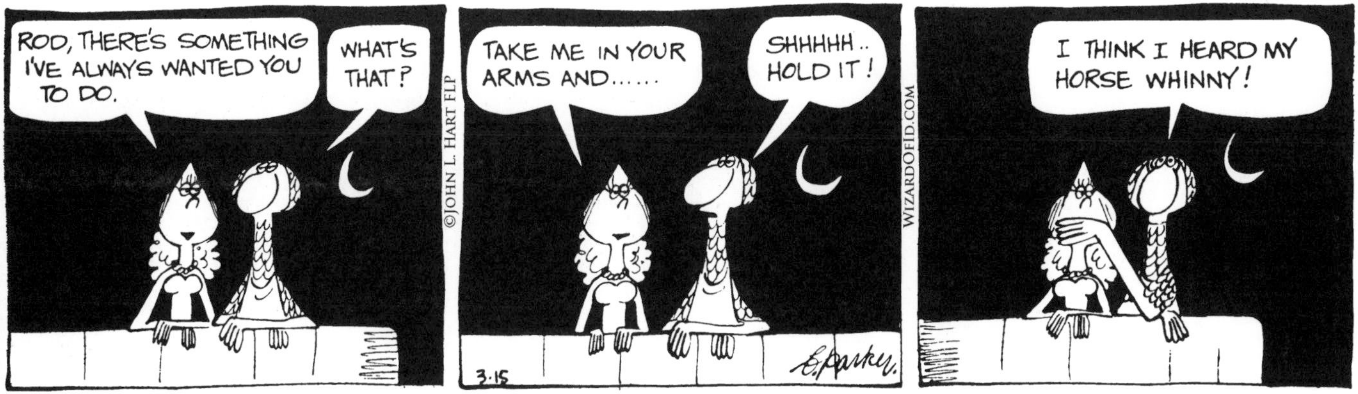
ROD, THERE'S SOMETHING I'VE ALWAYS WANTED YOU TO DO.
WHAT'S THAT?
TAKE ME IN YOUR ARMS AND......
SHHHHH.. HOLD IT!
I THINK I HEARD MY HORSE WHINNY!
©JOHN L. HART FLP
WIZARDOFID.COM
3·15

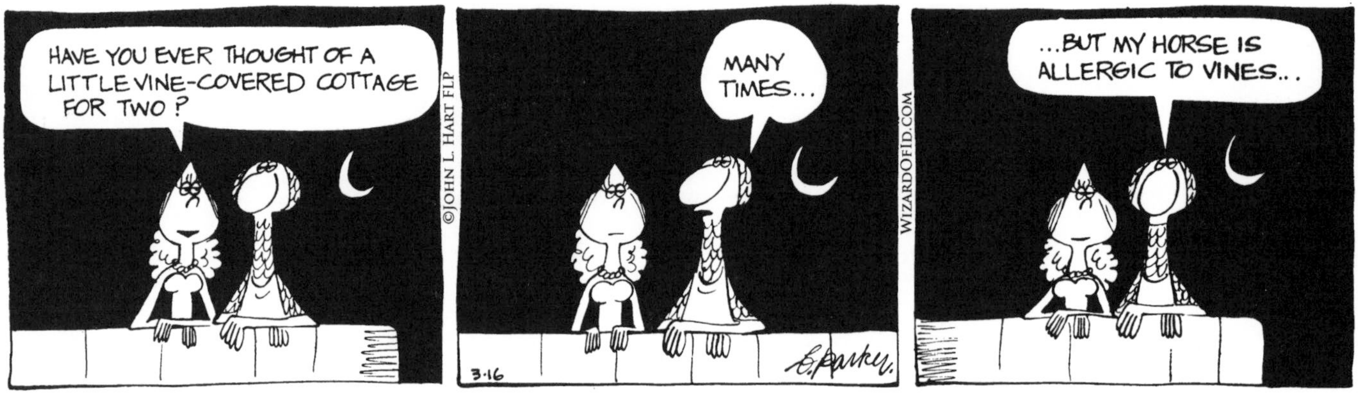
HAVE YOU EVER THOUGHT OF A LITTLE VINE-COVERED COTTAGE FOR TWO ?
©JOHN L. HART FLP
MANY TIMES...
3·16
B. Parker.
WIZARDOFID.COM
...BUT MY HORSE IS ALLERGIC TO VINES...

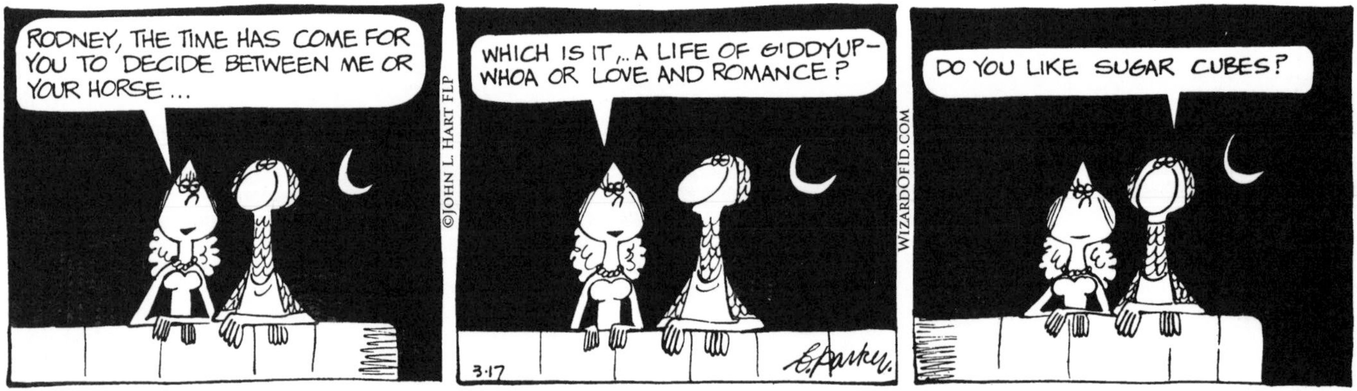
RODNEY, THE TIME HAS COME FOR YOU TO DECIDE BETWEEN ME OR YOUR HORSE ...
©JOHN L. HART FLP
WHICH IS IT,.. A LIFE OF GIDDYUP-WHOA OR LOVE AND ROMANCE ?
3·17
B. Parker.
WIZARDOFID.COM
DO YOU LIKE SUGAR CUBES?

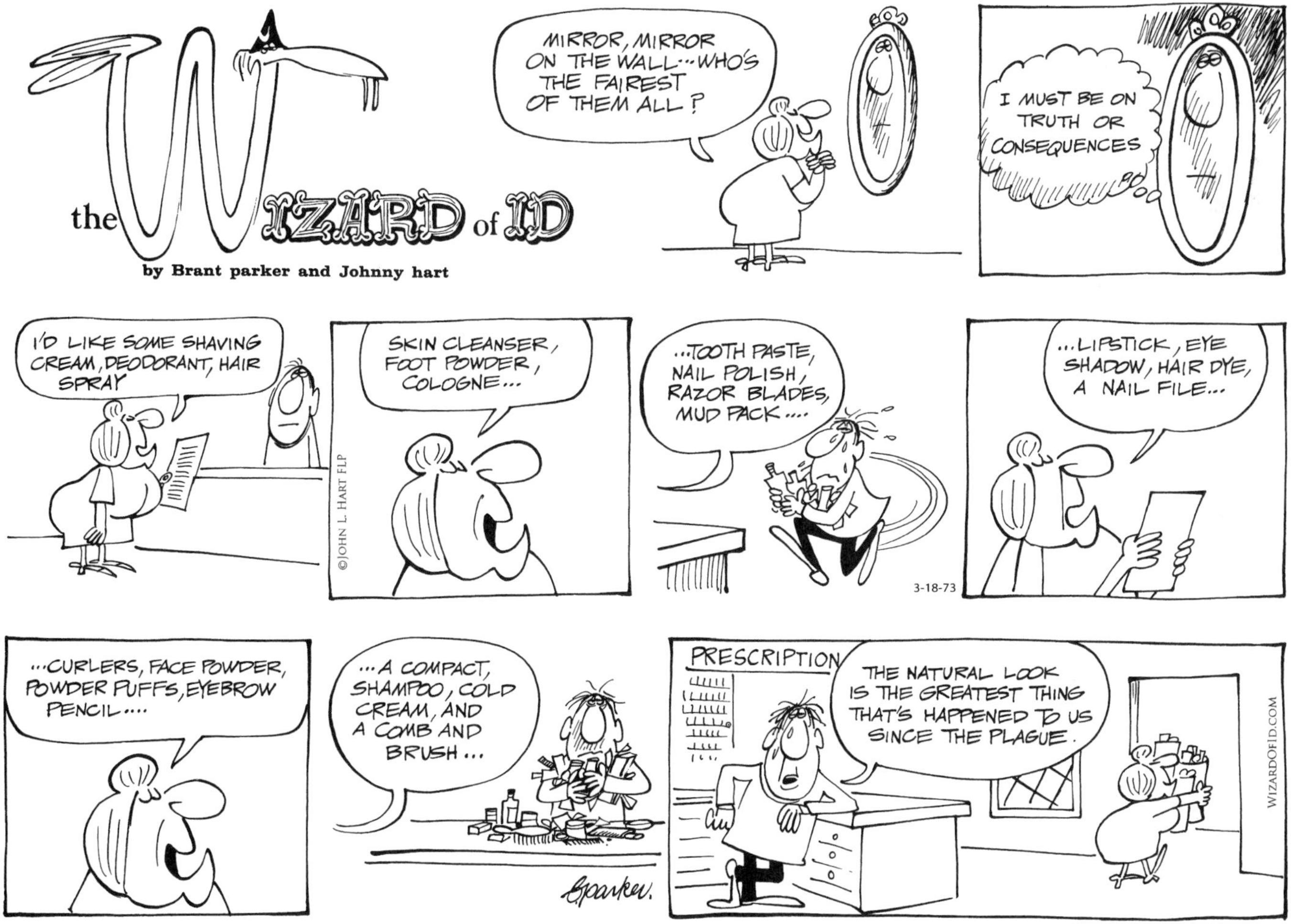
the WIZARD of ID
by Brant parker and Johnny hart
MIRROR, MIRROR ON THE WALL... WHO'S THE FAIREST OF THEM ALL ?
I MUST BE ON TRUTH OR CONSEQUENCES
I'D LIKE SOME SHAVING CREAM, DEODORANT, HAIR SPRAY
©JOHN L. HART FLP
SKIN CLEANSER, FOOT POWDER, COLOGNE...
...TOOTH PASTE, NAIL POLISH, RAZOR BLADES, MUD PACK....
3-18-73
...LIPSTICK, EYE SHADOW, HAIR DYE, A NAIL FILE...
...CURLERS, FACE POWDER, POWDER PUFFS, EYEBROW PENCIL....
...A COMPACT, SHAMPOO, COLD CREAM, AND A COMB AND BRUSH...
Bparker.
PRESCRIPTION
THE NATURAL LOOK IS THE GREATEST THING THAT'S HAPPENED TO US SINCE THE PLAGUE.
WIZARDOFID.COM

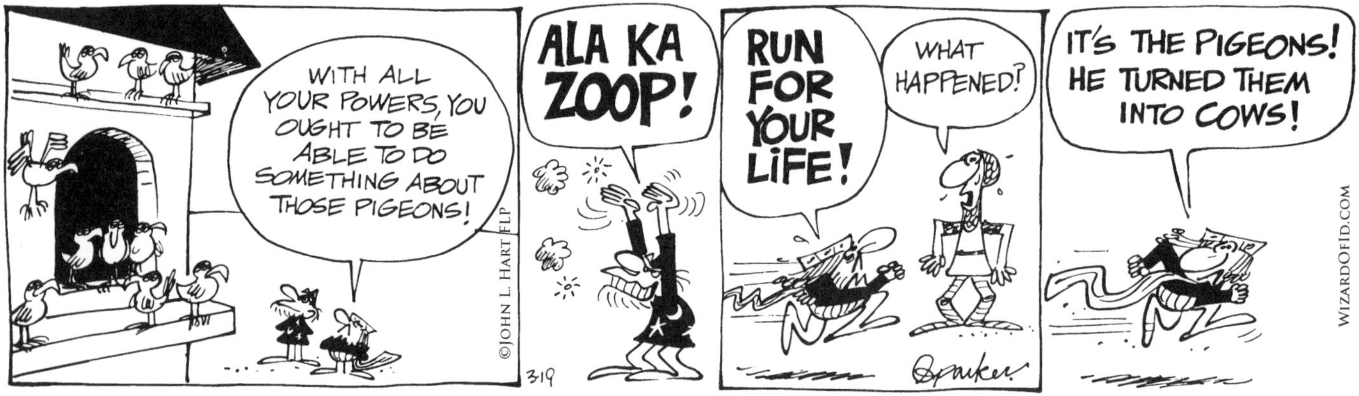
WITH ALL YOUR POWERS, YOU OUGHT TO BE ABLE TO DO SOMETHING ABOUT THOSE PIGEONS!
©JOHN L. HART FLP
3-19
ALA KA ZOOP!
RUN FOR YOUR LIFE!
WHAT HAPPENED?
IT'S THE PIGEONS! HE TURNED THEM INTO COWS!
WIZARDOFID.COM

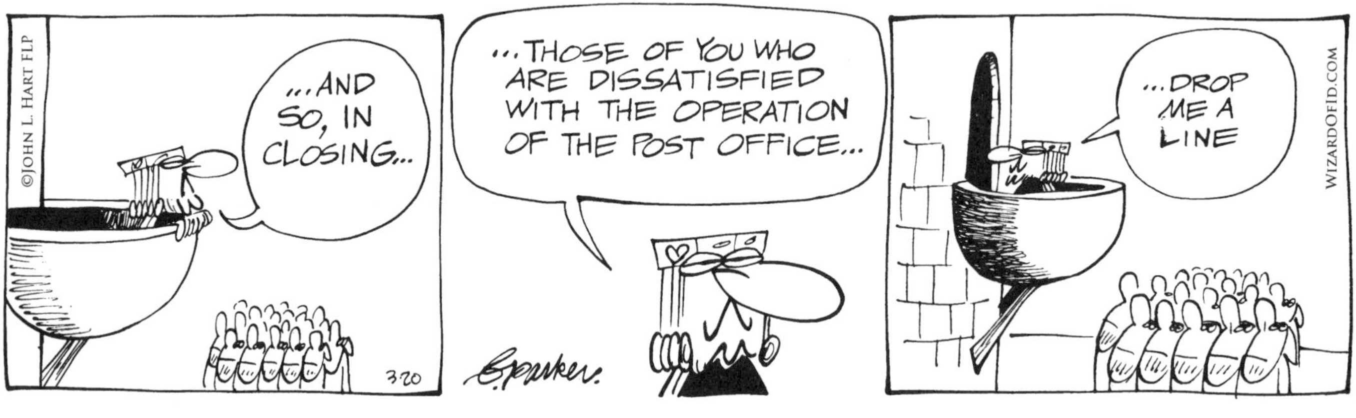
©JOHN L. HART FLP
...AND SO, IN CLOSING...
3-20
...THOSE OF YOU WHO ARE DISSATISFIED WITH THE OPERATION OF THE POST OFFICE...
...DROP ME A LINE
WIZARDOFID.COM

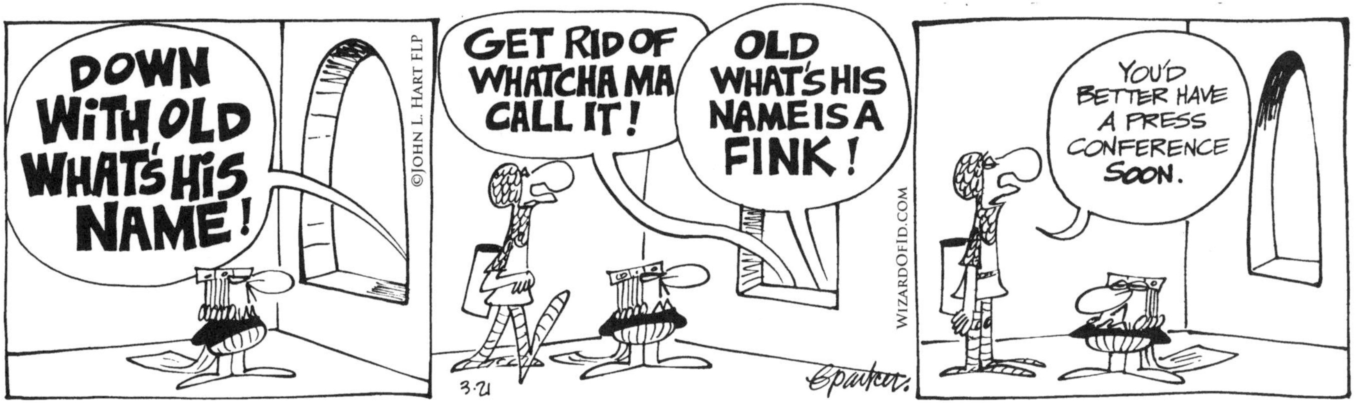
DOWN WITH OLD WHAT'S HIS NAME!
©JOHN L. HART FLP
GET RID OF WHATCHA MA CALL IT!
OLD WHAT'S HIS NAME IS A FINK!
3·21
B.parker.
WIZARDOFID.COM
YOU'D BETTER HAVE A PRESS CONFERENCE SOON.

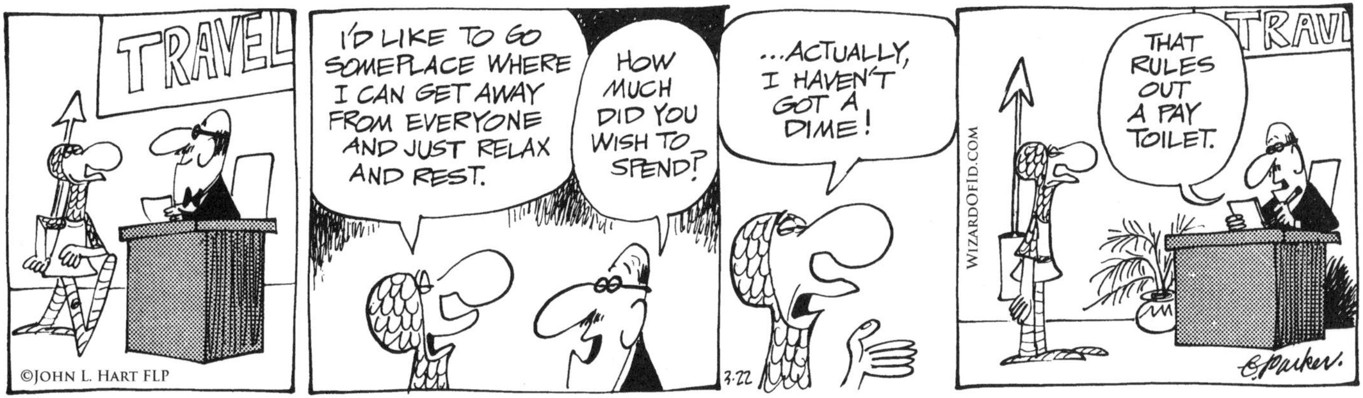
TRAVEL
©JOHN L. HART FLP
I'D LIKE TO GO SOMEPLACE WHERE I CAN GET AWAY FROM EVERYONE AND JUST RELAX AND REST.
HOW MUCH DID YOU WISH TO SPEND?
...ACTUALLY, I HAVEN'T GOT A DIME!
3·22
WIZARDOFID.COM
TRAV
THAT RULES OUT A PAY TOILET.
B.Parker.

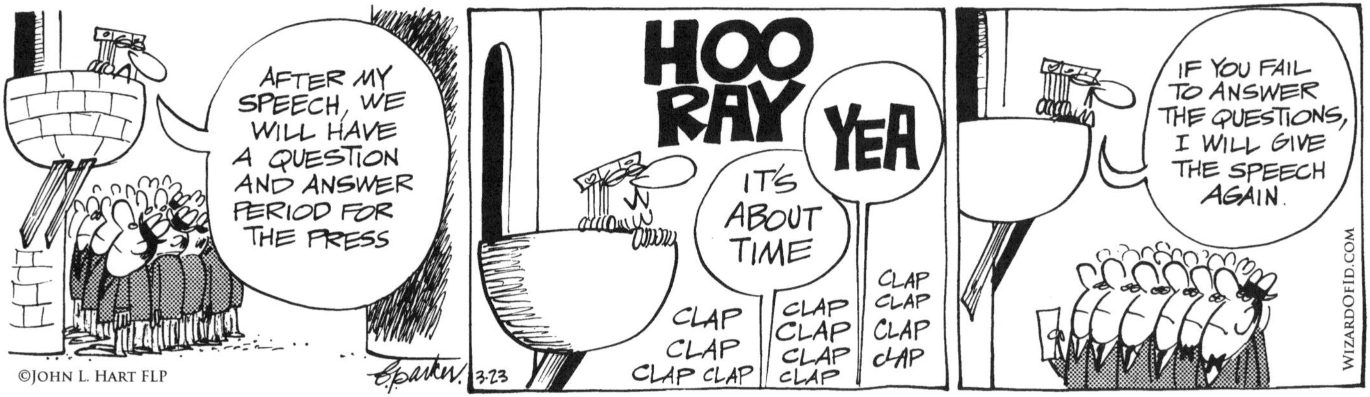
AFTER MY SPEECH, WE WILL HAVE A QUESTION AND ANSWER PERIOD FOR THE PRESS
HOO RAY
YEA
IT'S ABOUT TIME
CLAP CLAP CLAP CLAP
CLAP CLAP CLAP CLAP
CLAP CLAP CLAP CLAP
IF YOU FAIL TO ANSWER THE QUESTIONS, I WILL GIVE THE SPEECH AGAIN.
WIZARDOFID.COM

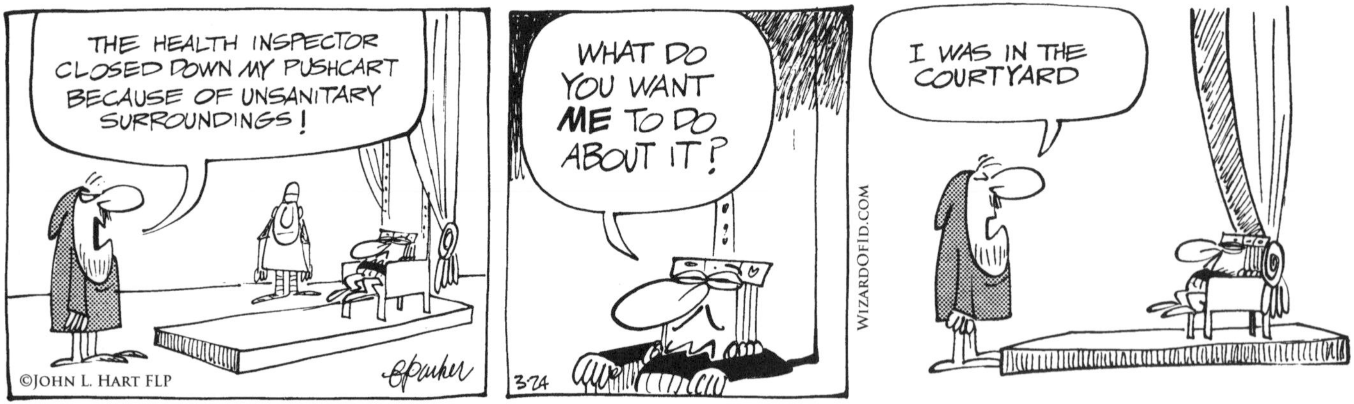
THE HEALTH INSPECTOR CLOSED DOWN MY PUSHCART BECAUSE OF UNSANITARY SURROUNDINGS!
WHAT DO YOU WANT ME TO DO ABOUT IT?
I WAS IN THE COURTYARD
WIZARDOFID.COM

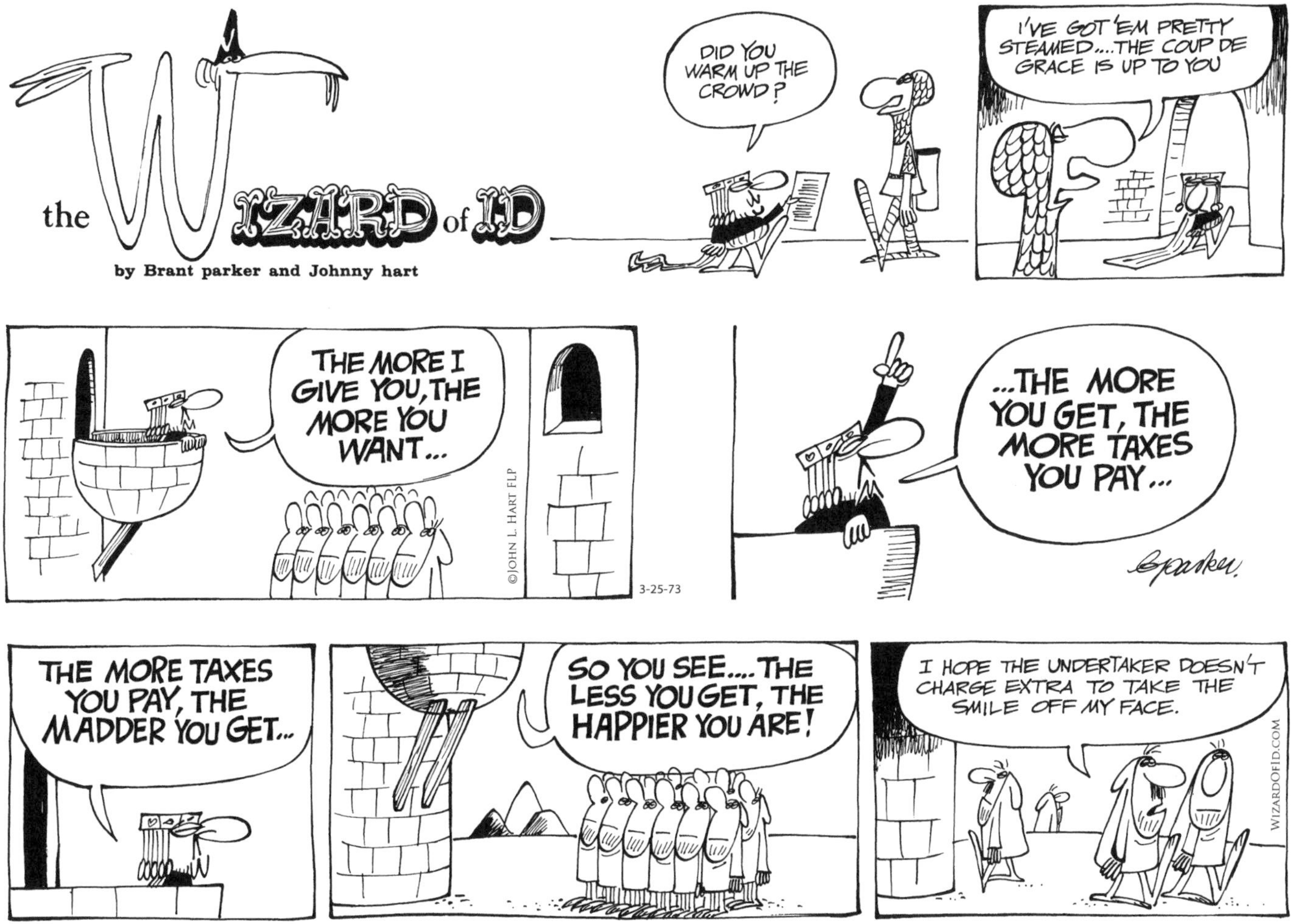
the WIZARD of ID
by Brant parker and Johnny hart
DID YOU WARM UP THE CROWD?
I'VE GOT 'EM PRETTY STEAMED....THE COUP DE GRACE IS UP TO YOU
THE MORE I GIVE YOU, THE MORE YOU WANT...
©JOHN L. HART FLP
3-25-73
...THE MORE YOU GET, THE MORE TAXES YOU PAY...
Bparker.
THE MORE TAXES YOU PAY, THE MADDER YOU GET...
SO YOU SEE.... THE LESS YOU GET, THE HAPPIER YOU ARE!
I HOPE THE UNDERTAKER DOESN'T CHARGE EXTRA TO TAKE THE SMILE OFF MY FACE.
WIZARDOFID.COM

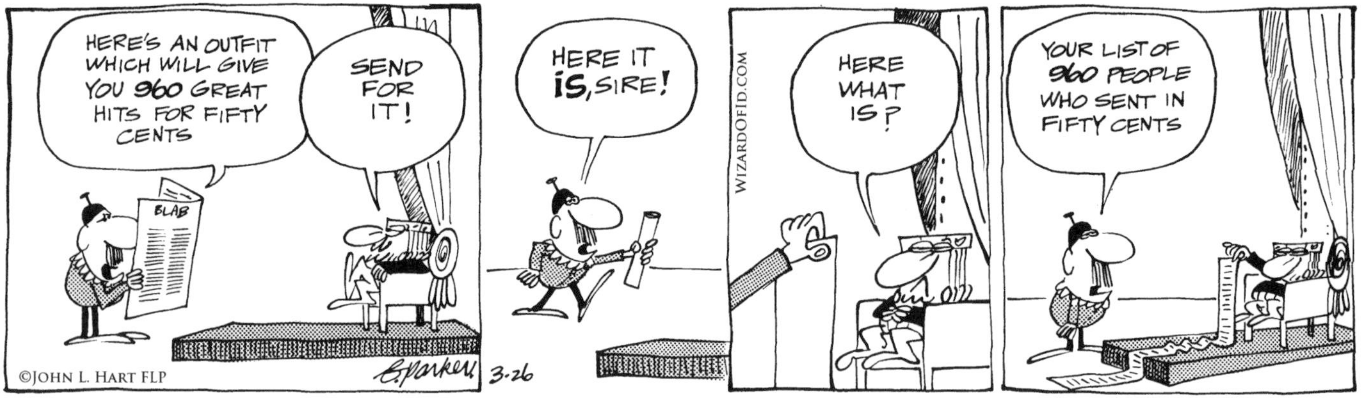
HERE'S AN OUTFIT WHICH WILL GIVE YOU 960 GREAT HITS FOR FIFTY CENTS
BLAB
SEND FOR IT!
HERE IT IS, SIRE!
HERE WHAT IS?
YOUR LIST OF 960 PEOPLE WHO SENT IN FIFTY CENTS
WIZARDOFID.COM
©JOHN L. HART FLP
3-26

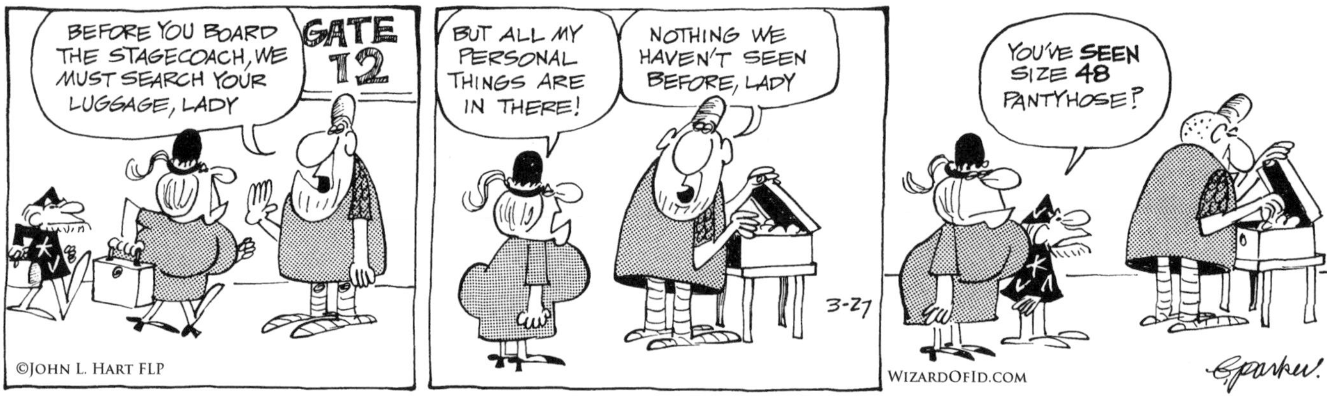
BEFORE YOU BOARD THE STAGECOACH, WE MUST SEARCH YOUR LUGGAGE, LADY
GATE 12
BUT ALL MY PERSONAL THINGS ARE IN THERE!
NOTHING WE HAVEN'T SEEN BEFORE, LADY
3-27
YOU'VE SEEN SIZE 48 PANTYHOSE?
©JOHN L. HART FLP
WIZARDOFID.COM

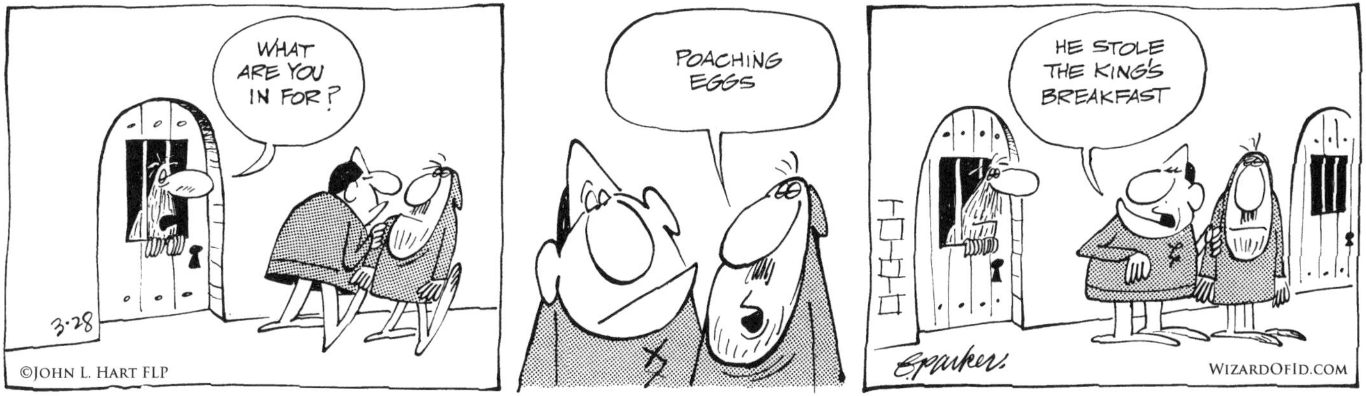
WHAT ARE YOU IN FOR?
3-28
©JOHN L. HART FLP
POACHING EGGS
HE STOLE THE KING'S BREAKFAST
WIZARDOFID.COM

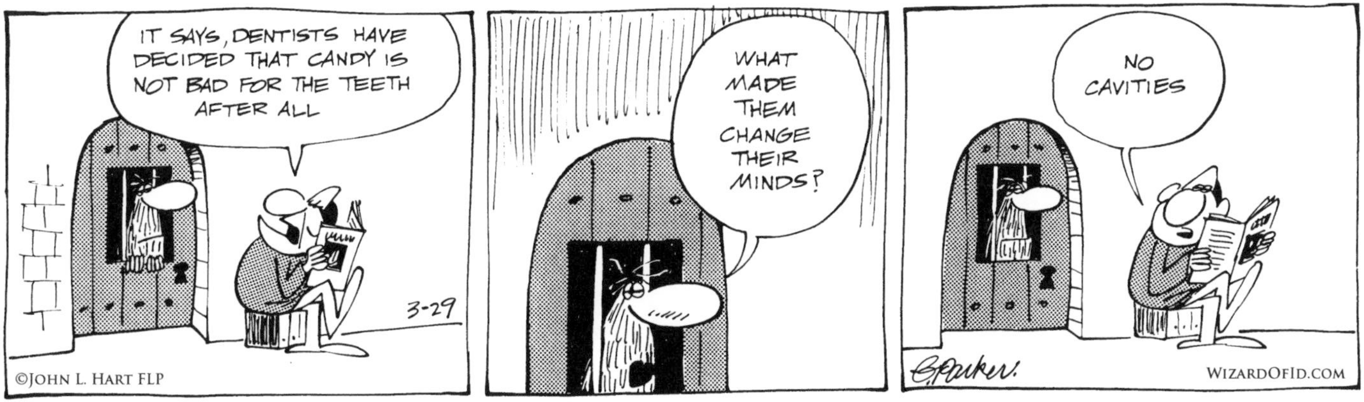
IT SAYS, DENTISTS HAVE DECIDED THAT CANDY IS NOT BAD FOR THE TEETH AFTER ALL
3-29
©JOHN L. HART FLP
WHAT MADE THEM CHANGE THEIR MINDS?
NO CAVITIES
WIZARDOFID.COM

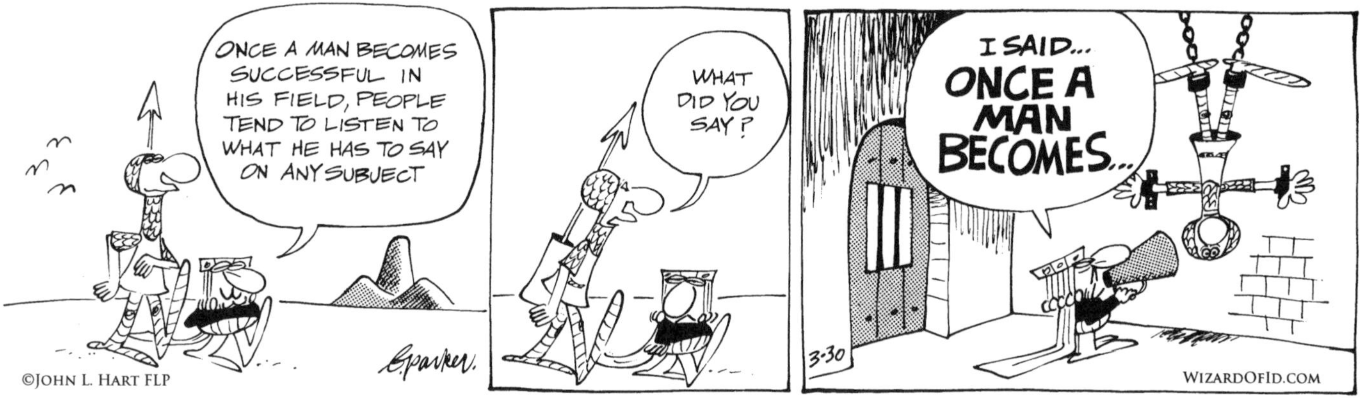
ONCE A MAN BECOMES SUCCESSFUL IN HIS FIELD, PEOPLE TEND TO LISTEN TO WHAT HE HAS TO SAY ON ANY SUBUECT
WHAT DID YOU SAY ?
I SAID... ONCE A MAN BECOMES...
3-30
©JOHN L. HART FLP
WIZARDOFID.COM

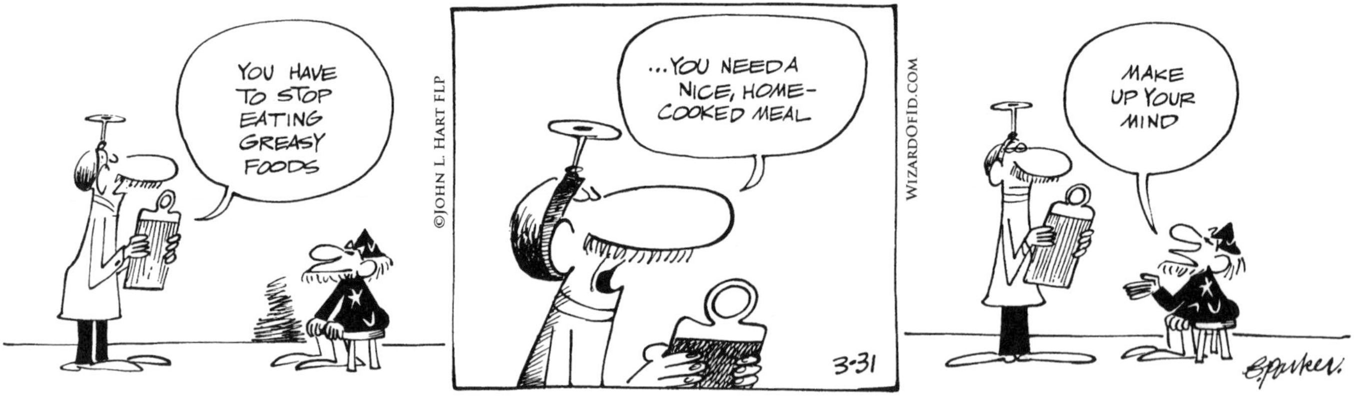
YOU HAVE TO STOP EATING GREASY FOODS
...YOU NEED A NICE, HOME-COOKED MEAL
MAKE UP YOUR MIND
3-31
©JOHN L. HART FLP
WIZARDOFID.COM

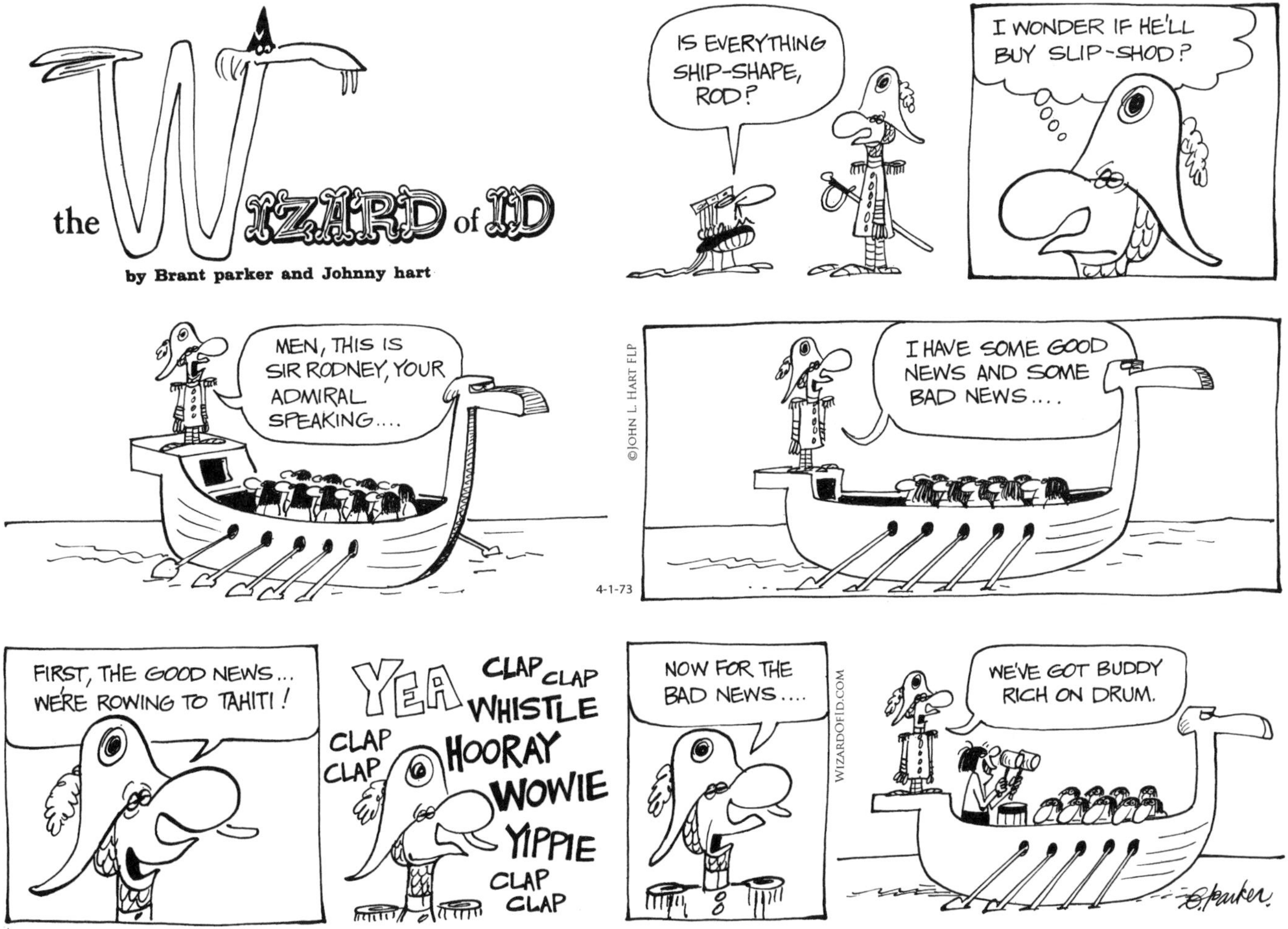
the WIZARD of ID
by Brant parker and Johnny hart
IS EVERYTHING SHIP-SHAPE, ROD?
I WONDER IF HE'LL BUY SLIP-SHOD?
MEN, THIS IS SIR RODNEY, YOUR ADMIRAL SPEAKING....
©JOHN L. HART FLP
4-1-73
I HAVE SOME GOOD NEWS AND SOME BAD NEWS....
FIRST, THE GOOD NEWS... WE'RE ROWING TO TAHITI!
YEA
CLAP CLAP
WHISTLE
CLAP CLAP
HOORAY
WOWIE
YIPPIE
CLAP CLAP
NOW FOR THE BAD NEWS....
WIZARDOFID.COM
WE'VE GOT BUDDY RICH ON DRUM.
B. parker

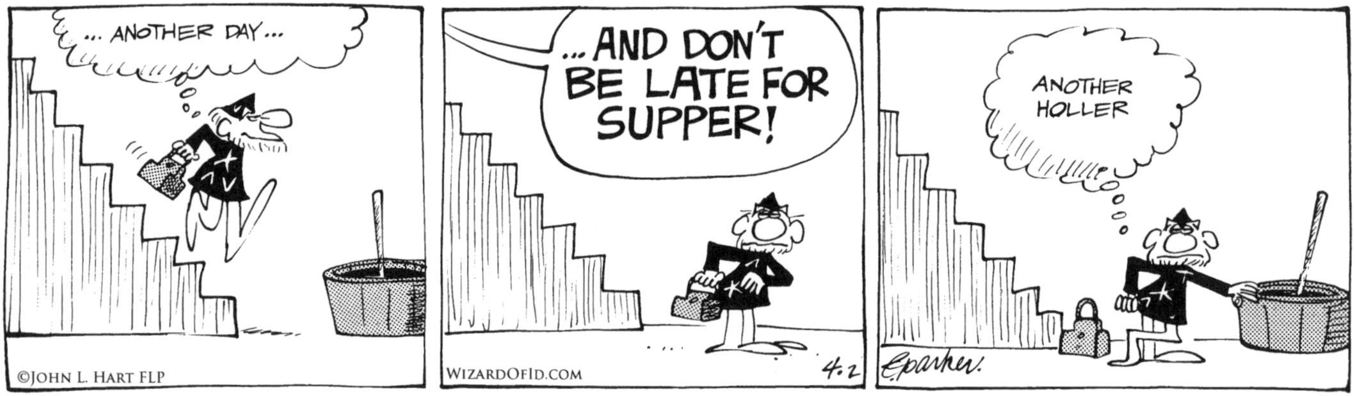
... ANOTHER DAY ...
©JOHN L. HART FLP
... AND DON'T BE LATE FOR SUPPER!
WIZARDOFID.COM
4-2
ANOTHER HOLLER

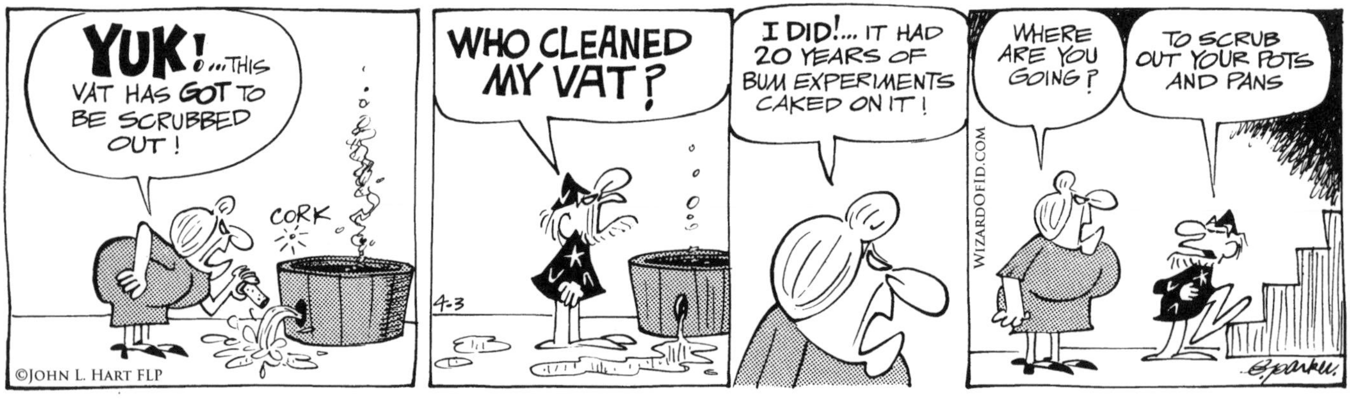
YUK! ... THIS VAT HAS GOT TO BE SCRUBBED OUT!
CORK
©JOHN L. HART FLP
WHO CLEANED MY VAT?
4-3
I DID!... IT HAD 20 YEARS OF BUM EXPERIMENTS CAKED ON IT!
WIZARDOFID.COM
WHERE ARE YOU GOING?
TO SCRUB OUT YOUR POTS AND PANS

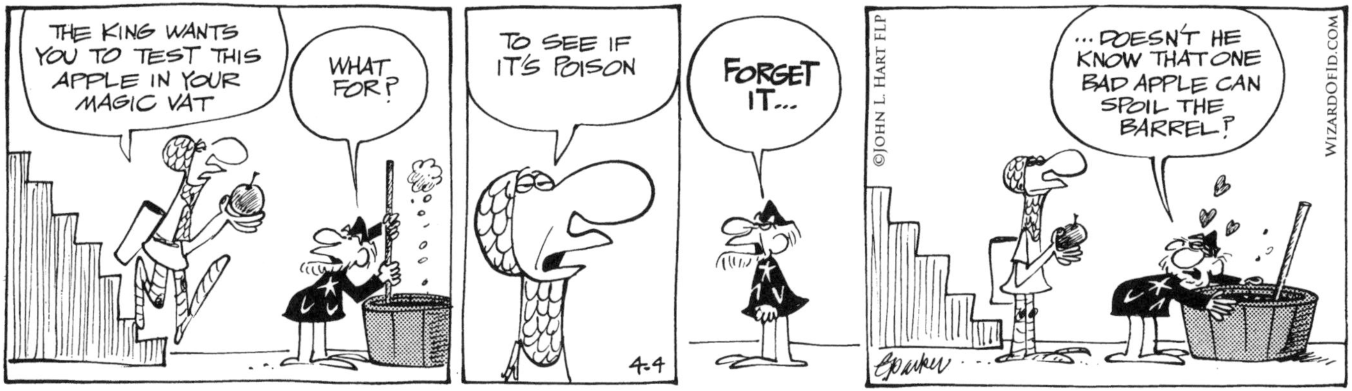
THE KING WANTS YOU TO TEST THIS APPLE IN YOUR MAGIC VAT
WHAT FOR?
TO SEE IF IT'S POISON
FORGET IT...
4.4
©JOHN L. HART FLP
...DOESN'T HE KNOW THAT ONE BAD APPLE CAN SPOIL THE BARREL?
WIZARDOFID.COM

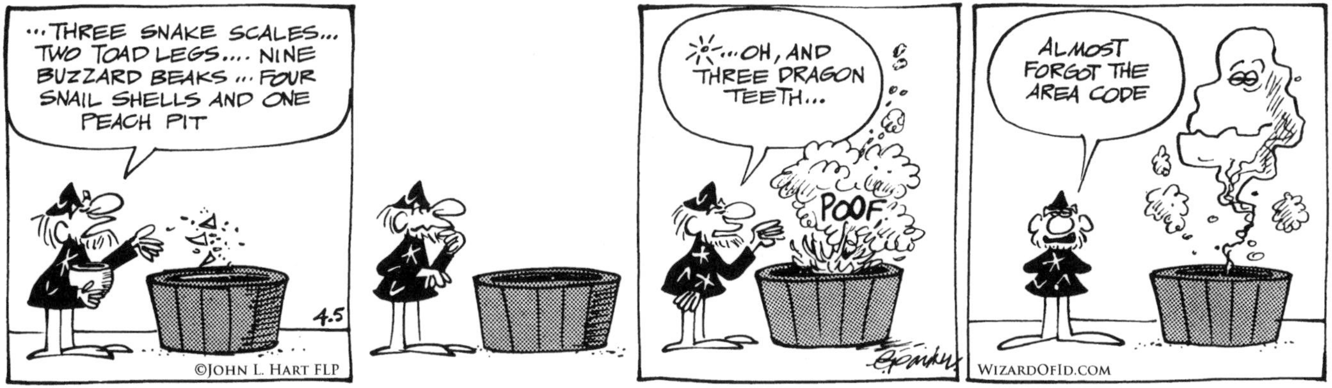
...THREE SNAKE SCALES... TWO TOAD LEGS.... NINE BUZZARD BEAKS ... FOUR SNAIL SHELLS AND ONE PEACH PIT
4.5
©JOHN L. HART FLP
...OH, AND THREE DRAGON TEETH...
POOF
ALMOST FORGOT THE AREA CODE
WIZARDOFID.COM

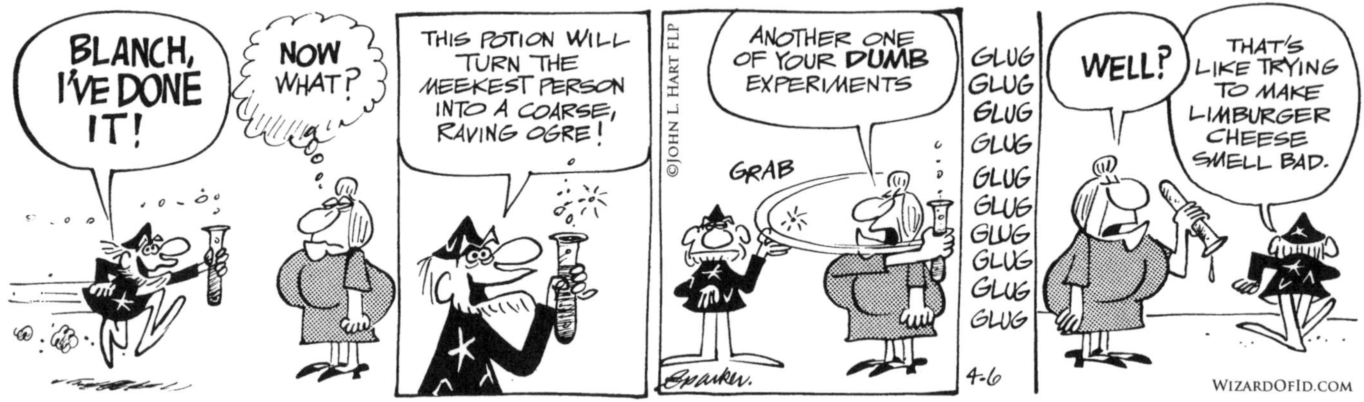
BLANCH, I'VE DONE IT!
NOW WHAT?
THIS POTION WILL TURN THE MEEKEST PERSON INTO A COARSE, RAVING OGRE!
©JOHN L. HART FLP
ANOTHER ONE OF YOUR DUMB EXPERIMENTS
GRAB
GLUG GLUG GLUG GLUG GLUG GLUG GLUG GLUG GLUG GLUG
4-6
WELL?
THAT'S LIKE TRYING TO MAKE LIMBURGER CHEESE SMELL BAD.
WIZARDOFID.COM

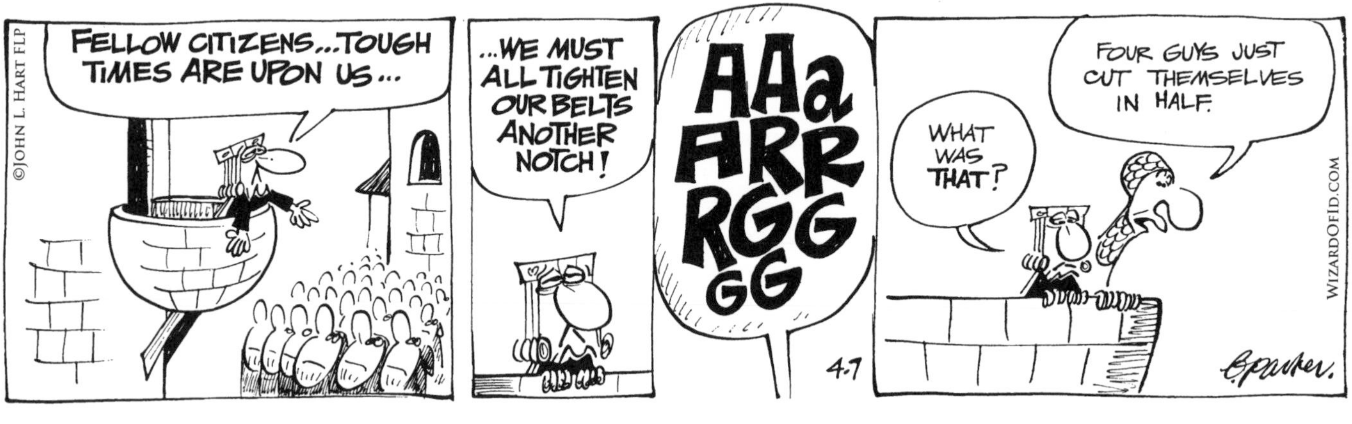
©JOHN L. HART FLP
FELLOW CITIZENS...TOUGH TIMES ARE UPON US...
...WE MUST ALL TIGHTEN OUR BELTS ANOTHER NOTCH!
AAa ARR RGG GG
4-7
WHAT WAS THAT?
FOUR GUYS JUST CUT THEMSELVES IN HALF.
WIZARDOFID.COM

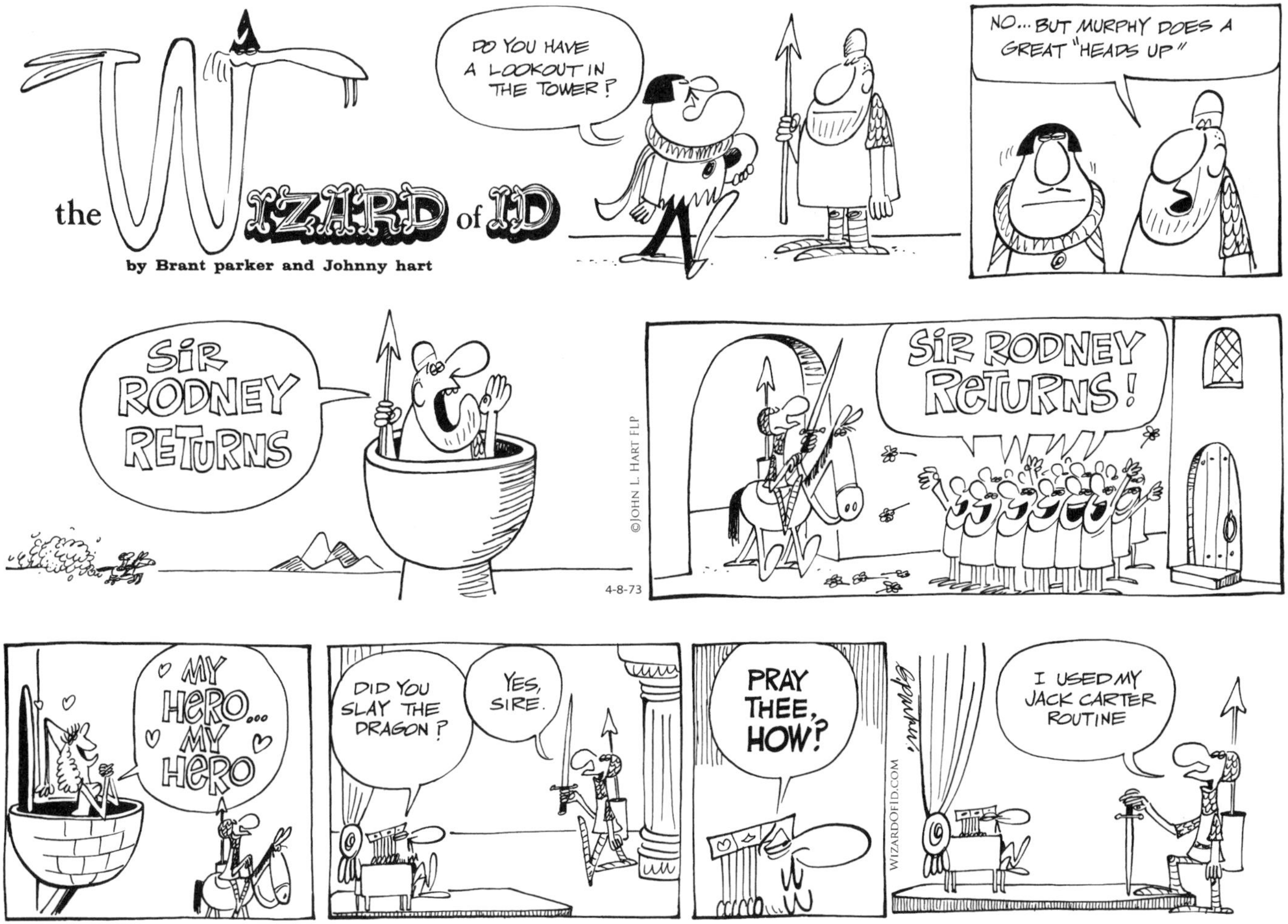

the WIZARD of ID
by Brant parker and Johnny hart
DO YOU HAVE A LOOKOUT IN THE TOWER?
NO... BUT MURPHY DOES A GREAT "HEADS UP"
SIR RODNEY RETURNS
SIR RODNEY RETURNS!
©JOHN L. HART FLP
4-8-73
MY HERO... MY HERO
DID YOU SLAY THE DRAGON?
YES, SIRE.
PRAY THEE, HOW?
WIZARDOFID.COM
I USED MY JACK CARTER ROUTINE

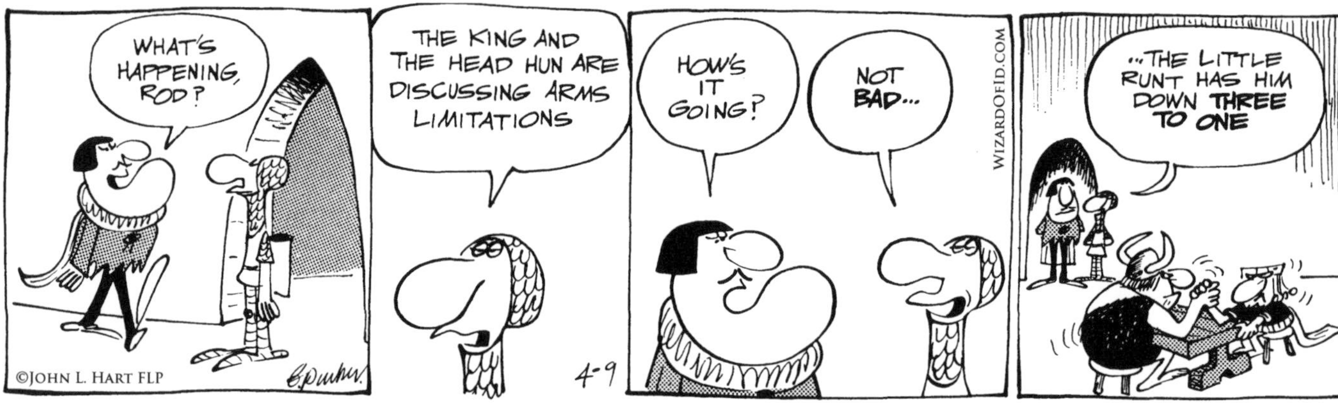
WHAT'S HAPPENING, ROD?
THE KING AND THE HEAD HUN ARE DISCUSSING ARMS LIMITATIONS
HOW'S IT GOING?
NOT BAD...
...THE LITTLE RUNT HAS HIM DOWN THREE TO ONE
©JOHN L. HART FLP
4-9
WIZARDOFID.COM

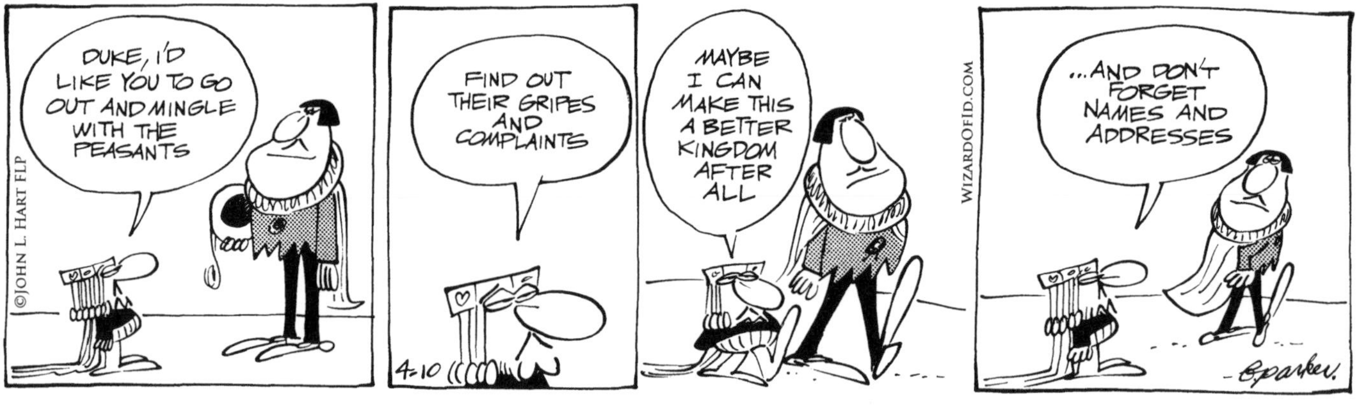
DUKE, I'D LIKE YOU TO GO OUT AND MINGLE WITH THE PEASANTS
FIND OUT THEIR GRIPES AND COMPLAINTS
MAYBE I CAN MAKE THIS A BETTER KINGDOM AFTER ALL
...AND DON'T FORGET NAMES AND ADDRESSES
©JOHN L. HART FLP
4-10
WIZARDOFID.COM

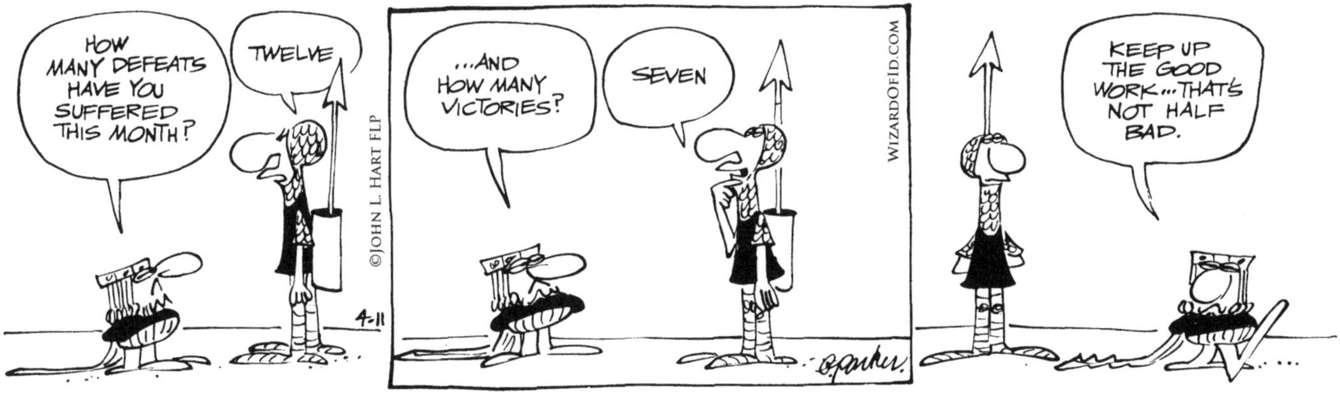
HOW MANY DEFEATS HAVE YOU SUFFERED THIS MONTH?
TWELVE
©JOHN L. HART FLP
4-11
...AND HOW MANY VICTORIES?
SEVEN
WIZARDOFID.COM
KEEP UP THE GOOD WORK... THAT'S NOT HALF BAD.

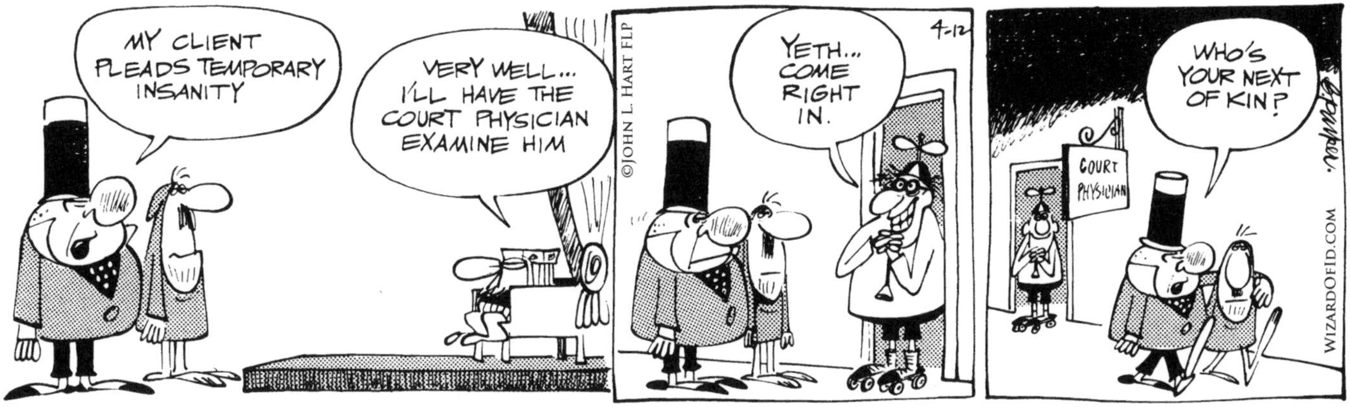
MY CLIENT PLEADS TEMPORARY INSANITY
VERY WELL... I'LL HAVE THE COURT PHYSICIAN EXAMINE HIM
©JOHN L. HART FLP
4-12
YETH... COME RIGHT IN.
COURT PHYSICIAN
WHO'S YOUR NEXT OF KIN?
WIZARDOFID.COM

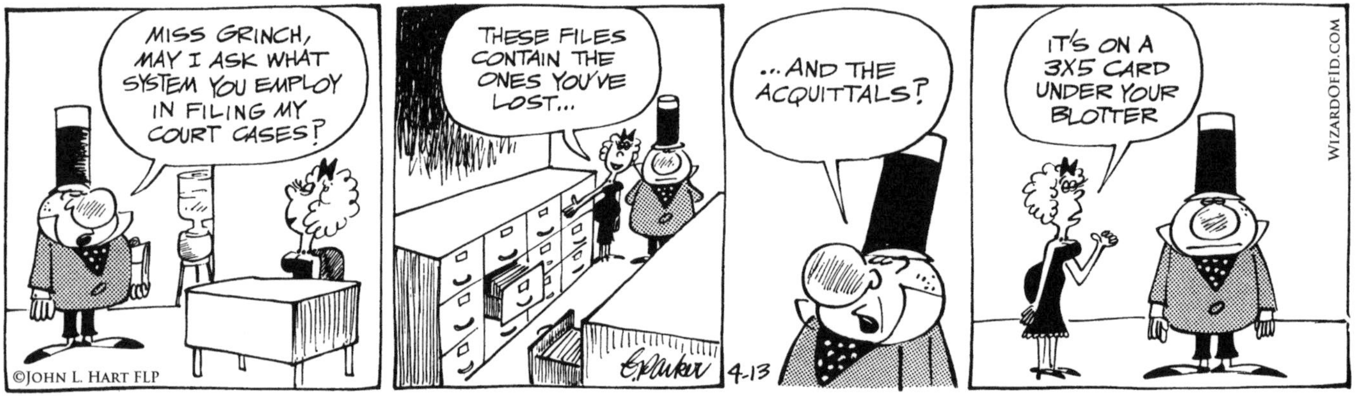
MISS GRINCH, MAY I ASK WHAT SYSTEM YOU EMPLOY IN FILING MY COURT CASES?
©JOHN L. HART FLP
THESE FILES CONTAIN THE ONES YOU'VE LOST...
B.Parker
4-13
...AND THE ACQUITTALS?
IT'S ON A 3X5 CARD UNDER YOUR BLOTTER
WIZARDOFID.COM

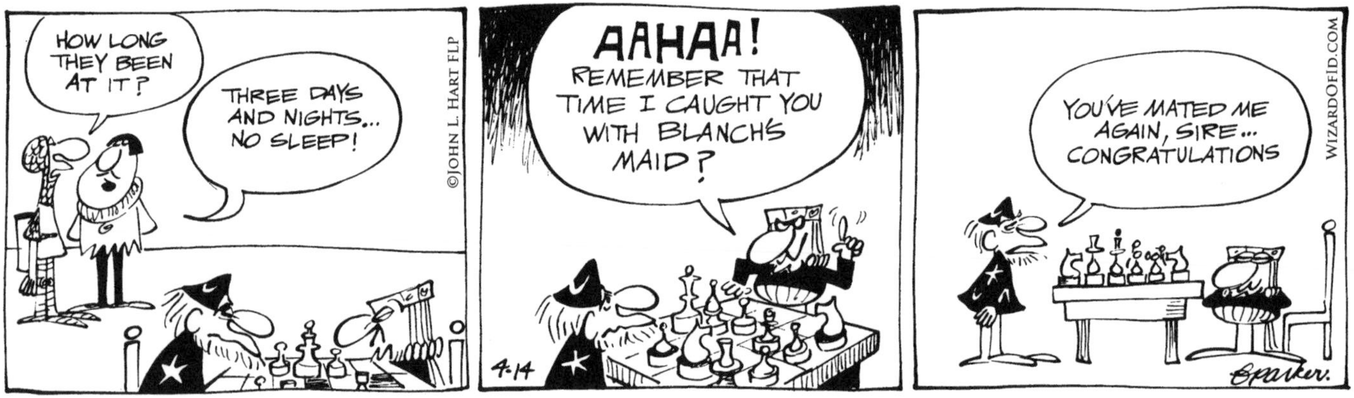
HOW LONG THEY BEEN AT IT?
THREE DAYS AND NIGHTS... NO SLEEP!
©JOHN L. HART FLP
AAHAA! REMEMBER THAT TIME I CAUGHT YOU WITH BLANCH'S MAID?
4-14
YOU'VE MATED ME AGAIN, SIRE... CONGRATULATIONS
WIZARDOFID.COM
B.Parker.

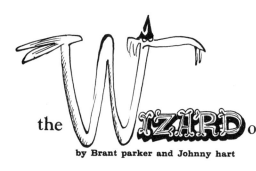

the WIZARD of ID

by Brant parker and Johnny hart

WHY DON'T YOU CLEAN OUT THAT VAT?... IT SMELLS TERRIBLE!

I'LL BET NEWTON'S OLD LADY NEVER COMPLAINED ABOUT SOUR APPLES

ARISE, OH SPIRIT!

HELLO... THIS IS YOUR SPIRIT SPEAKING. I AM SORRY, BUT ALL OF MY LINES ARE TEMPORARILY BUSY...

©JOHN L. HART FLP

THIS IS DUE TO THE FACT THAT I AM UNDERSTAFFED, OVERWORKED AND UNDERPAID...

...HOWEVER, WITH ANY LUCK, I SHOULD BE FREE SOMETIME LATER TODAY.

IN THE MEANTIME, IF YOU HAVE AN URGENT INCANTATION, YOU MAY SPEAK IT INTO THE VAT, WHEN YOU HEAR THE TONE

...REMEMBER, DON'T START SPEAKING UNTIL YOU HEAR THE......

GGRRRR

4-15-73

WIZARDOFID.COM

UH.... THANK YOU FOR WAITING... MY LINES ARE FREE NOW.

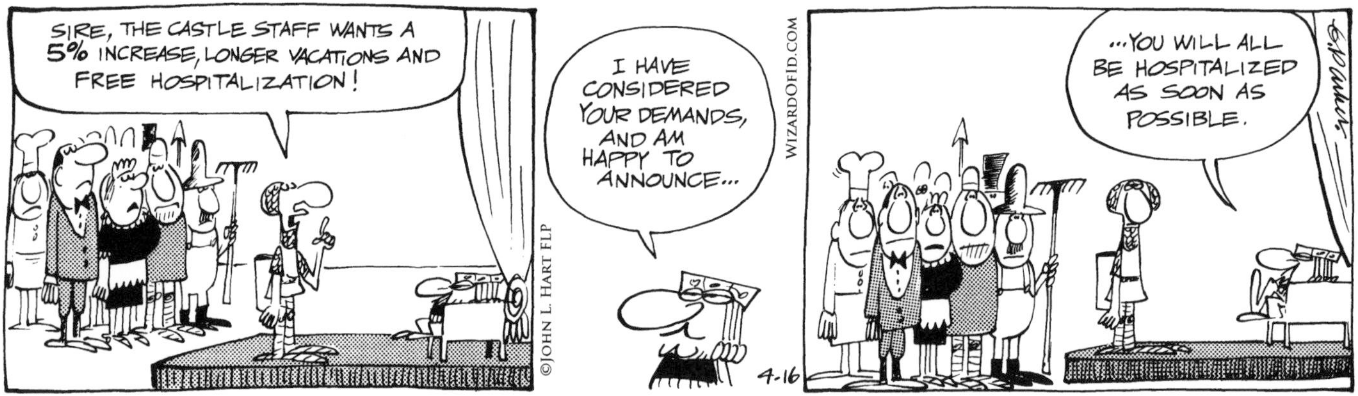
SIRE, THE CASTLE STAFF WANTS A 5% INCREASE, LONGER VACATIONS AND FREE HOSPITALIZATION!
©JOHN L. HART FLP
I HAVE CONSIDERED YOUR DEMANDS, AND AM HAPPY TO ANNOUNCE...
4-16
WIZARDOFID.COM
...YOU WILL ALL BE HOSPITALIZED AS SOON AS POSSIBLE.

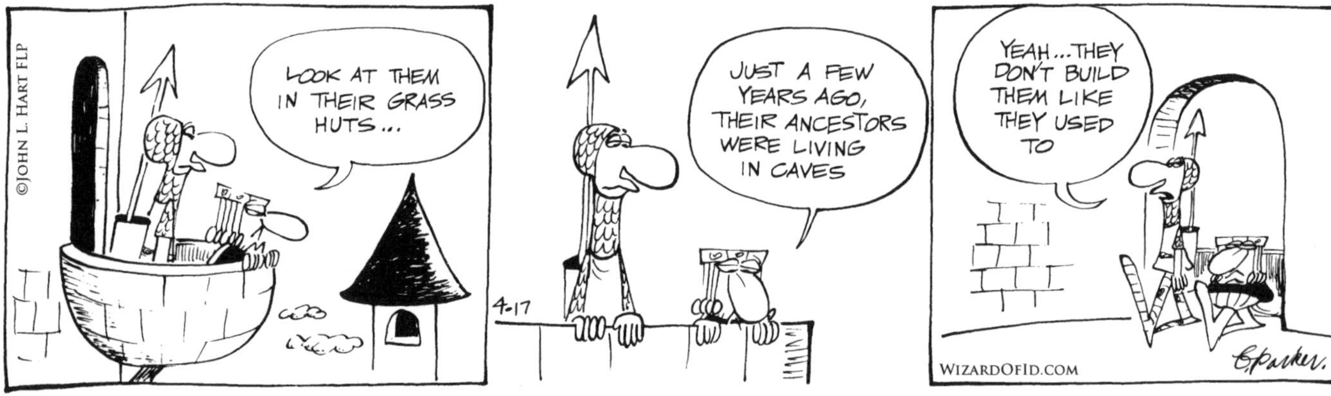
©JOHN L. HART FLP
LOOK AT THEM IN THEIR GRASS HUTS...
4-17
JUST A FEW YEARS AGO, THEIR ANCESTORS WERE LIVING IN CAVES
YEAH...THEY DON'T BUILD THEM LIKE THEY USED TO
WIZARDOFID.COM

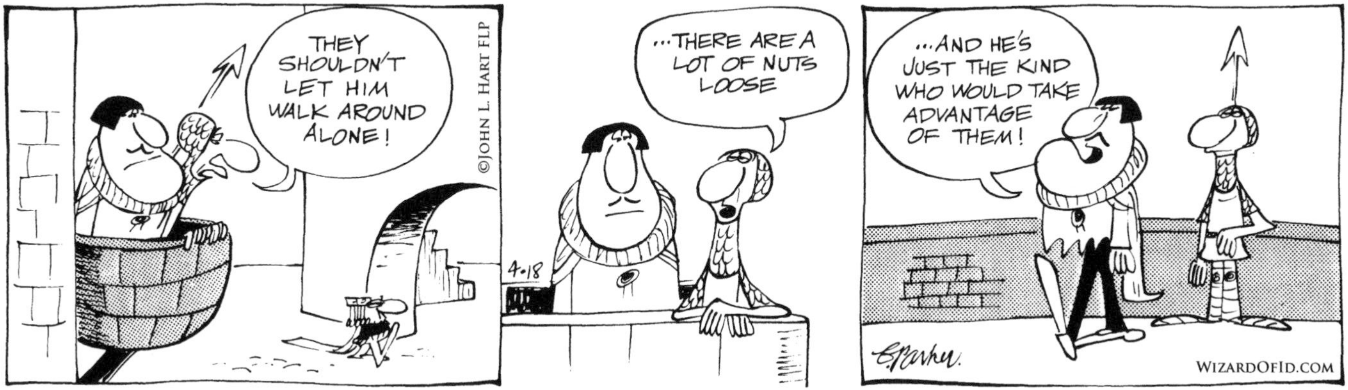
THEY SHOULDN'T LET HIM WALK AROUND ALONE!
©JOHN L. HART FLP
4-18
...THERE ARE A LOT OF NUTS LOOSE
...AND HE'S JUST THE KIND WHO WOULD TAKE ADVANTAGE OF THEM!
B.Parker.
WIZARDOFID.COM

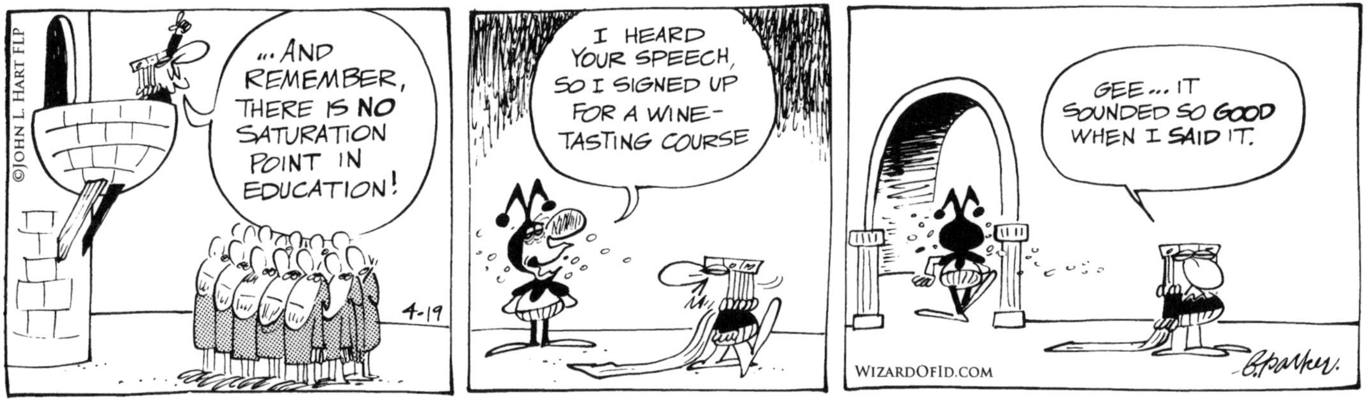
©JOHN L. HART FLP
...AND REMEMBER, THERE IS **NO** SATURATION POINT IN EDUCATION!
4-19
I HEARD YOUR SPEECH, SO I SIGNED UP FOR A WINE-TASTING COURSE
GEE... IT SOUNDED SO **GOOD** WHEN I **SAID** IT.
WIZARDOFID.COM
B.Parker.

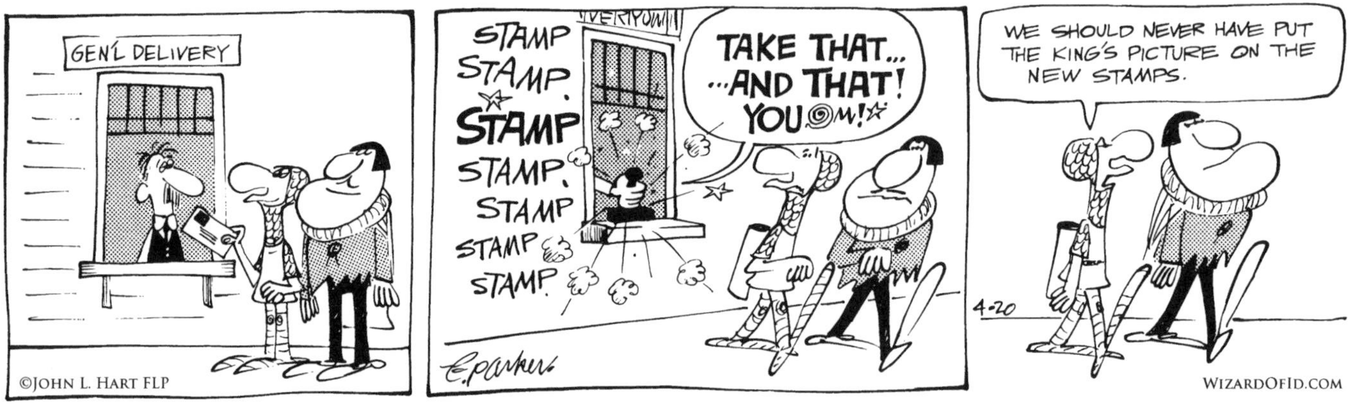
GEN'L DELIVERY
©JOHN L. HART FLP
STAMP STAMP STAMP STAMP STAMP STAMP STAMP
TAKE THAT... ...AND THAT! YOU
E. parker
WE SHOULD NEVER HAVE PUT THE KING'S PICTURE ON THE NEW STAMPS.
4-20
WIZARDOFID.COM

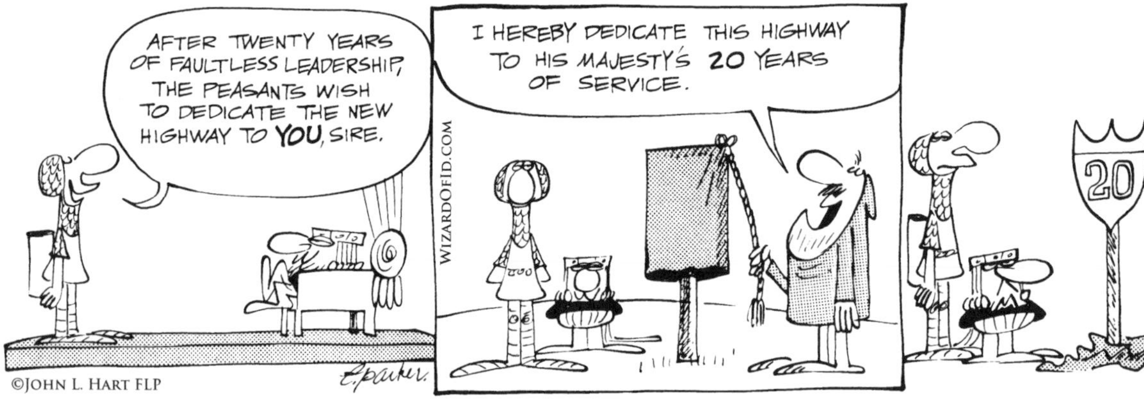
AFTER TWENTY YEARS OF FAULTLESS LEADERSHIP, THE PEASANTS WISH TO DEDICATE THE NEW HIGHWAY TO YOU, SIRE.
©JOHN L. HART FLP
E. parker
WIZARDOFID.COM
I HEREBY DEDICATE THIS HIGHWAY TO HIS MAJESTY'S 20 YEARS OF SERVICE.
20
PULL

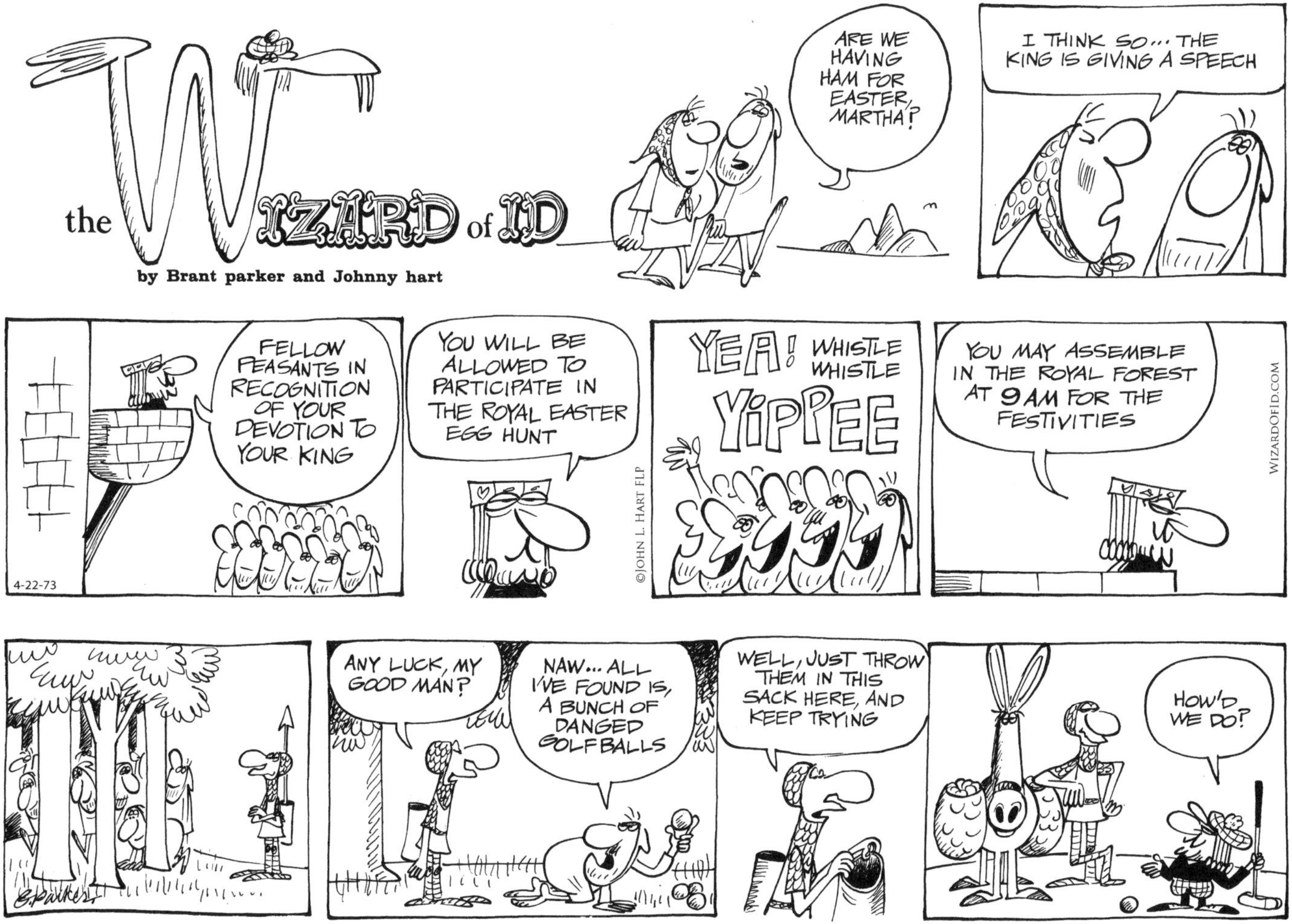

the WIZARD of ID
by Brant parker and Johnny hart
ARE WE HAVING HAM FOR EASTER, MARTHA?
I THINK SO... THE KING IS GIVING A SPEECH
4-22-73
FELLOW PEASANTS IN RECOGNITION OF YOUR DEVOTION TO YOUR KING
YOU WILL BE ALLOWED TO PARTICIPATE IN THE ROYAL EASTER EGG HUNT
©JOHN L. HART FLP
YEA! WHISTLE WHISTLE
YIPPEE
YOU MAY ASSEMBLE IN THE ROYAL FOREST AT 9 AM FOR THE FESTIVITIES
WIZARDOFID.COM
B.PARKER
ANY LUCK, MY GOOD MAN?
NAW... ALL I'VE FOUND IS, A BUNCH OF DANGED GOLF BALLS
WELL, JUST THROW THEM IN THIS SACK HERE, AND KEEP TRYING
HOW'D WE DO?

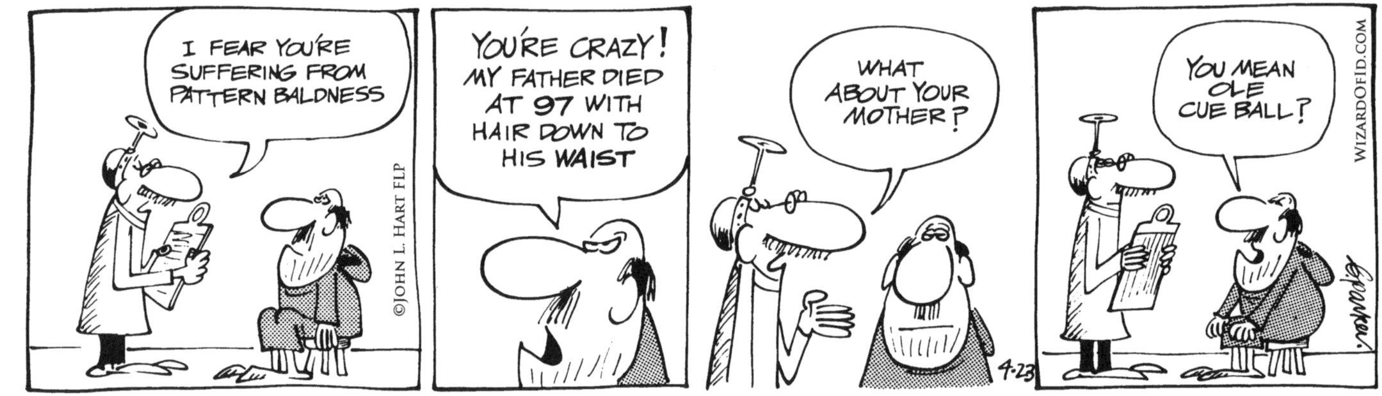
I FEAR YOU'RE SUFFERING FROM PATTERN BALDNESS
YOU'RE CRAZY! MY FATHER DIED AT 97 WITH HAIR DOWN TO HIS WAIST
WHAT ABOUT YOUR MOTHER?
YOU MEAN OLE CUE BALL?
©JOHN L. HART FLP
WIZARDOFID.COM
4·23

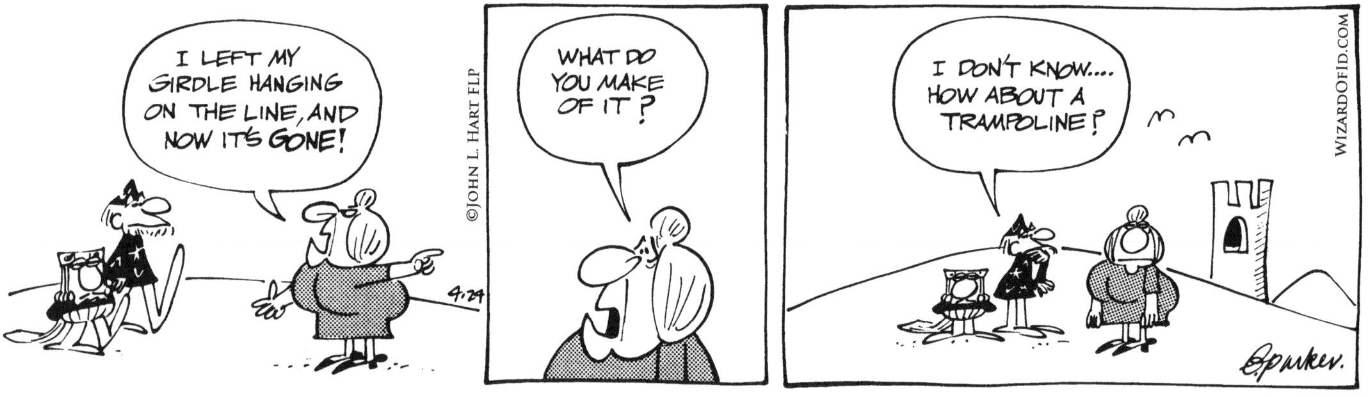
I LEFT MY GIRDLE HANGING ON THE LINE, AND NOW IT'S GONE!
WHAT DO YOU MAKE OF IT?
I DON'T KNOW.... HOW ABOUT A TRAMPOLINE?
©JOHN L. HART FLP
WIZARDOFID.COM
4·24

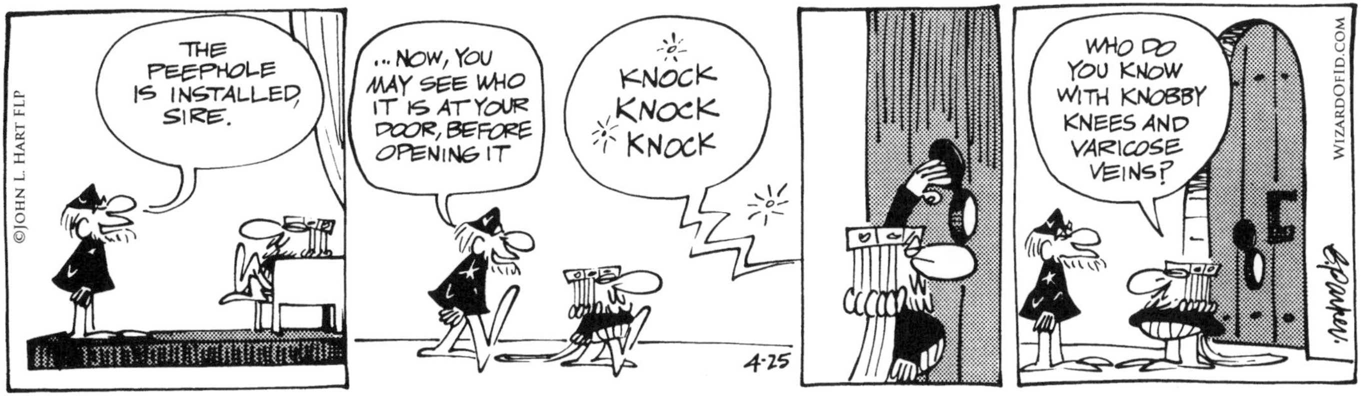
©JOHN L. HART FLP
THE PEEPHOLE IS INSTALLED, SIRE.
...NOW, YOU MAY SEE WHO IT IS AT YOUR DOOR, BEFORE OPENING IT
KNOCK KNOCK KNOCK
4-25
WHO DO YOU KNOW WITH KNOBBY KNEES AND VARICOSE VEINS?
WIZARDOFID.COM

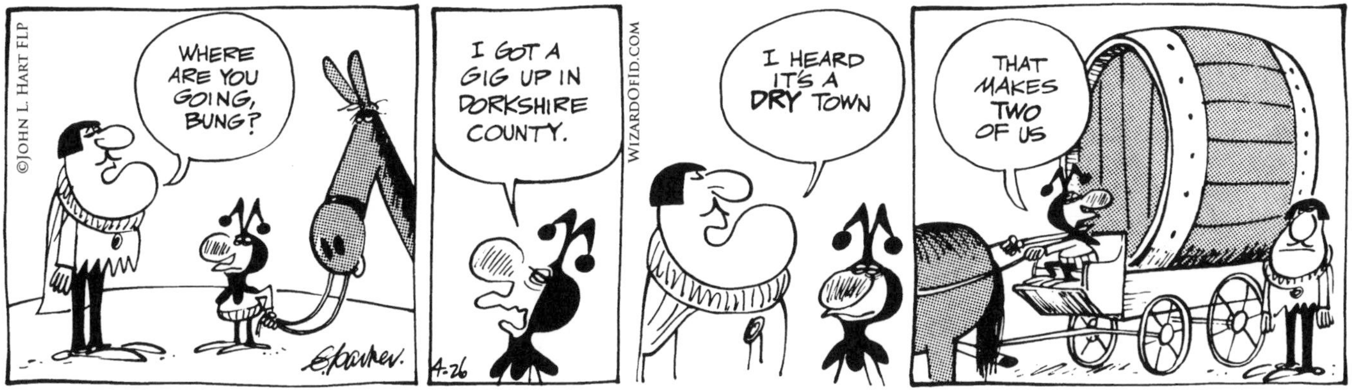
©JOHN L. HART FLP
WHERE ARE YOU GOING, BUNG?
I GOT A GIG UP IN DORKSHIRE COUNTY.
4-26
WIZARDOFID.COM
I HEARD IT'S A DRY TOWN
THAT MAKES TWO OF US

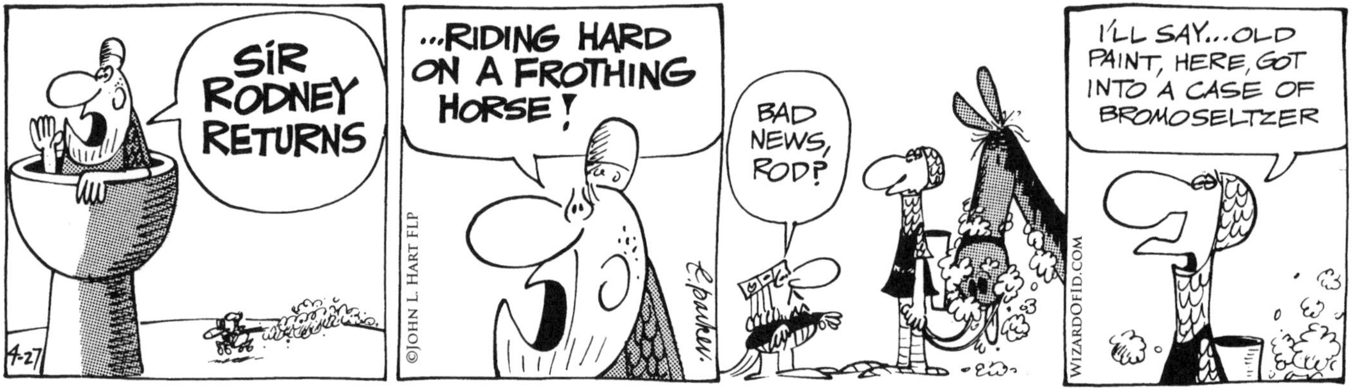
SIR RODNEY RETURNS
...RIDING HARD ON A FROTHING HORSE!
BAD NEWS, ROD?
I'LL SAY...OLD PAINT, HERE, GOT INTO A CASE OF BROMOSELTZER
4-27
©JOHN L. HART FLP
WIZARDOFID.COM

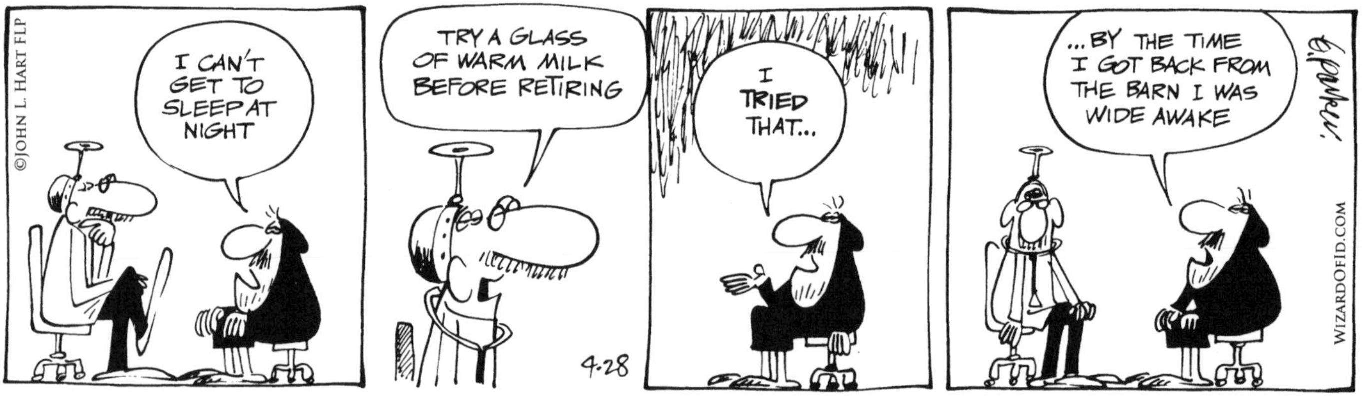
I CAN'T GET TO SLEEP AT NIGHT
TRY A GLASS OF WARM MILK BEFORE RETIRING
I TRIED THAT...
...BY THE TIME I GOT BACK FROM THE BARN I WAS WIDE AWAKE
4-28
©JOHN L. HART FLP
WIZARDOFID.COM

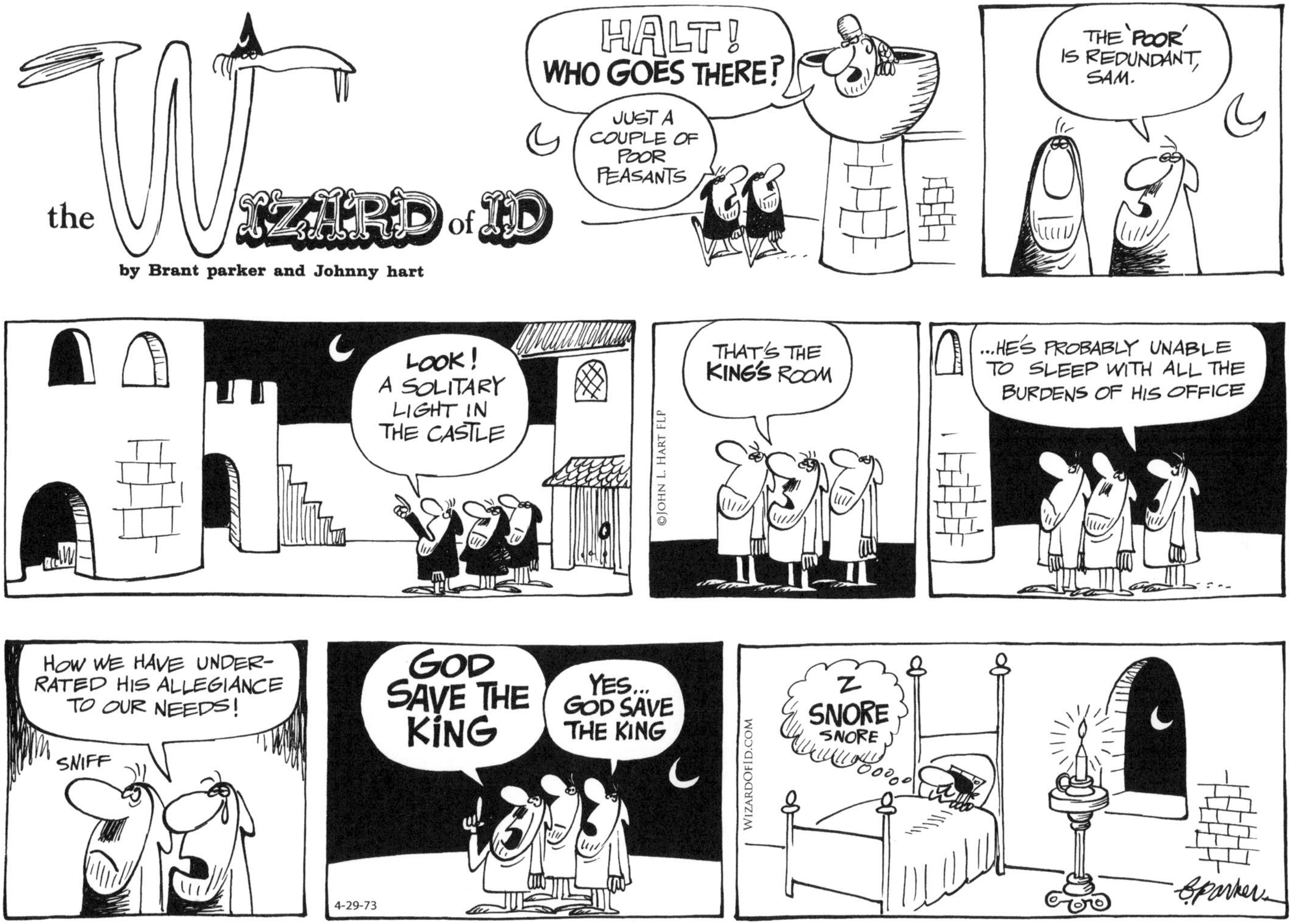
the WIZARD of ID
by Brant parker and Johnny hart
HALT! WHO GOES THERE?
JUST A COUPLE OF POOR PEASANTS
THE 'POOR' IS REDUNDANT, SAM.
LOOK! A SOLITARY LIGHT IN THE CASTLE
©JOHN L. HART FLP
THAT'S THE KING'S ROOM
...HE'S PROBABLY UNABLE TO SLEEP WITH ALL THE BURDENS OF HIS OFFICE
HOW WE HAVE UNDER-RATED HIS ALLEGIANCE TO OUR NEEDS!
SNIFF
GOD SAVE THE KING
YES... GOD SAVE THE KING
4-29-73
WIZARDOFID.COM
Z
SNORE
SNORE
B. parker

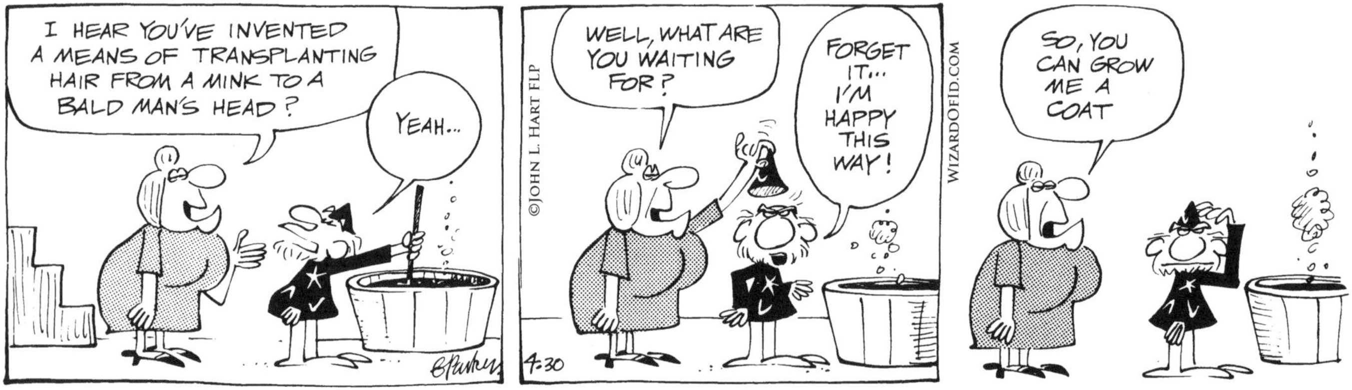
I HEAR YOU'VE INVENTED A MEANS OF TRANSPLANTING HAIR FROM A MINK TO A BALD MAN'S HEAD?
YEAH...
WELL, WHAT ARE YOU WAITING FOR?
FORGET IT... I'M HAPPY THIS WAY!
SO, YOU CAN GROW ME A COAT
©JOHN L. HART FLP
WIZARDOFID.COM
4-30

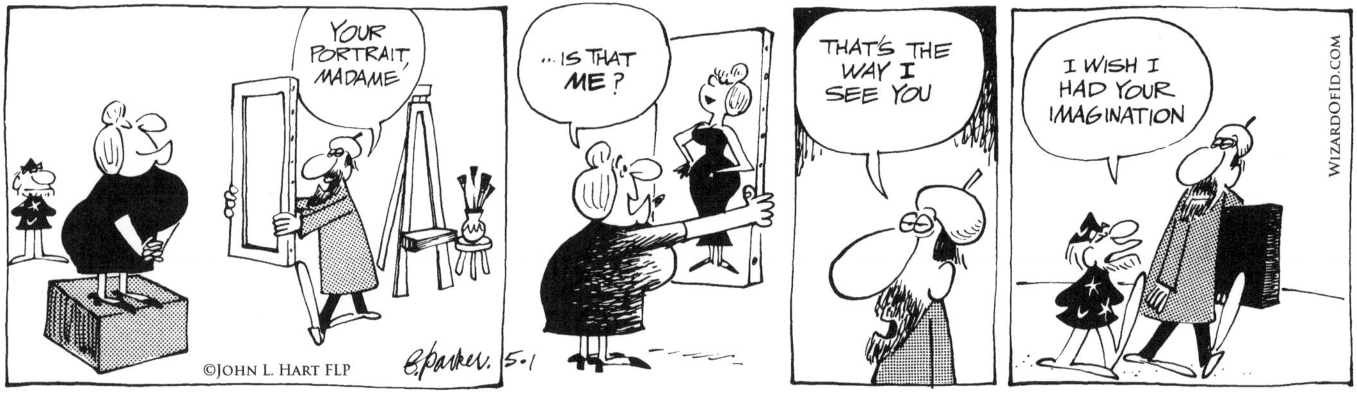
YOUR PORTRAIT, MADAME
...IS THAT **ME**?
THAT'S THE WAY **I** SEE YOU
I WISH I HAD YOUR IMAGINATION
©JOHN L. HART FLP
WIZARDOFID.COM
5-1

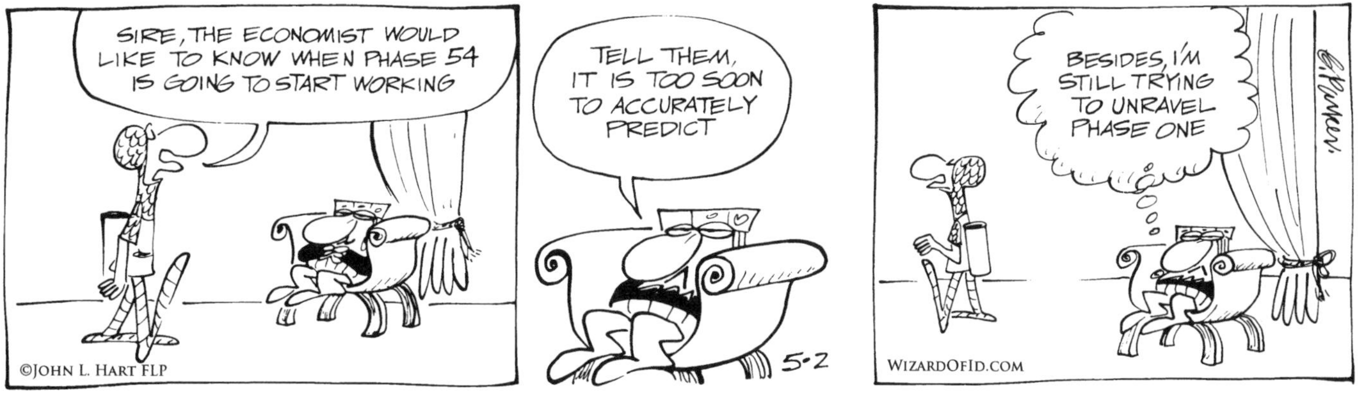
SIRE, THE ECONOMIST WOULD LIKE TO KNOW WHEN PHASE 54 IS GOING TO START WORKING
©JOHN L. HART FLP
TELL THEM, IT IS TOO SOON TO ACCURATELY PREDICT
5-2
BESIDES, I'M STILL TRYING TO UNRAVEL PHASE ONE
WIZARDOFID.COM

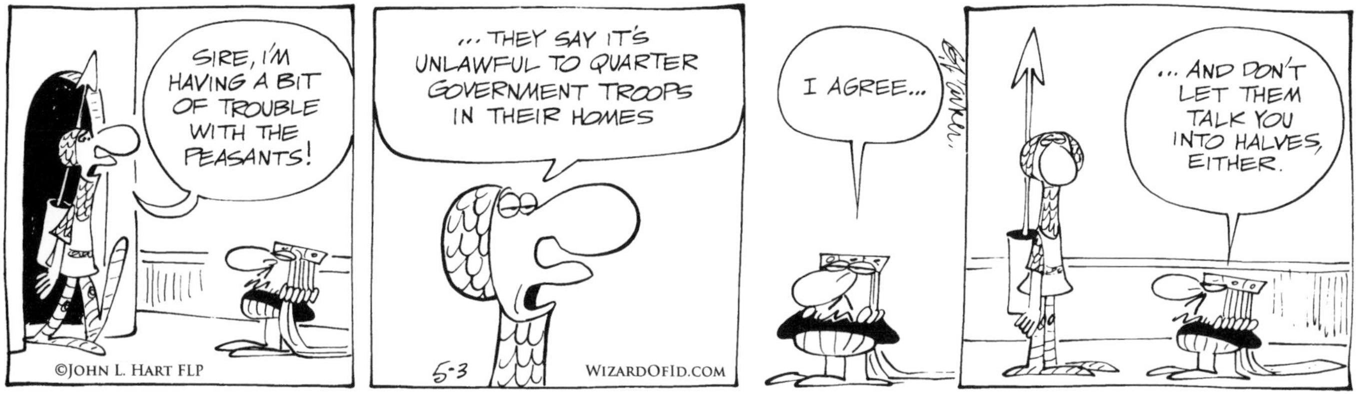
SIRE, I'M HAVING A BIT OF TROUBLE WITH THE PEASANTS!
©JOHN L. HART FLP
... THEY SAY IT'S UNLAWFUL TO QUARTER GOVERNMENT TROOPS IN THEIR HOMES
5-3
WIZARDOFID.COM
I AGREE...
... AND DON'T LET THEM TALK YOU INTO HALVES, EITHER.

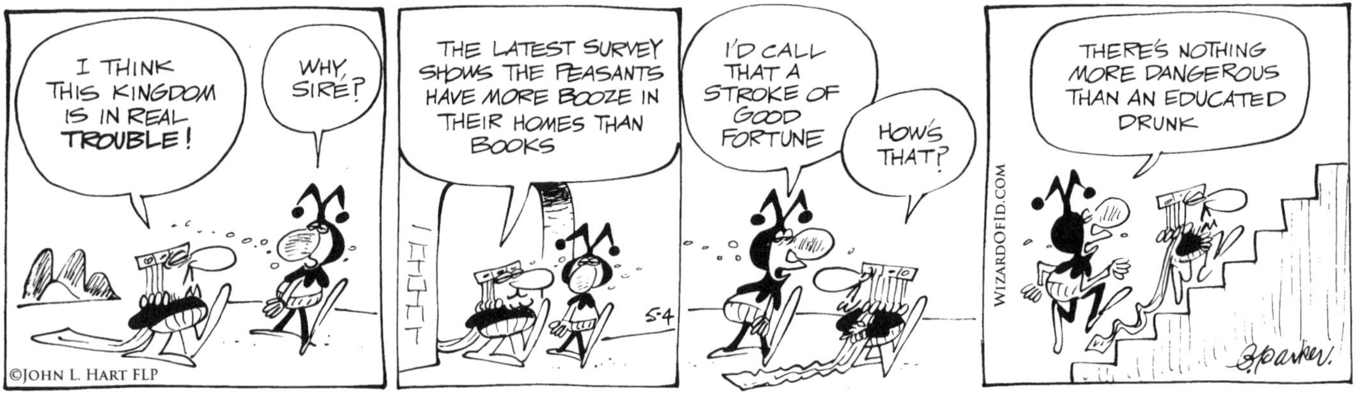
I THINK THIS KINGDOM IS IN REAL TROUBLE!
WHY, SIRE?
THE LATEST SURVEY SHOWS THE PEASANTS HAVE MORE BOOZE IN THEIR HOMES THAN BOOKS
I'D CALL THAT A STROKE OF GOOD FORTUNE
HOW'S THAT?
THERE'S NOTHING MORE DANGEROUS THAN AN EDUCATED DRUNK
©JOHN L. HART FLP
5·4
WIZARDOFID.COM

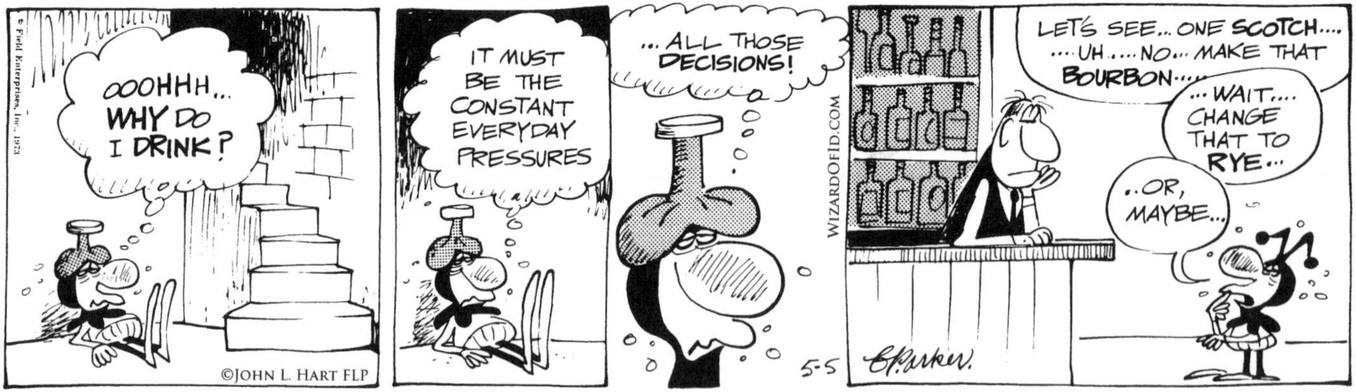
© Field Enterprises, Inc., 1973
OOOHHH... WHY DO I DRINK?
IT MUST BE THE CONSTANT EVERYDAY PRESSURES
...ALL THOSE DECISIONS!
LET'S SEE... ONE SCOTCH.... ....UH.....NO... MAKE THAT BOURBON.....
...WAIT.... CHANGE THAT TO RYE...
..OR, MAYBE...
©JOHN L. HART FLP
5·5
WIZARDOFID.COM

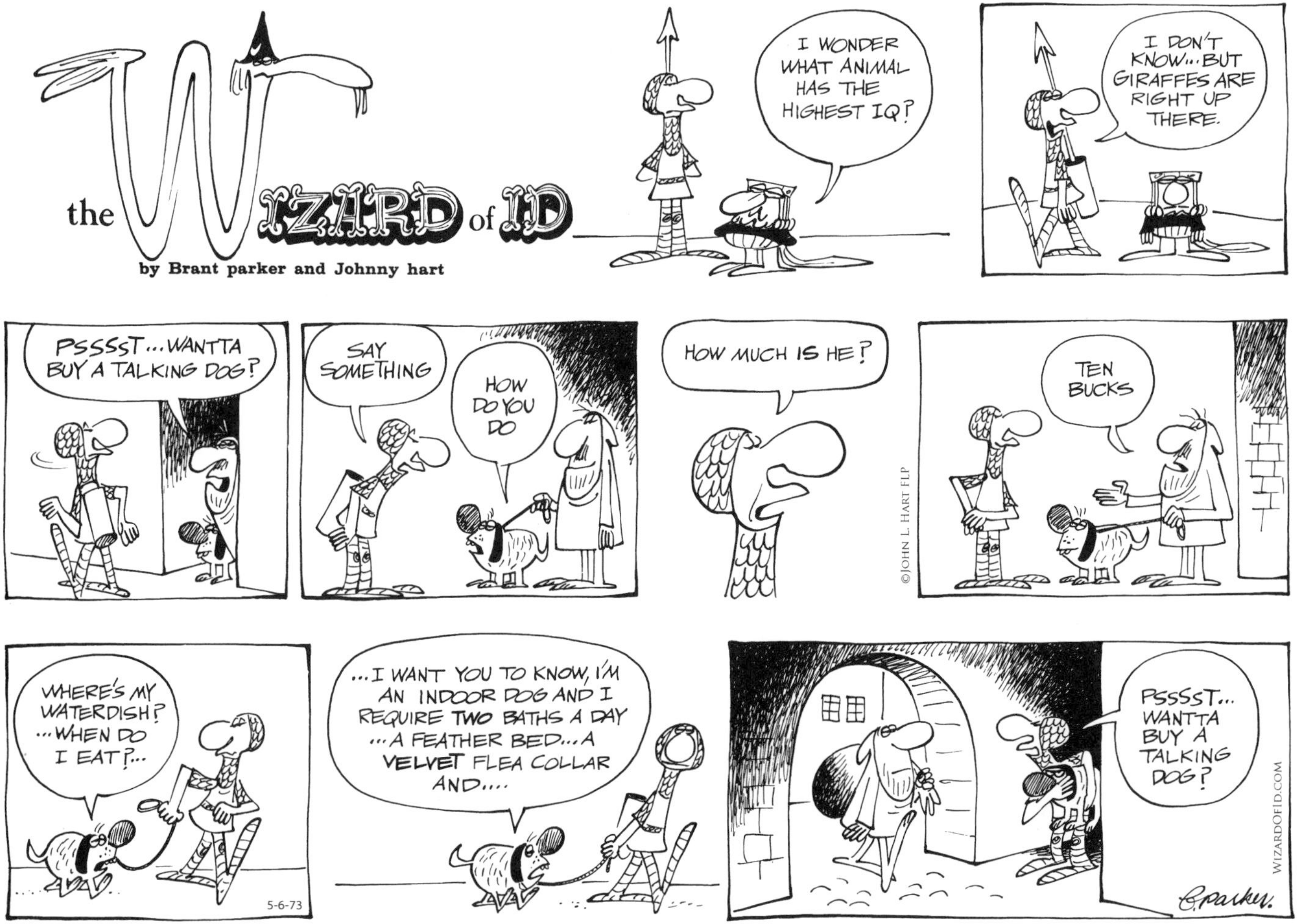

the Wizard of Id
by Brant parker and Johnny hart
I WONDER WHAT ANIMAL HAS THE HIGHEST IQ?
I DON'T KNOW... BUT GIRAFFES ARE RIGHT UP THERE.
PSSSST... WANTTA BUY A TALKING DOG?
SAY SOMETHING
HOW DO YOU DO
HOW MUCH IS HE?
©JOHN L. HART FLP
TEN BUCKS
WHERE'S MY WATERDISH? ...WHEN DO I EAT?...
5-6-73
...I WANT YOU TO KNOW, I'M AN INDOOR DOG AND I REQUIRE TWO BATHS A DAY ...A FEATHER BED... A VELVET FLEA COLLAR AND....
PSSSST... WANTTA BUY A TALKING DOG?
WIZARDOFID.COM
B. parker.

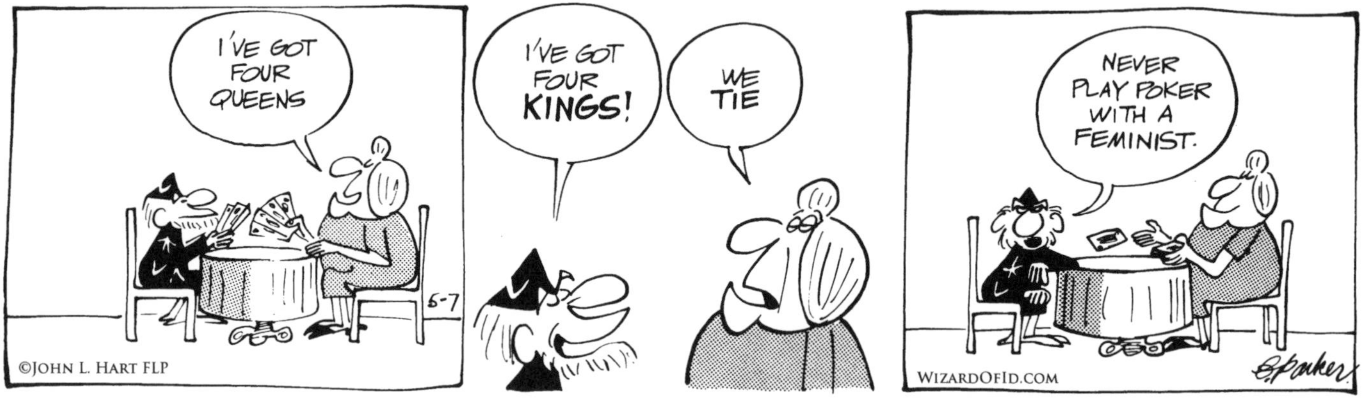
I'VE GOT FOUR QUEENS
I'VE GOT FOUR **KINGS**!
WE TIE
NEVER PLAY POKER WITH A FEMINIST.
5-7
©JOHN L. HART FLP
WIZARDOFID.COM

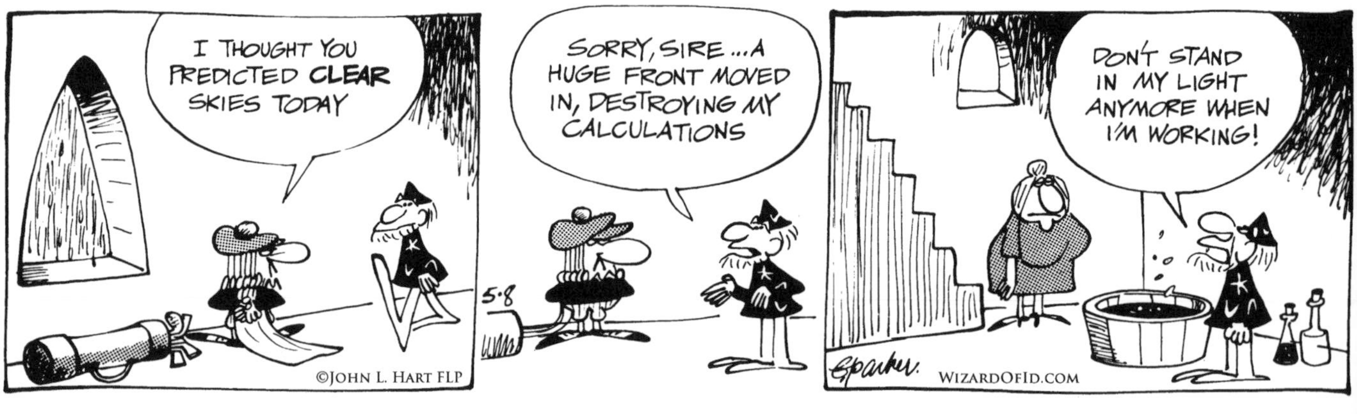
I THOUGHT YOU PREDICTED **CLEAR** SKIES TODAY
SORRY, SIRE ... A HUGE FRONT MOVED IN, DESTROYING MY CALCULATIONS
DON'T STAND IN MY LIGHT ANYMORE WHEN I'M WORKING!
5·8
©JOHN L. HART FLP
WIZARDOFID.COM

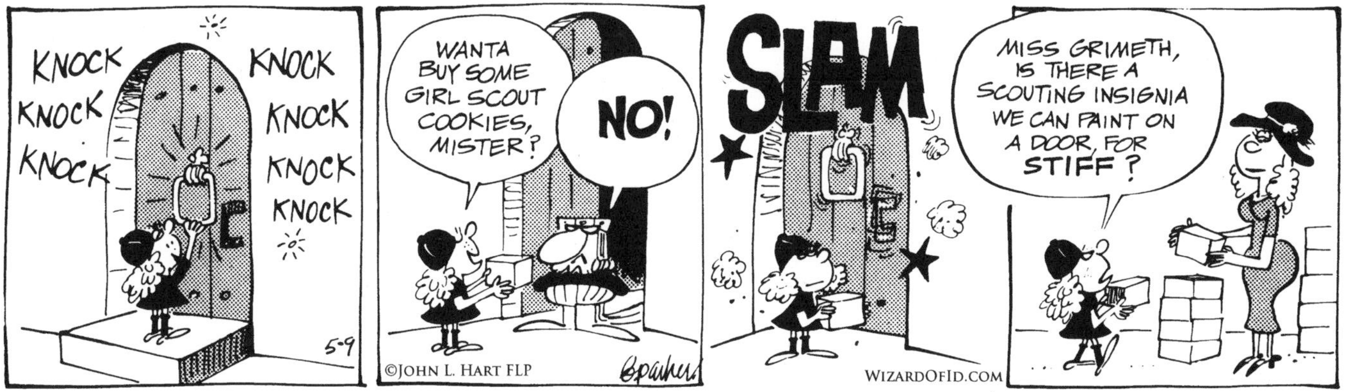
KNOCK KNOCK KNOCK
KNOCK KNOCK KNOCK KNOCK
5-9
WANTA BUY SOME GIRL SCOUT COOKIES, MISTER?
NO!
©JOHN L. HART FLP
SLAM
WIZARDOFID.COM
MISS GRIMETH, IS THERE A SCOUTING INSIGNIA WE CAN PAINT ON A DOOR, FOR STIFF?

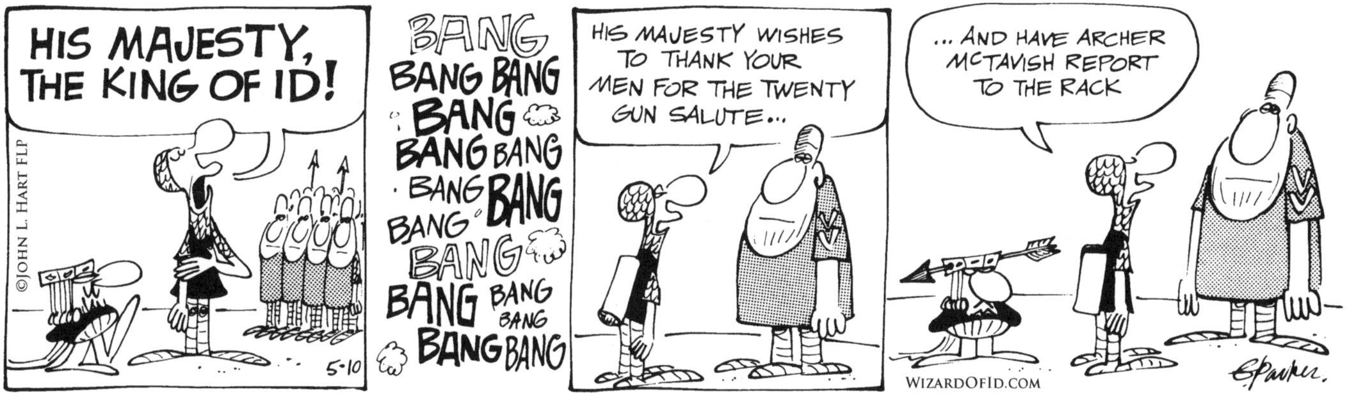
HIS MAJESTY, THE KING OF ID!
©JOHN L. HART FLP
5-10
BANG BANG BANG BANG BANG BANG BANG BANG BANG BANG BANG BANG BANG BANG BANG BANG BANG
HIS MAJESTY WISHES TO THANK YOUR MEN FOR THE TWENTY GUN SALUTE...
... AND HAVE ARCHER McTAVISH REPORT TO THE RACK
WIZARDOFID.COM

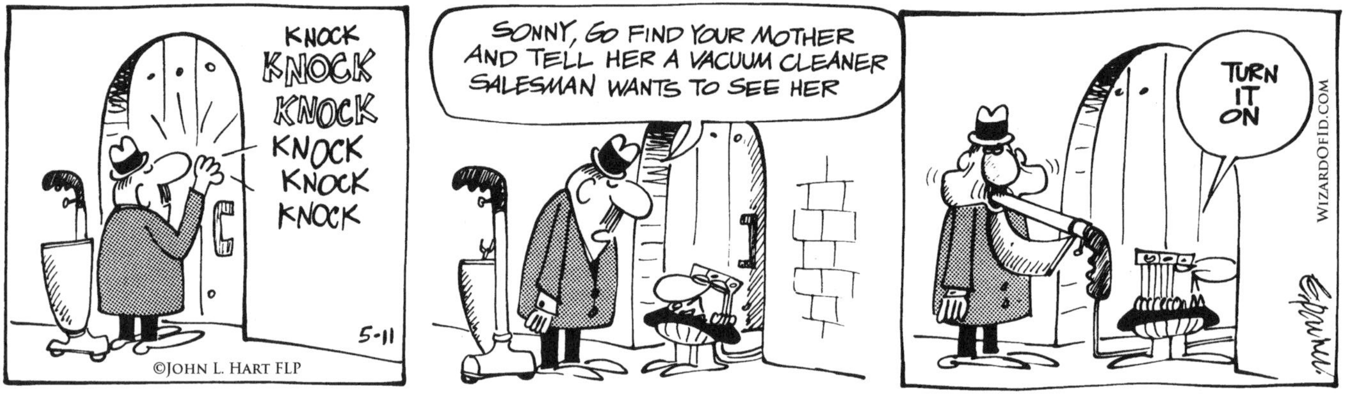
KNOCK
KNOCK
KNOCK
KNOCK
KNOCK
KNOCK
5-11
©JOHN L. HART FLP
SONNY, GO FIND YOUR MOTHER AND TELL HER A VACUUM CLEANER SALESMAN WANTS TO SEE HER
TURN IT ON
WIZARDOFID.COM

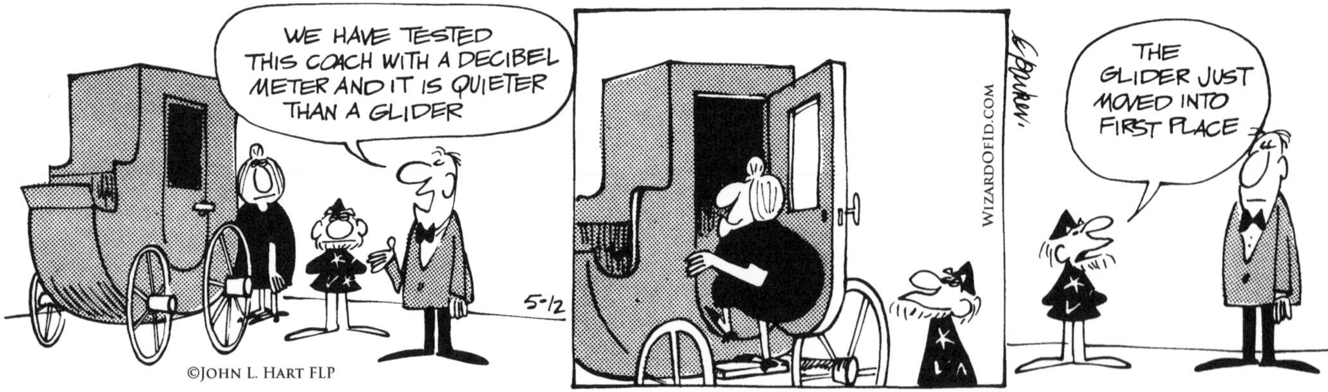
WE HAVE TESTED THIS COACH WITH A DECIBEL METER AND IT IS QUIETER THAN A GLIDER
5-12
©JOHN L. HART FLP
WIZARDOFID.COM
THE GLIDER JUST MOVED INTO FIRST PLACE

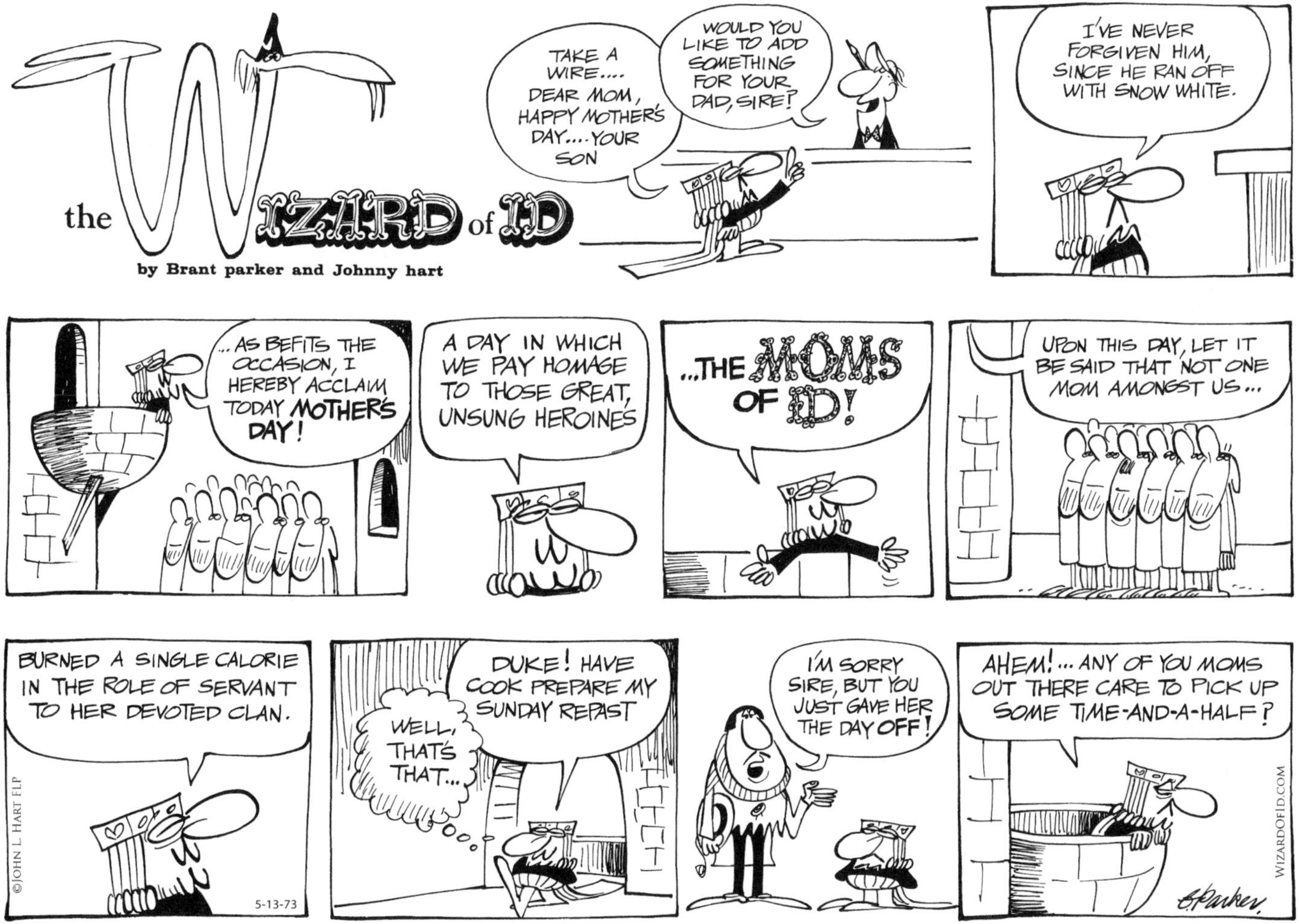
the WIZARD of ID
by Brant parker and Johnny hart
TAKE A WIRE.... DEAR MOM, HAPPY MOTHER'S DAY.... YOUR SON
WOULD YOU LIKE TO ADD SOMETHING FOR YOUR DAD, SIRE?
I'VE NEVER FORGIVEN HIM, SINCE HE RAN OFF WITH SNOW WHITE.
...AS BEFITS THE OCCASION, I HEREBY ACCLAIM TODAY MOTHER'S DAY!
A DAY IN WHICH WE PAY HOMAGE TO THOSE GREAT, UNSUNG HEROINES
...THE MOMS OF ID!
UPON THIS DAY, LET IT BE SAID THAT NOT ONE MOM AMONGST US...
BURNED A SINGLE CALORIE IN THE ROLE OF SERVANT TO HER DEVOTED CLAN.
©JOHN L. HART FLP
5-13-73
WELL, THAT'S THAT...
DUKE! HAVE COOK PREPARE MY SUNDAY REPAST
I'M SORRY SIRE, BUT YOU JUST GAVE HER THE DAY OFF!
AHEM!... ANY OF YOU MOMS OUT THERE CARE TO PICK UP SOME TIME-AND-A-HALF?
B Parker
WIZARDOFID.COM

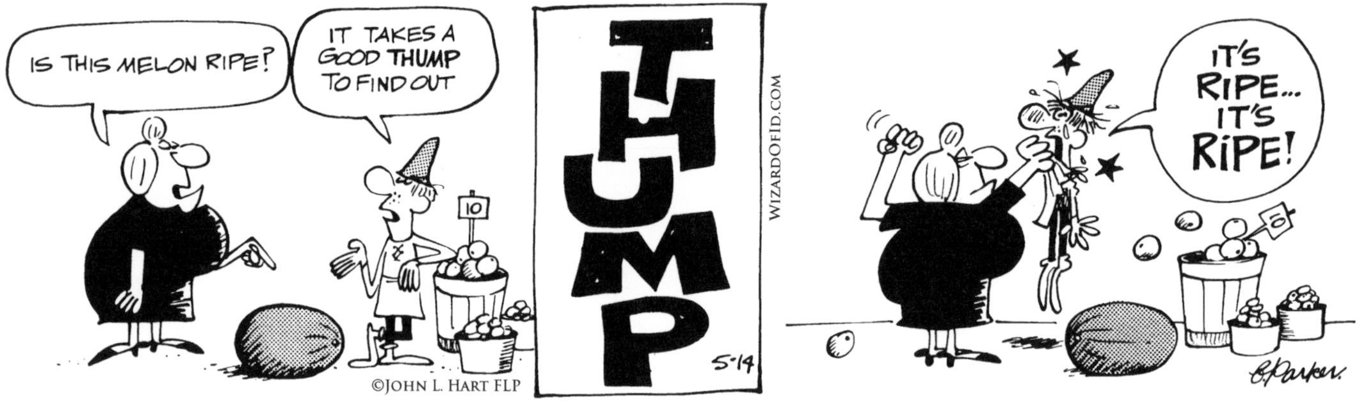
IS THIS MELON RIPE?
IT TAKES A GOOD THUMP TO FIND OUT
10
THUMP
WIZARDOFID.COM
5-14
IT'S RIPE... IT'S RIPE!
©JOHN L. HART FLP

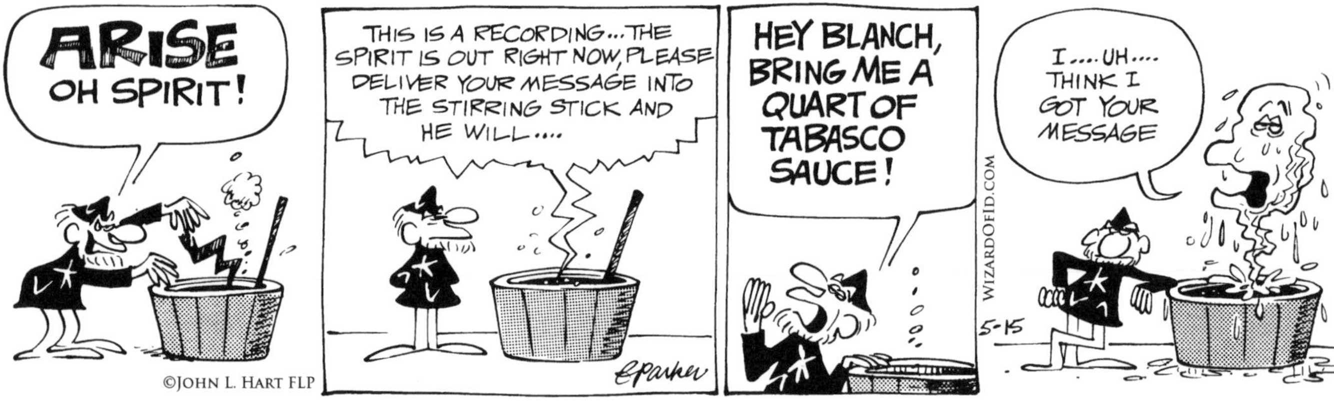
ARISE OH SPIRIT!
THIS IS A RECORDING... THE SPIRIT IS OUT RIGHT NOW, PLEASE DELIVER YOUR MESSAGE INTO THE STIRRING STICK AND HE WILL....
HEY BLANCH, BRING ME A QUART OF TABASCO SAUCE!
WIZARDOFID.COM
5-15
I.... UH.... THINK I GOT YOUR MESSAGE
©JOHN L. HART FLP

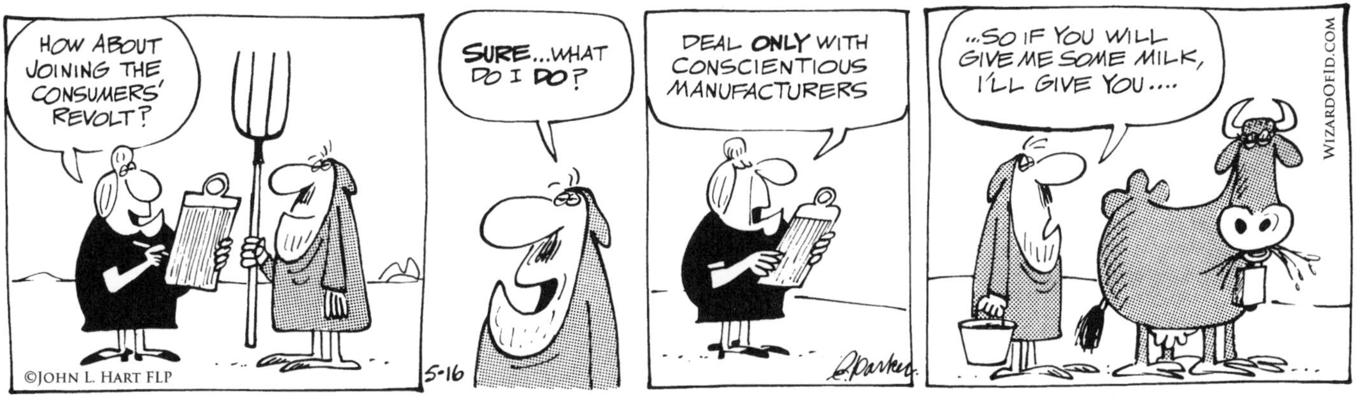
HOW ABOUT JOINING THE CONSUMERS' REVOLT?
SURE...WHAT DO I DO?
DEAL ONLY WITH CONSCIENTIOUS MANUFACTURERS
...SO IF YOU WILL GIVE ME SOME MILK, I'LL GIVE YOU....
©JOHN L. HART FLP
5-16
WIZARDOFID.COM

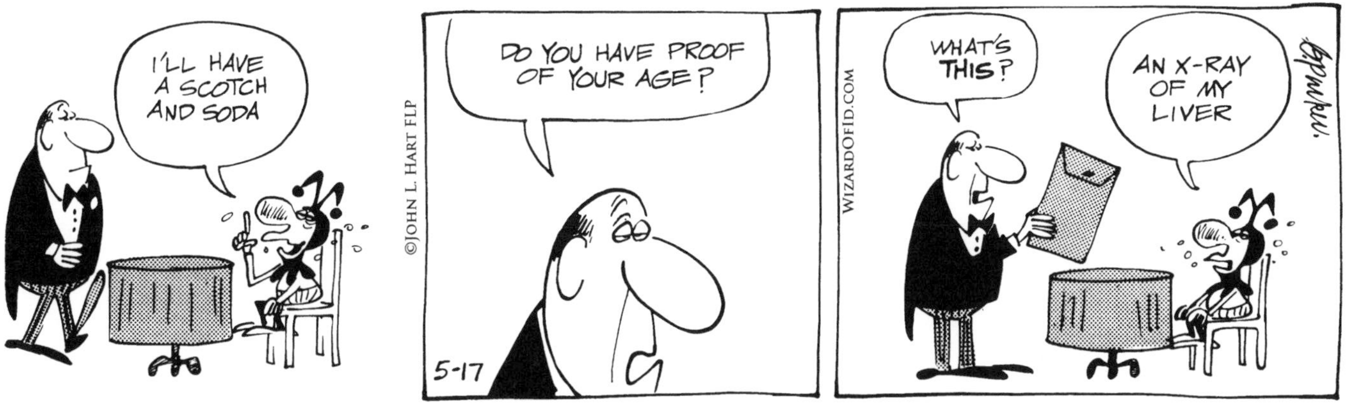
I'LL HAVE A SCOTCH AND SODA
DO YOU HAVE PROOF OF YOUR AGE?
WHAT'S THIS?
AN X-RAY OF MY LIVER
©JOHN L. HART FLP
5-17
WIZARDOFID.COM

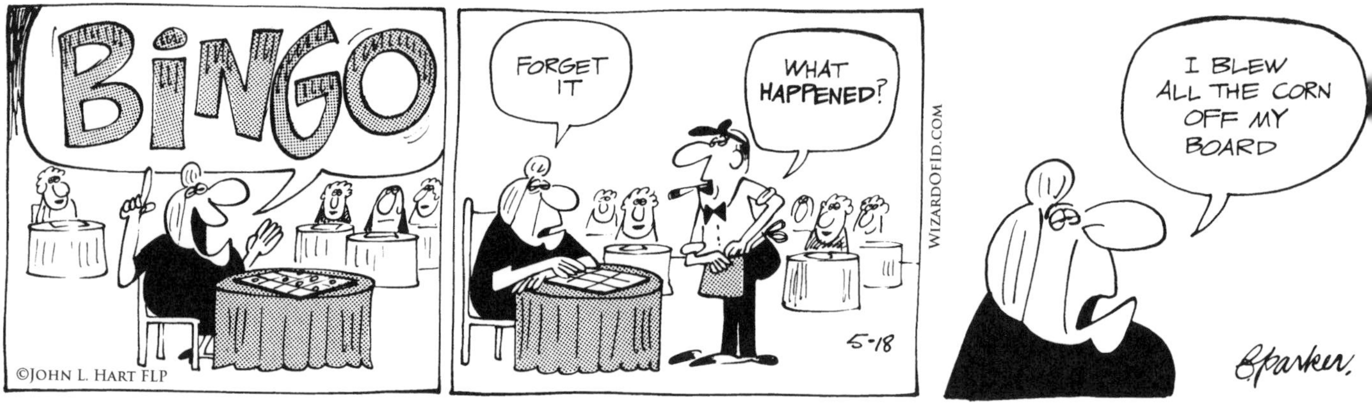
BINGO
FORGET IT
WHAT HAPPENED?
I BLEW ALL THE CORN OFF MY BOARD
5-18
©JOHN L. HART FLP
WIZARDOFID.COM
B.Parker.

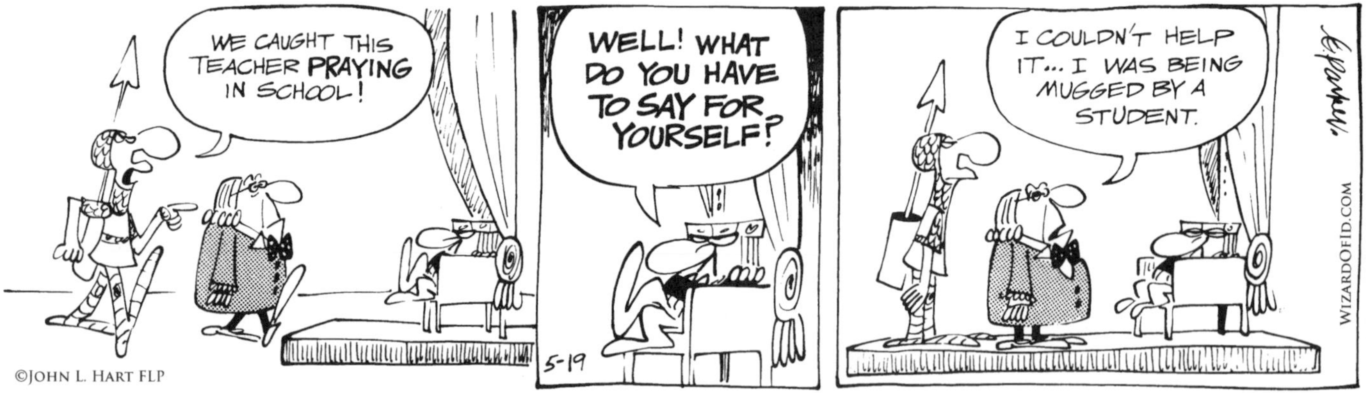
WE CAUGHT THIS TEACHER PRAYING IN SCHOOL!
WELL! WHAT DO YOU HAVE TO SAY FOR YOURSELF?
I COULDN'T HELP IT... I WAS BEING MUGGED BY A STUDENT.
5-19
©JOHN L. HART FLP
WIZARDOFID.COM
B.Parker.

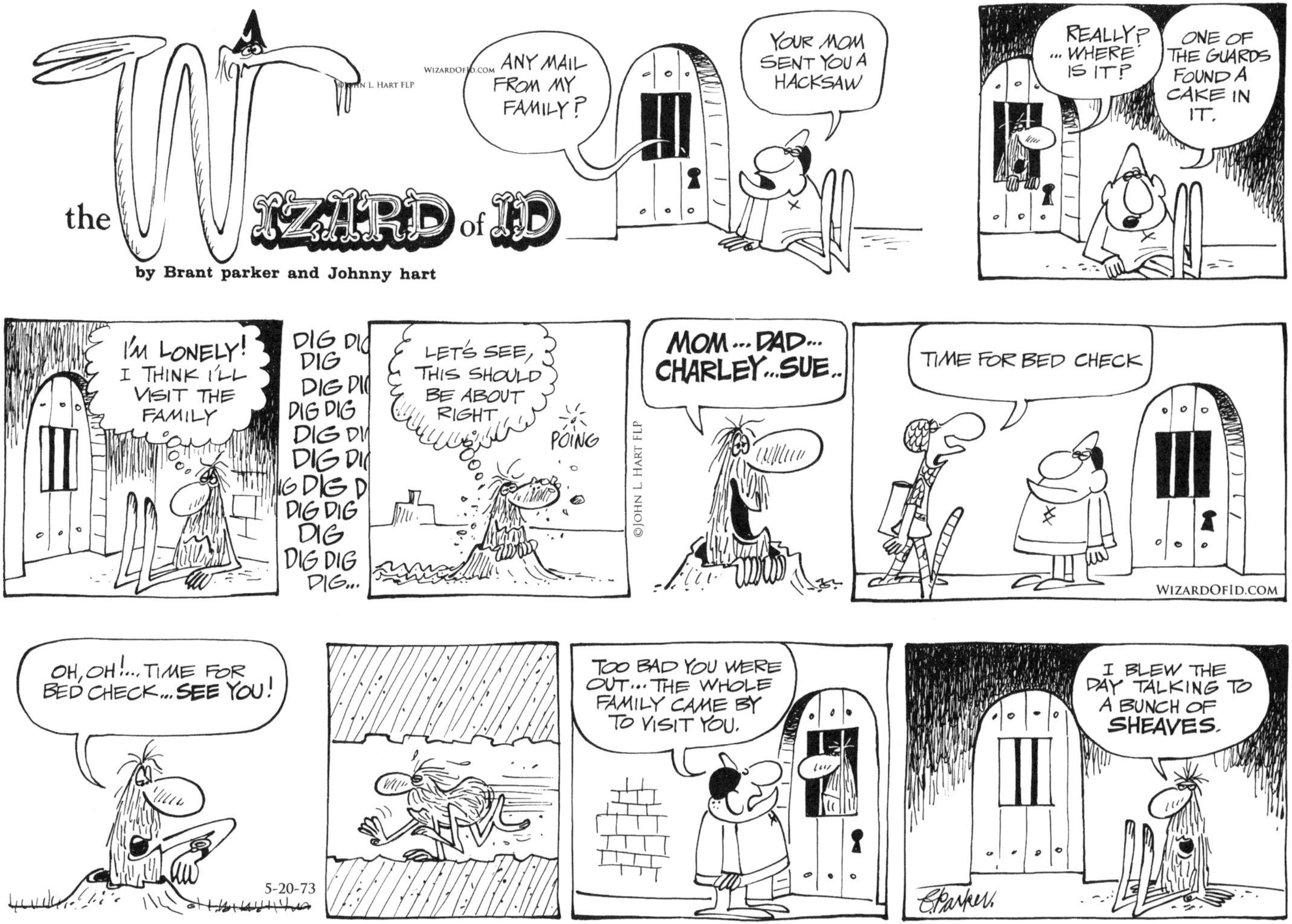
the Wizard of Id
by Brant parker and Johnny hart
©John L. Hart FLP
WizardOfId.com
ANY MAIL FROM MY FAMILY?
YOUR MOM SENT YOU A HACKSAW
REALLY? ...WHERE IS IT?
ONE OF THE GUARDS FOUND A CAKE IN IT.
I'M LONELY! I THINK I'LL VISIT THE FAMILY
DIG DIG DIG DIG DIG DIG DIG DIG DIG DIG DIG DIG DIG DIG DIG DIG DIG DIG DIG DIG DIG...
LET'S SEE, THIS SHOULD BE ABOUT RIGHT
POING
©John L. Hart FLP
MOM...DAD... CHARLEY...SUE..
TIME FOR BED CHECK
WizardOfId.com
OH, OH!... TIME FOR BED CHECK... SEE YOU!
5-20-73
TOO BAD YOU WERE OUT... THE WHOLE FAMILY CAME BY TO VISIT YOU.
I BLEW THE DAY TALKING TO A BUNCH OF SHEAVES.
B. Parker

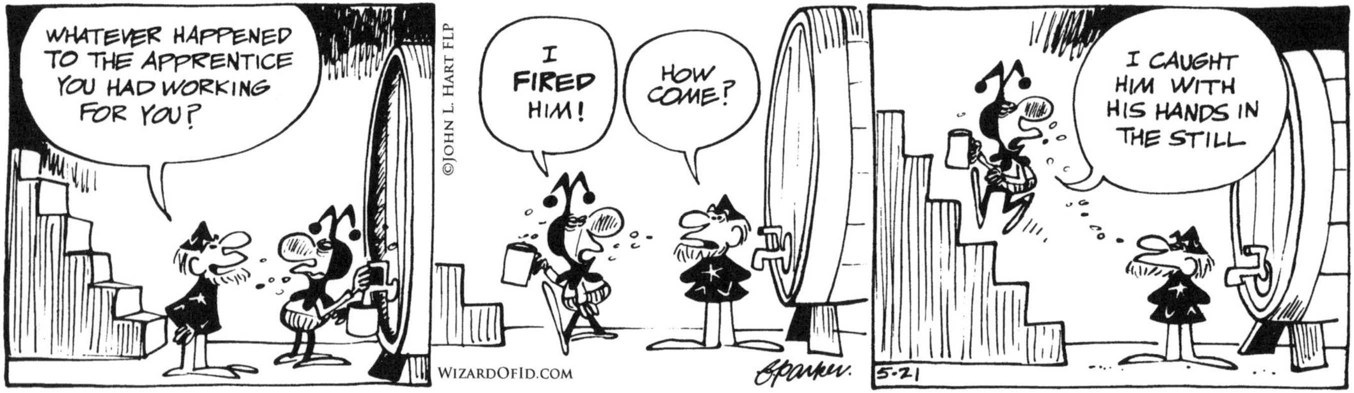
WHATEVER HAPPENED TO THE APPRENTICE YOU HAD WORKING FOR YOU?
©JOHN L. HART FLP
I FIRED HIM!
HOW COME?
I CAUGHT HIM WITH HIS HANDS IN THE STILL
WIZARDOFID.COM
5-21

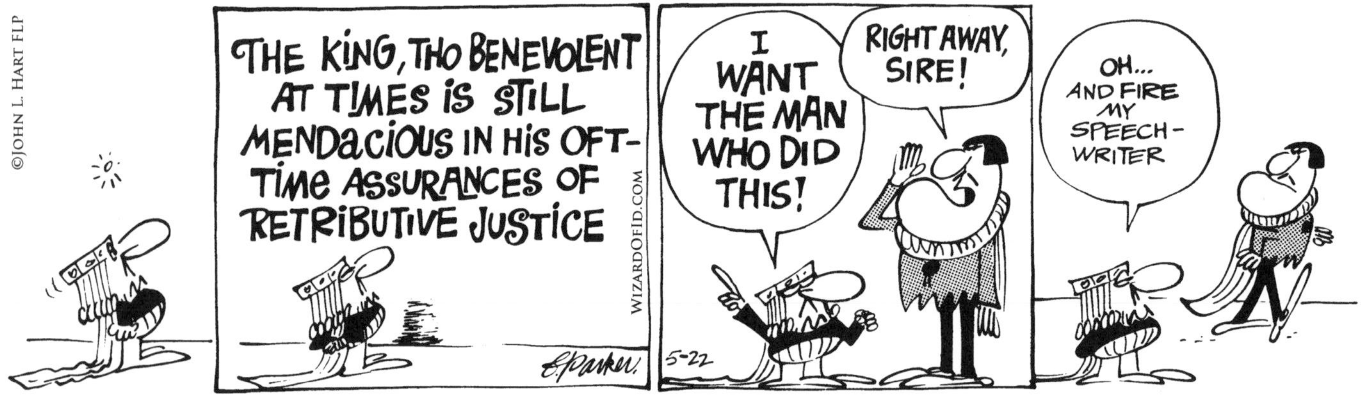
©JOHN L. HART FLP
THE KING, THO BENEVOLENT AT TIMES IS STILL MENDACIOUS IN HIS OFT-TIME ASSURANCES OF RETRIBUTIVE JUSTICE
WIZARDOFID.COM
I WANT THE MAN WHO DID THIS!
RIGHT AWAY, SIRE!
5-22
OH... AND FIRE MY SPEECH-WRITER

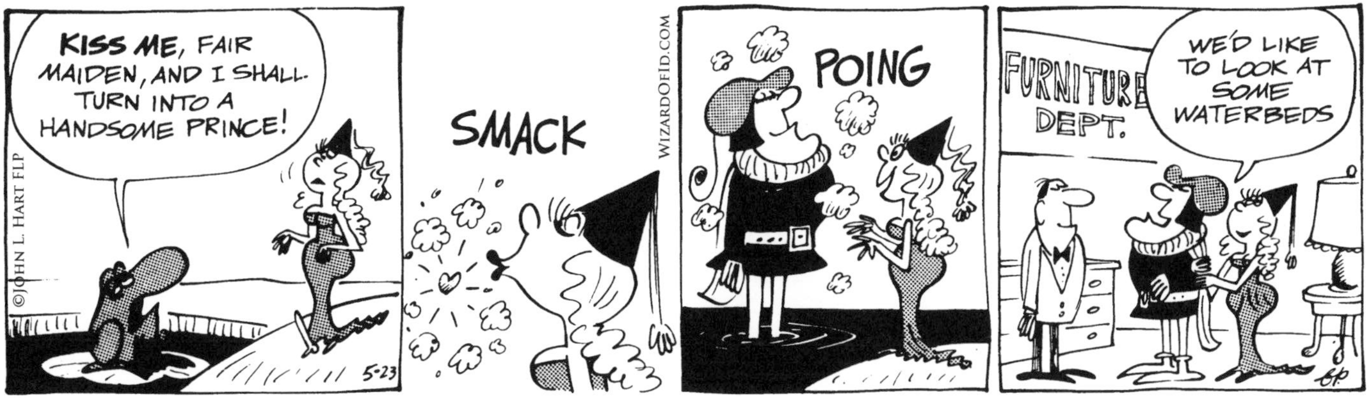
KISS ME, FAIR MAIDEN, AND I SHALL TURN INTO A HANDSOME PRINCE!
©JOHN L. HART FLP
5-23
SMACK
WIZARDOFID.COM
POING
FURNITURE DEPT.
WE'D LIKE TO LOOK AT SOME WATERBEDS

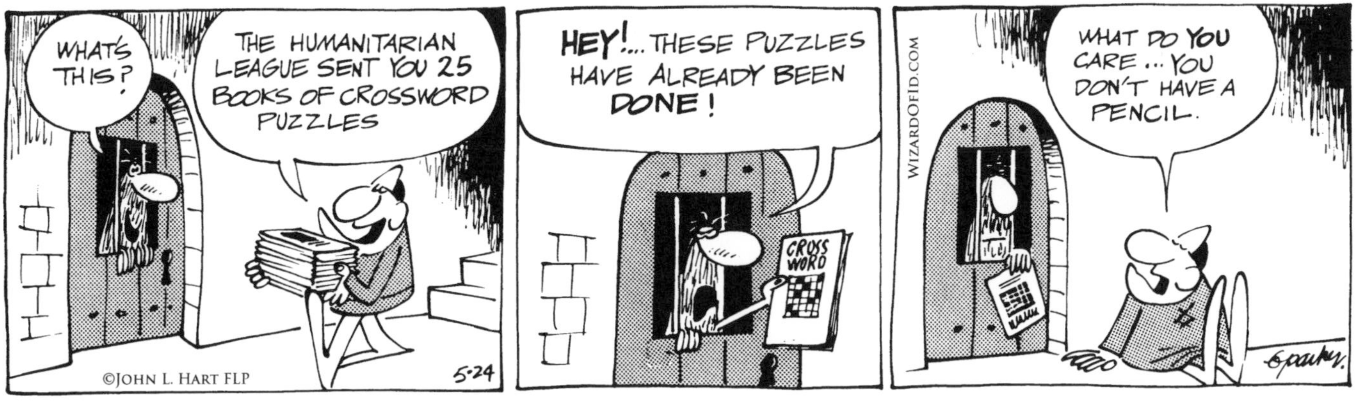
WHAT'S THIS?
THE HUMANITARIAN LEAGUE SENT YOU 25 BOOKS OF CROSSWORD PUZZLES
©JOHN L. HART FLP
5-24
HEY!... THESE PUZZLES HAVE ALREADY BEEN DONE!
CROSS WORD
WIZARDOFID.COM
WHAT DO YOU CARE... YOU DON'T HAVE A PENCIL.

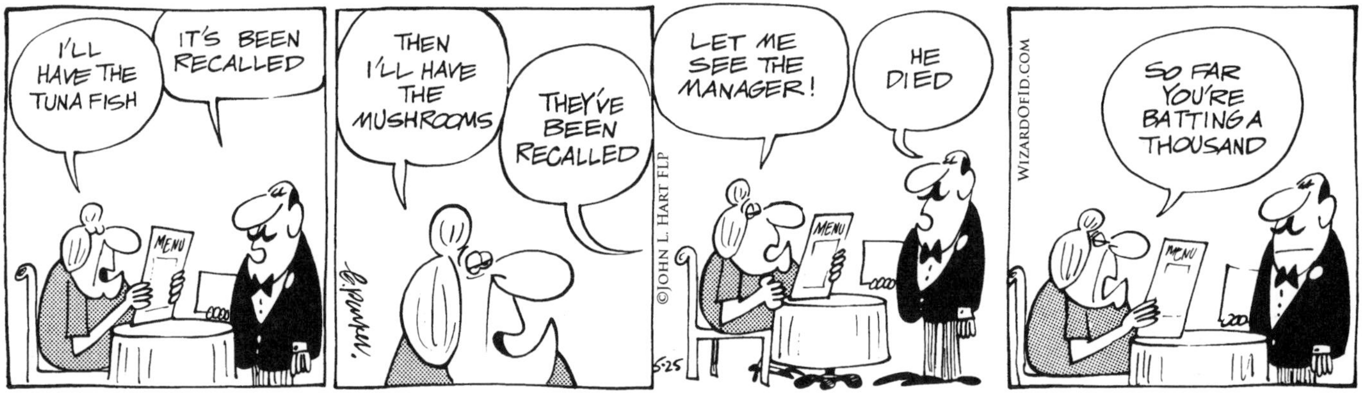
I'LL HAVE THE TUNA FISH
IT'S BEEN RECALLED
THEN I'LL HAVE THE MUSHROOMS
THEY'VE BEEN RECALLED
©JOHN L. HART FLP
5-25
LET ME SEE THE MANAGER!
HE DIED
WIZARDOFID.COM
SO FAR YOU'RE BATTING A THOUSAND
MENU

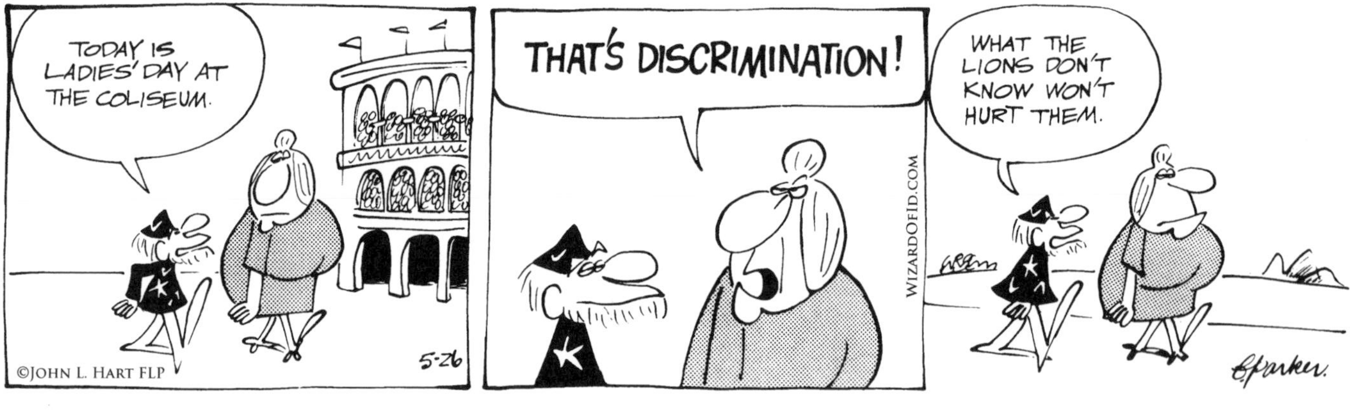
TODAY IS LADIES' DAY AT THE COLISEUM.
©JOHN L. HART FLP
5-26
THAT'S DISCRIMINATION!
WIZARDOFID.COM
WHAT THE LIONS DON'T KNOW WON'T HURT THEM.

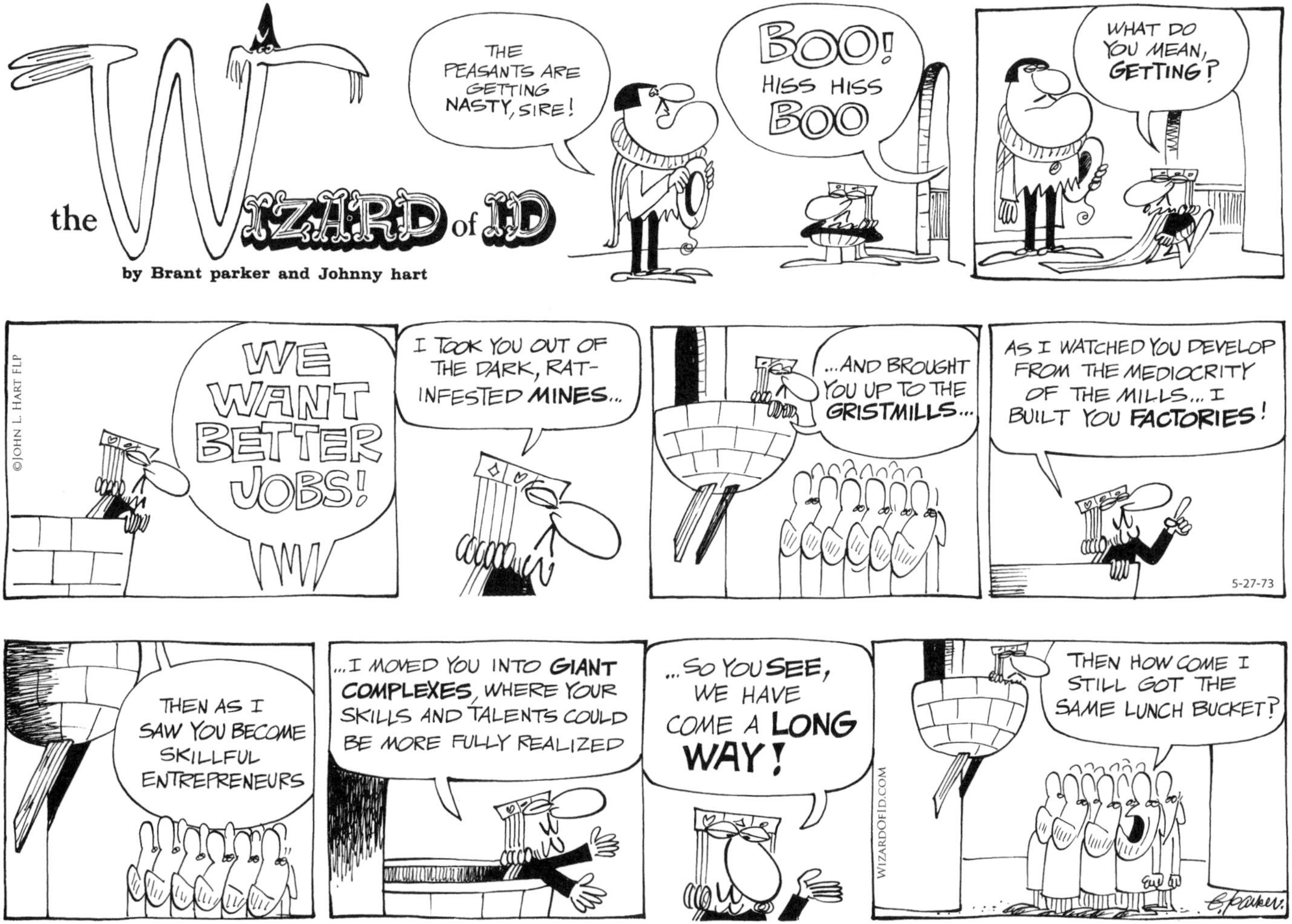
the WIZARD of ID
by Brant parker and Johnny hart
THE PEASANTS ARE GETTING NASTY, SIRE!
BOO! HISS HISS BOO
WHAT DO YOU MEAN, GETTING?
©JOHN L. HART FLP
WE WANT BETTER JOBS!
I TOOK YOU OUT OF THE DARK, RAT-INFESTED MINES...
...AND BROUGHT YOU UP TO THE GRISTMILLS...
AS I WATCHED YOU DEVELOP FROM THE MEDIOCRITY OF THE MILLS... I BUILT YOU FACTORIES!
5-27-73
THEN AS I SAW YOU BECOME SKILLFUL ENTREPRENEURS
...I MOVED YOU INTO GIANT COMPLEXES, WHERE YOUR SKILLS AND TALENTS COULD BE MORE FULLY REALIZED
...SO YOU SEE, WE HAVE COME A LONG WAY!
WIZARDOFID.COM
THEN HOW COME I STILL GOT THE SAME LUNCH BUCKET?
B. parker

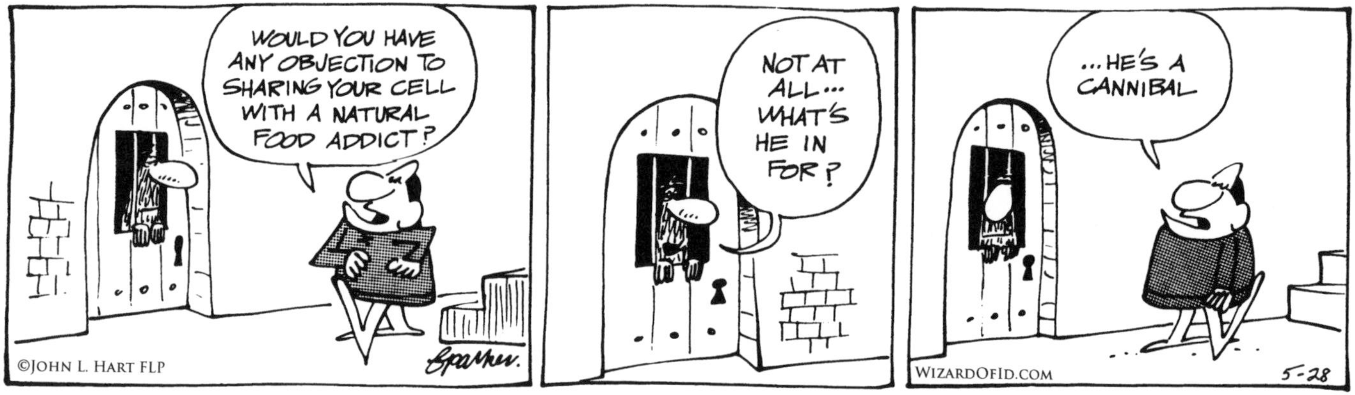
©JOHN L. HART FLP
WOULD YOU HAVE ANY OBJECTION TO SHARING YOUR CELL WITH A NATURAL FOOD ADDICT?
NOT AT ALL... WHAT'S HE IN FOR?
...HE'S A CANNIBAL
WIZARDOFID.COM
5-28

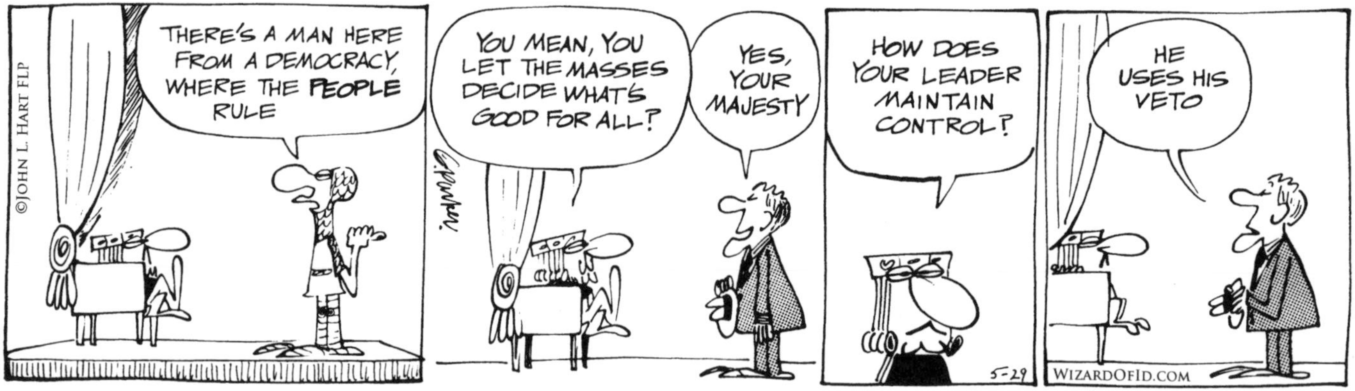
©JOHN L. HART FLP
THERE'S A MAN HERE FROM A DEMOCRACY, WHERE THE PEOPLE RULE
YOU MEAN, YOU LET THE MASSES DECIDE WHAT'S GOOD FOR ALL?
YES, YOUR MAJESTY
HOW DOES YOUR LEADER MAINTAIN CONTROL?
HE USES HIS VETO
5-29
WIZARDOFID.COM

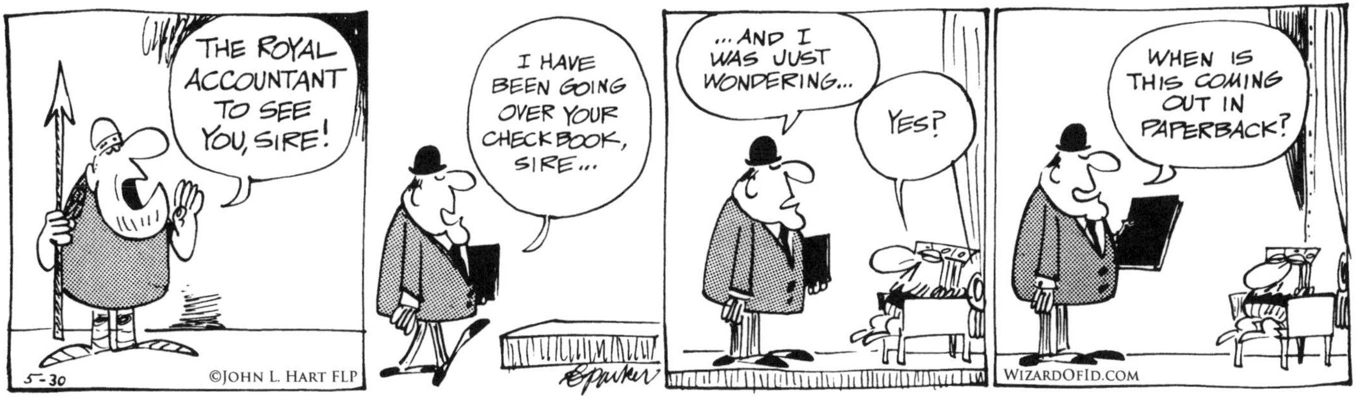
THE ROYAL ACCOUNTANT TO SEE YOU, SIRE!
I HAVE BEEN GOING OVER YOUR CHECKBOOK, SIRE...
...AND I WAS JUST WONDERING...
YES?
WHEN IS THIS COMING OUT IN PAPERBACK?
5-30
©JOHN L. HART FLP
WIZARDOFID.COM

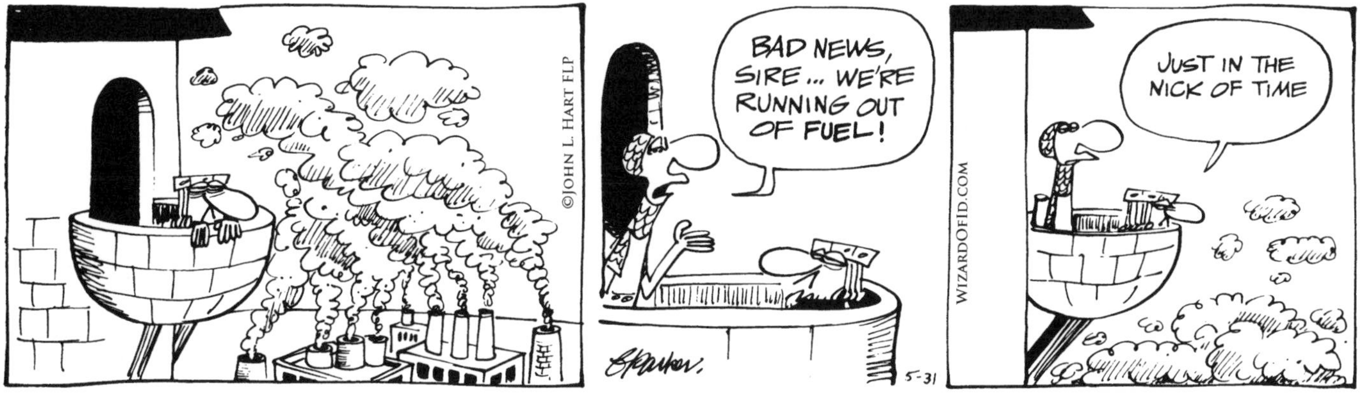
©JOHN L. HART FLP
BAD NEWS, SIRE... WE'RE RUNNING OUT OF FUEL!
5-31
WIZARDOFID.COM
JUST IN THE NICK OF TIME

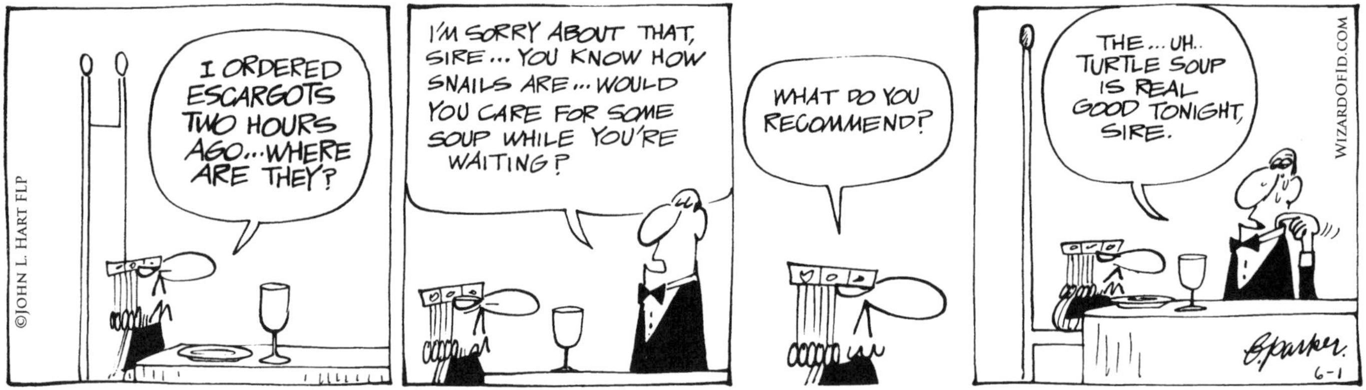
I ORDERED ESCARGOTS TWO HOURS AGO... WHERE ARE THEY?
I'M SORRY ABOUT THAT, SIRE... YOU KNOW HOW SNAILS ARE... WOULD YOU CARE FOR SOME SOUP WHILE YOU'RE WAITING?
WHAT DO YOU RECOMMEND?
THE... UH.. TURTLE SOUP IS REAL GOOD TONIGHT, SIRE.
©JOHN L. HART FLP
WIZARDOFID.COM
6-1

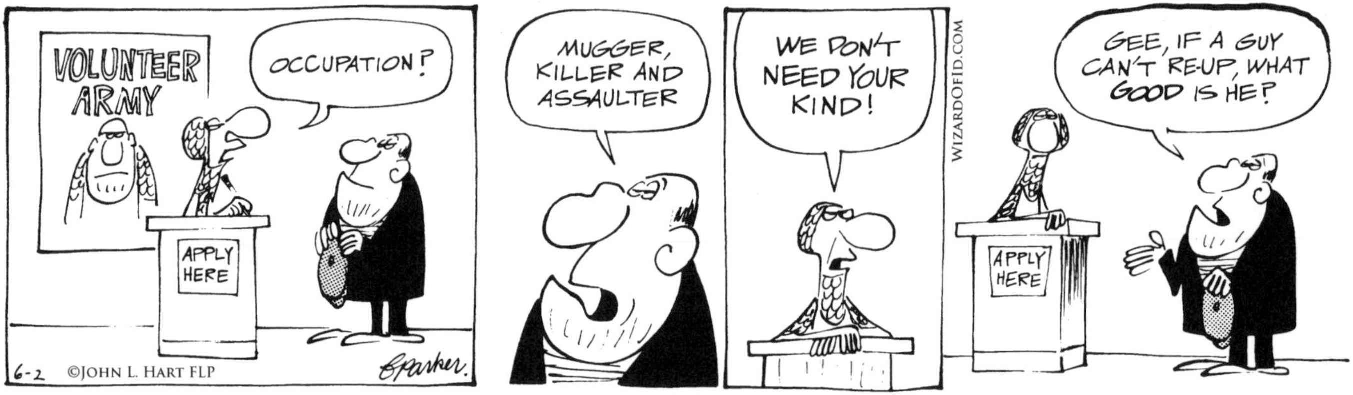
VOLUNTEER ARMY
APPLY HERE
OCCUPATION?
MUGGER, KILLER AND ASSAULTER
WE DON'T NEED YOUR KIND!
GEE, IF A GUY CAN'T RE-UP, WHAT GOOD IS HE?
6-2 ©JOHN L. HART FLP
WIZARDOFID.COM

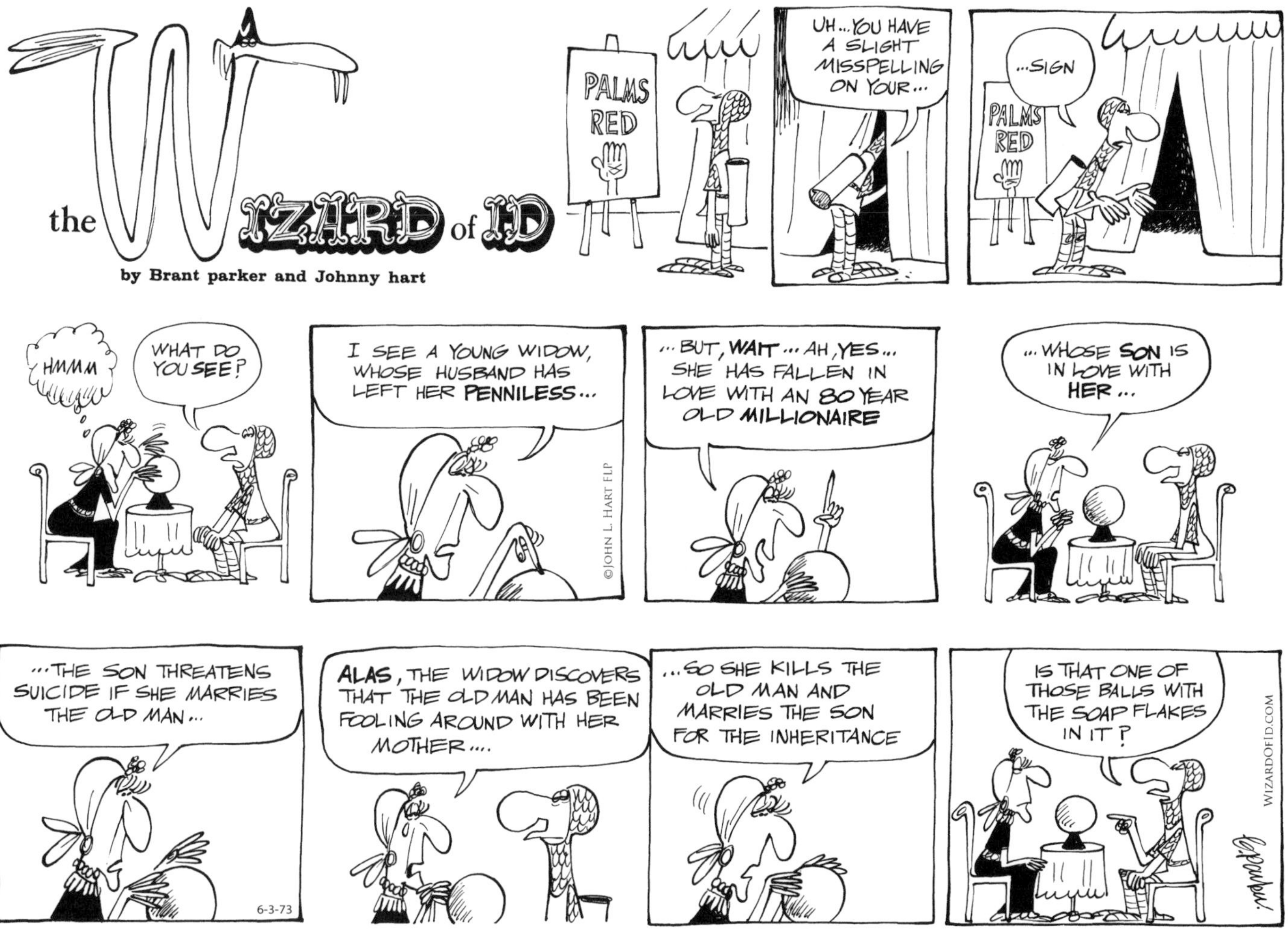the WIZARD of ID
by Brant parker and Johnny hart
PALMS RED
UH... YOU HAVE A SLIGHT MISSPELLING ON YOUR...
...SIGN
PALMS RED
HMMM
WHAT DO YOU SEE?
I SEE A YOUNG WIDOW, WHOSE HUSBAND HAS LEFT HER PENNILESS...
©JOHN L. HART FLP
...BUT, WAIT... AH, YES... SHE HAS FALLEN IN LOVE WITH AN 80 YEAR OLD MILLIONAIRE
...WHOSE SON IS IN LOVE WITH HER...
...THE SON THREATENS SUICIDE IF SHE MARRIES THE OLD MAN...
6-3-73
ALAS, THE WIDOW DISCOVERS THAT THE OLD MAN HAS BEEN FOOLING AROUND WITH HER MOTHER....
...SO SHE KILLS THE OLD MAN AND MARRIES THE SON FOR THE INHERITANCE
IS THAT ONE OF THOSE BALLS WITH THE SOAP FLAKES IN IT?
WIZARDOFID.COM

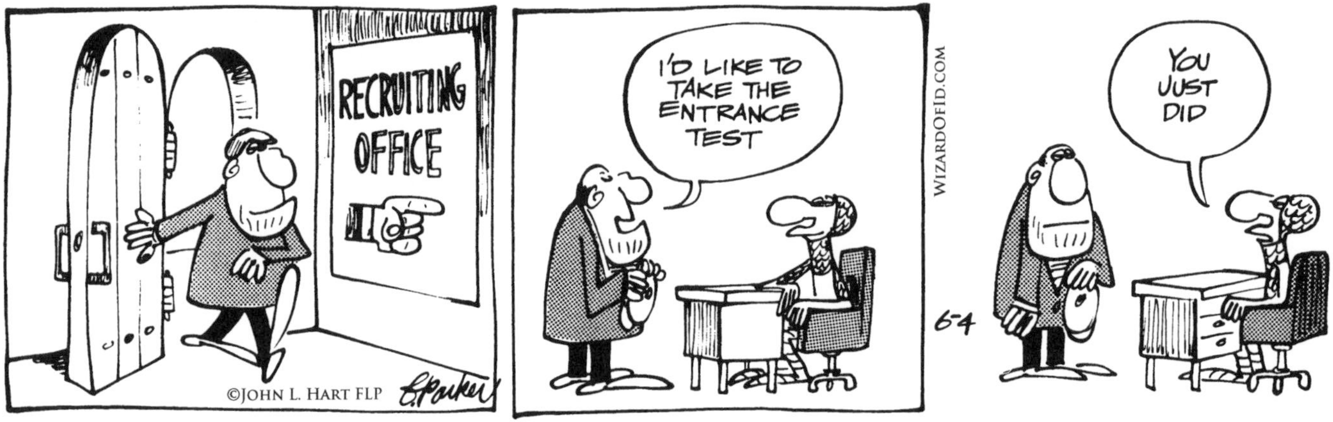
RECRUITING OFFICE
©JOHN L. HART FLP
I'D LIKE TO TAKE THE ENTRANCE TEST
WIZARDOFID.COM
6-4
YOU JUST DID

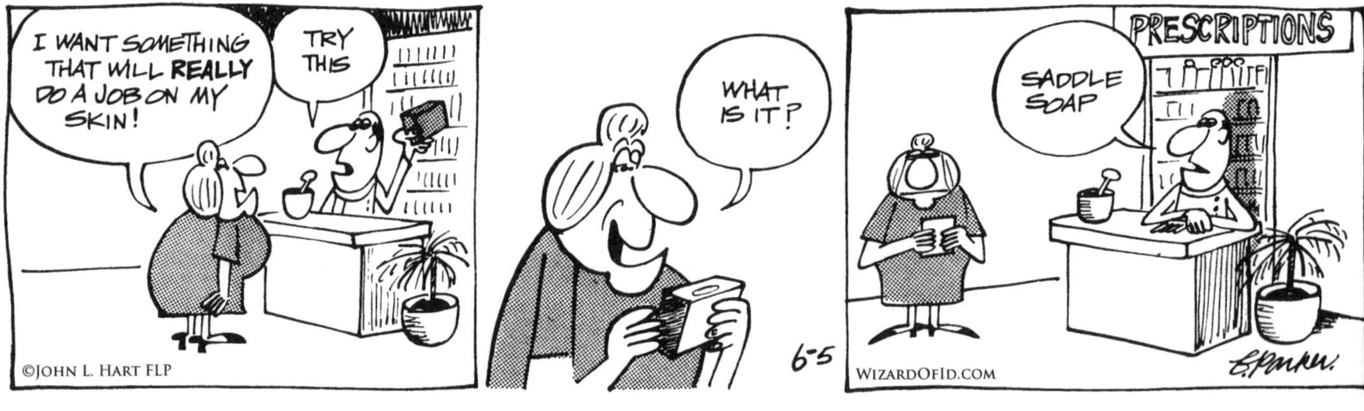
I WANT SOMETHING THAT WILL **REALLY** DO A JOB ON MY SKIN!
TRY THIS
©JOHN L. HART FLP
WHAT IS IT?
6-5
PRESCRIPTIONS
SADDLE SOAP
WIZARDOFID.COM

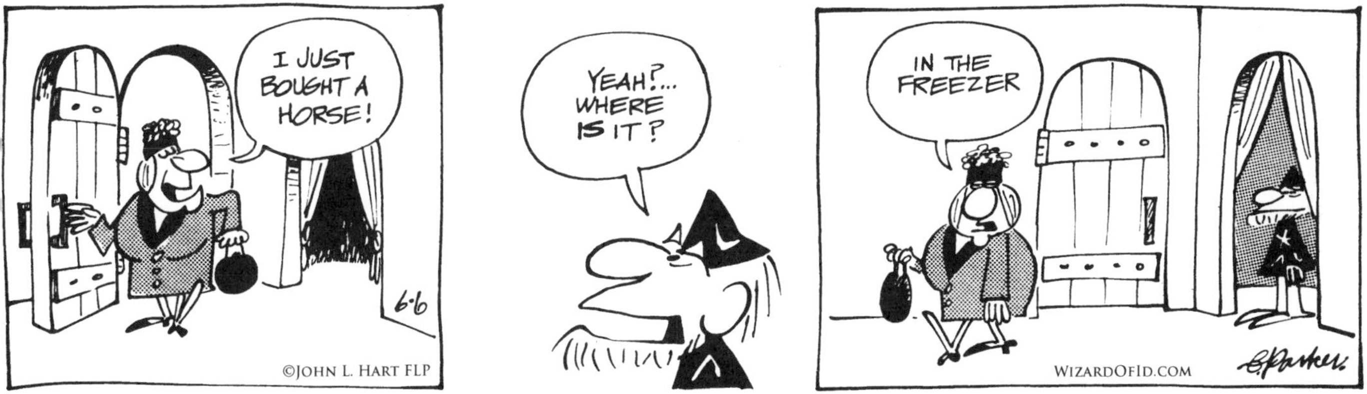
I JUST BOUGHT A HORSE!
6-6
©JOHN L. HART FLP
YEAH?... WHERE IS IT?
IN THE FREEZER
WIZARDOFID.COM
B. Parker

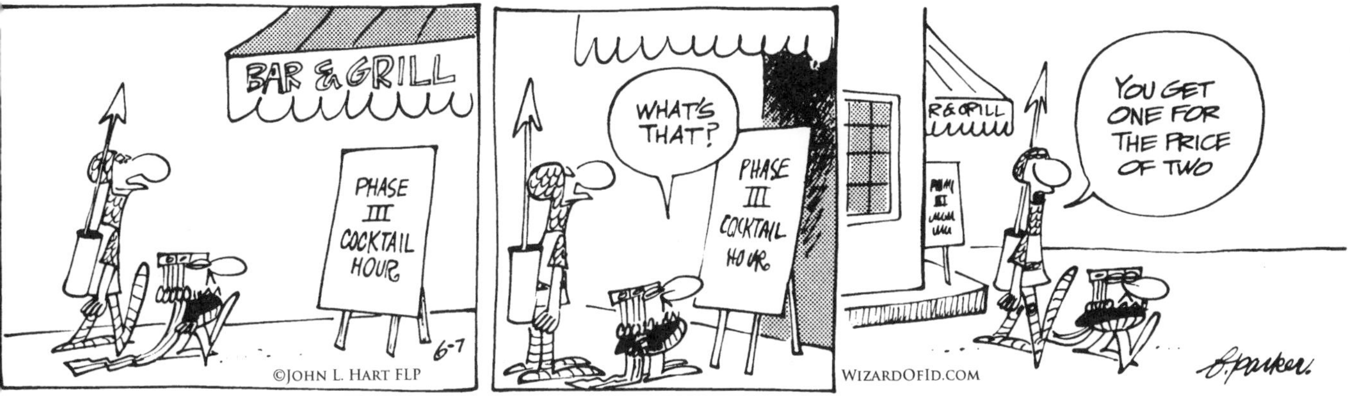
BAR & GRILL
PHASE III COCKTAIL HOUR
6-7
©JOHN L. HART FLP
WHAT'S THAT?
PHASE III COCKTAIL HOUR
R & GRILL
YOU GET ONE FOR THE PRICE OF TWO
WIZARDOFID.COM
B. Parker

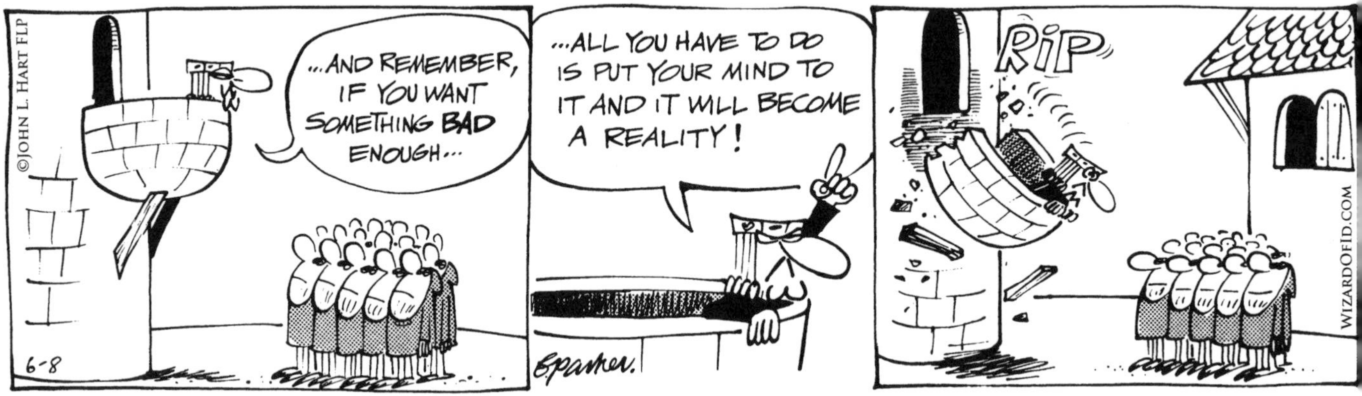
©JOHN L. HART FLP
6-8
...AND REMEMBER, IF YOU WANT SOMETHING BAD ENOUGH...
...ALL YOU HAVE TO DO IS PUT YOUR MIND TO IT AND IT WILL BECOME A REALITY!
RIP
WIZARDOFID.COM

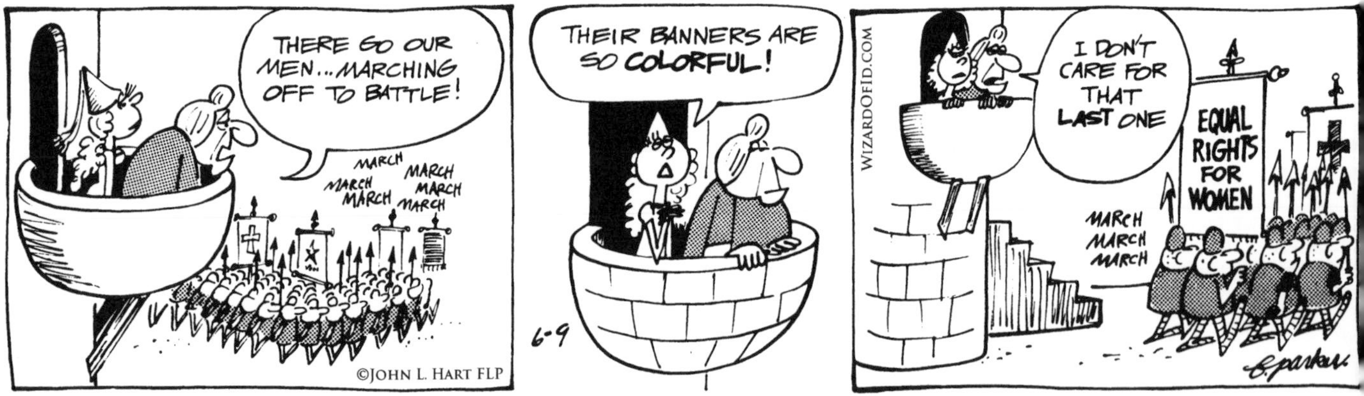
THERE GO OUR MEN...MARCHING OFF TO BATTLE!
MARCH MARCH MARCH MARCH MARCH MARCH
©JOHN L. HART FLP
6-9
THEIR BANNERS ARE SO COLORFUL!
WIZARDOFID.COM
I DON'T CARE FOR THAT LAST ONE
EQUAL RIGHTS FOR WOMEN
MARCH MARCH MARCH

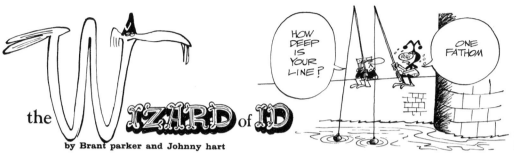

the WIZARD of ID

by Brant parker and Johnny hart

©JOHN L. HART FLP

HOW DEEP IS YOUR LINE?

ONE FATHOM

HOW DEEP IS THAT?

BARRING THE CORK... ABOUT 36 SHOTGLASSES

WIZ

YES?

WHAT THE HECK IS A **FATHOM**?

6-10-73

I'LL LOOK IT UP.

WHAT ARE YOU LOOKING UP?

fath'om

OH, I KNOW **THAT**... WE HAD IT IN **SCHOOL**!

A FATHOM IS: THE EXTENDED LENGTH OF ONE'S ARMS, FROM FINGER TIP TO FINGER TIP, AND/OR SIX FEET.

...OF COURSE, IF YOUR ARMS WERE **THAT** LONG, THEY WOULD PROBABLY GO AROUND ME **TWICE**!

WIZARDOFID.COM

I FIND THAT HARD TO **FATHOM**

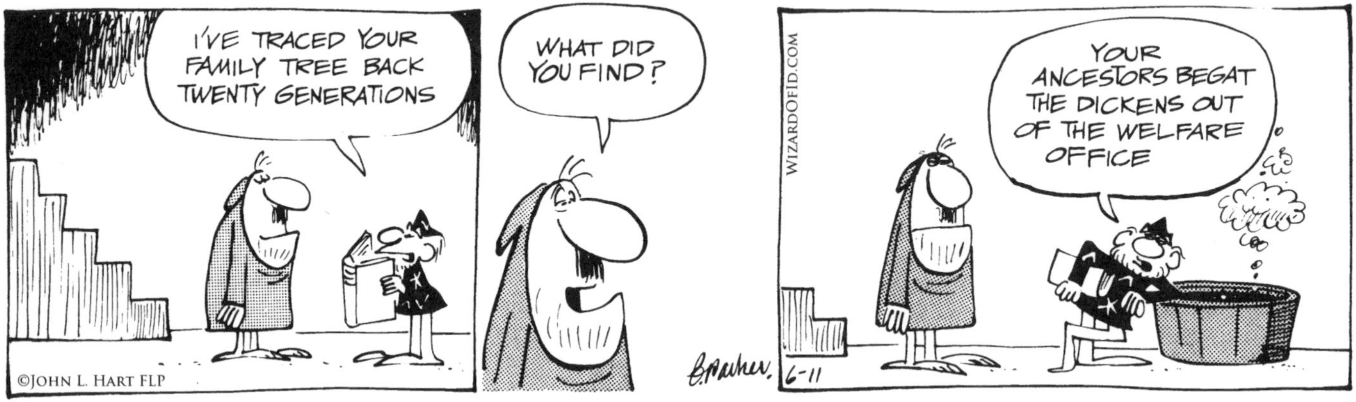
I'VE TRACED YOUR FAMILY TREE BACK TWENTY GENERATIONS
WHAT DID YOU FIND?
YOUR ANCESTORS BEGAT THE DICKENS OUT OF THE WELFARE OFFICE
©JOHN L. HART FLP
WIZARDOFID.COM
6-11

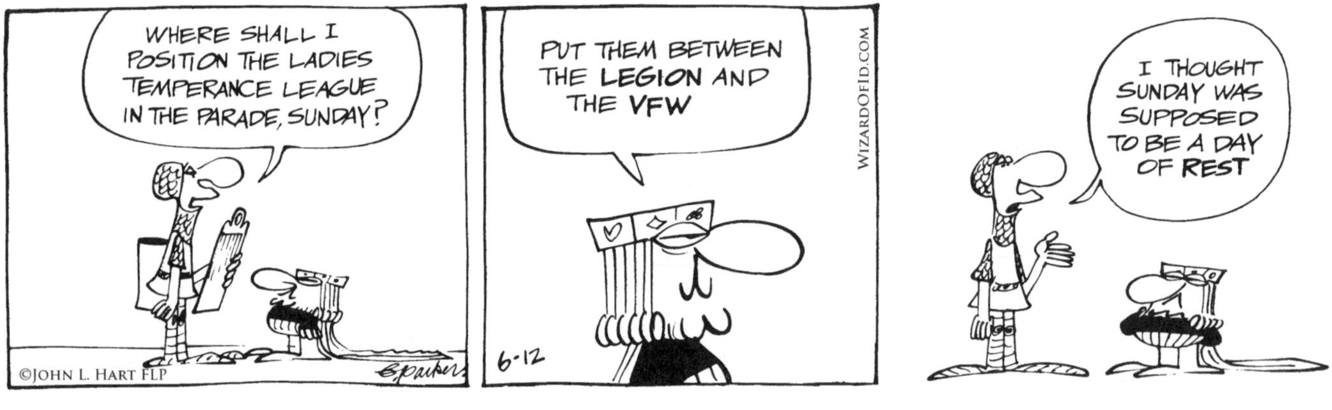
WHERE SHALL I POSITION THE LADIES TEMPERANCE LEAGUE IN THE PARADE, SUNDAY?
PUT THEM BETWEEN THE **LEGION** AND THE **VFW**
I THOUGHT SUNDAY WAS SUPPOSED TO BE A DAY OF **REST**
©JOHN L. HART FLP
WIZARDOFID.COM
6-12

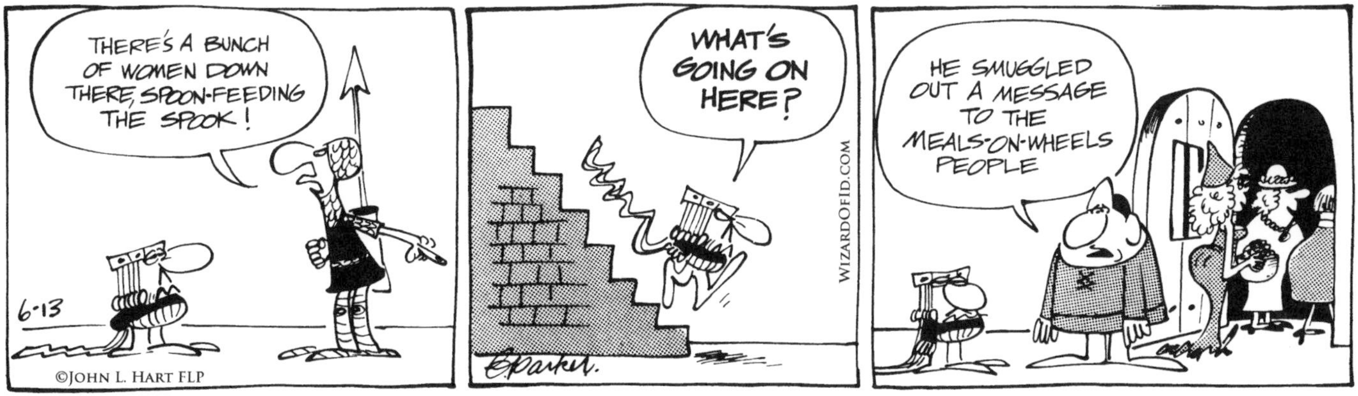
THERE'S A BUNCH OF WOMEN DOWN THERE, SPOON-FEEDING THE SPOOK!
6-13
©JOHN L. HART FLP
WHAT'S GOING ON HERE?
WIZARDOFID.COM
HE SMUGGLED OUT A MESSAGE TO THE MEALS-ON-WHEELS PEOPLE

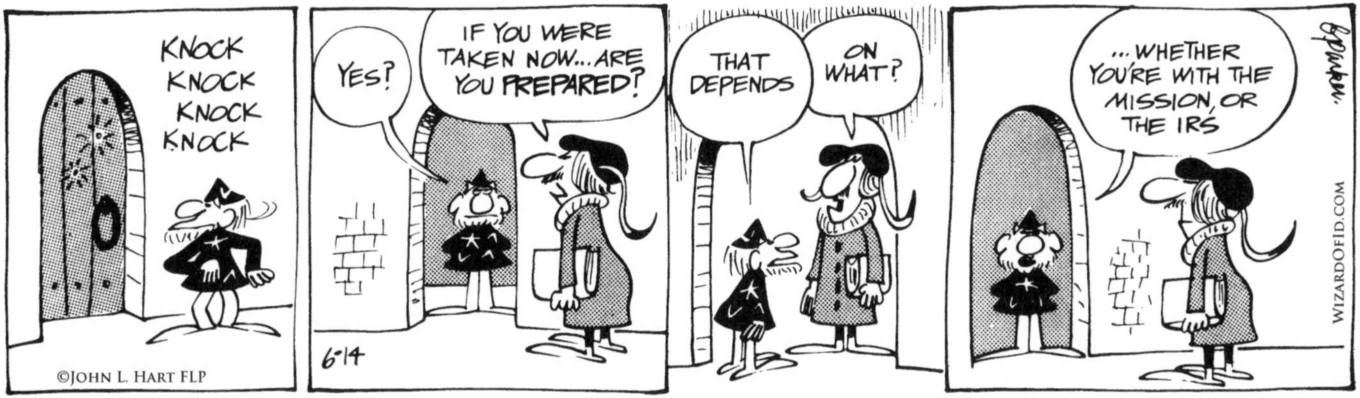
KNOCK KNOCK KNOCK KNOCK
©JOHN L. HART FLP
YES?
IF YOU WERE TAKEN NOW... ARE YOU PREPARED?
6-14
THAT DEPENDS
ON WHAT?
...WHETHER YOU'RE WITH THE MISSION, OR THE IRS
WIZARDOFID.COM

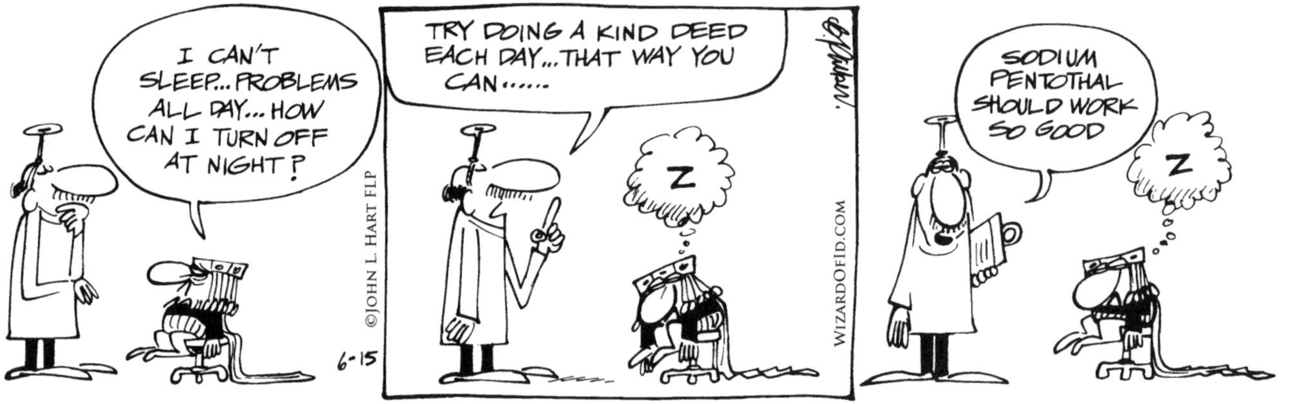
I CAN'T SLEEP... PROBLEMS ALL DAY... HOW CAN I TURN OFF AT NIGHT?
TRY DOING A KIND DEED EACH DAY... THAT WAY YOU CAN......
Z
SODIUM PENTOTHAL SHOULD WORK SO GOOD
Z
©JOHN L. HART FLP
WIZARDOFID.COM
6-15

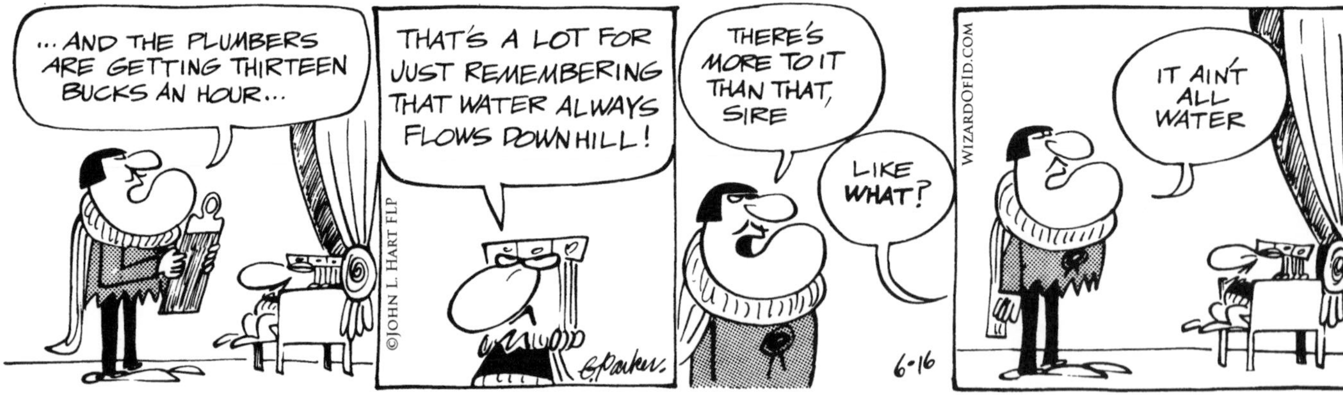
...AND THE PLUMBERS ARE GETTING THIRTEEN BUCKS AN HOUR...
THAT'S A LOT FOR JUST REMEMBERING THAT WATER ALWAYS FLOWS DOWNHILL!
THERE'S MORE TO IT THAN THAT, SIRE
LIKE WHAT?
IT AIN'T ALL WATER
©JOHN L. HART FLP
WIZARDOFID.COM
6-16

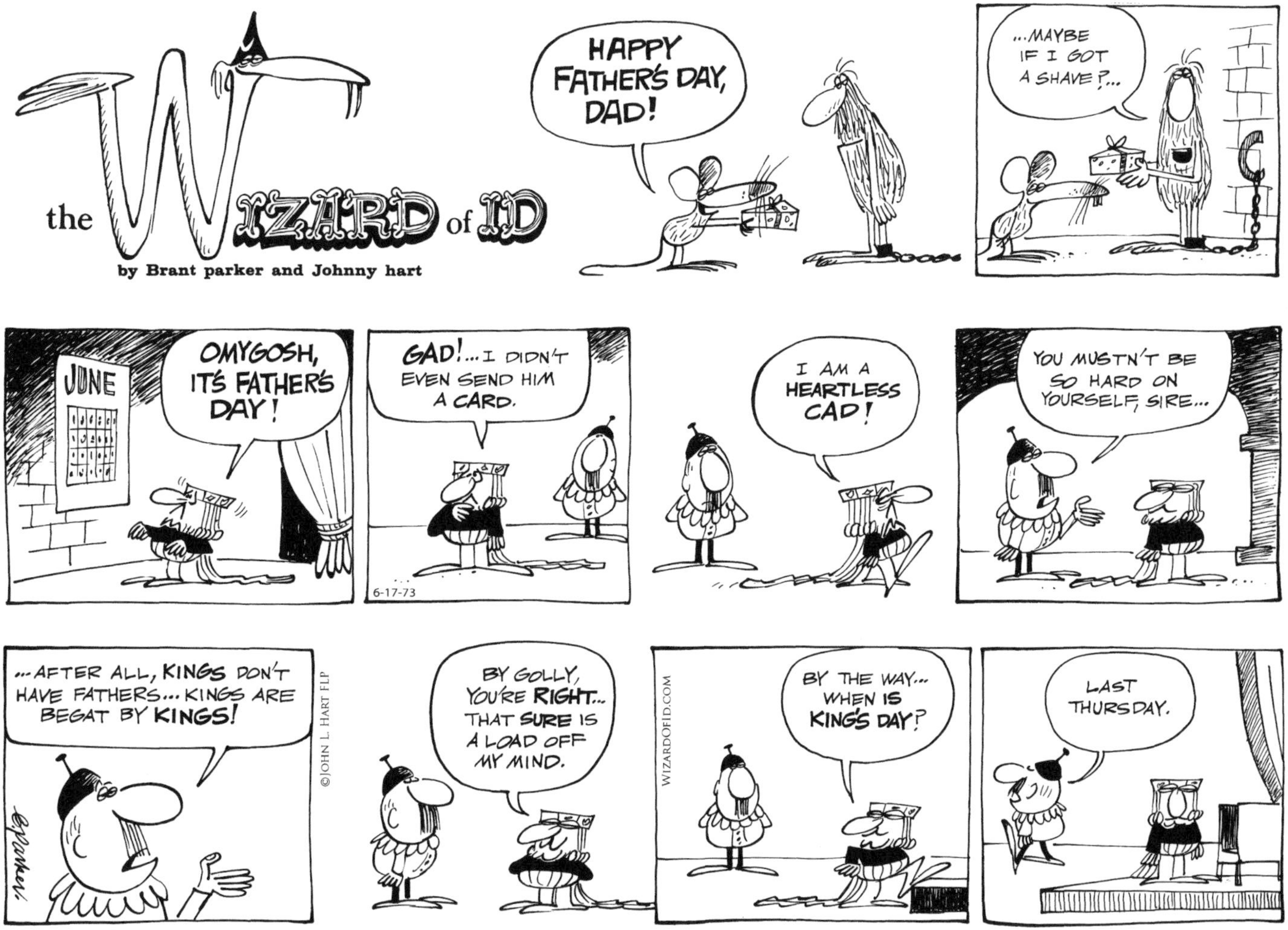
the WIZARD of ID
by Brant parker and Johnny hart
HAPPY FATHER'S DAY, DAD!
...MAYBE IF I GOT A SHAVE?...
JUNE
OMYGOSH, IT'S FATHER'S DAY!
GAD!... I DIDN'T EVEN SEND HIM A CARD.
6-17-73
I AM A HEARTLESS CAD!
YOU MUSTN'T BE SO HARD ON YOURSELF, SIRE...
...AFTER ALL, KINGS DON'T HAVE FATHERS... KINGS ARE BEGAT BY KINGS!
parker
©JOHN L. HART FLP
BY GOLLY, YOU'RE RIGHT... THAT SURE IS A LOAD OFF MY MIND.
WIZARDOFID.COM
BY THE WAY... WHEN IS KING'S DAY?
LAST THURSDAY.

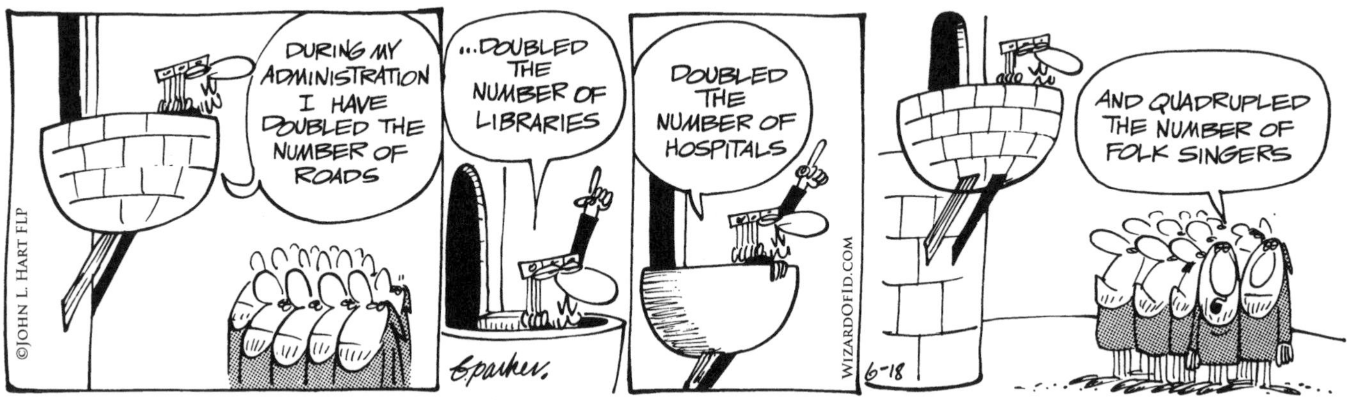
©JOHN L. HART FLP
DURING MY ADMINISTRATION I HAVE DOUBLED THE NUMBER OF ROADS
...DOUBLED THE NUMBER OF LIBRARIES
DOUBLED THE NUMBER OF HOSPITALS
WIZARDOFID.COM
AND QUADRUPLED THE NUMBER OF FOLK SINGERS
6-18

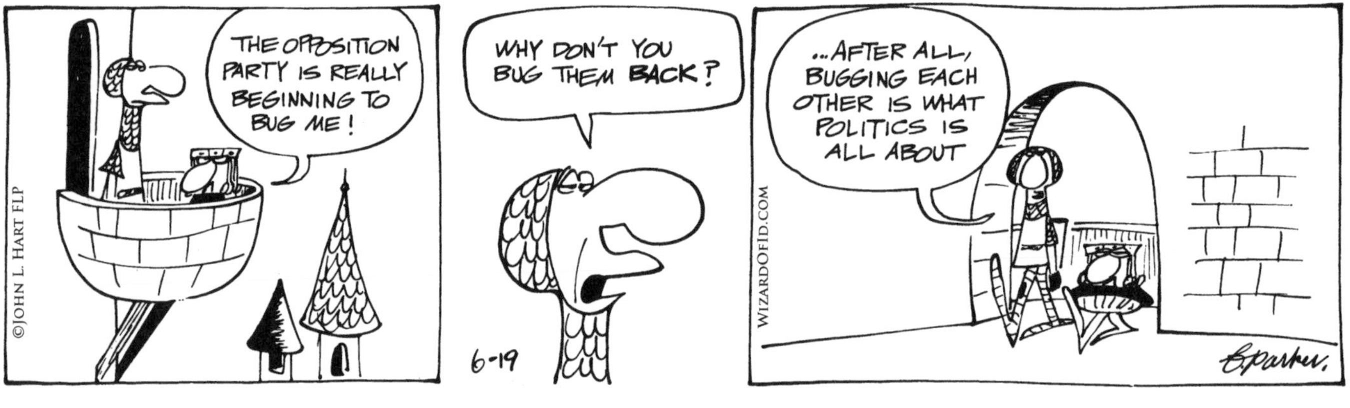
©JOHN L. HART FLP
THE OPPOSITION PARTY IS REALLY BEGINNING TO BUG ME!
WHY DON'T YOU BUG THEM BACK?
6-19
WIZARDOFID.COM
...AFTER ALL, BUGGING EACH OTHER IS WHAT POLITICS IS ALL ABOUT

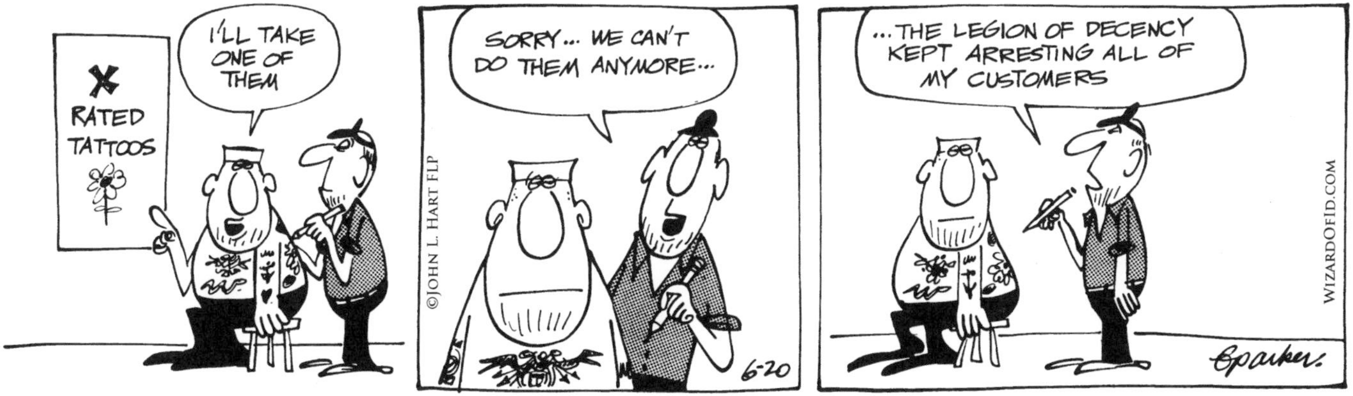
X RATED TATTOOS
I'LL TAKE ONE OF THEM
SORRY... WE CAN'T DO THEM ANYMORE...
...THE LEGION OF DECENCY KEPT ARRESTING ALL OF MY CUSTOMERS
©JOHN L. HART FLP
6-20
WIZARDOFID.COM

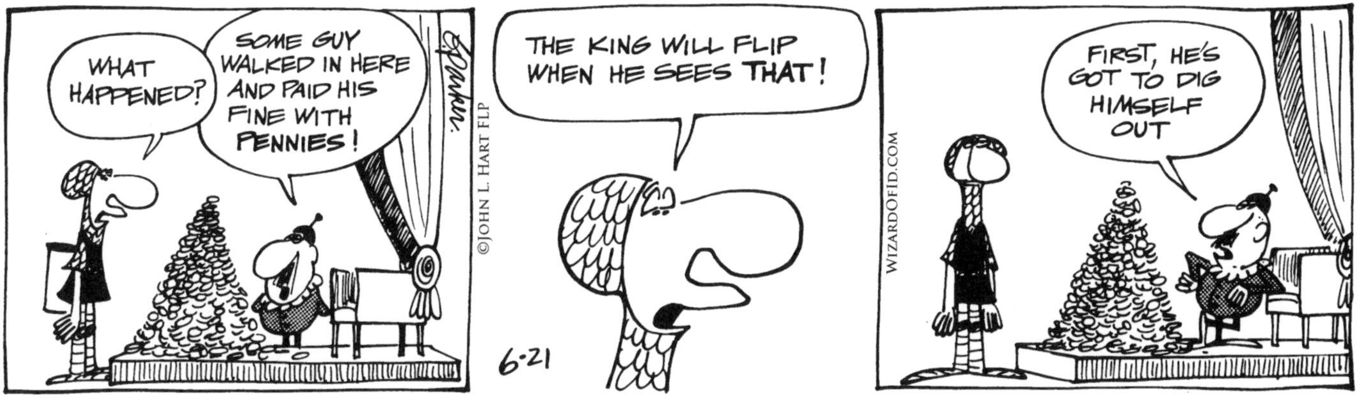
WHAT HAPPENED?
SOME GUY WALKED IN HERE AND PAID HIS FINE WITH PENNIES!
THE KING WILL FLIP WHEN HE SEES THAT!
FIRST, HE'S GOT TO DIG HIMSELF OUT
©JOHN L. HART FLP
6-21
WIZARDOFID.COM

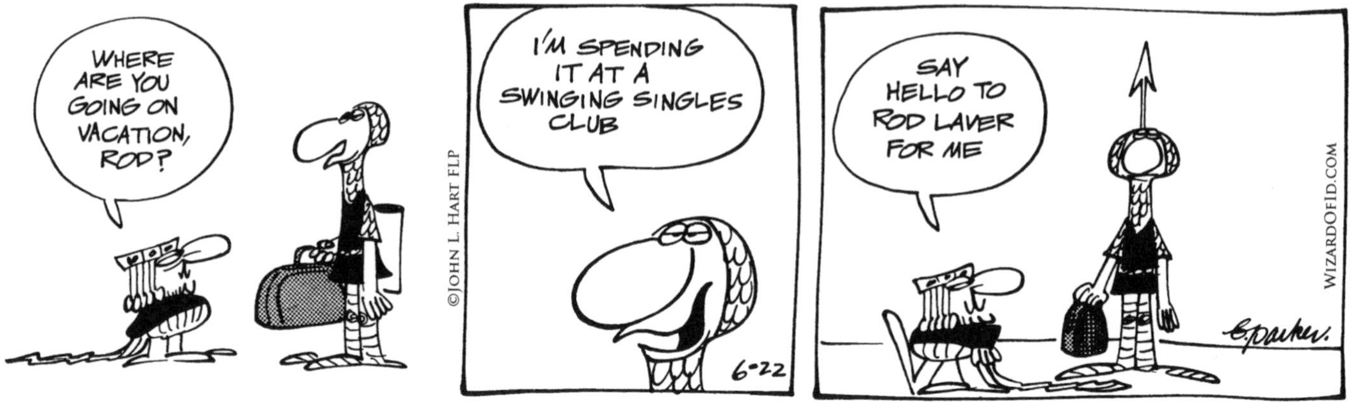
WHERE ARE YOU GOING ON VACATION, ROD?
I'M SPENDING IT AT A SWINGING SINGLES CLUB
SAY HELLO TO ROD LAVER FOR ME
6-22
©JOHN L. HART FLP
WIZARDOFID.COM

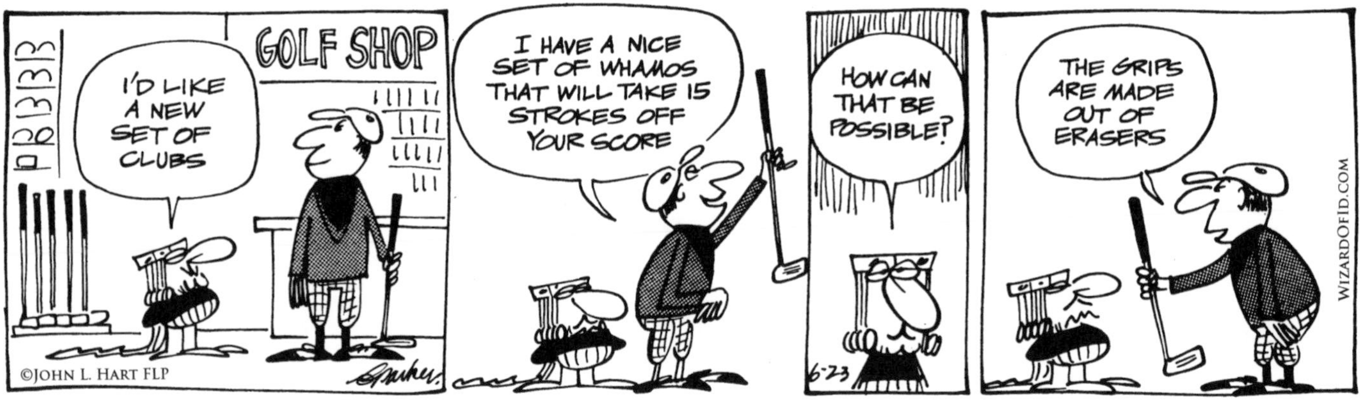
GOLF SHOP
I'D LIKE A NEW SET OF CLUBS
I HAVE A NICE SET OF WHAMOS THAT WILL TAKE 15 STROKES OFF YOUR SCORE
HOW CAN THAT BE POSSIBLE?
THE GRIPS ARE MADE OUT OF ERASERS
6-23
©JOHN L. HART FLP
WIZARDOFID.COM

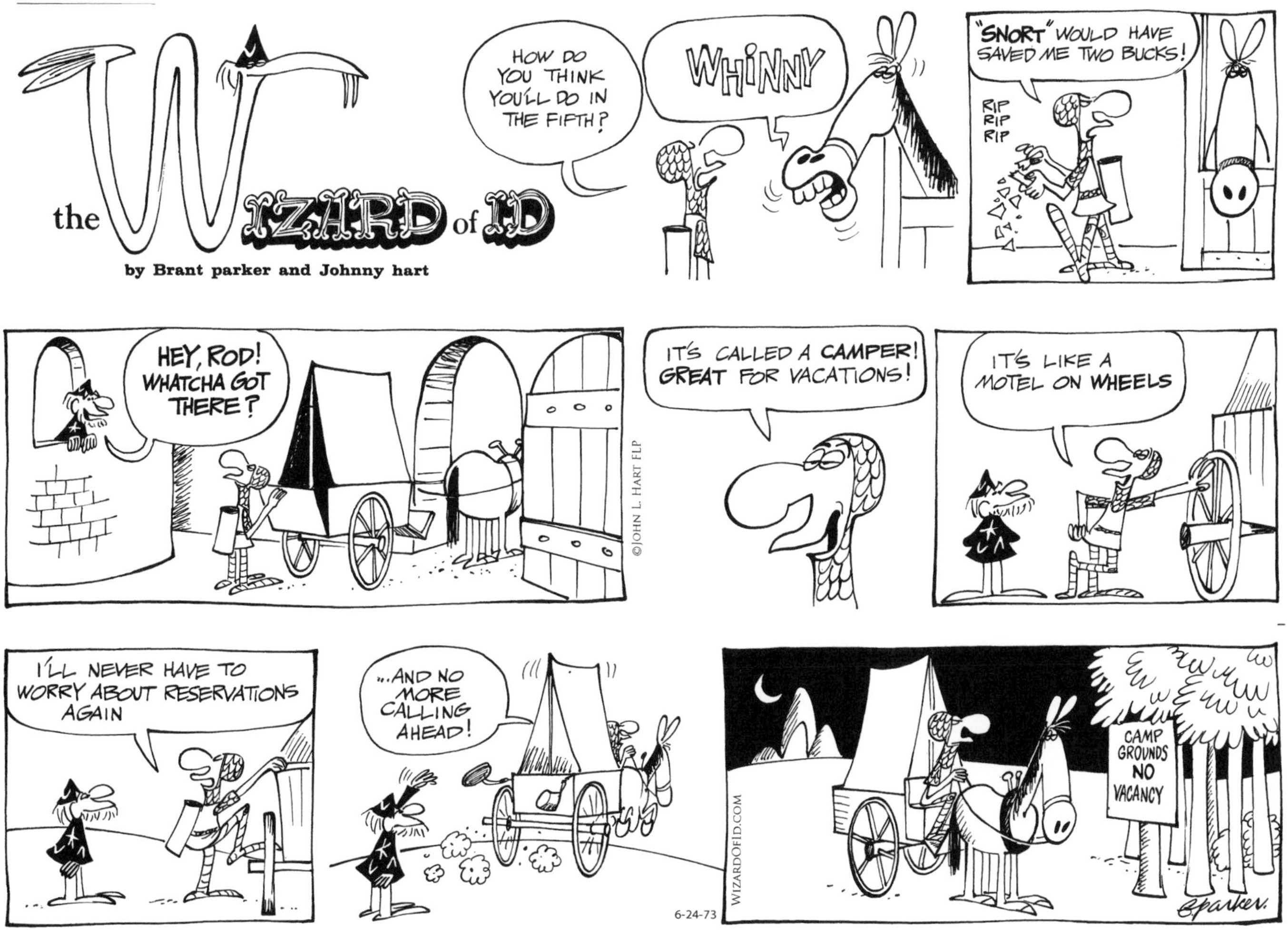
the WIZARD of ID
by Brant parker and Johnny hart
HOW DO YOU THINK YOU'LL DO IN THE FIFTH?
WHINNY
"SNORT" WOULD HAVE SAVED ME TWO BUCKS!
RIP RIP RIP
HEY, ROD! WHATCHA GOT THERE?
©JOHN L. HART FLP
IT'S CALLED A CAMPER! GREAT FOR VACATIONS!
IT'S LIKE A MOTEL ON WHEELS
I'LL NEVER HAVE TO WORRY ABOUT RESERVATIONS AGAIN
...AND NO MORE CALLING AHEAD!
6-24-73
WIZARDOFID.COM
CAMP GROUNDS NO VACANCY
parker

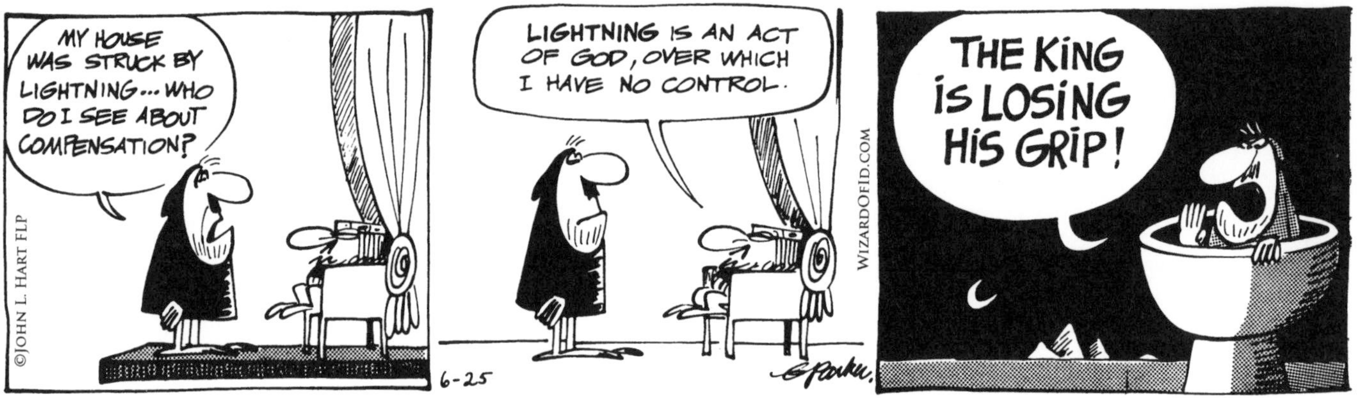
MY HOUSE WAS STRUCK BY LIGHTNING... WHO DO I SEE ABOUT COMPENSATION?
LIGHTNING IS AN ACT OF GOD, OVER WHICH I HAVE NO CONTROL.
THE KING IS LOSING HIS GRIP!
©JOHN L. HART FLP
WIZARDOFID.COM
6-25

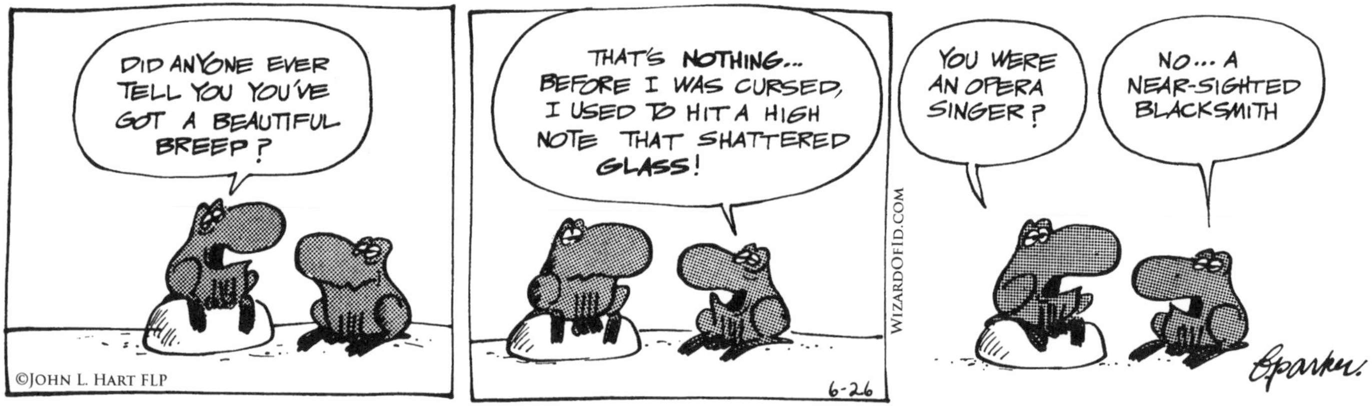
DID ANYONE EVER TELL YOU YOU'VE GOT A BEAUTIFUL BREEP?
THAT'S NOTHING... BEFORE I WAS CURSED, I USED TO HIT A HIGH NOTE THAT SHATTERED GLASS!
YOU WERE AN OPERA SINGER?
NO... A NEAR-SIGHTED BLACKSMITH
©JOHN L. HART FLP
WIZARDOFID.COM
6-26

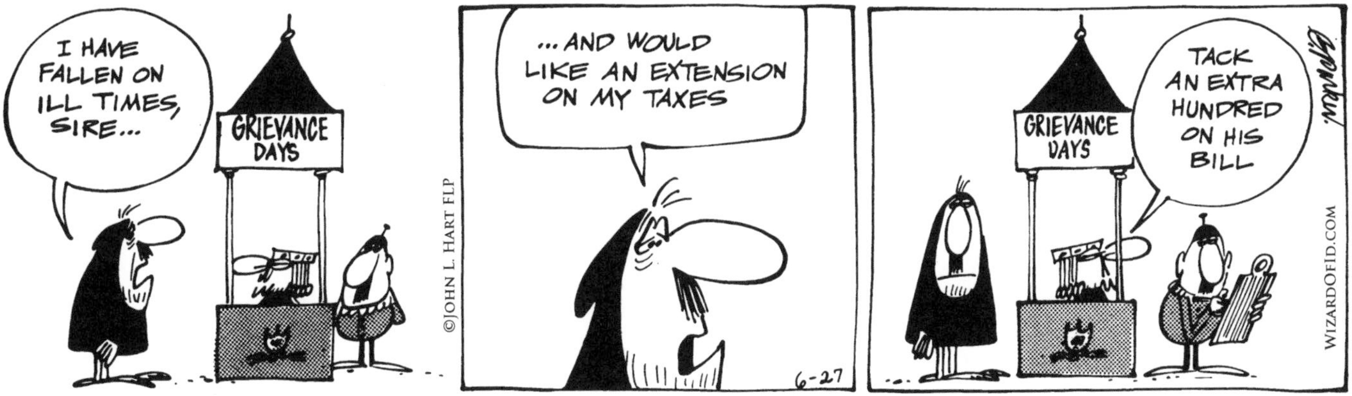
I HAVE FALLEN ON ILL TIMES, SIRE...
GRIEVANCE DAYS
©JOHN L. HART FLP
...AND WOULD LIKE AN EXTENSION ON MY TAXES
6-27
GRIEVANCE DAYS
TACK AN EXTRA HUNDRED ON HIS BILL
WIZARDOFID.COM

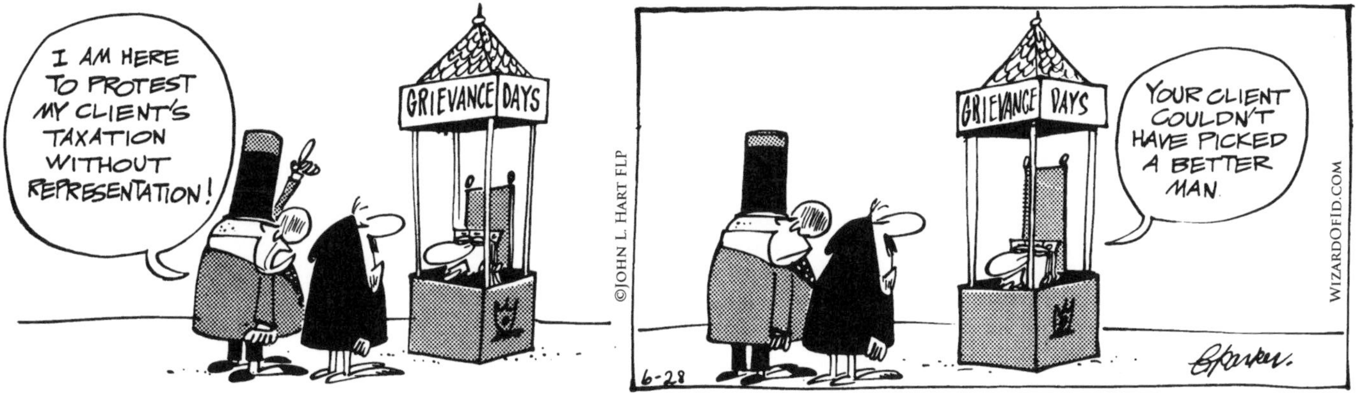
I AM HERE TO PROTEST MY CLIENT'S TAXATION WITHOUT REPRESENTATION!
GRIEVANCE DAYS
©JOHN L. HART FLP
GRIEVANCE DAYS
YOUR CLIENT COULDN'T HAVE PICKED A BETTER MAN.
WIZARDOFID.COM
6-28

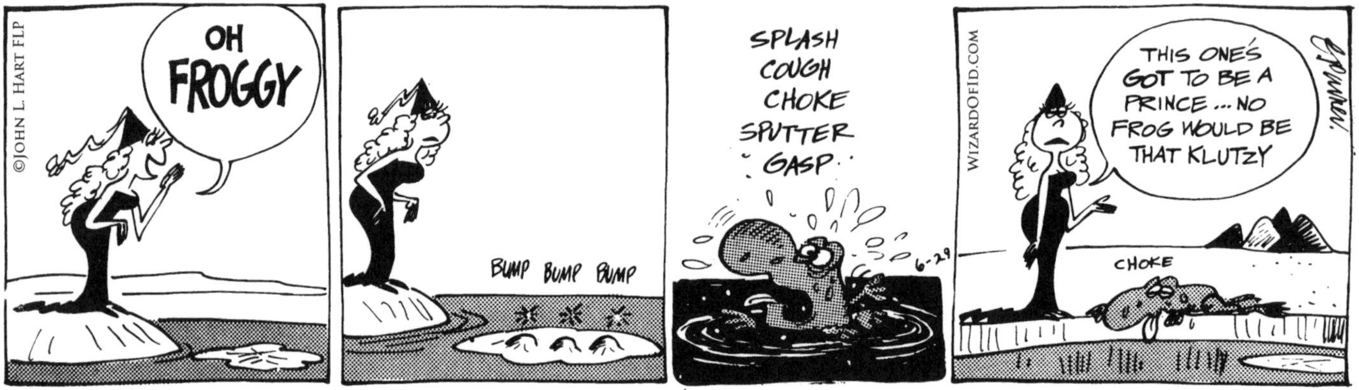
©JOHN L. HART FLP
OH FROGGY
BUMP BUMP BUMP
SPLASH
COUGH
CHOKE
SPUTTER
GASP
6-29
WIZARDOFID.COM
THIS ONE'S GOT TO BE A PRINCE ... NO FROG WOULD BE THAT KLUTZY
CHOKE

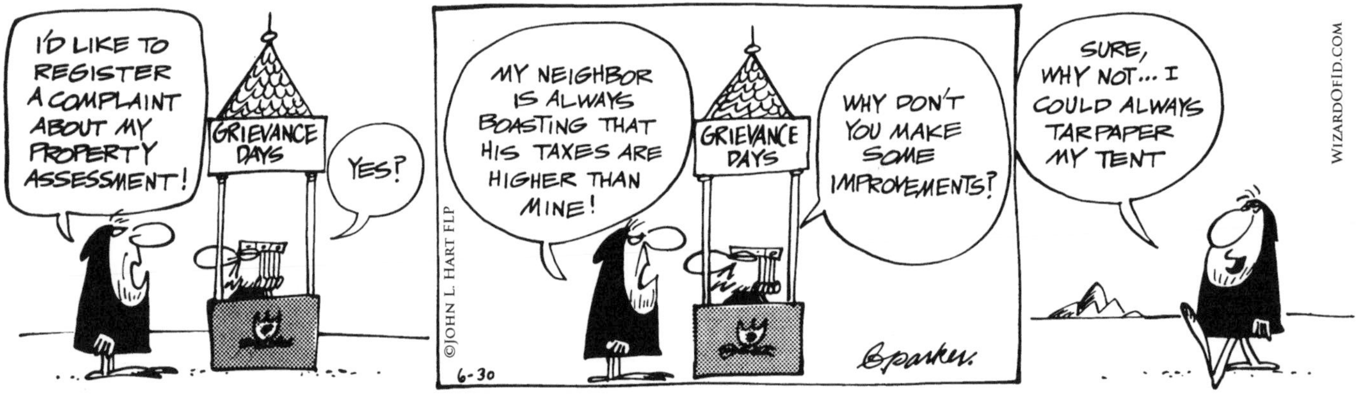
I'D LIKE TO REGISTER A COMPLAINT ABOUT MY PROPERTY ASSESSMENT!
GRIEVANCE DAYS
YES?
©JOHN L. HART FLP
MY NEIGHBOR IS ALWAYS BOASTING THAT HIS TAXES ARE HIGHER THAN MINE!
GRIEVANCE DAYS
WHY DON'T YOU MAKE SOME IMPROVEMENTS?
6-30
SURE, WHY NOT... I COULD ALWAYS TARPAPER MY TENT
WIZARDOFID.COM

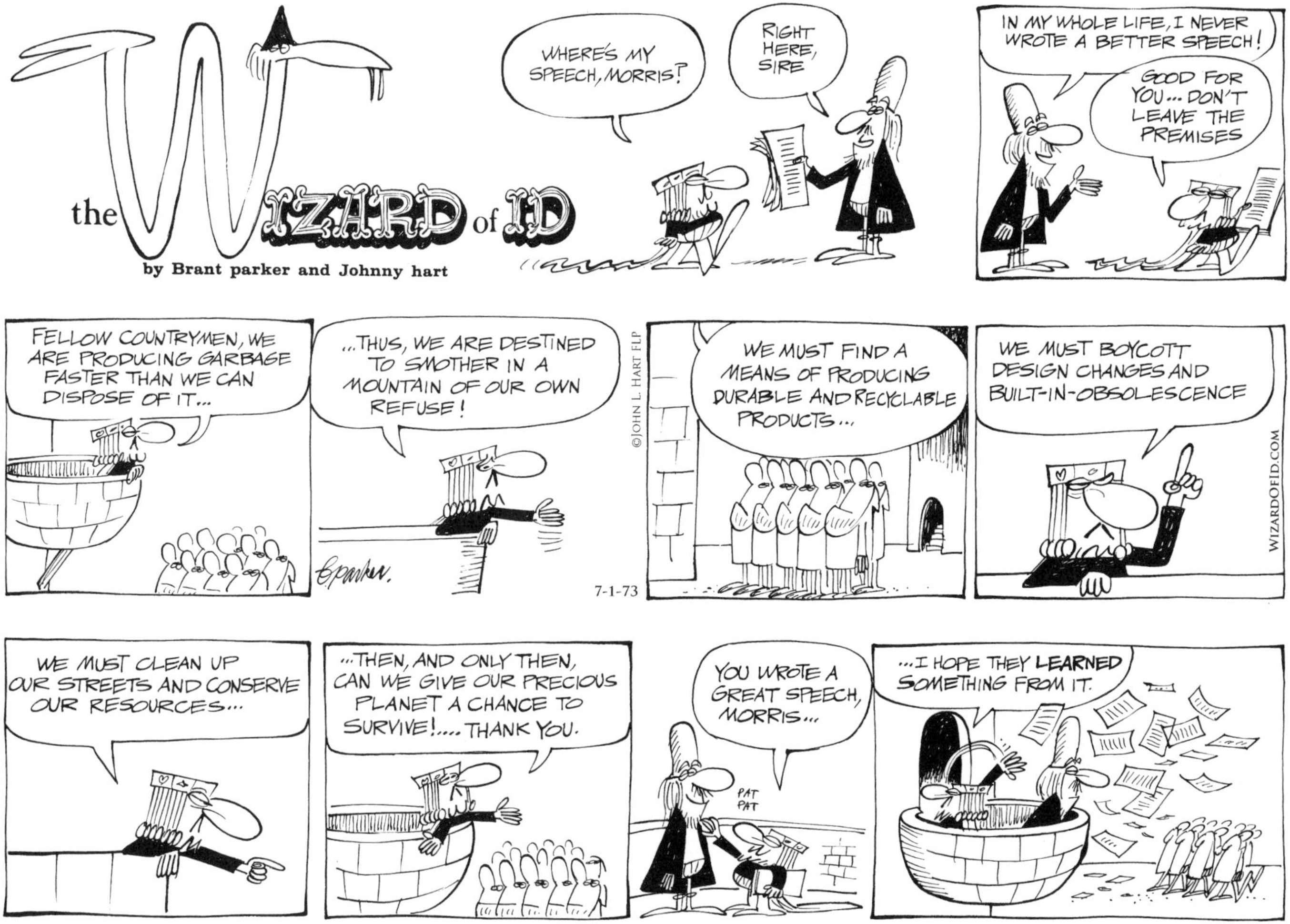
the WIZARD of ID
by Brant parker and Johnny hart
WHERE'S MY SPEECH, MORRIS?
RIGHT HERE, SIRE
IN MY WHOLE LIFE, I NEVER WROTE A BETTER SPEECH!
GOOD FOR YOU... DON'T LEAVE THE PREMISES
FELLOW COUNTRYMEN, WE ARE PRODUCING GARBAGE FASTER THAN WE CAN DISPOSE OF IT...
...THUS, WE ARE DESTINED TO SMOTHER IN A MOUNTAIN OF OUR OWN REFUSE!
©JOHN L. HART FLP
7-1-73
WE MUST FIND A MEANS OF PRODUCING DURABLE AND RECYCLABLE PRODUCTS...
WE MUST BOYCOTT DESIGN CHANGES AND BUILT-IN-OBSOLESCENCE
WIZARDOFID.COM
WE MUST CLEAN UP OUR STREETS AND CONSERVE OUR RESOURCES...
...THEN, AND ONLY THEN, CAN WE GIVE OUR PRECIOUS PLANET A CHANCE TO SURVIVE!.... THANK YOU.
YOU WROTE A GREAT SPEECH, MORRIS...
PAT PAT
...I HOPE THEY LEARNED SOMETHING FROM IT.

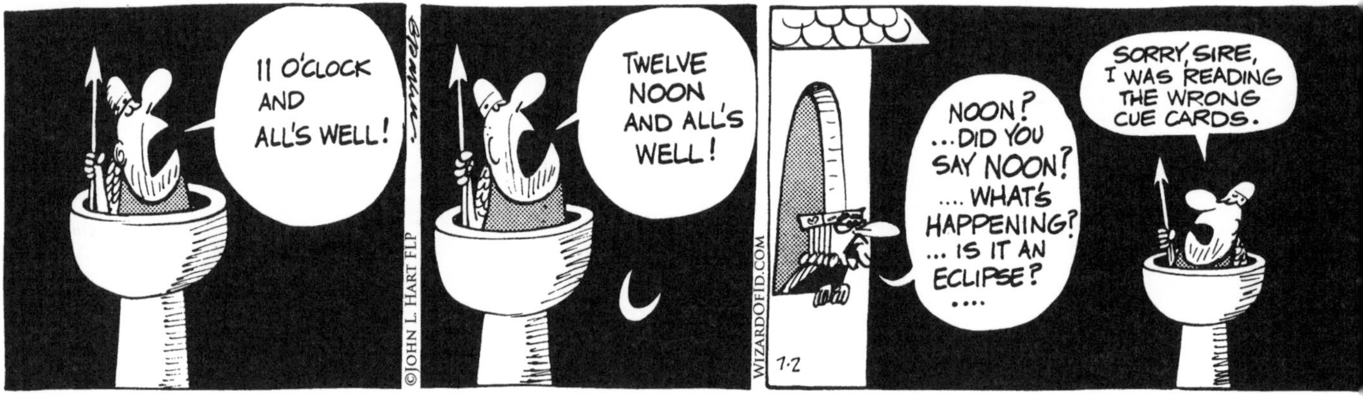
11 O'CLOCK AND ALL'S WELL!
TWELVE NOON AND ALL'S WELL!
NOON? ...DID YOU SAY NOON? .... WHAT'S HAPPENING? ... IS IT AN ECLIPSE? ....
SORRY, SIRE, I WAS READING THE WRONG CUE CARDS.
©JOHN L. HART FLP
WIZARDOFID.COM
7·2

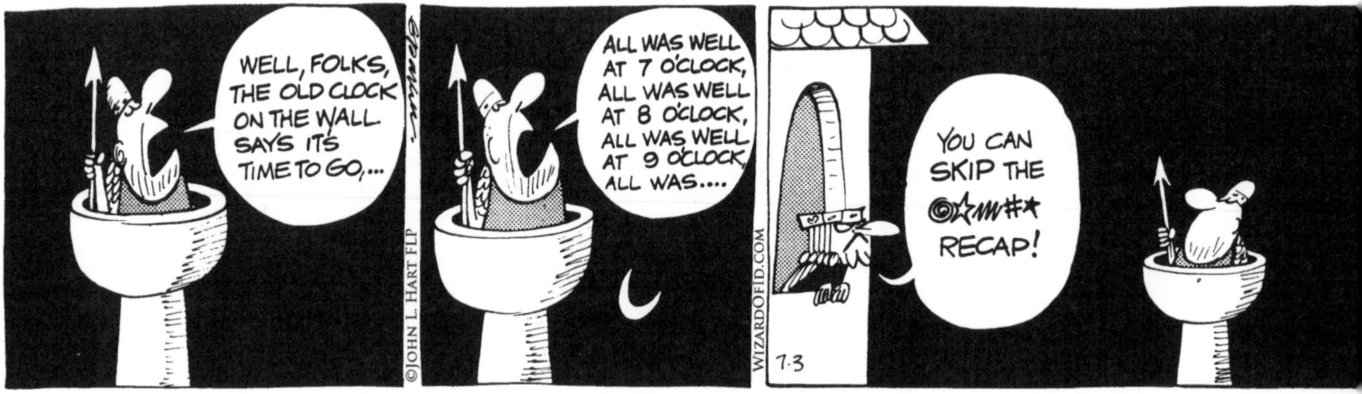
WELL, FOLKS, THE OLD CLOCK ON THE WALL SAYS IT'S TIME TO GO,...
ALL WAS WELL AT 7 O'CLOCK, ALL WAS WELL AT 8 O'CLOCK, ALL WAS WELL AT 9 O'CLOCK, ALL WAS....
YOU CAN SKIP THE @☆##* RECAP!
©JOHN L. HART FLP
WIZARDOFID.COM
7·3

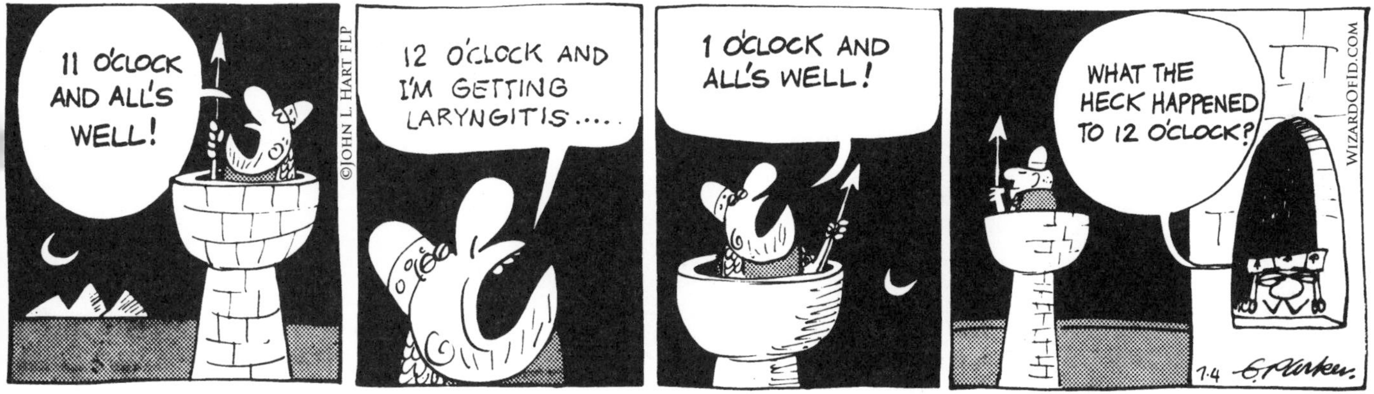
11 O'CLOCK AND ALL'S WELL!
©JOHN L. HART FLP
12 O'CLOCK AND I'M GETTING LARYNGITIS.....
1 O'CLOCK AND ALL'S WELL!
WHAT THE HECK HAPPENED TO 12 O'CLOCK?
WIZARDOFID.COM
7·4

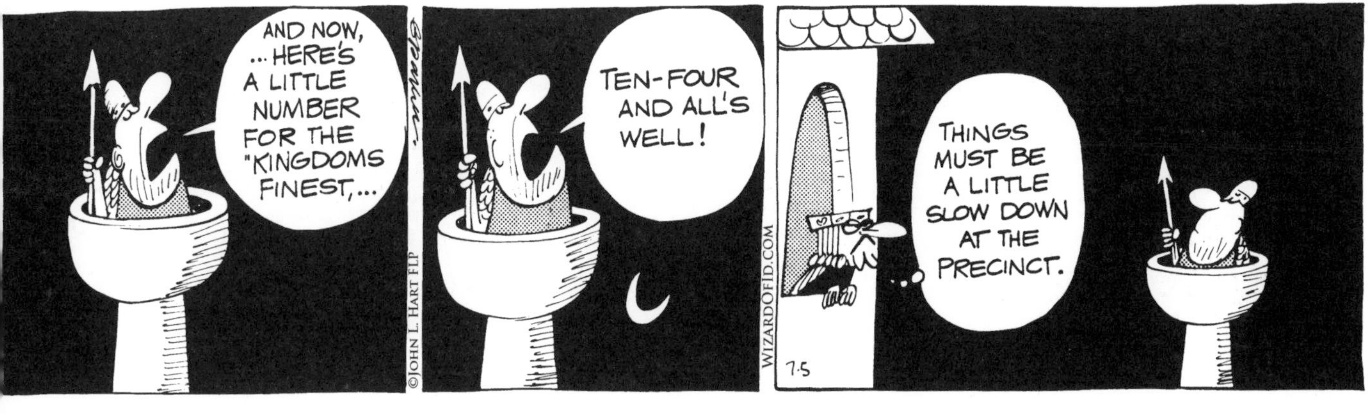
AND NOW, ... HERE'S A LITTLE NUMBER FOR THE "KINGDOMS FINEST,...
©JOHN L. HART FLP
TEN-FOUR AND ALL'S WELL!
WIZARDOFID.COM
THINGS MUST BE A LITTLE SLOW DOWN AT THE PRECINCT.
7·5

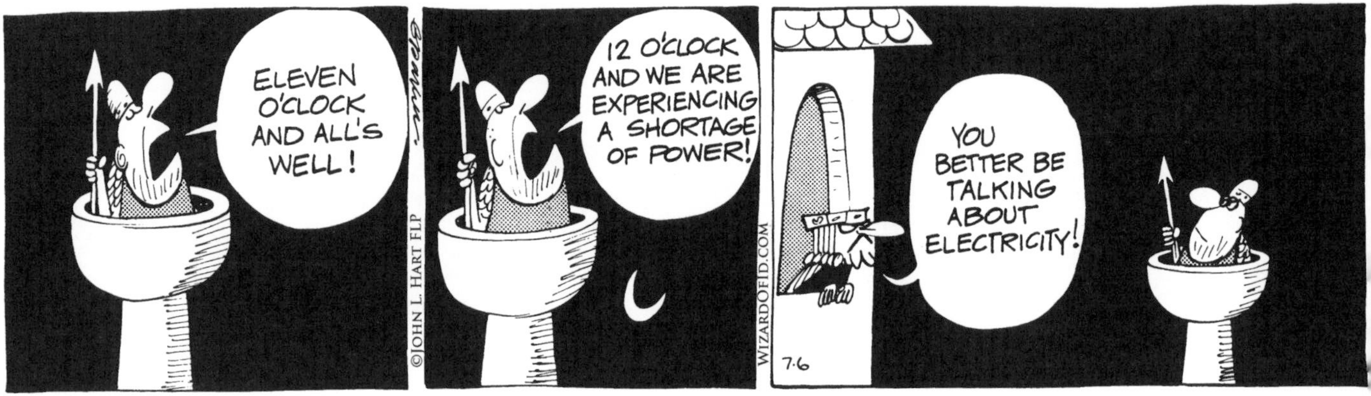
ELEVEN O'CLOCK AND ALL'S WELL!
12 O'CLOCK AND WE ARE EXPERIENCING A SHORTAGE OF POWER!
©JOHN L. HART FLP
WIZARDOFID.COM
YOU BETTER BE TALKING ABOUT ELECTRICITY!
7·6

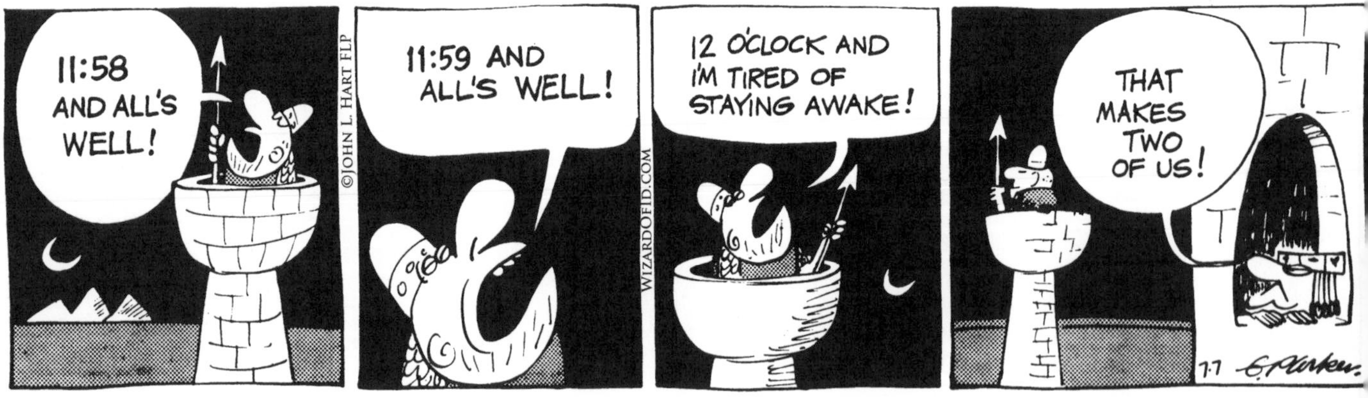
11:58 AND ALL'S WELL!
©JOHN L. HART FLP
11:59 AND ALL'S WELL!
WIZARDOFID.COM
12 O'CLOCK AND I'M TIRED OF STAYING AWAKE!
THAT MAKES TWO OF US!
7·7

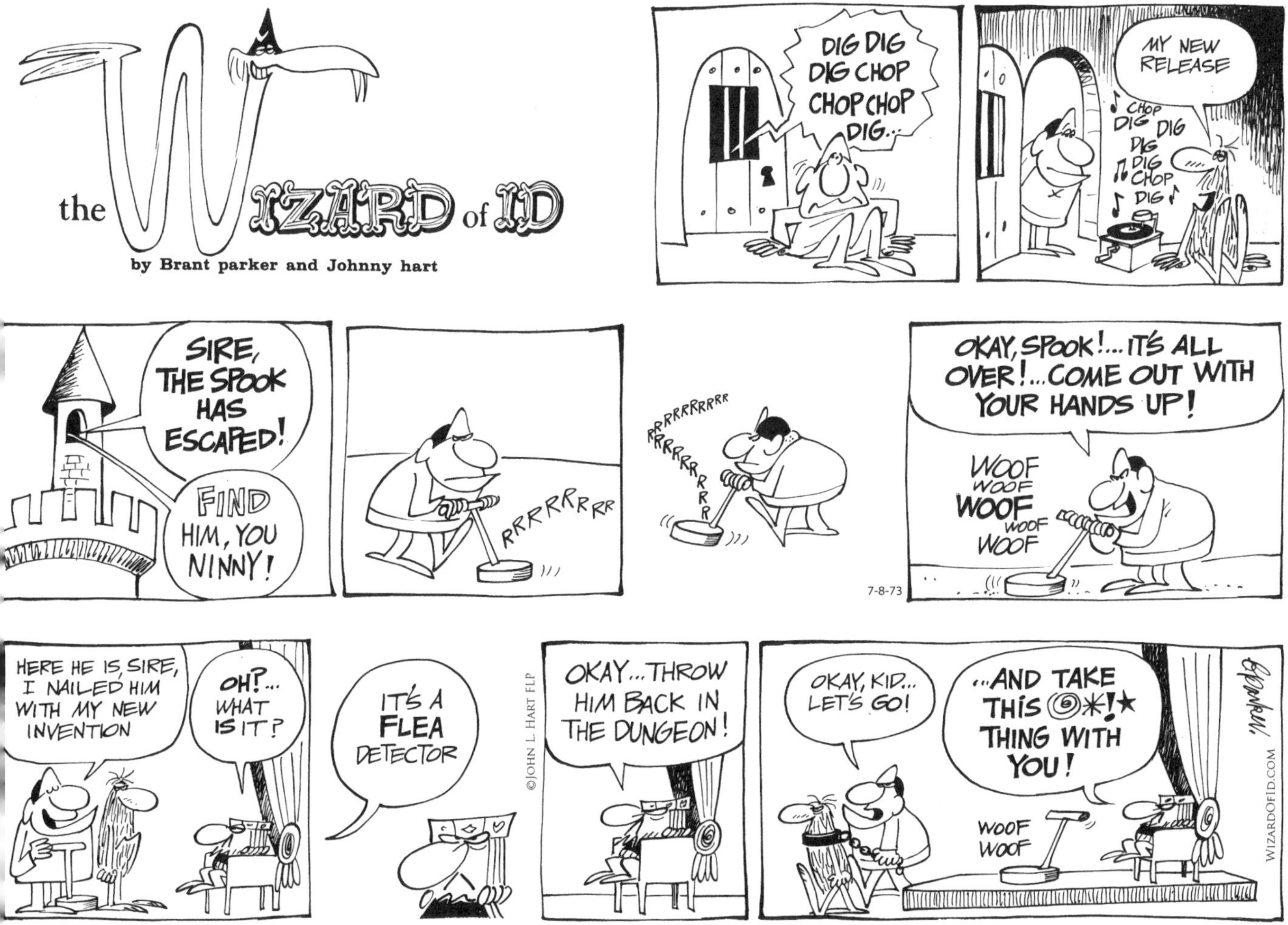

the WIZARD of ID
by Brant parker and Johnny hart
DIG DIG DIG CHOP CHOP CHOP DIG...
MY NEW RELEASE
CHOP DIG DIG DIG DIG CHOP DIG
SIRE, THE SPOOK HAS ESCAPED!
FIND HIM, YOU NINNY!
RRRRRRRRR
RRRRRRRRRR RRRRRRRRR
OKAY, SPOOK!... IT'S ALL OVER!...COME OUT WITH YOUR HANDS UP!
WOOF WOOF WOOF WOOF WOOF
7-8-73
HERE HE IS, SIRE, I NAILED HIM WITH MY NEW INVENTION
OH?... WHAT IS IT?
IT'S A FLEA DETECTOR
©JOHN L. HART FLP
OKAY... THROW HIM BACK IN THE DUNGEON!
OKAY, KID... LET'S GO!
...AND TAKE THIS ◎✱!★ THING WITH YOU!
WOOF WOOF
WIZARDOFID.COM

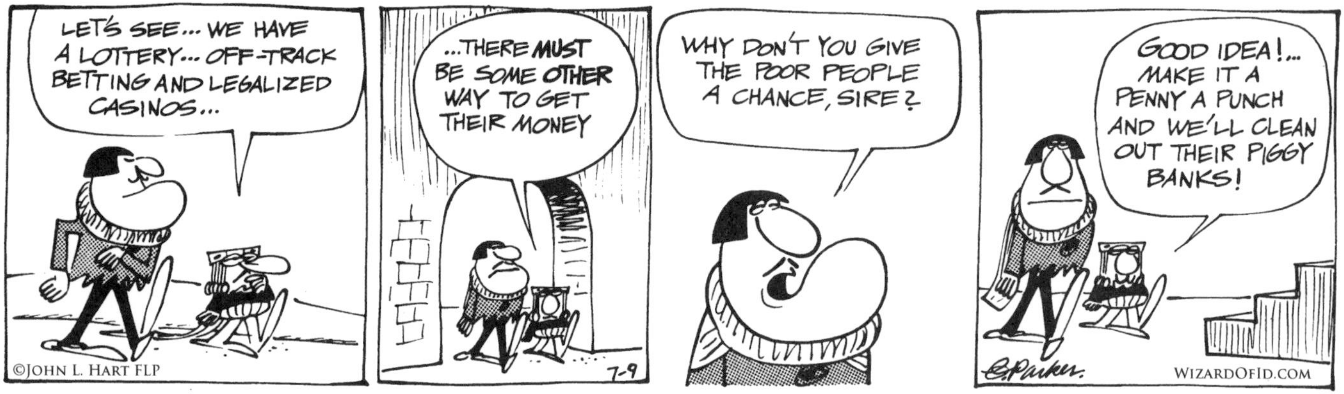
LET'S SEE... WE HAVE A LOTTERY... OFF-TRACK BETTING AND LEGALIZED CASINOS...
©JOHN L. HART FLP
...THERE MUST BE SOME OTHER WAY TO GET THEIR MONEY
7-9
WHY DON'T YOU GIVE THE POOR PEOPLE A CHANCE, SIRE?
GOOD IDEA!... MAKE IT A PENNY A PUNCH AND WE'LL CLEAN OUT THEIR PIGGY BANKS!
WIZARDOFID.COM

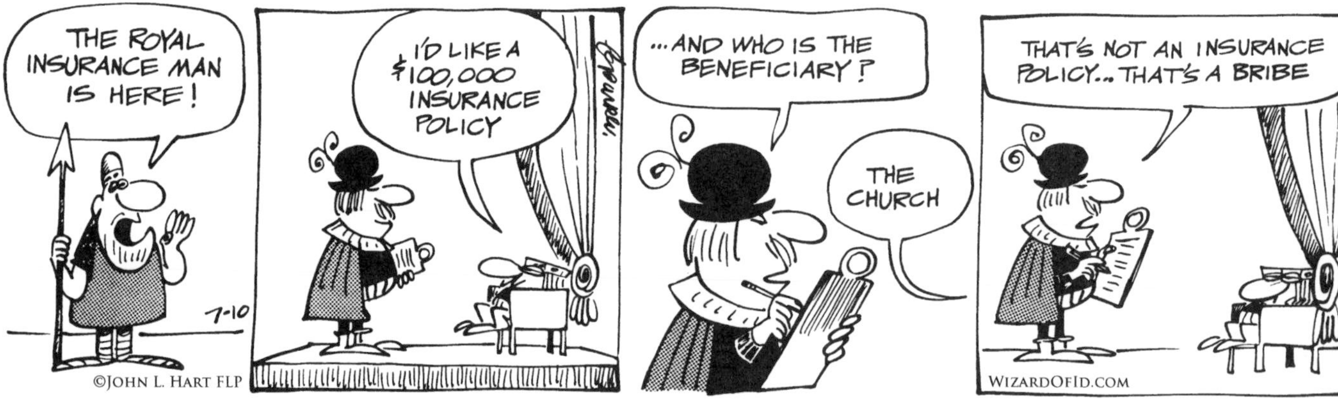
THE ROYAL INSURANCE MAN IS HERE!
7-10
©JOHN L. HART FLP
I'D LIKE A $100,000 INSURANCE POLICY
...AND WHO IS THE BENEFICIARY?
THE CHURCH
THAT'S NOT AN INSURANCE POLICY... THAT'S A BRIBE
WIZARDOFID.COM

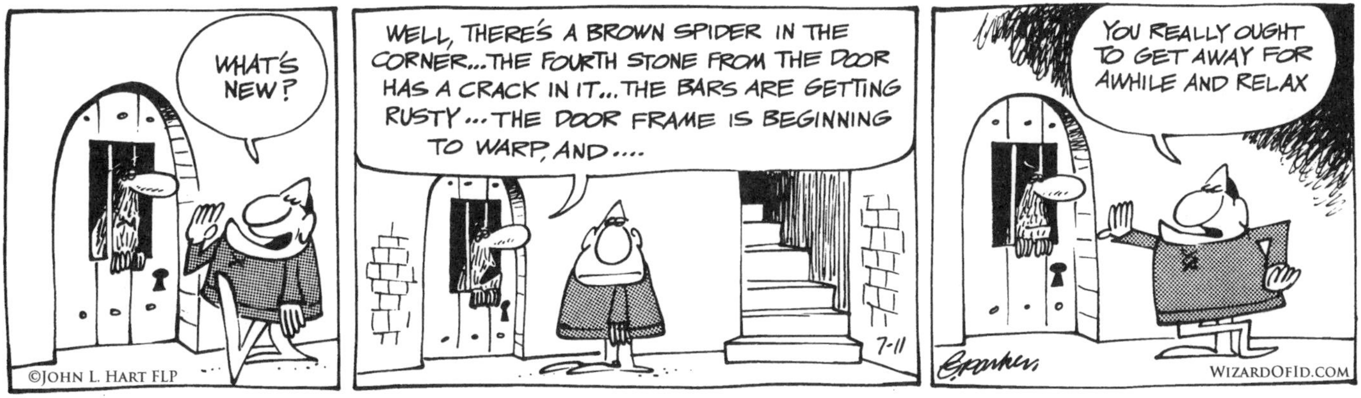

WHAT'S NEW?
WELL, THERE'S A BROWN SPIDER IN THE CORNER...THE FOURTH STONE FROM THE DOOR HAS A CRACK IN IT...THE BARS ARE GETTING RUSTY...THE DOOR FRAME IS BEGINNING TO WARP, AND....
7-11
YOU REALLY OUGHT TO GET AWAY FOR AWHILE AND RELAX

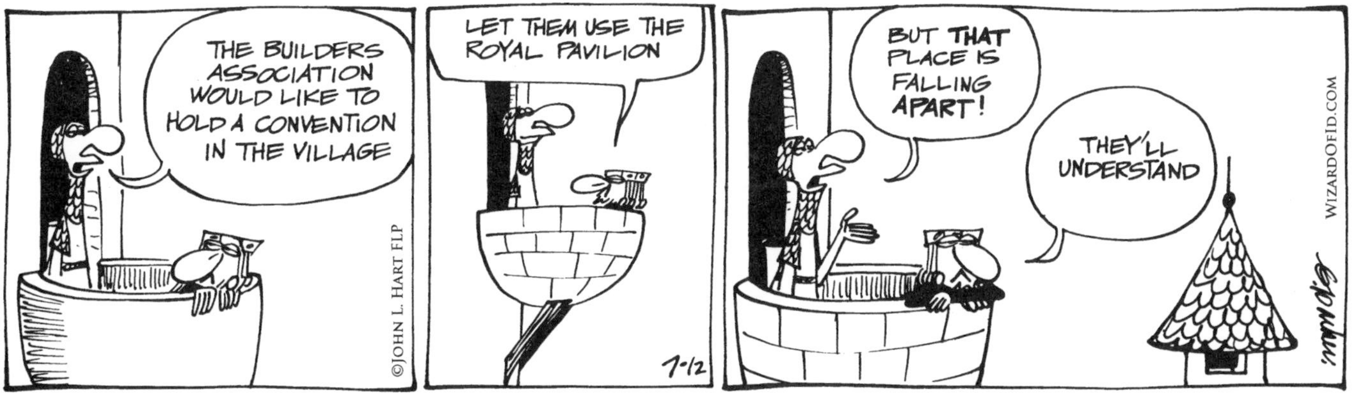

THE BUILDERS ASSOCIATION WOULD LIKE TO HOLD A CONVENTION IN THE VILLAGE
LET THEM USE THE ROYAL PAVILION
7-12
BUT THAT PLACE IS FALLING APART!
THEY'LL UNDERSTAND

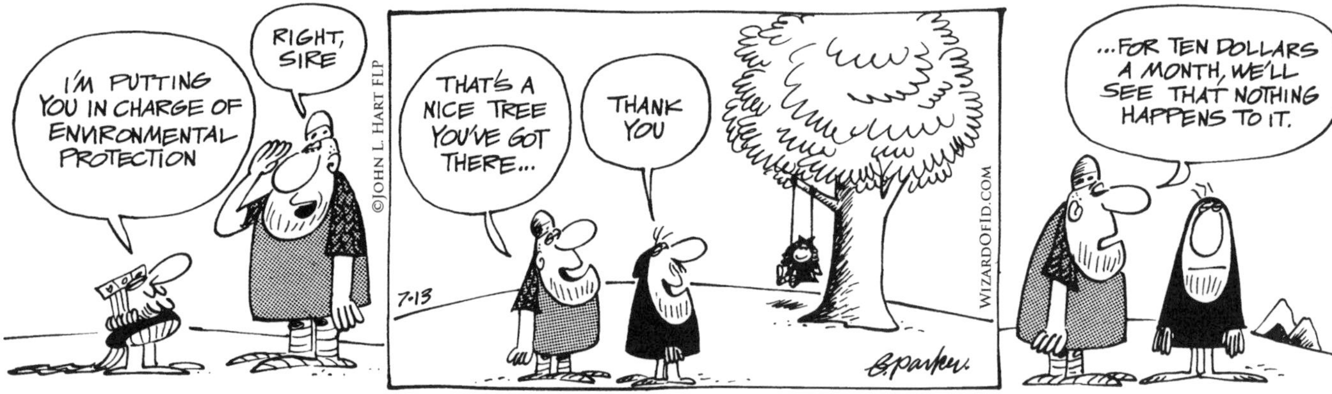
I'M PUTTING YOU IN CHARGE OF ENVIRONMENTAL PROTECTION
RIGHT, SIRE
©JOHN L. HART FLP
THAT'S A NICE TREE YOU'VE GOT THERE...
THANK YOU
7-13
WIZARDOFID.COM
...FOR TEN DOLLARS A MONTH, WE'LL SEE THAT NOTHING HAPPENS TO IT.

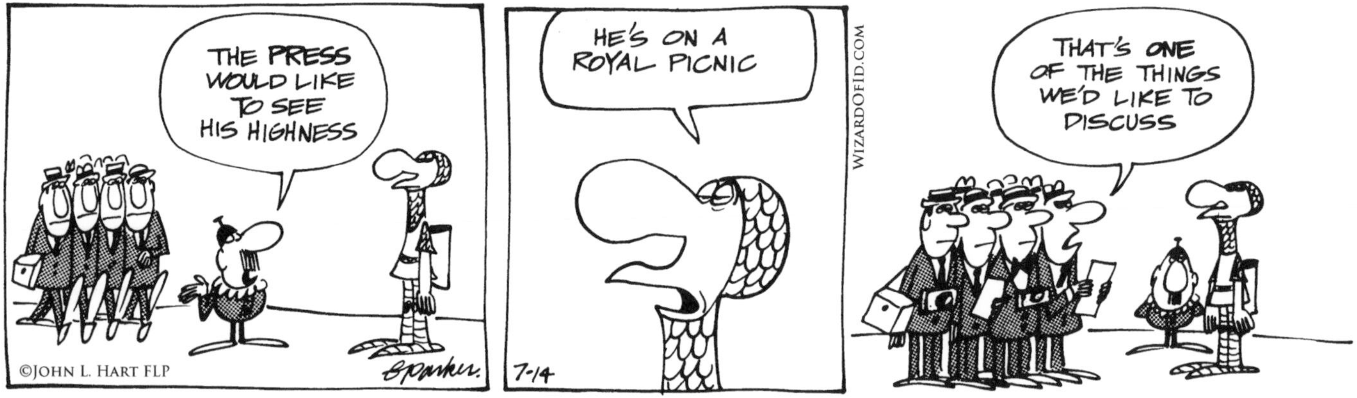
THE PRESS WOULD LIKE TO SEE HIS HIGHNESS
©JOHN L. HART FLP
HE'S ON A ROYAL PICNIC
7-14
WIZARDOFID.COM
THAT'S ONE OF THE THINGS WE'D LIKE TO DISCUSS

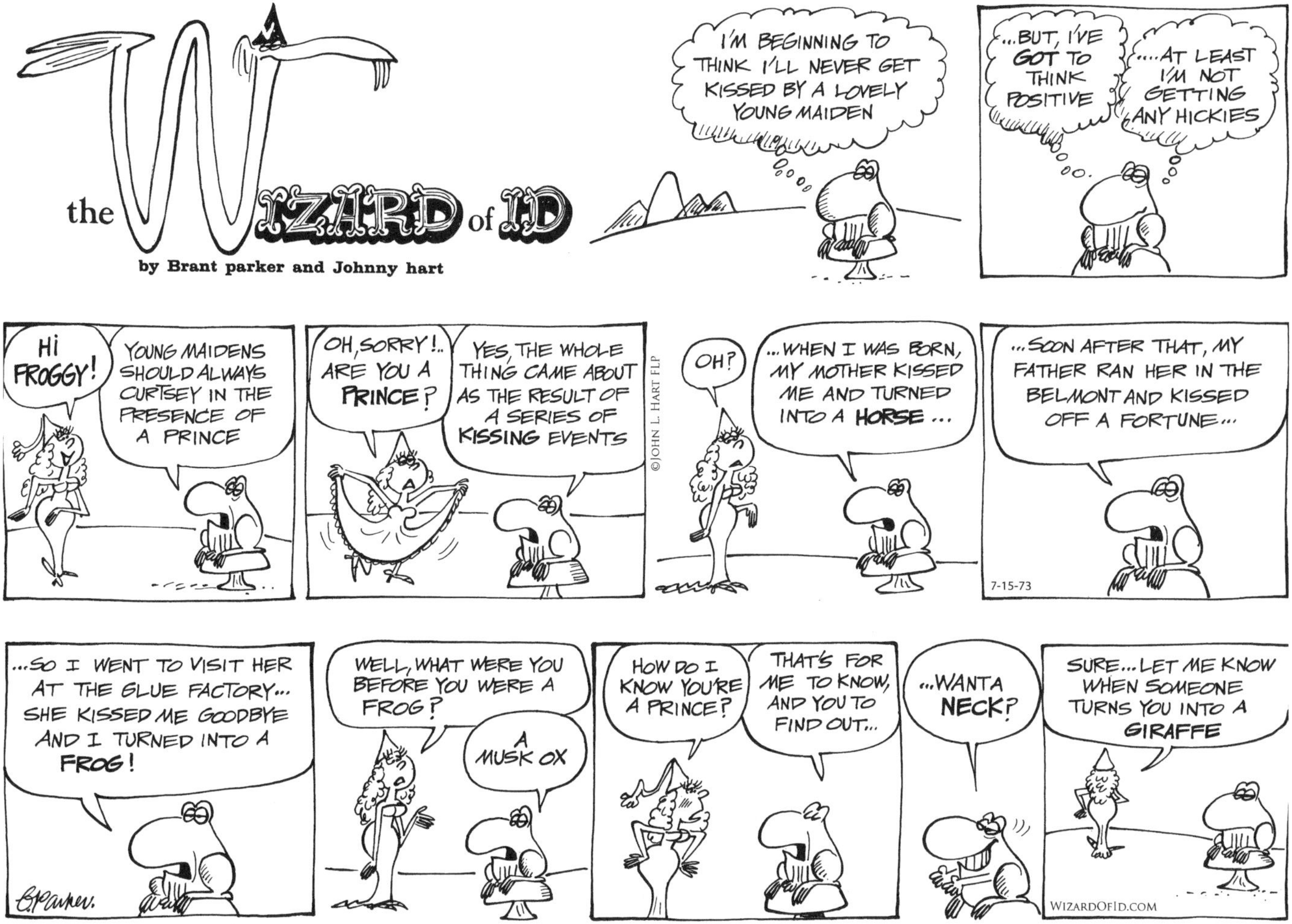
the WIZARD of ID
by Brant parker and Johnny hart
I'M BEGINNING TO THINK I'LL NEVER GET KISSED BY A LOVELY YOUNG MAIDEN
...BUT, I'VE GOT TO THINK POSITIVE
....AT LEAST I'M NOT GETTING ANY HICKIES
Hi FROGGY!
YOUNG MAIDENS SHOULD ALWAYS CURTSEY IN THE PRESENCE OF A PRINCE
OH, SORRY!.. ARE YOU A PRINCE?
YES, THE WHOLE THING CAME ABOUT AS THE RESULT OF A SERIES OF KISSING EVENTS
©JOHN L. HART FLP
OH?
...WHEN I WAS BORN, MY MOTHER KISSED ME AND TURNED INTO A HORSE...
...SOON AFTER THAT, MY FATHER RAN HER IN THE BELMONT AND KISSED OFF A FORTUNE...
7-15-73
...SO I WENT TO VISIT HER AT THE GLUE FACTORY... SHE KISSED ME GOODBYE AND I TURNED INTO A FROG!
B. Parker.
WELL, WHAT WERE YOU BEFORE YOU WERE A FROG?
A MUSK OX
HOW DO I KNOW YOU'RE A PRINCE?
THAT'S FOR ME TO KNOW, AND YOU TO FIND OUT...
...WANTA NECK?
SURE... LET ME KNOW WHEN SOMEONE TURNS YOU INTO A GIRAFFE
WIZARDOFID.COM

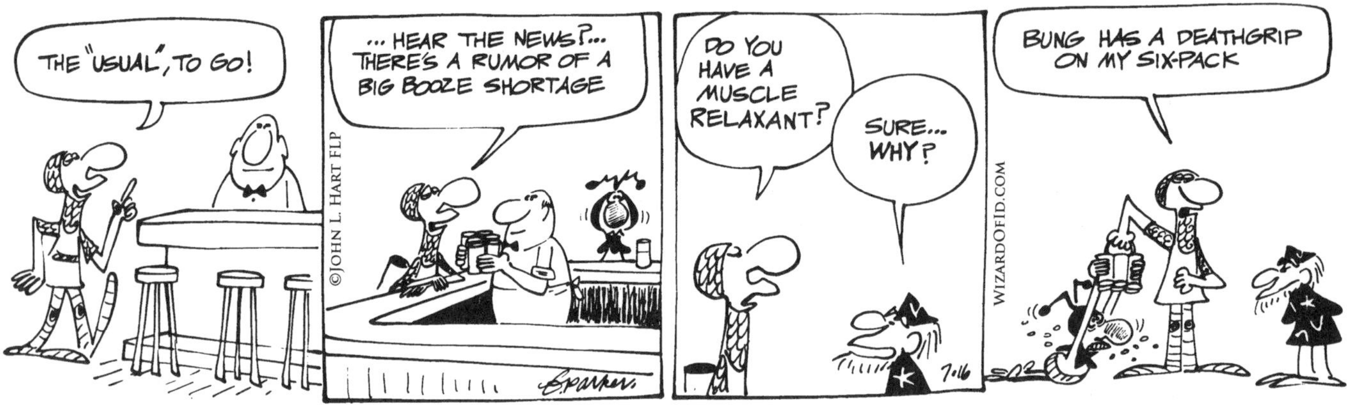
THE "USUAL", TO GO!
... HEAR THE NEWS?... THERE'S A RUMOR OF A BIG BOOZE SHORTAGE
©JOHN L. HART FLP
DO YOU HAVE A MUSCLE RELAXANT?
SURE... WHY?
7-16
WIZARDOFID.COM
BUNG HAS A DEATHGRIP ON MY SIX-PACK

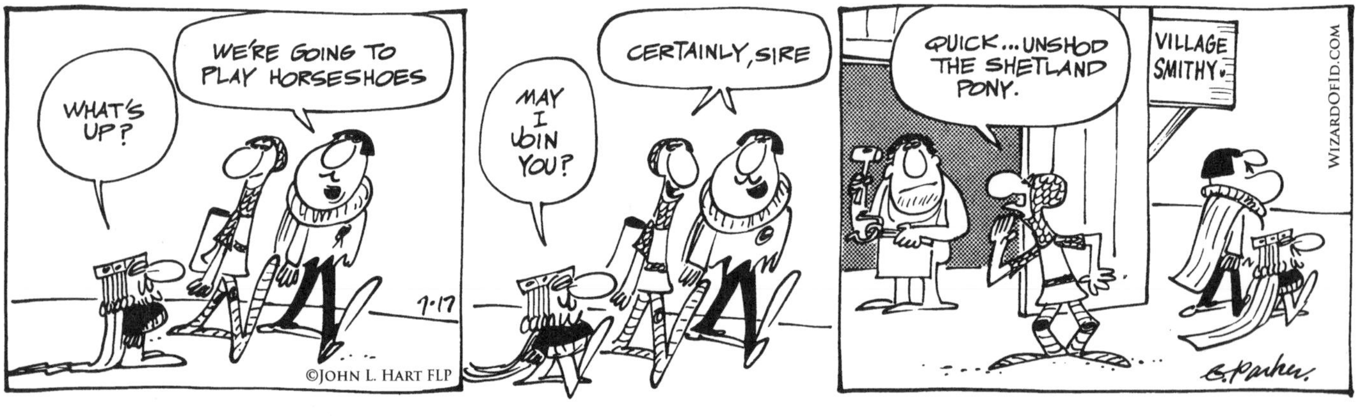
WHAT'S UP?
WE'RE GOING TO PLAY HORSESHOES
7-17
©JOHN L. HART FLP
MAY I JOIN YOU?
CERTAINLY, SIRE
QUICK... UNSHOD THE SHETLAND PONY.
VILLAGE SMITHY
WIZARDOFID.COM

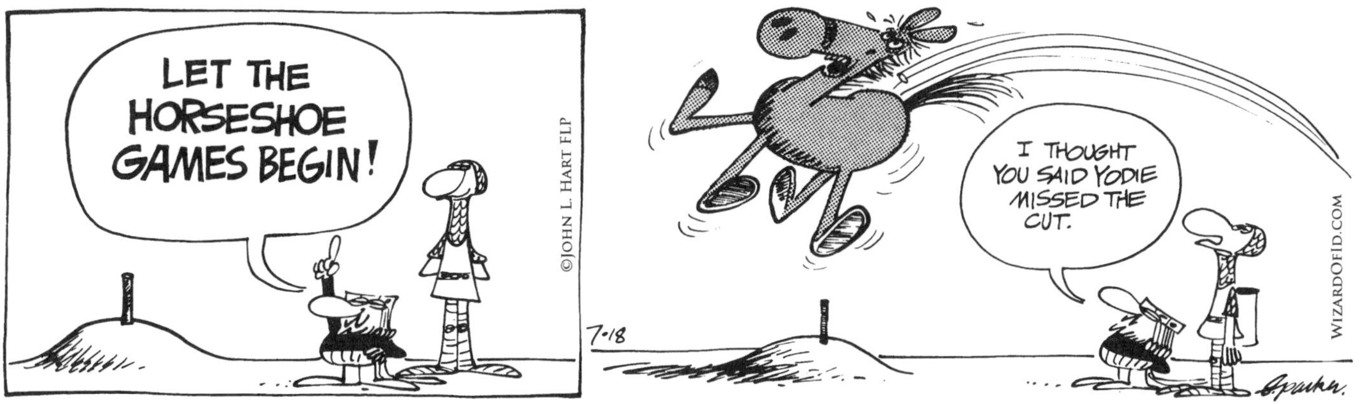
LET THE HORSESHOE GAMES BEGIN!
©JOHN L. HART FLP
7-18
I THOUGHT YOU SAID YODIE MISSED THE CUT.
WIZARDOFID.COM

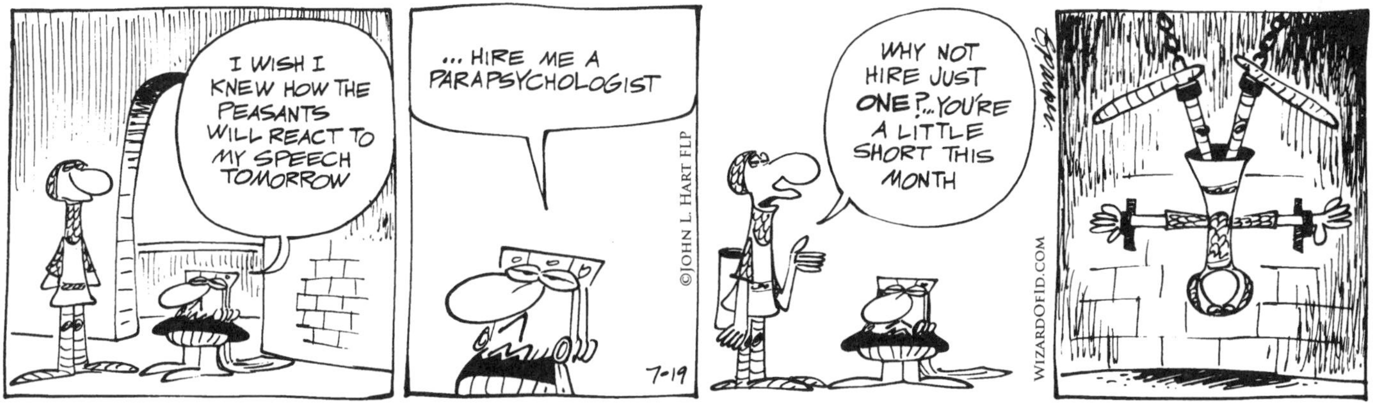
I WISH I KNEW HOW THE PEASANTS WILL REACT TO MY SPEECH TOMORROW
... HIRE ME A PARAPSYCHOLOGIST
©JOHN L. HART FLP
7-19
WHY NOT HIRE JUST ONE?... YOU'RE A LITTLE SHORT THIS MONTH
WIZARDOFID.COM

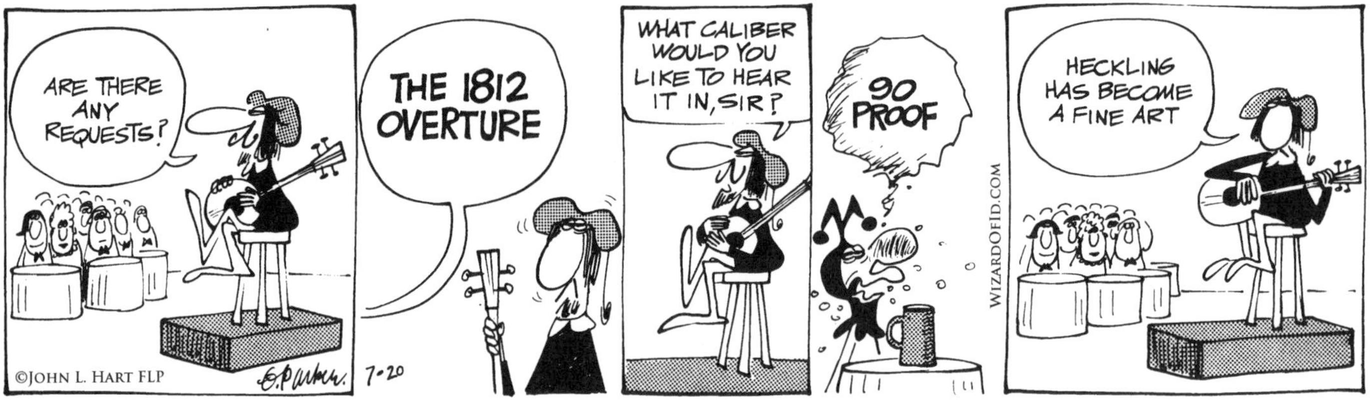
ARE THERE ANY REQUESTS?
THE 1812 OVERTURE
WHAT CALIBER WOULD YOU LIKE TO HEAR IT IN, SIR?
90 PROOF
HECKLING HAS BECOME A FINE ART
©JOHN L. HART FLP
7-20
WIZARDOFID.COM

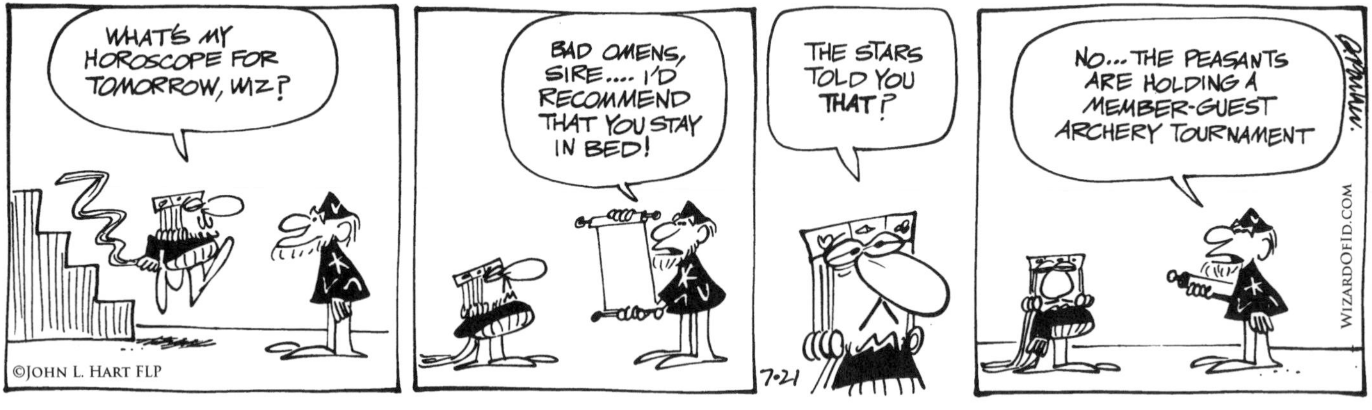
WHAT'S MY HOROSCOPE FOR TOMORROW, WIZ?
BAD OMENS, SIRE.... I'D RECOMMEND THAT YOU STAY IN BED!
THE STARS TOLD YOU THAT?
NO... THE PEASANTS ARE HOLDING A MEMBER-GUEST ARCHERY TOURNAMENT
©JOHN L. HART FLP
7-21
WIZARDOFID.COM

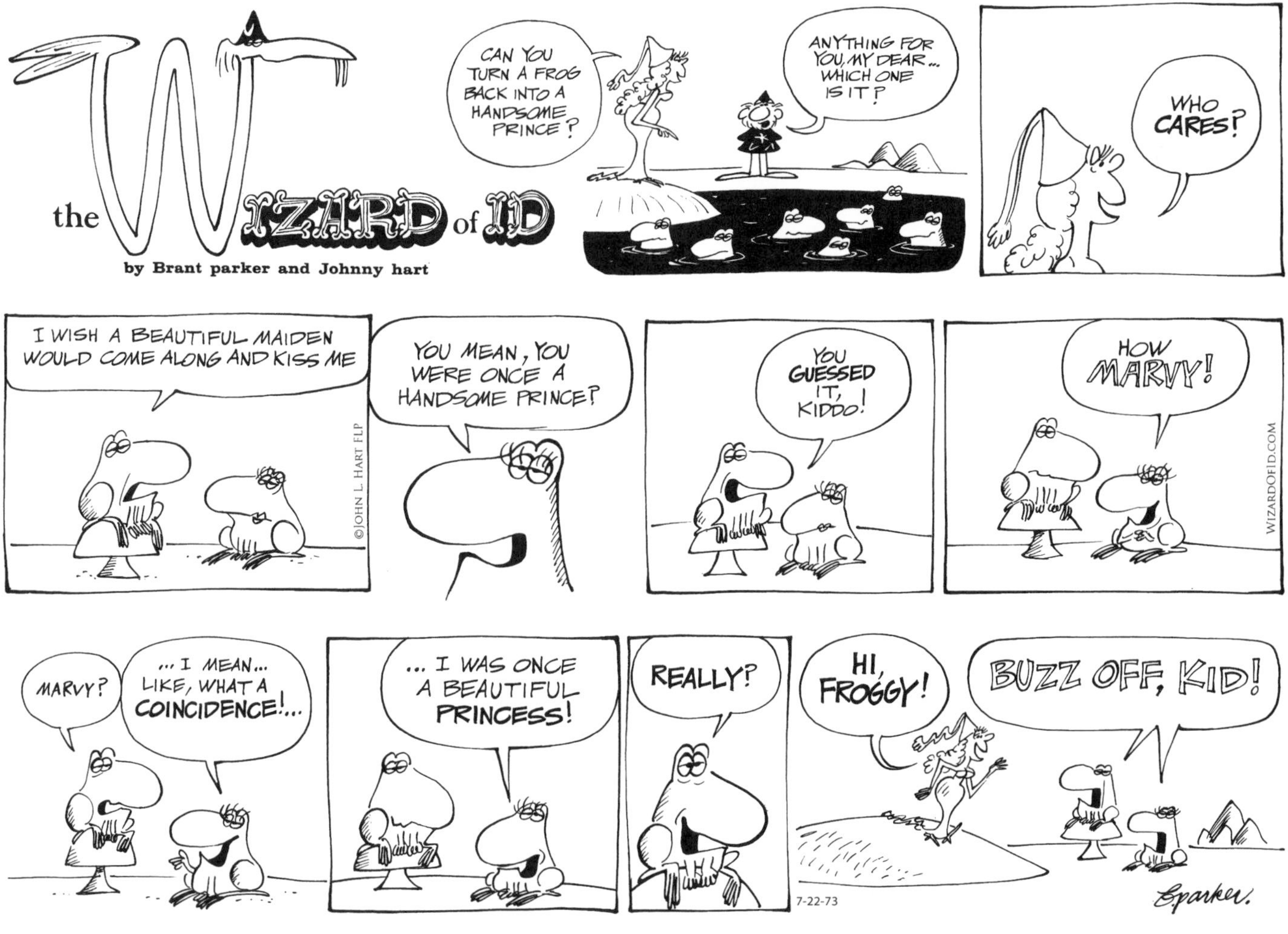
the WIZARD of ID
by Brant parker and Johnny hart
CAN YOU TURN A FROG BACK INTO A HANDSOME PRINCE?
ANYTHING FOR YOU, MY DEAR... WHICH ONE IS IT?
WHO CARES?
I WISH A BEAUTIFUL MAIDEN WOULD COME ALONG AND KISS ME
©JOHN L. HART FLP
YOU MEAN, YOU WERE ONCE A HANDSOME PRINCE?
YOU GUESSED IT, KIDDO!
HOW MARVY!
WIZARDOFID.COM
MARVY?
... I MEAN... LIKE, WHAT A COINCIDENCE!...
... I WAS ONCE A BEAUTIFUL PRINCESS!
REALLY?
HI, FROGGY!
BUZZ OFF, KID!
7-22-73
Bparker.

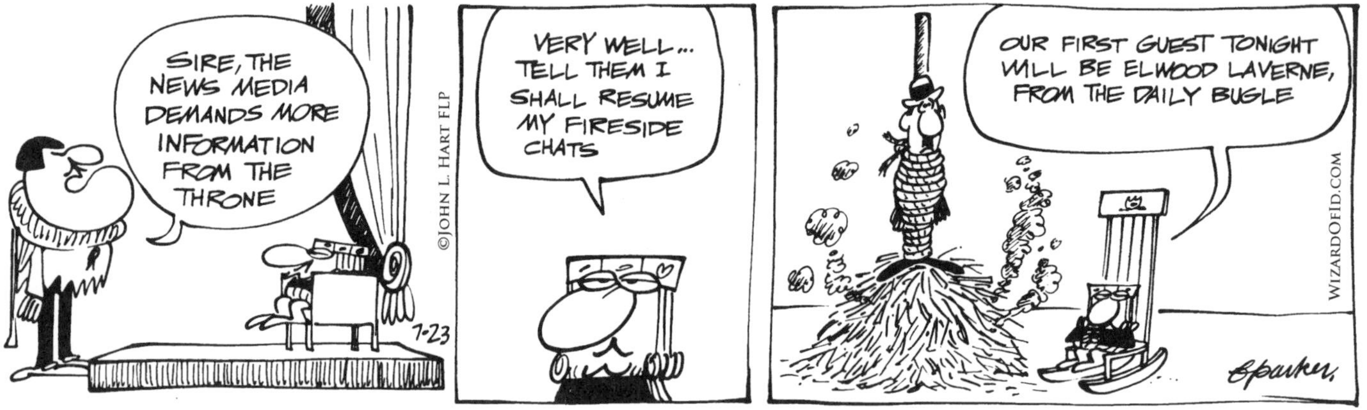
SIRE, THE NEWS MEDIA DEMANDS MORE INFORMATION FROM THE THRONE
©JOHN L. HART FLP
7-23
VERY WELL... TELL THEM I SHALL RESUME MY FIRESIDE CHATS
OUR FIRST GUEST TONIGHT WILL BE ELWOOD LAVERNE, FROM THE DAILY BUGLE
WIZARDOFID.COM

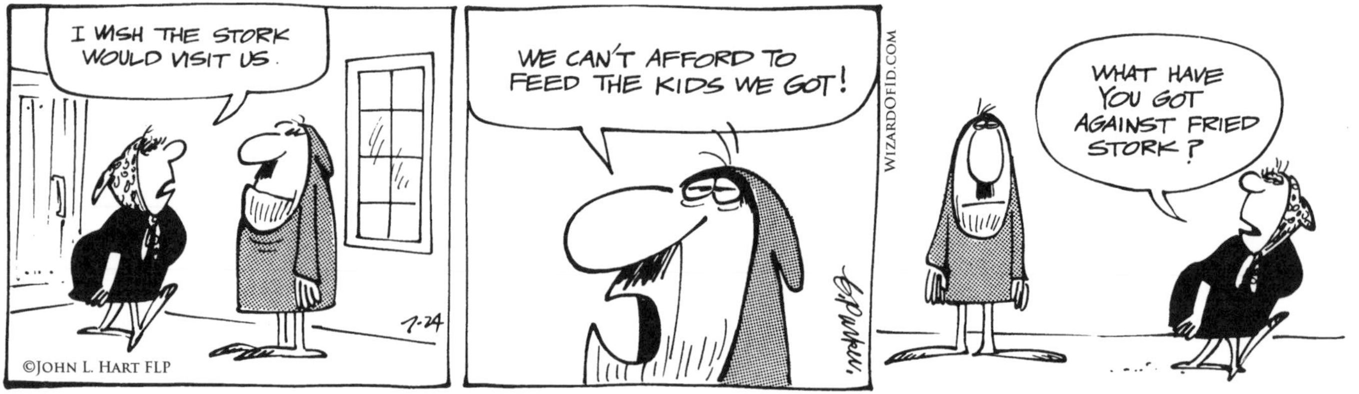
I WISH THE STORK WOULD VISIT US.
7-24
©JOHN L. HART FLP
WE CAN'T AFFORD TO FEED THE KIDS WE GOT!
WIZARDOFID.COM
WHAT HAVE YOU GOT AGAINST FRIED STORK?

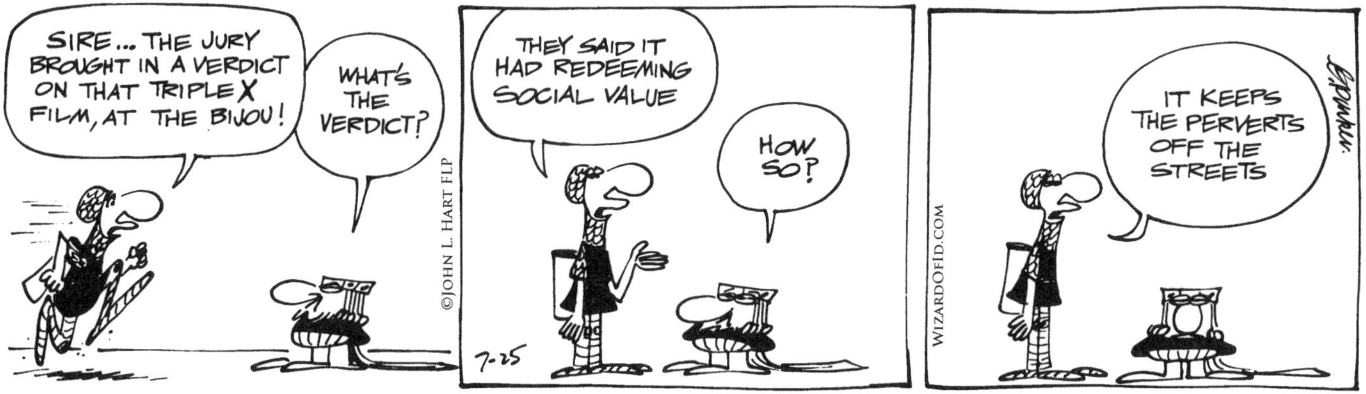
SIRE... THE JURY BROUGHT IN A VERDICT ON THAT TRIPLE X FILM, AT THE BIJOU!
WHAT'S THE VERDICT?
©JOHN L. HART FLP
THEY SAID IT HAD REDEEMING SOCIAL VALUE
HOW SO?
7-25
WIZARDOFID.COM
IT KEEPS THE PERVERTS OFF THE STREETS

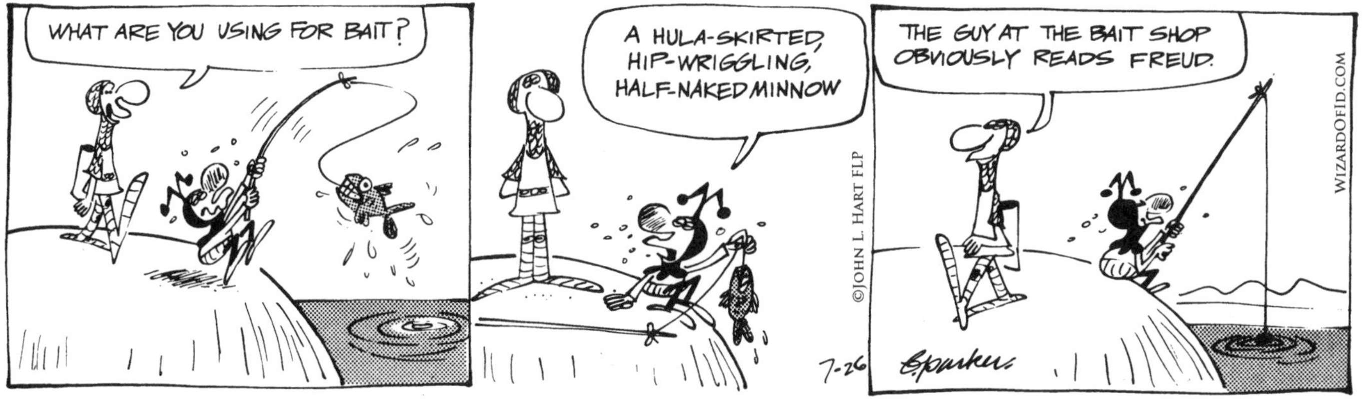
WHAT ARE YOU USING FOR BAIT?
A HULA-SKIRTED, HIP-WRIGGLING, HALF-NAKED MINNOW
©JOHN L. HART FLP
7-26
THE GUY AT THE BAIT SHOP OBVIOUSLY READS FREUD.
WIZARDOFID.COM

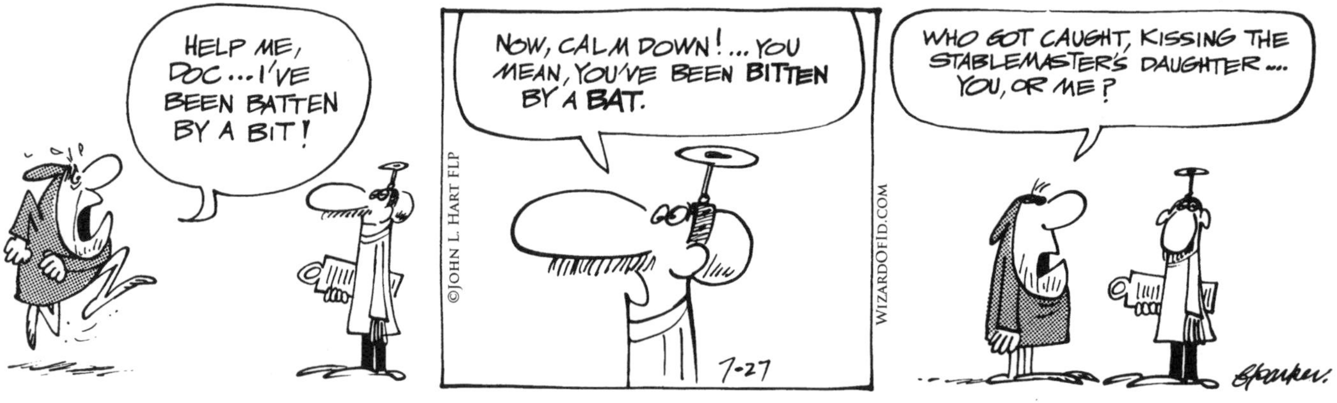
HELP ME, DOC... I'VE BEEN BATTEN BY A BIT!
©JOHN L. HART FLP
NOW, CALM DOWN! ... YOU MEAN, YOU'VE BEEN BITTEN BY A BAT.
7-27
WIZARDOFID.COM
WHO GOT CAUGHT, KISSING THE STABLEMASTER'S DAUGHTER.... YOU, OR ME?

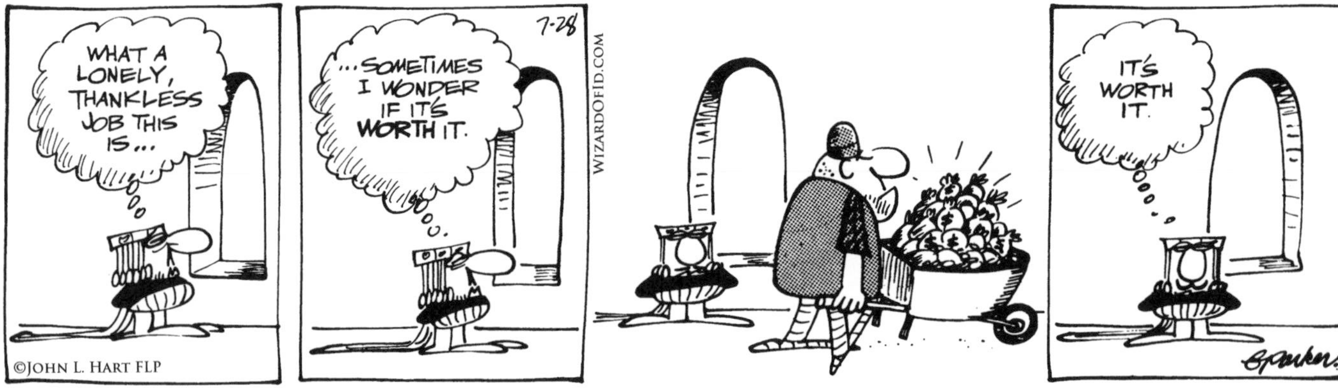
WHAT A LONELY, THANKLESS JOB THIS IS...
©JOHN L. HART FLP
...SOMETIMES I WONDER IF IT'S WORTH IT.
7-28
WIZARDOFID.COM
IT'S WORTH IT.

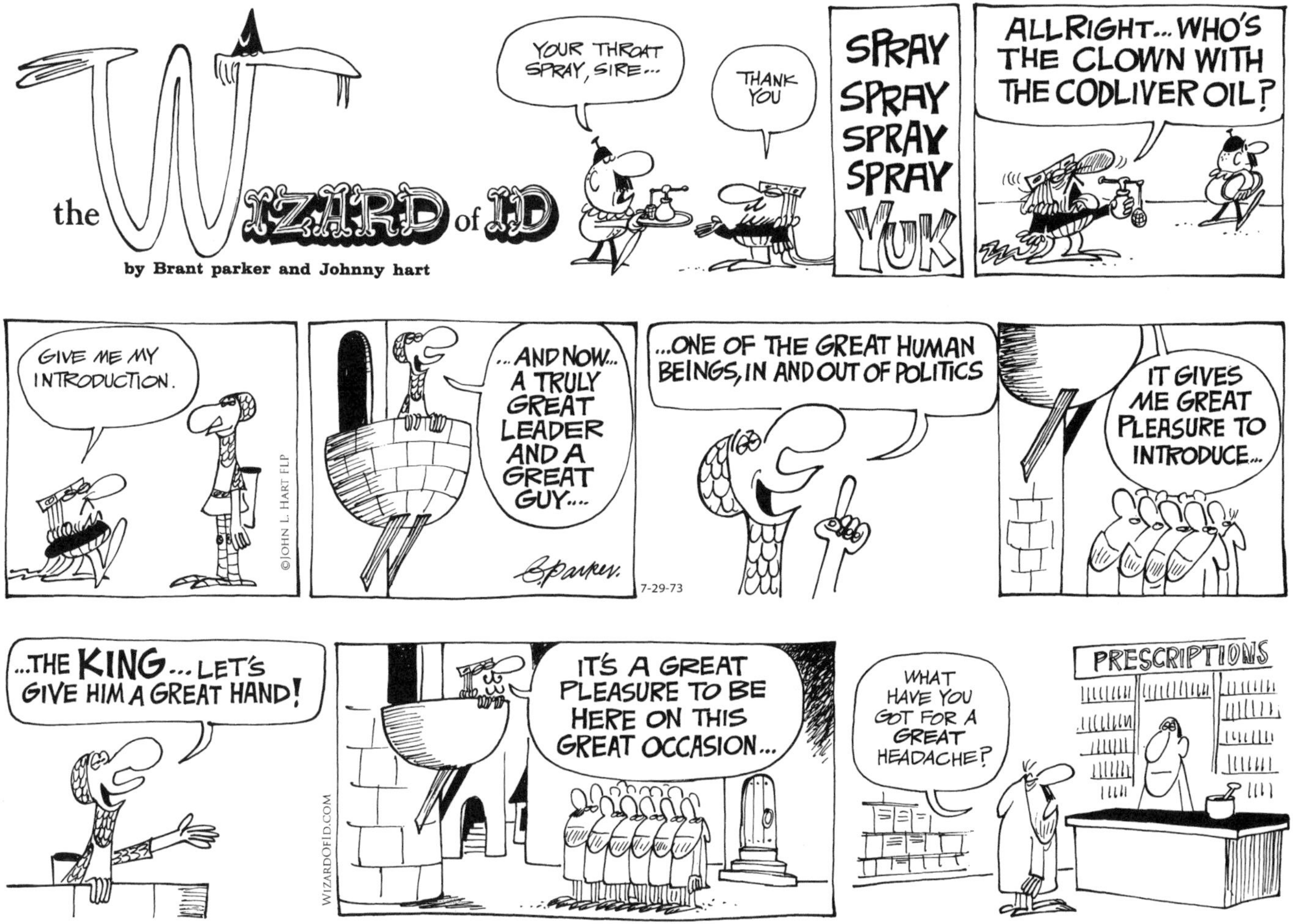
the WIZARD of ID
by Brant parker and Johnny hart
YOUR THROAT SPRAY, SIRE...
THANK YOU
SPRAY SPRAY SPRAY SPRAY
YUK
ALL RIGHT... WHO'S THE CLOWN WITH THE CODLIVER OIL?
GIVE ME MY INTRODUCTION.
©JOHN L. HART FLP
...AND NOW... A TRULY GREAT LEADER AND A GREAT GUY....
B parker
7-29-73
...ONE OF THE GREAT HUMAN BEINGS, IN AND OUT OF POLITICS
IT GIVES ME GREAT PLEASURE TO INTRODUCE...
...THE KING... LET'S GIVE HIM A GREAT HAND!
WIZARDOFID.COM
IT'S A GREAT PLEASURE TO BE HERE ON THIS GREAT OCCASION...
WHAT HAVE YOU GOT FOR A GREAT HEADACHE?
PRESCRIPTIONS

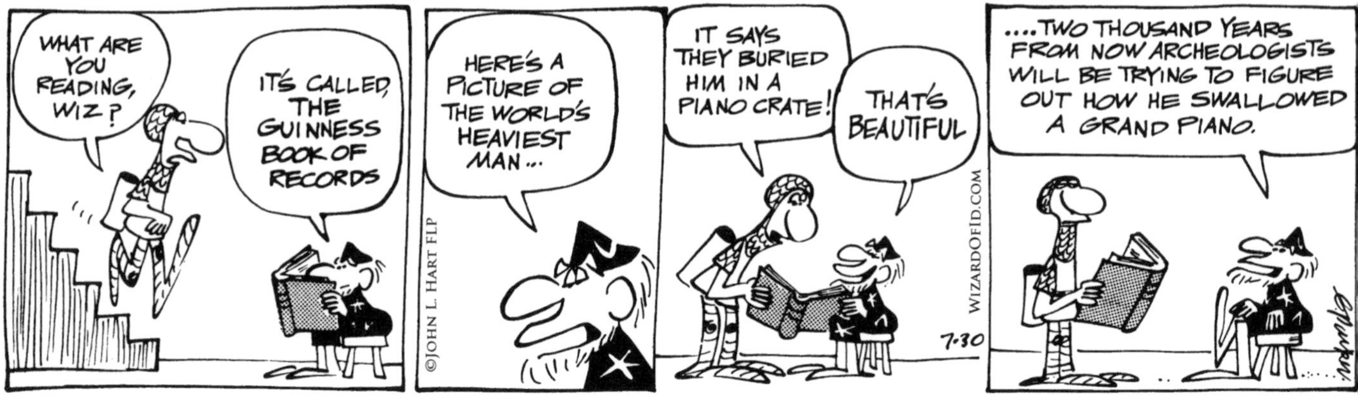
WHAT ARE YOU READING, WIZ?
IT'S CALLED THE GUINNESS BOOK OF RECORDS
©JOHN L. HART FLP
HERE'S A PICTURE OF THE WORLD'S HEAVIEST MAN...
IT SAYS THEY BURIED HIM IN A PIANO CRATE!
THAT'S BEAUTIFUL
WIZARDOFID.COM
7-30
....TWO THOUSAND YEARS FROM NOW ARCHEOLOGISTS WILL BE TRYING TO FIGURE OUT HOW HE SWALLOWED A GRAND PIANO.

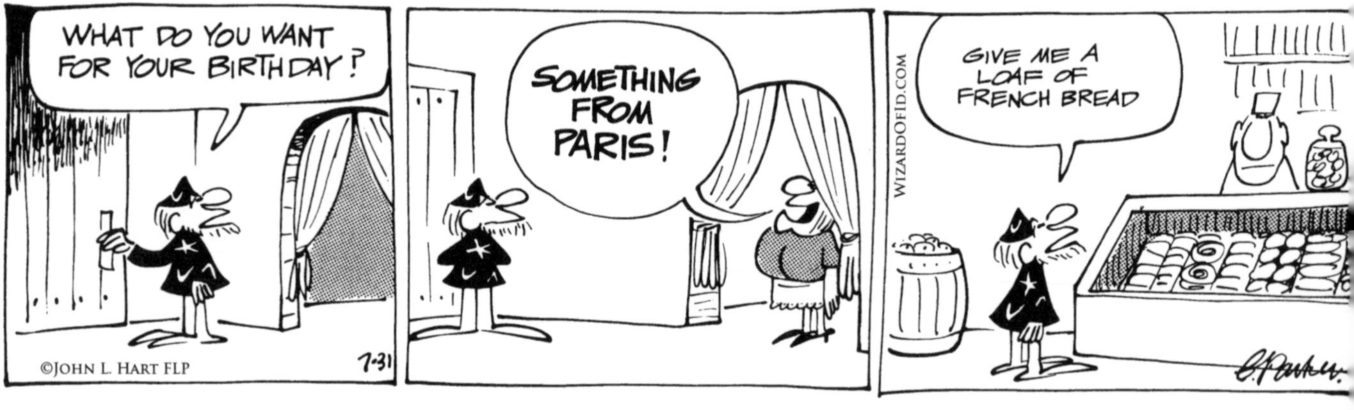
WHAT DO YOU WANT FOR YOUR BIRTHDAY?
©JOHN L. HART FLP
7-31
SOMETHING FROM PARIS!
WIZARDOFID.COM
GIVE ME A LOAF OF FRENCH BREAD

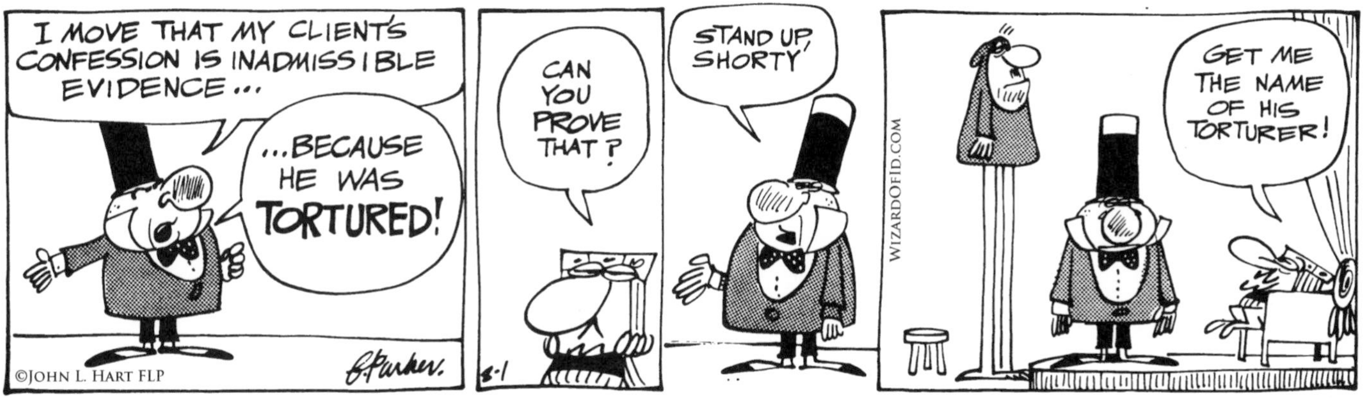
I MOVE THAT MY CLIENT'S CONFESSION IS INADMISSIBLE EVIDENCE...
...BECAUSE HE WAS TORTURED!
©JOHN L. HART FLP
CAN YOU PROVE THAT?
8-1
STAND UP, SHORTY
WIZARDOFID.COM
GET ME THE NAME OF HIS TORTURER!

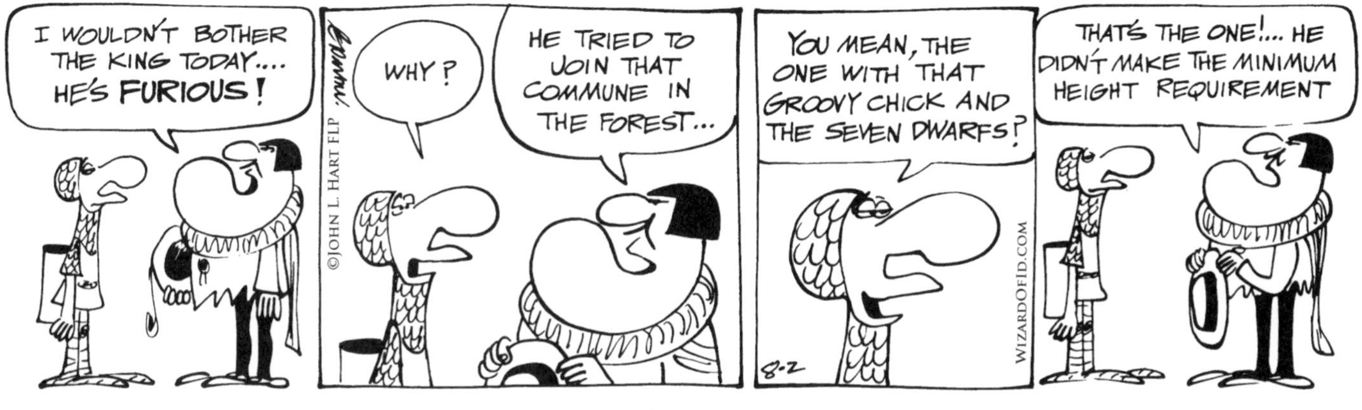
I WOULDN'T BOTHER THE KING TODAY.... HE'S FURIOUS!
©JOHN L. HART FLP
WHY?
HE TRIED TO JOIN THAT COMMUNE IN THE FOREST...
YOU MEAN, THE ONE WITH THAT GROOVY CHICK AND THE SEVEN DWARFS?
8-2
WIZARDOFID.COM
THAT'S THE ONE!.... HE DIDN'T MAKE THE MINIMUM HEIGHT REQUIREMENT

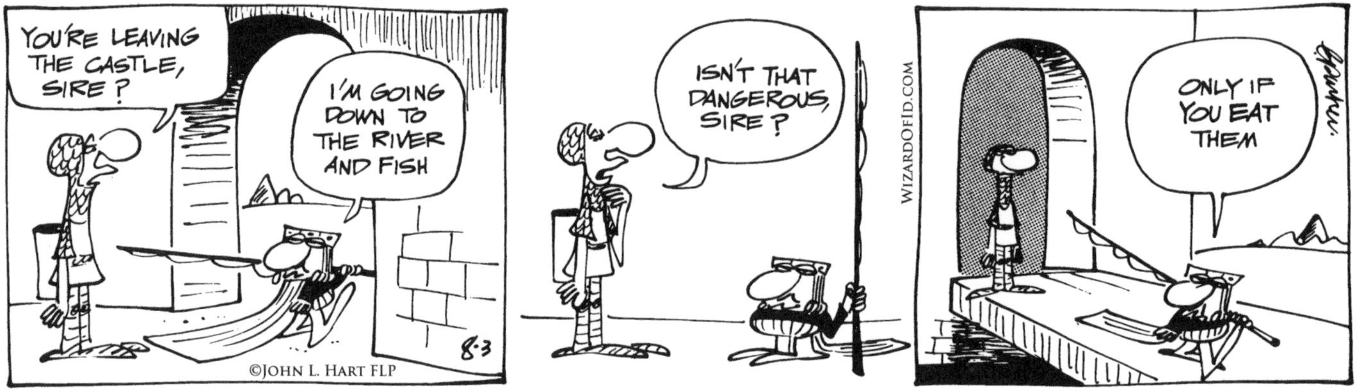
YOU'RE LEAVING THE CASTLE, SIRE?
I'M GOING DOWN TO THE RIVER AND FISH
8·3
©JOHN L. HART FLP
ISN'T THAT DANGEROUS, SIRE?
WIZARDOFID.COM
ONLY IF YOU EAT THEM

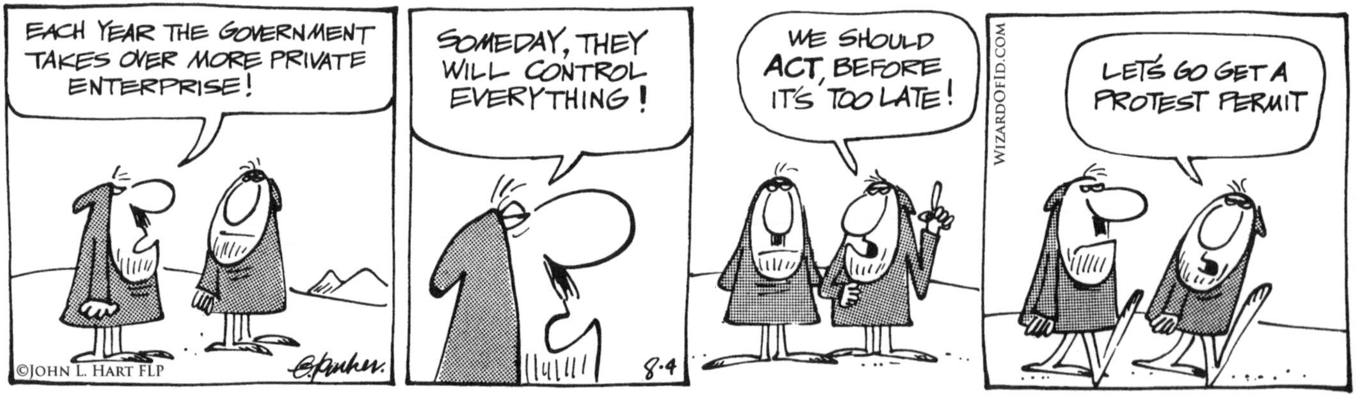
EACH YEAR THE GOVERNMENT TAKES OVER MORE PRIVATE ENTERPRISE!
©JOHN L. HART FLP
SOMEDAY, THEY WILL CONTROL EVERYTHING!
8·4
WE SHOULD ACT, BEFORE IT'S TOO LATE!
WIZARDOFID.COM
LET'S GO GET A PROTEST PERMIT

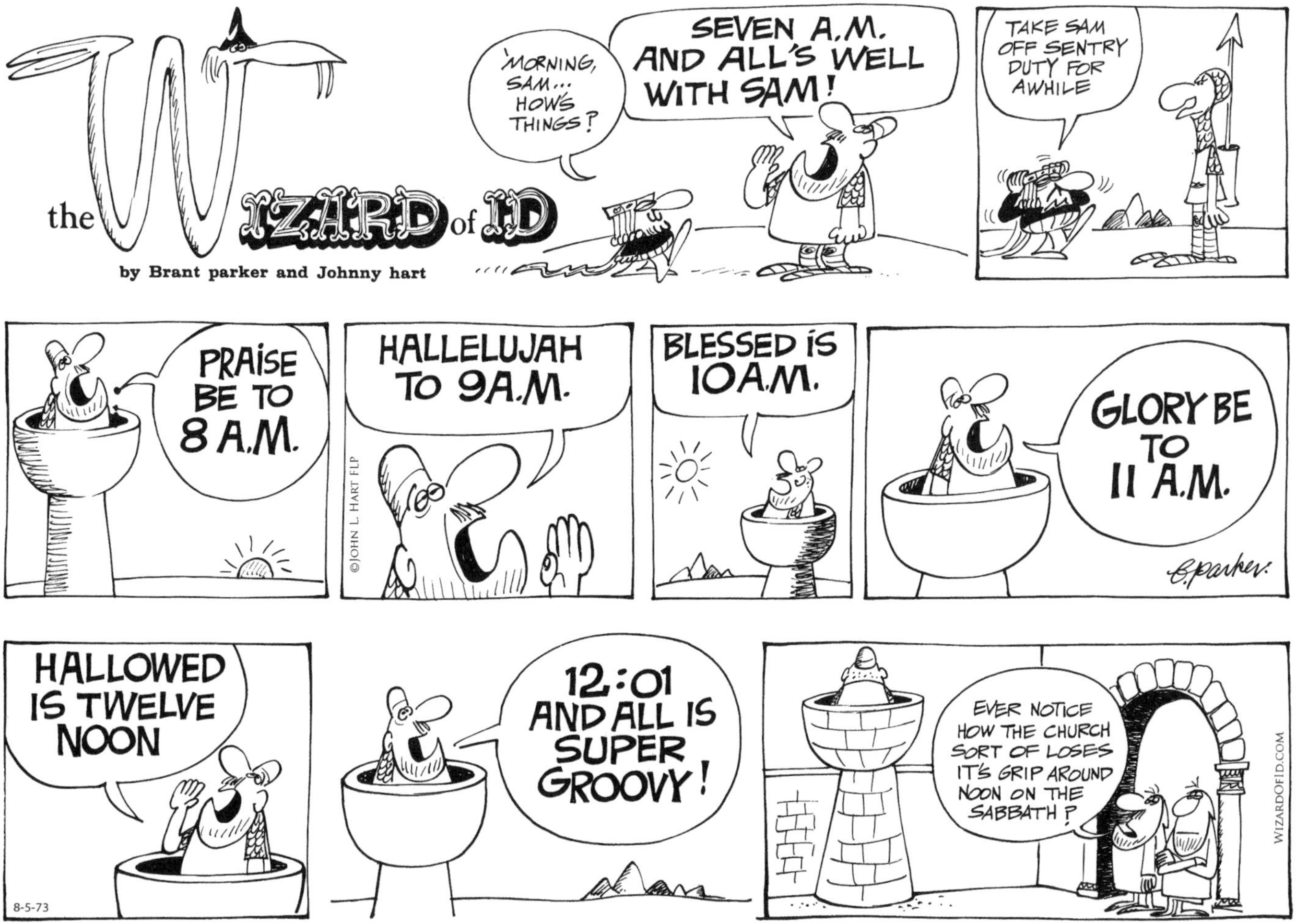
the WIZARD of ID
by Brant parker and Johnny hart
'MORNING, SAM... HOW'S THINGS?
SEVEN A.M. AND ALL'S WELL WITH SAM!
TAKE SAM OFF SENTRY DUTY FOR AWHILE
PRAISE BE TO 8 A.M.
HALLELUJAH TO 9A.M.
©JOHN L. HART FLP
BLESSED IS 10A.M.
GLORY BE TO 11 A.M.
B.parker.
HALLOWED IS TWELVE NOON
8-5-73
12:01 AND ALL IS SUPER GROOVY!
EVER NOTICE HOW THE CHURCH SORT OF LOSES IT'S GRIP AROUND NOON ON THE SABBATH?
WIZARDOFID.COM

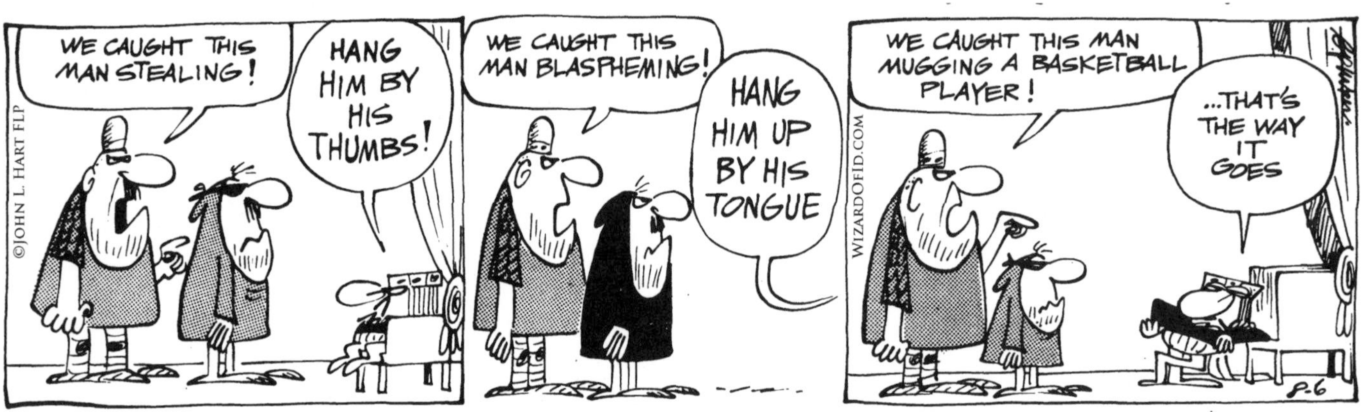
WE CAUGHT THIS MAN STEALING!
HANG HIM BY HIS THUMBS!
WE CAUGHT THIS MAN BLASPHEMING!
HANG HIM UP BY HIS TONGUE
WE CAUGHT THIS MAN MUGGING A BASKETBALL PLAYER!
...THAT'S THE WAY IT GOES
©JOHN L. HART FLP
WIZARDOFID.COM
8-6

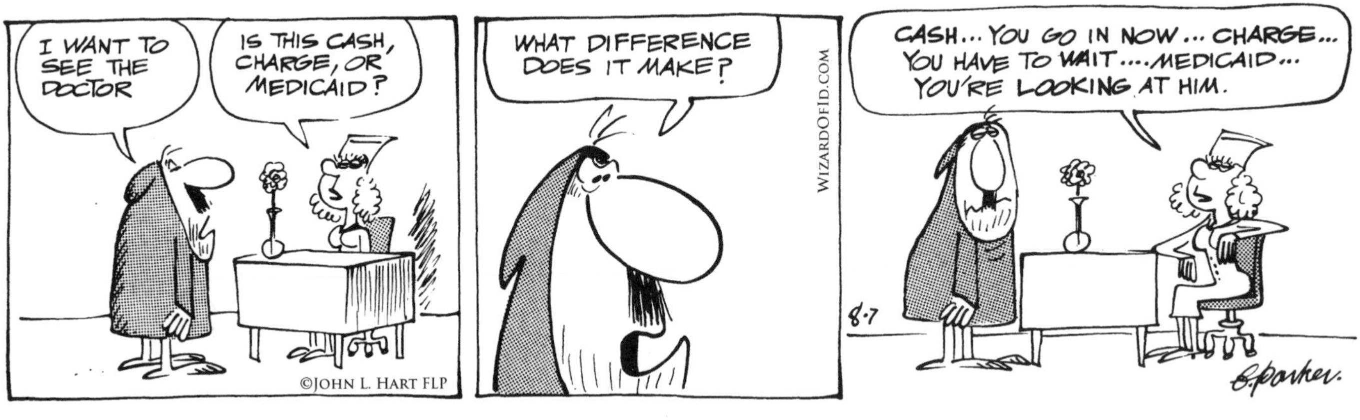
I WANT TO SEE THE DOCTOR
IS THIS CASH, CHARGE, OR MEDICAID?
WHAT DIFFERENCE DOES IT MAKE?
CASH... YOU GO IN NOW... CHARGE... YOU HAVE TO WAIT.....MEDICAID... YOU'RE LOOKING AT HIM.
©JOHN L. HART FLP
WIZARDOFID.COM
8-7

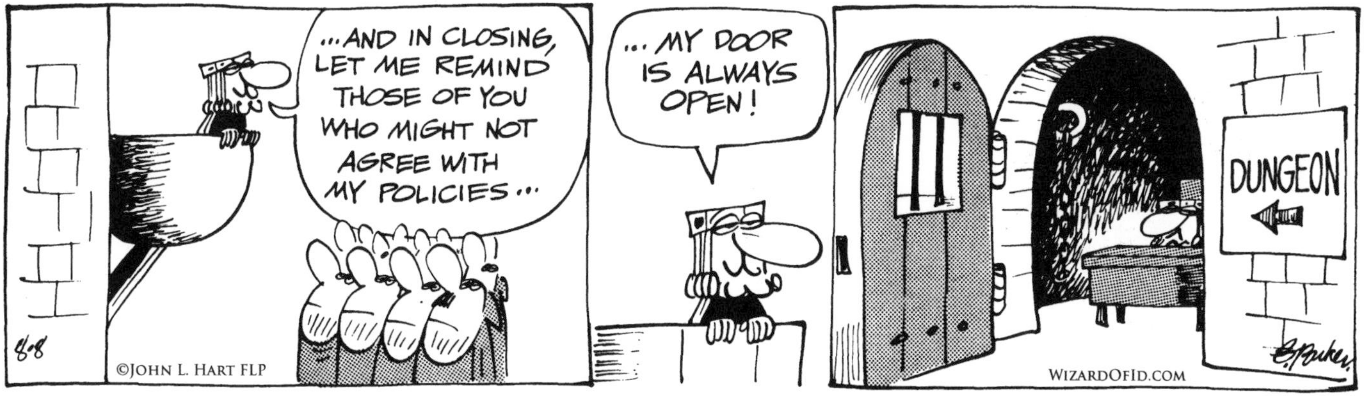
...AND IN CLOSING, LET ME REMIND THOSE OF YOU WHO MIGHT NOT AGREE WITH MY POLICIES...
...MY DOOR IS ALWAYS OPEN!
DUNGEON
8-8
©JOHN L. HART FLP
WIZARDOFID.COM

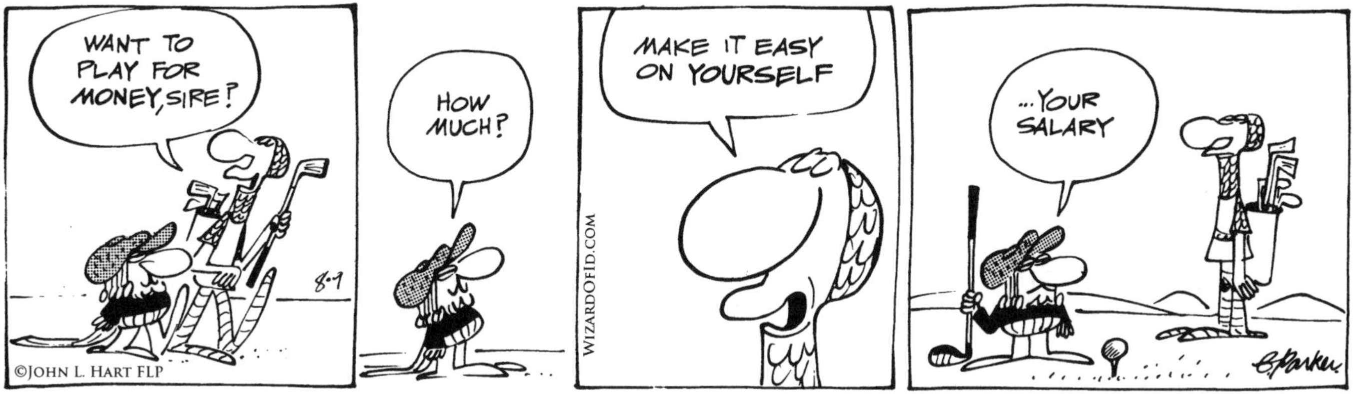
WANT TO PLAY FOR MONEY, SIRE?
HOW MUCH?
MAKE IT EASY ON YOURSELF
...YOUR SALARY
8-9
©JOHN L. HART FLP
WIZARDOFID.COM

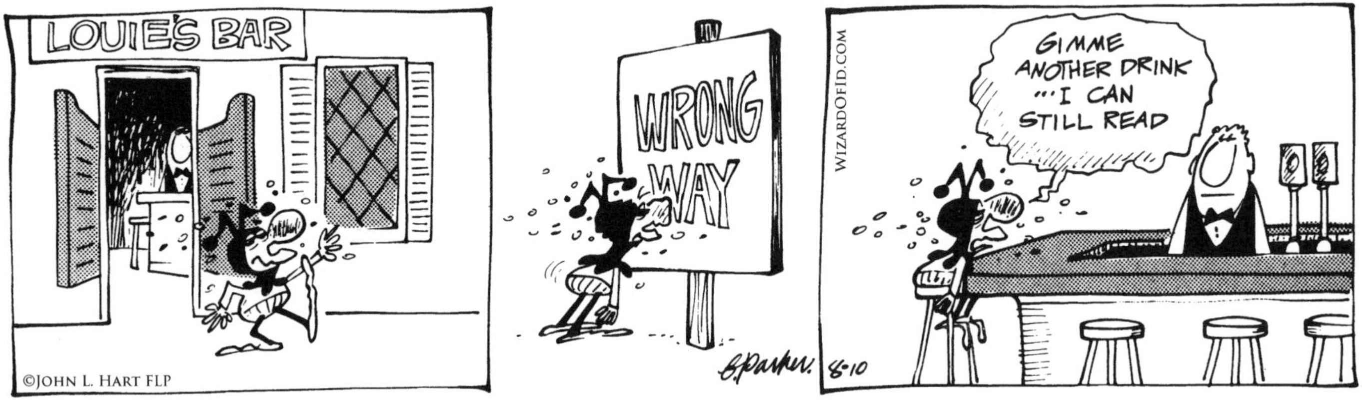
LOUIE'S BAR
WRONG WAY
GIMME ANOTHER DRINK ...I CAN STILL READ
WIZARDOFID.COM
©JOHN L. HART FLP
8-10

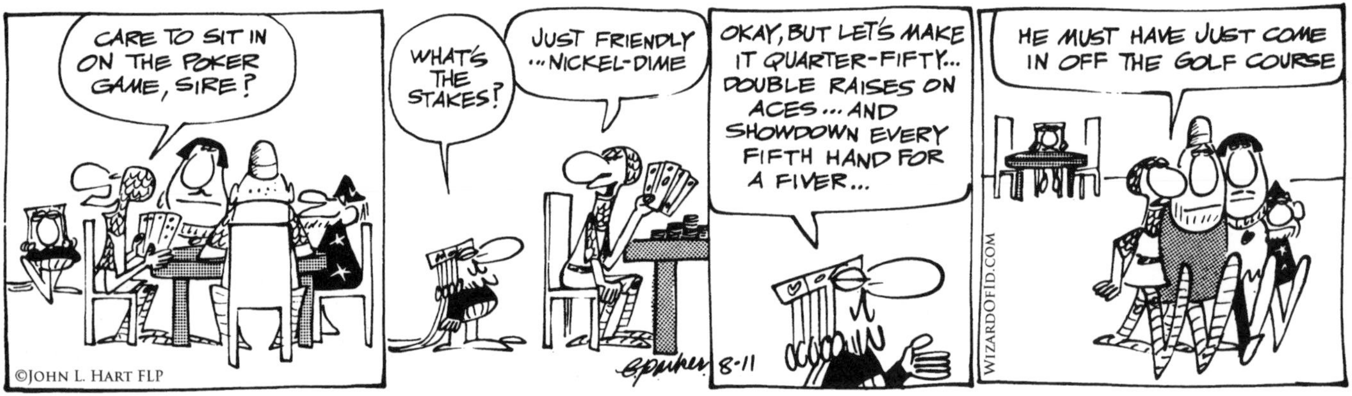
CARE TO SIT IN ON THE POKER GAME, SIRE?
WHAT'S THE STAKES?
JUST FRIENDLY ...NICKEL-DIME
OKAY, BUT LET'S MAKE IT QUARTER-FIFTY... DOUBLE RAISES ON ACES ... AND SHOWDOWN EVERY FIFTH HAND FOR A FIVER...
HE MUST HAVE JUST COME IN OFF THE GOLF COURSE
WIZARDOFID.COM
©JOHN L. HART FLP
8-11

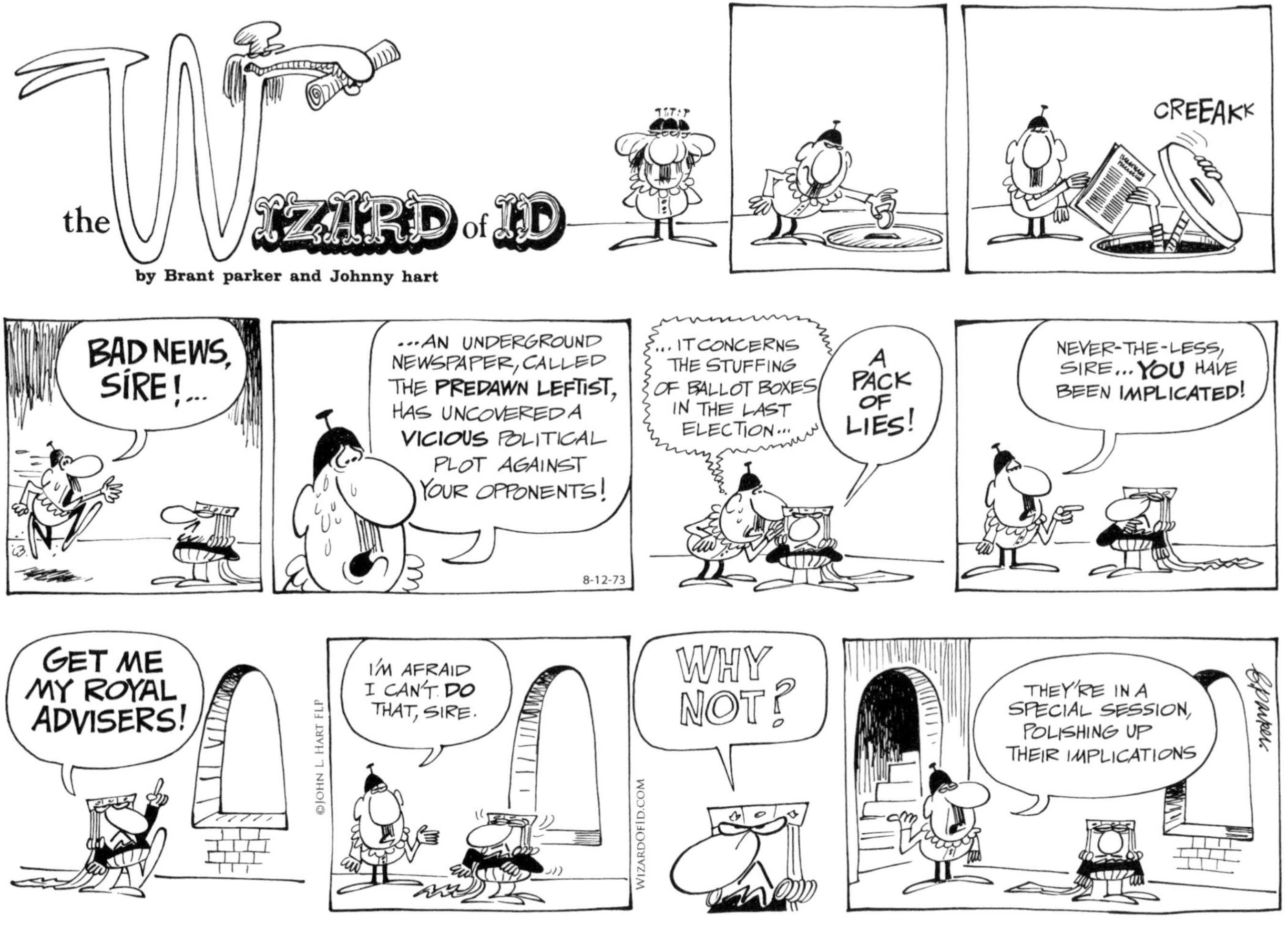
the WIZARD of ID
by Brant parker and Johnny hart
CREEAKK
BAD NEWS, SIRE!...
...AN UNDERGROUND NEWSPAPER, CALLED THE PREDAWN LEFTIST, HAS UNCOVERED A VICIOUS POLITICAL PLOT AGAINST YOUR OPPONENTS!
8-12-73
...IT CONCERNS THE STUFFING OF BALLOT BOXES IN THE LAST ELECTION...
A PACK OF LIES!
NEVER-THE-LESS, SIRE... YOU HAVE BEEN IMPLICATED!
GET ME MY ROYAL ADVISERS!
©JOHN L. HART FLP
I'M AFRAID I CAN'T DO THAT, SIRE.
WIZARDOFID.COM
WHY NOT?
THEY'RE IN A SPECIAL SESSION, POLISHING UP THEIR IMPLICATIONS

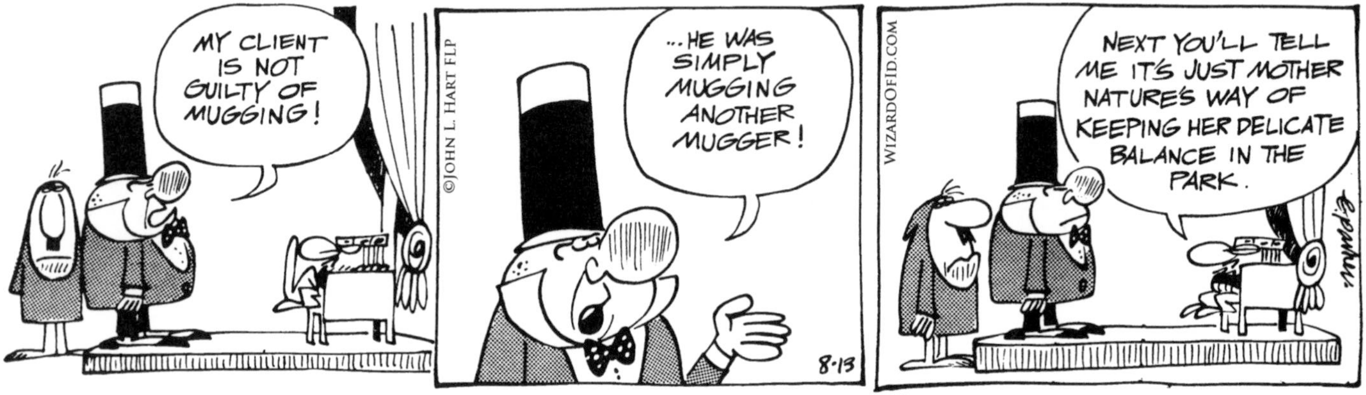
MY CLIENT IS NOT GUILTY OF MUGGING!
©JOHN L. HART FLP
...HE WAS SIMPLY MUGGING ANOTHER MUGGER!
8-13
WIZARDOFID.COM
NEXT YOU'LL TELL ME IT'S JUST MOTHER NATURE'S WAY OF KEEPING HER DELICATE BALANCE IN THE PARK.

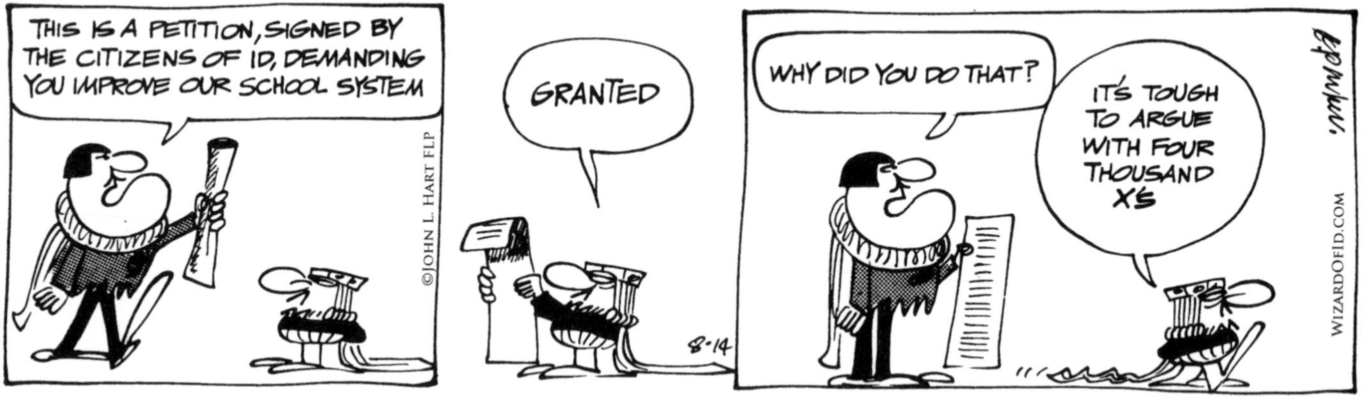
THIS IS A PETITION, SIGNED BY THE CITIZENS OF ID, DEMANDING YOU IMPROVE OUR SCHOOL SYSTEM
©JOHN L. HART FLP
GRANTED
8-14
WHY DID YOU DO THAT?
IT'S TOUGH TO ARGUE WITH FOUR THOUSAND X'S
WIZARDOFID.COM

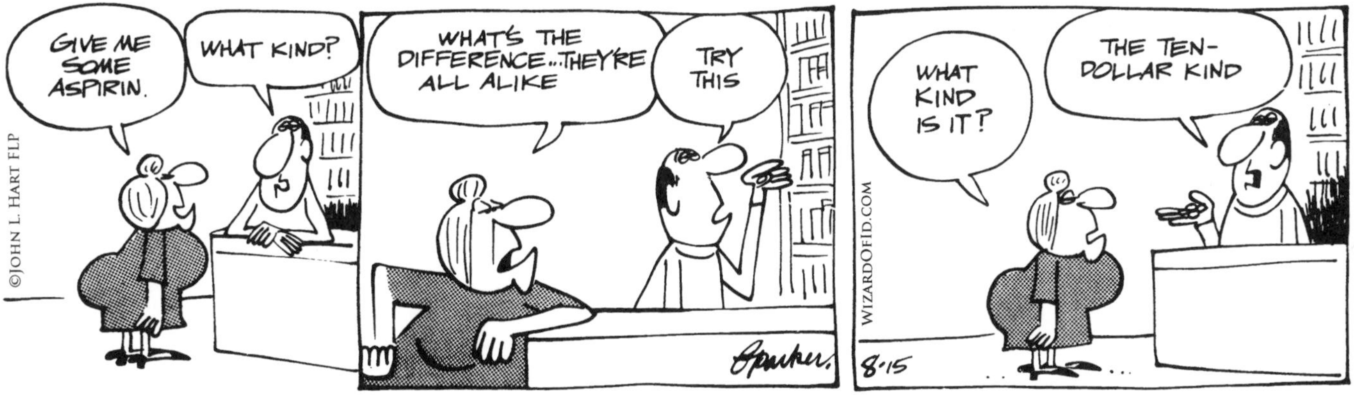

©JOHN L. HART FLP
GIVE ME SOME ASPIRIN.
WHAT KIND?
WHAT'S THE DIFFERENCE...THEY'RE ALL ALIKE
TRY THIS
WIZARDOFID.COM
WHAT KIND IS IT?
THE TEN-DOLLAR KIND
8-15

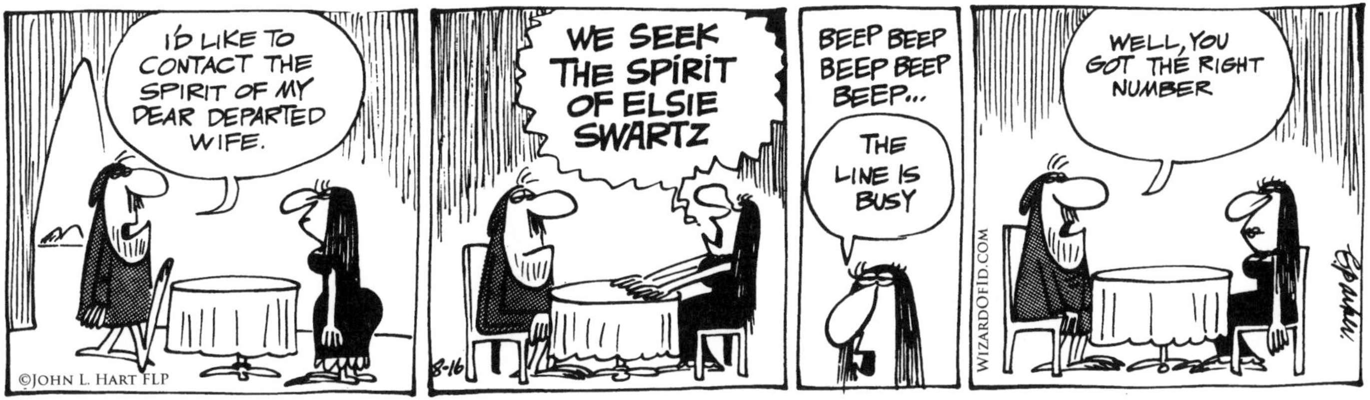

I'D LIKE TO CONTACT THE SPIRIT OF MY DEAR DEPARTED WIFE.
©JOHN L. HART FLP
WE SEEK THE SPIRIT OF ELSIE SWARTZ
8-16
BEEP BEEP BEEP BEEP BEEP...
THE LINE IS BUSY
WIZARDOFID.COM
WELL, YOU GOT THE RIGHT NUMBER

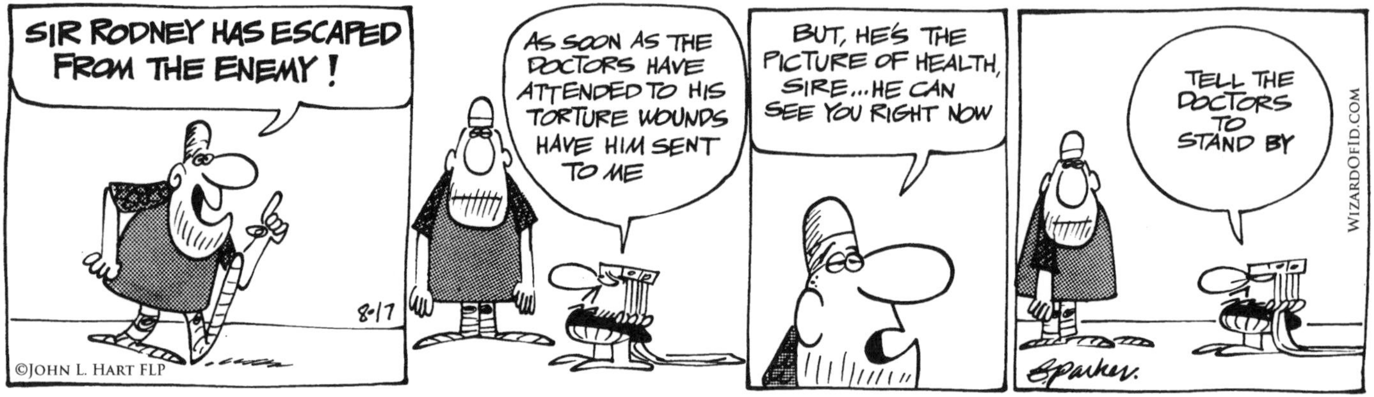
SIR RODNEY HAS ESCAPED FROM THE ENEMY !
8-17
©JOHN L. HART FLP
AS SOON AS THE DOCTORS HAVE ATTENDED TO HIS TORTURE WOUNDS HAVE HIM SENT TO ME
BUT, HE'S THE PICTURE OF HEALTH, SIRE... HE CAN SEE YOU RIGHT NOW
TELL THE DOCTORS TO STAND BY
WIZARDOFID.COM

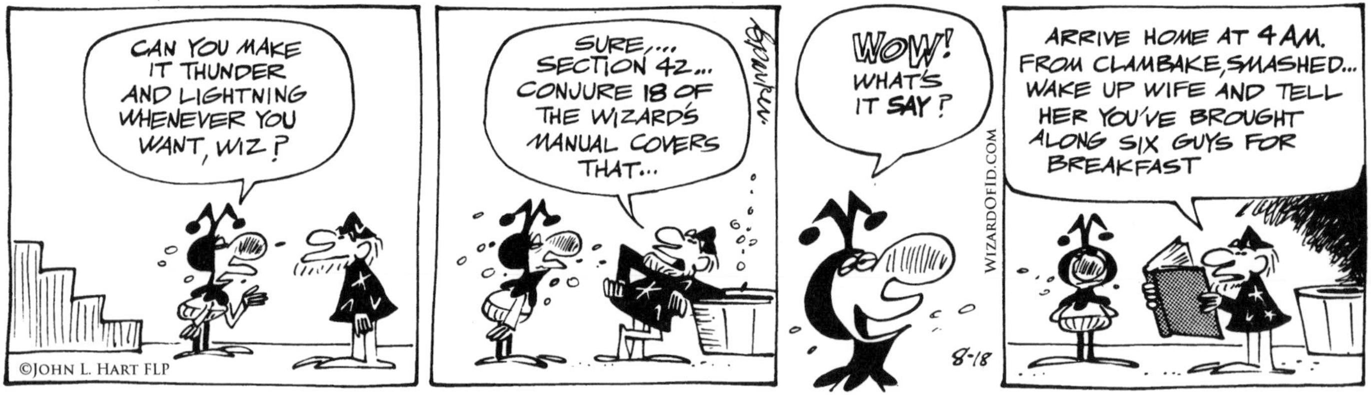
CAN YOU MAKE IT THUNDER AND LIGHTNING WHENEVER YOU WANT, WIZ ?
©JOHN L. HART FLP
SURE,... SECTION 42... CONJURE 18 OF THE WIZARD'S MANUAL COVERS THAT...
WOW! WHAT'S IT SAY ?
8-18
WIZARDOFID.COM
ARRIVE HOME AT 4 A.M. FROM CLAMBAKE, SMASHED... WAKE UP WIFE AND TELL HER YOU'VE BROUGHT ALONG SIX GUYS FOR BREAKFAST

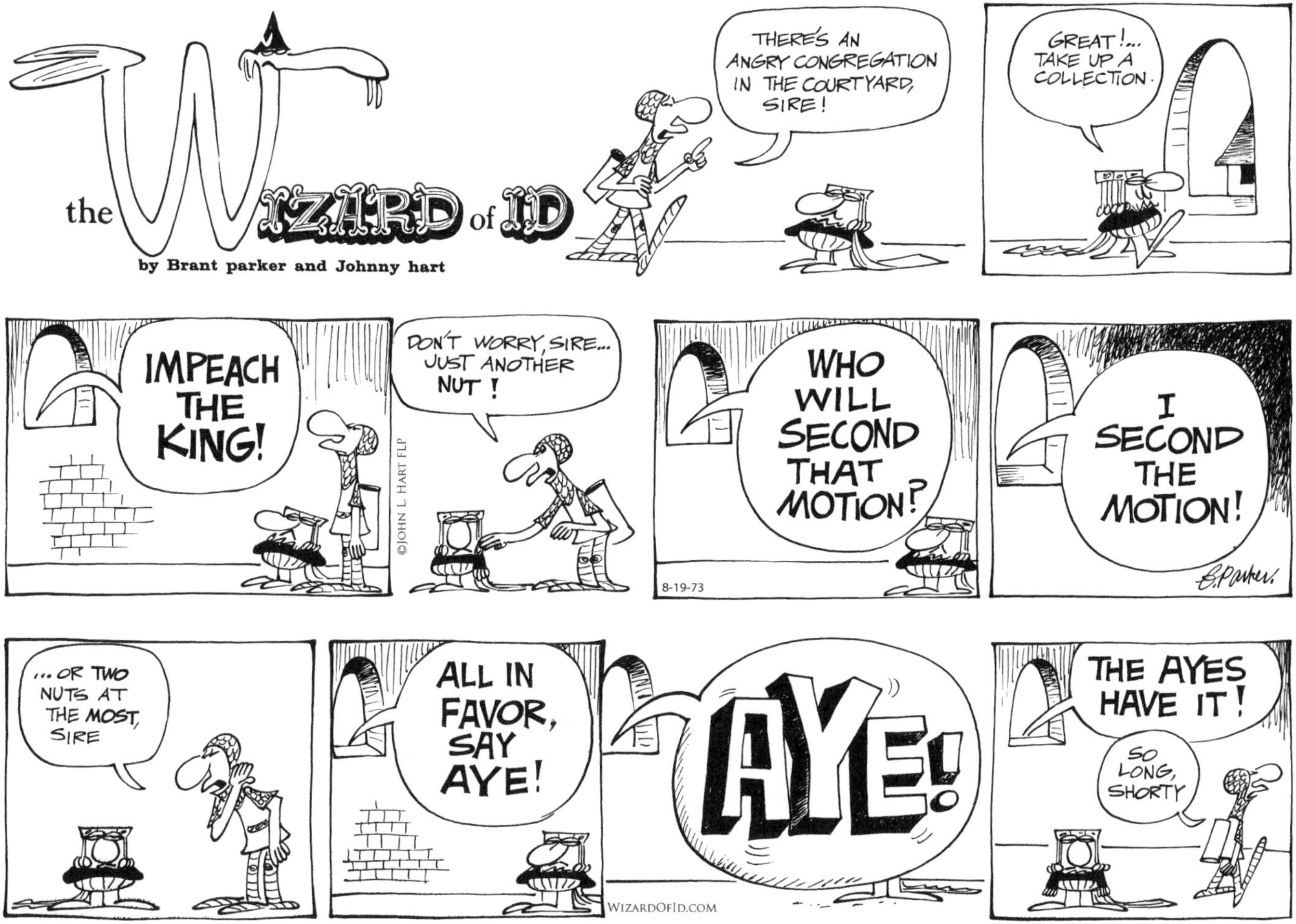
the WIZARD of ID
by Brant parker and Johnny hart
THERE'S AN ANGRY CONGREGATION IN THE COURTYARD, SIRE!
GREAT!... TAKE UP A COLLECTION.
IMPEACH THE KING!
©JOHN L. HART FLP
DON'T WORRY, SIRE... JUST ANOTHER NUT!
WHO WILL SECOND THAT MOTION?
8-19-73
I SECOND THE MOTION!
B. Parker
...OR TWO NUTS AT THE MOST, SIRE
ALL IN FAVOR, SAY AYE!
AYE!
WIZARDOFID.COM
THE AYES HAVE IT!
SO LONG, SHORTY

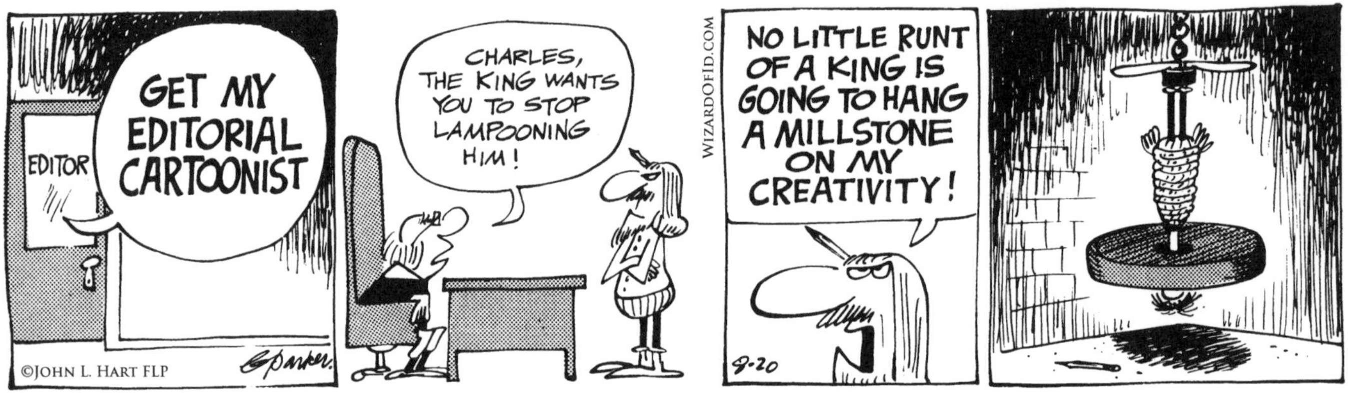

EDITOR
GET MY EDITORIAL CARTOONIST
CHARLES, THE KING WANTS YOU TO STOP LAMPOONING HIM!
WIZARDOFID.COM
NO LITTLE RUNT OF A KING IS GOING TO HANG A MILLSTONE ON MY CREATIVITY!
8-20
©JOHN L. HART FLP

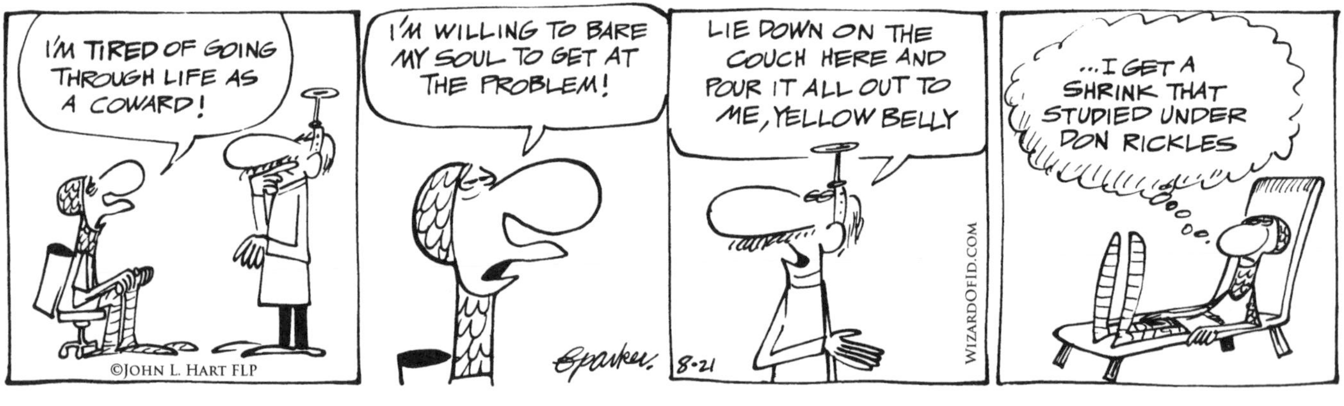

I'M TIRED OF GOING THROUGH LIFE AS A COWARD!
I'M WILLING TO BARE MY SOUL TO GET AT THE PROBLEM!
LIE DOWN ON THE COUCH HERE AND POUR IT ALL OUT TO ME, YELLOW BELLY
...I GET A SHRINK THAT STUDIED UNDER DON RICKLES
8-21
WIZARDOFID.COM
©JOHN L. HART FLP

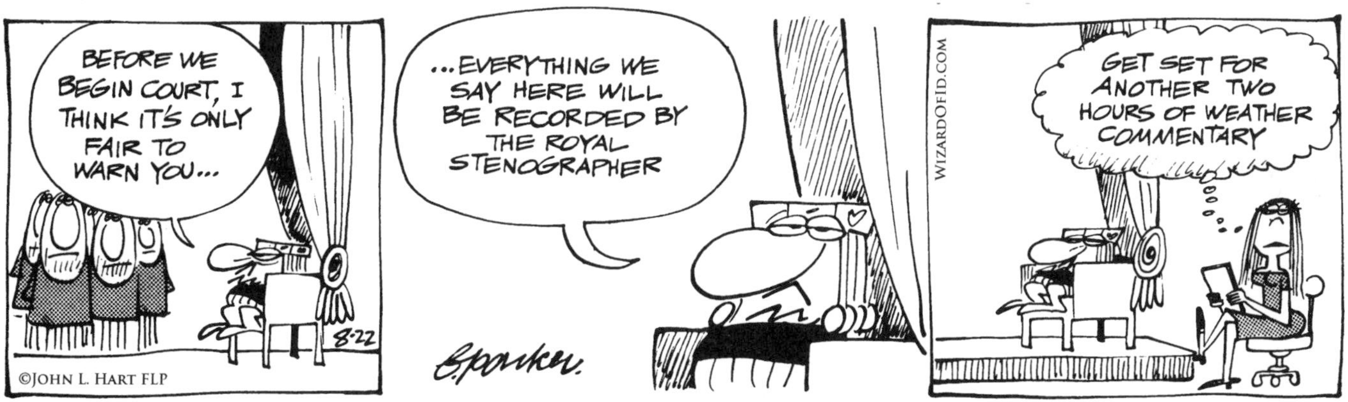
BEFORE WE BEGIN COURT, I THINK IT'S ONLY FAIR TO WARN YOU...
8-22
...EVERYTHING WE SAY HERE WILL BE RECORDED BY THE ROYAL STENOGRAPHER
WIZARDOFID.COM
GET SET FOR ANOTHER TWO HOURS OF WEATHER COMMENTARY
©JOHN L. HART FLP

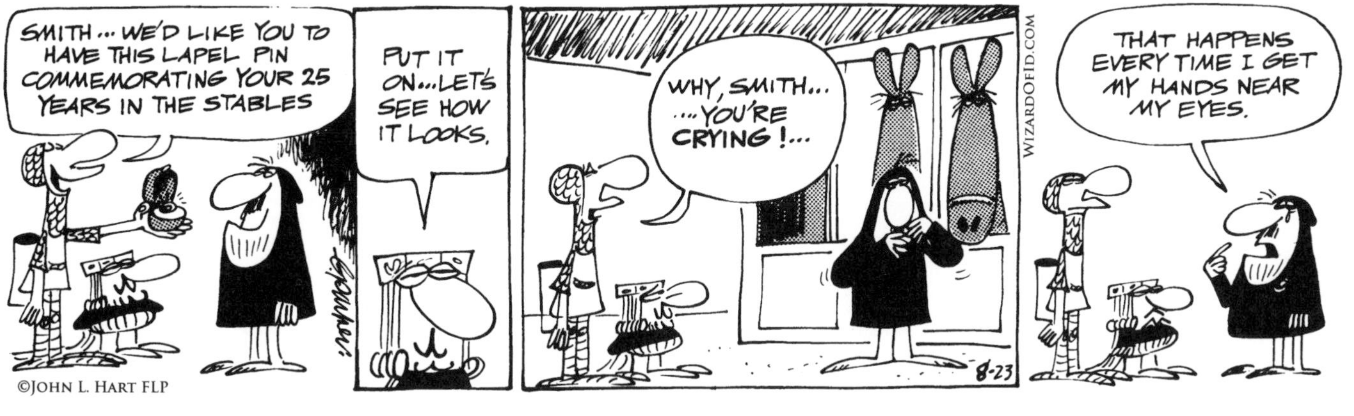
SMITH... WE'D LIKE YOU TO HAVE THIS LAPEL PIN COMMEMORATING YOUR 25 YEARS IN THE STABLES
PUT IT ON...LET'S SEE HOW IT LOOKS.
WHY, SMITH... ...YOU'RE CRYING!...
8-23
WIZARDOFID.COM
THAT HAPPENS EVERY TIME I GET MY HANDS NEAR MY EYES.
©JOHN L. HART FLP

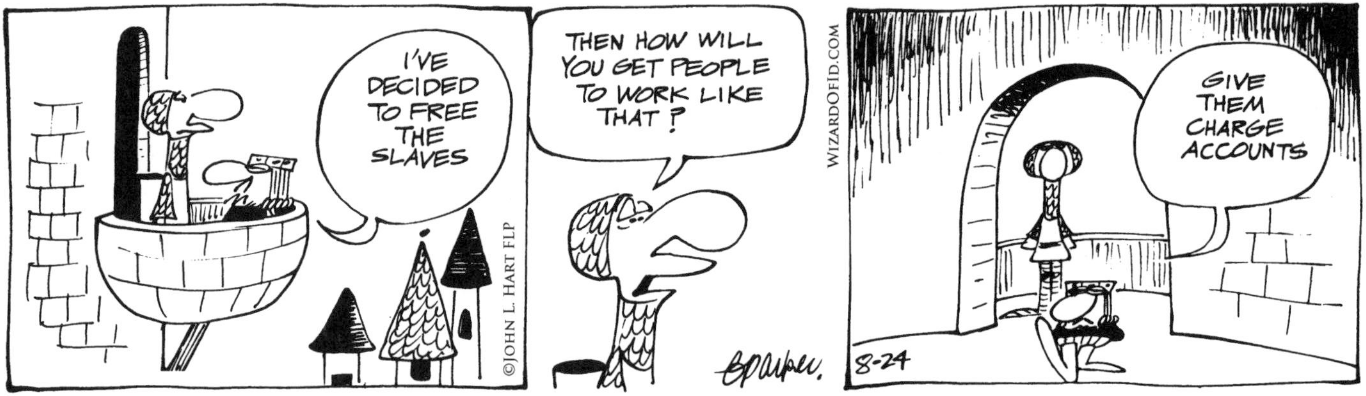
I'VE DECIDED TO FREE THE SLAVES
©JOHN L. HART FLP
THEN HOW WILL YOU GET PEOPLE TO WORK LIKE THAT ?
WIZARDOFID.COM
GIVE THEM CHARGE ACCOUNTS
8-24

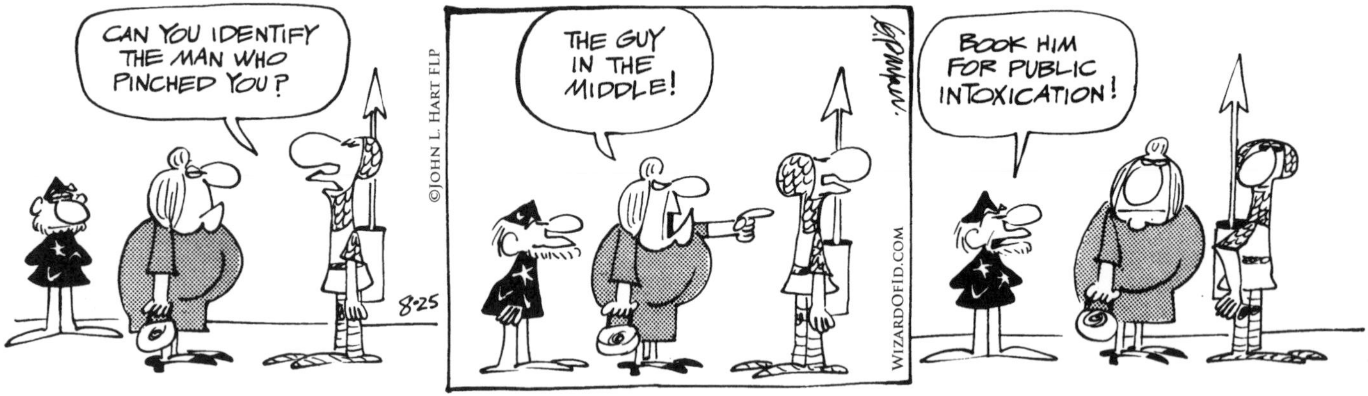
CAN YOU IDENTIFY THE MAN WHO PINCHED YOU ?
8-25
©JOHN L. HART FLP
THE GUY IN THE MIDDLE!
WIZARDOFID.COM
BOOK HIM FOR PUBLIC INTOXICATION!

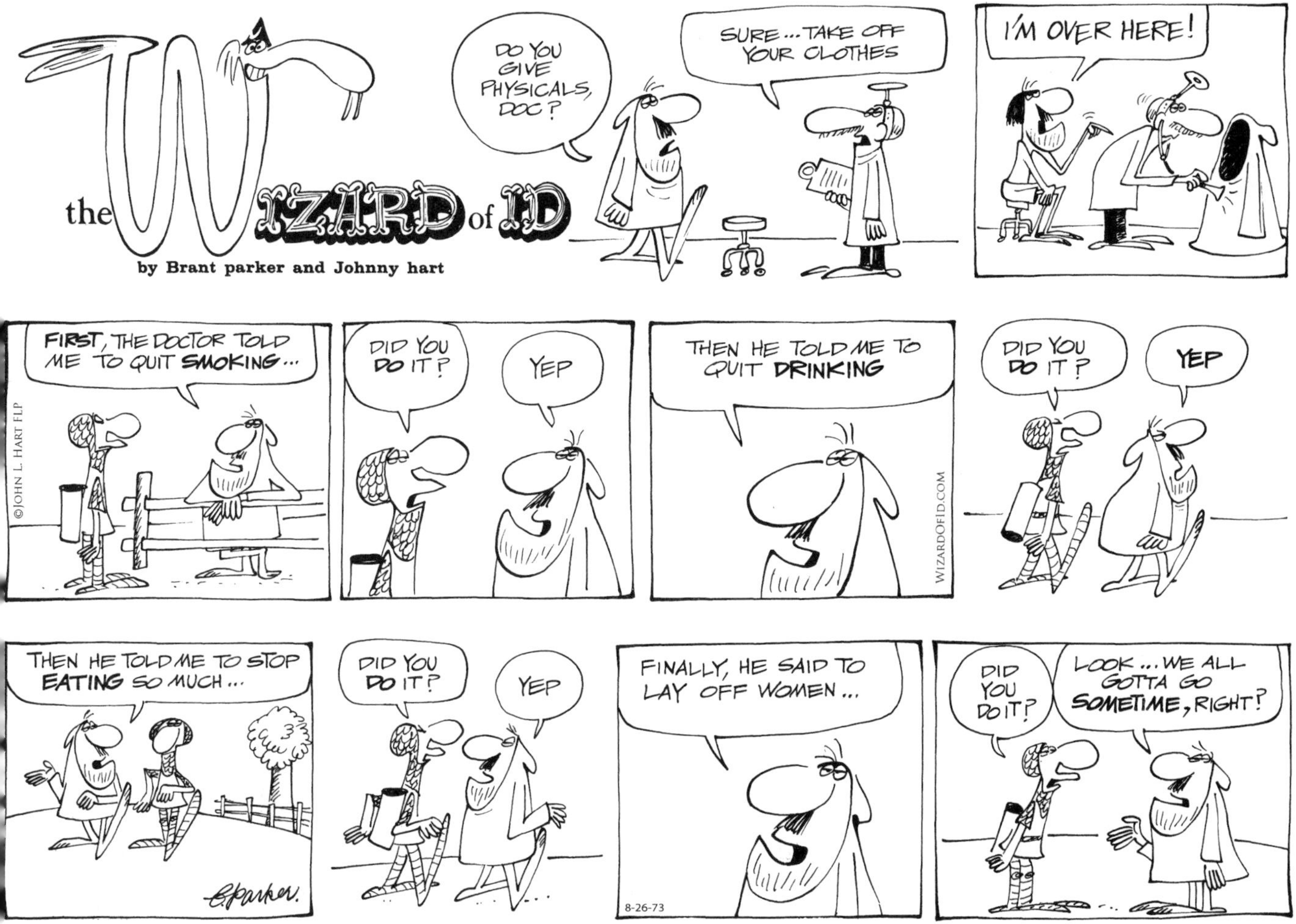
the WIZARD of ID
by Brant parker and Johnny hart
DO YOU GIVE PHYSICALS, DOC?
SURE ... TAKE OFF YOUR CLOTHES
I'M OVER HERE!
FIRST, THE DOCTOR TOLD ME TO QUIT SMOKING ...
DID YOU DO IT?
YEP
THEN HE TOLD ME TO QUIT DRINKING
DID YOU DO IT?
YEP
THEN HE TOLD ME TO STOP EATING SO MUCH ...
DID YOU DO IT?
YEP
FINALLY, HE SAID TO LAY OFF WOMEN ...
DID YOU DO IT?
LOOK ... WE ALL GOTTA GO SOMETIME, RIGHT?
©JOHN L. HART FLP
WIZARDOFID.COM
B. parker.
8-26-73

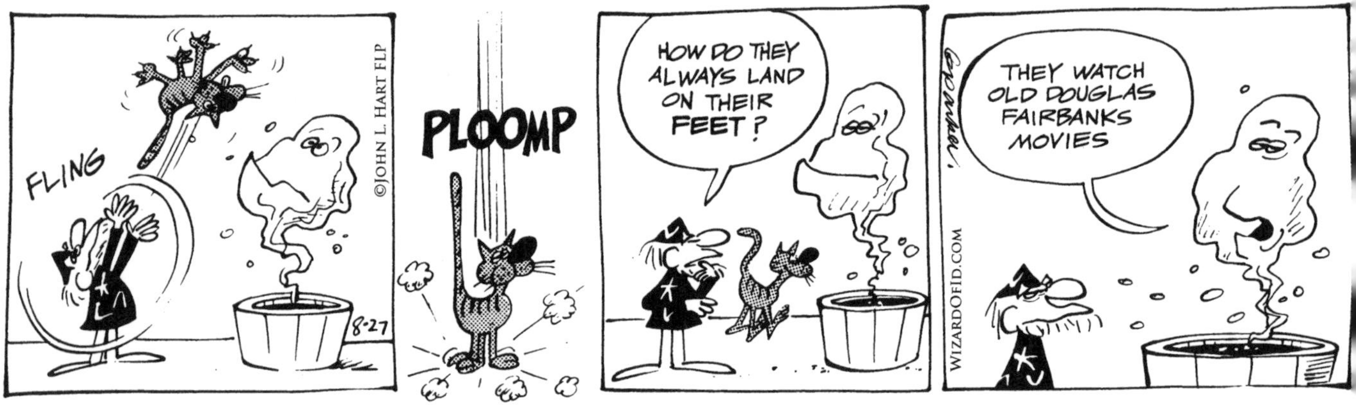
FLING
©JOHN L. HART FLP
8-27
PLOOMP
HOW DO THEY ALWAYS LAND ON THEIR FEET ?
WIZARDOFID.COM
THEY WATCH OLD DOUGLAS FAIRBANKS MOVIES

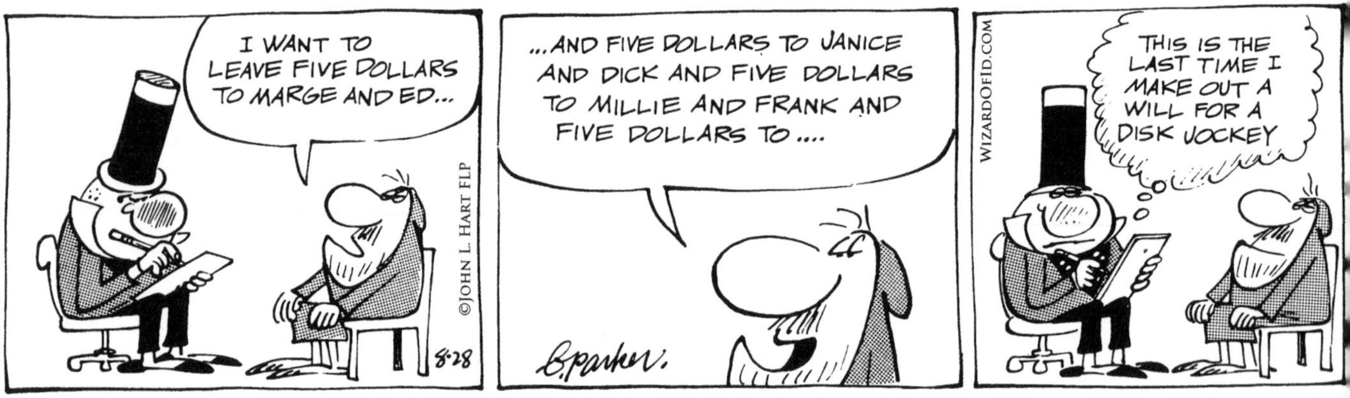
I WANT TO LEAVE FIVE DOLLARS TO MARGE AND ED...
©JOHN L. HART FLP
8-28
...AND FIVE DOLLARS TO JANICE AND DICK AND FIVE DOLLARS TO MILLIE AND FRANK AND FIVE DOLLARS TO....
B. parker.
WIZARDOFID.COM
THIS IS THE LAST TIME I MAKE OUT A WILL FOR A DISK JOCKEY

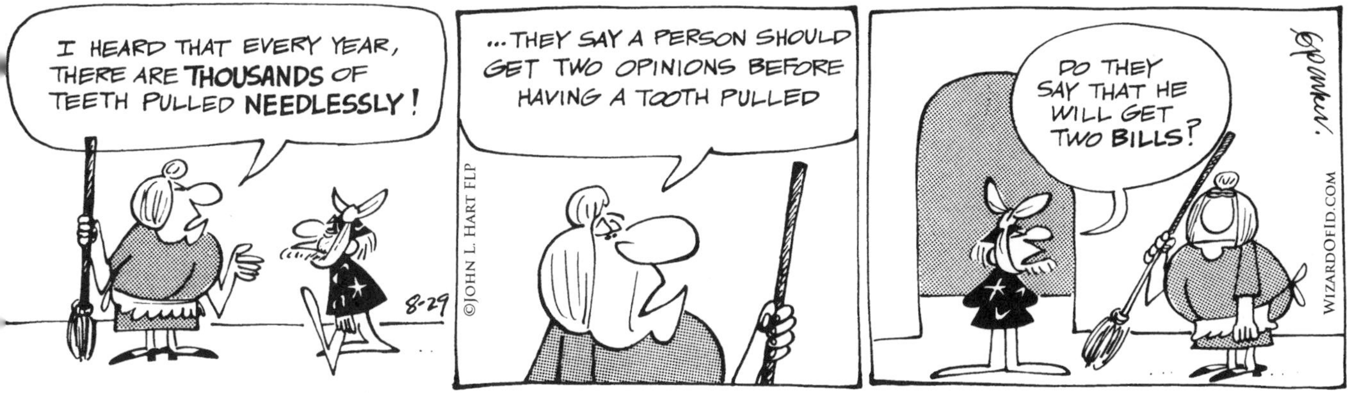
I HEARD THAT EVERY YEAR, THERE ARE **THOUSANDS** OF TEETH PULLED **NEEDLESSLY**!
8-29
©JOHN L. HART FLP
...THEY SAY A PERSON SHOULD GET TWO OPINIONS BEFORE HAVING A TOOTH PULLED
DO THEY SAY THAT HE WILL GET TWO **BILLS**?
WIZARDOFID.COM

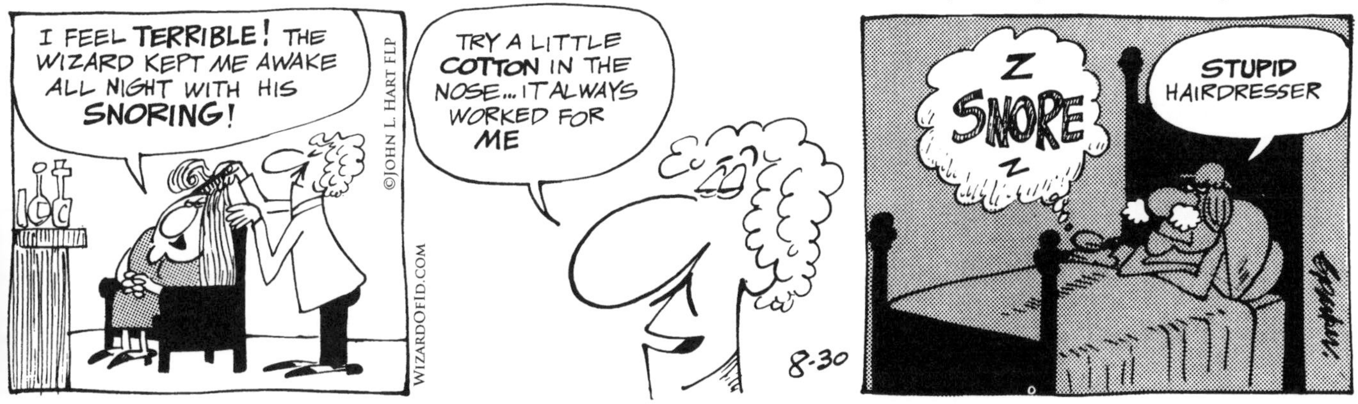
I FEEL **TERRIBLE**! THE WIZARD KEPT ME AWAKE ALL NIGHT WITH HIS **SNORING**!
©JOHN L. HART FLP
WIZARDOFID.COM
TRY A LITTLE **COTTON** IN THE NOSE...IT ALWAYS WORKED FOR **ME**
8-30
Z
SNORE
Z
STUPID HAIRDRESSER

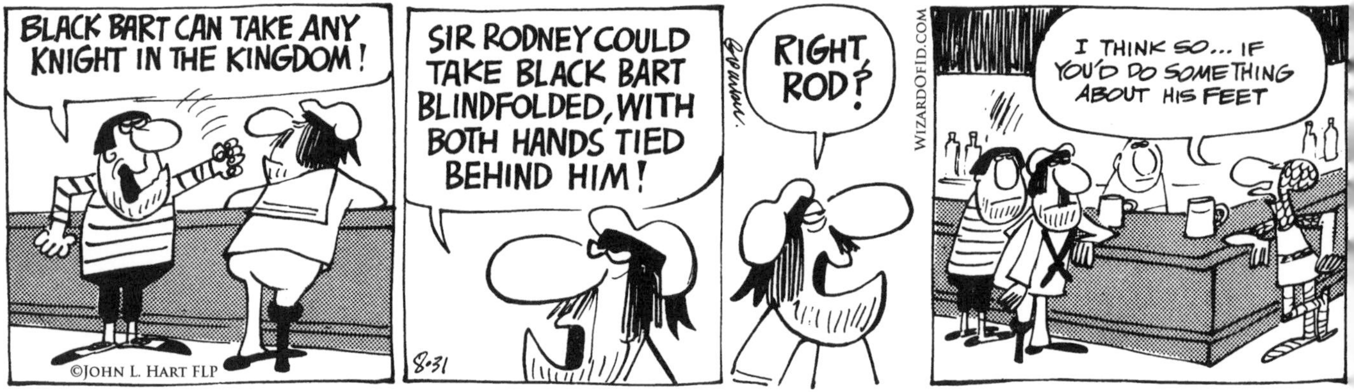
BLACK BART CAN TAKE ANY KNIGHT IN THE KINGDOM!
©JOHN L. HART FLP
SIR RODNEY COULD TAKE BLACK BART BLINDFOLDED, WITH BOTH HANDS TIED BEHIND HIM!
8-31
RIGHT, ROD?
WIZARDOFID.COM
I THINK SO... IF YOU'D DO SOMETHING ABOUT HIS FEET

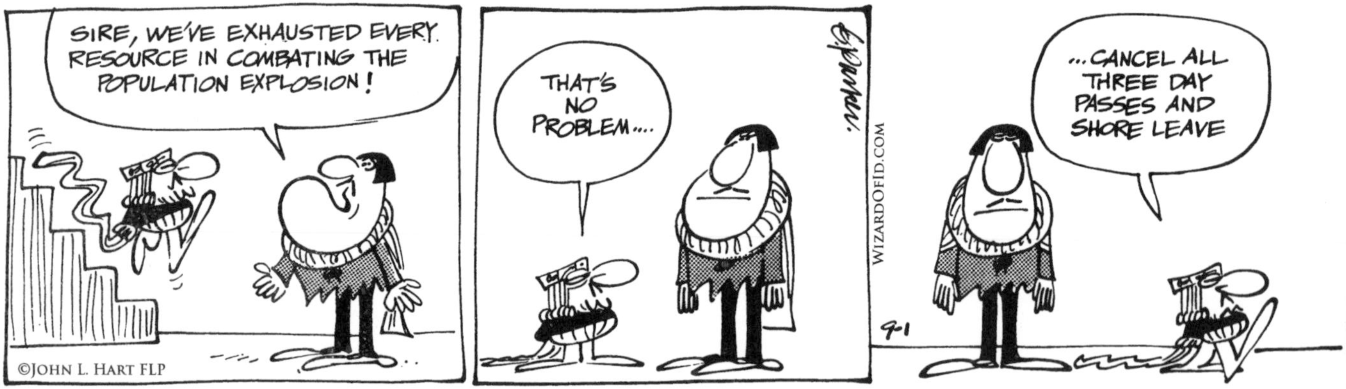
SIRE, WE'VE EXHAUSTED EVERY RESOURCE IN COMBATING THE POPULATION EXPLOSION!
©JOHN L. HART FLP
THAT'S NO PROBLEM....
WIZARDOFID.COM
9-1
...CANCEL ALL THREE DAY PASSES AND SHORE LEAVE

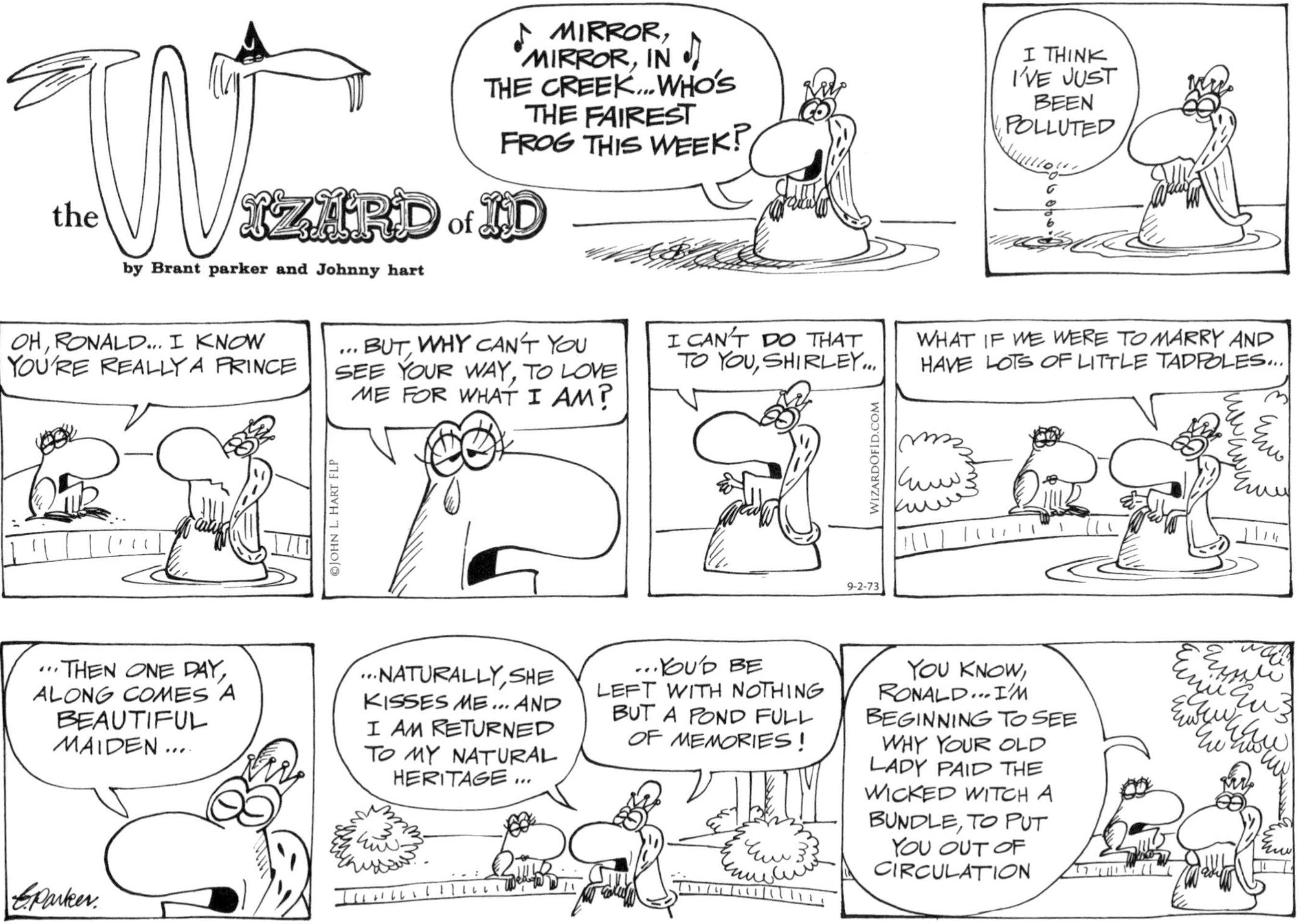
the WIZARD of ID
by Brant parker and Johnny hart
♪ MIRROR, MIRROR, IN THE CREEK...WHO'S THE FAIREST FROG THIS WEEK? ♪
I THINK I'VE JUST BEEN POLLUTED
OH, RONALD... I KNOW YOU'RE REALLY A PRINCE
... BUT, WHY CAN'T YOU SEE YOUR WAY, TO LOVE ME FOR WHAT I AM?
©JOHN L. HART FLP
I CAN'T DO THAT TO YOU, SHIRLEY...
WIZARDOFID.COM
9-2-73
WHAT IF WE WERE TO MARRY AND HAVE LOTS OF LITTLE TADPOLES...
...THEN ONE DAY, ALONG COMES A BEAUTIFUL MAIDEN...
B. Parker
...NATURALLY, SHE KISSES ME... AND I AM RETURNED TO MY NATURAL HERITAGE...
...YOU'D BE LEFT WITH NOTHING BUT A POND FULL OF MEMORIES!
YOU KNOW, RONALD... I'M BEGINNING TO SEE WHY YOUR OLD LADY PAID THE WICKED WITCH A BUNDLE, TO PUT YOU OUT OF CIRCULATION

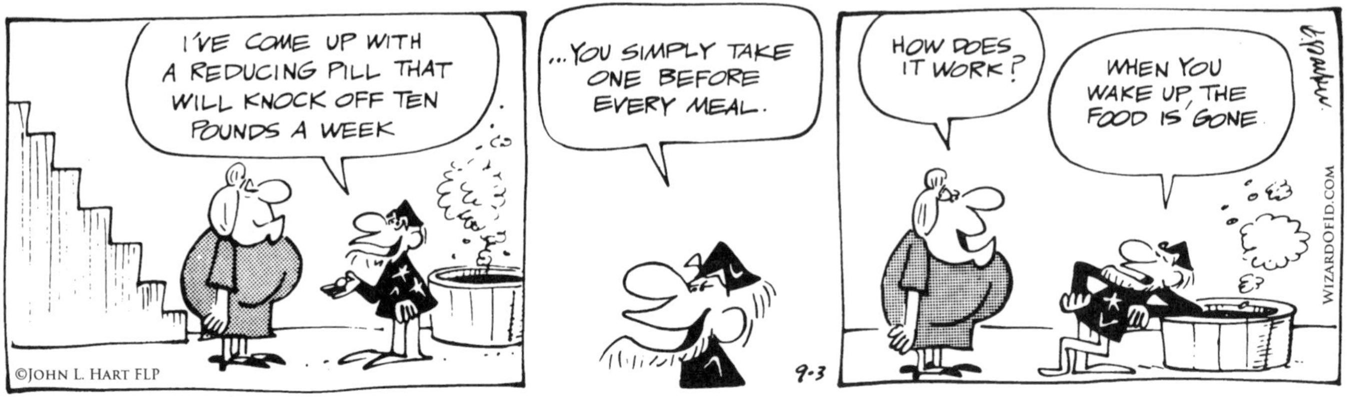
I'VE COME UP WITH A REDUCING PILL THAT WILL KNOCK OFF TEN POUNDS A WEEK
...YOU SIMPLY TAKE ONE BEFORE EVERY MEAL.
HOW DOES IT WORK?
WHEN YOU WAKE UP, THE FOOD IS GONE
©JOHN L. HART FLP
9-3
WIZARDOFID.COM

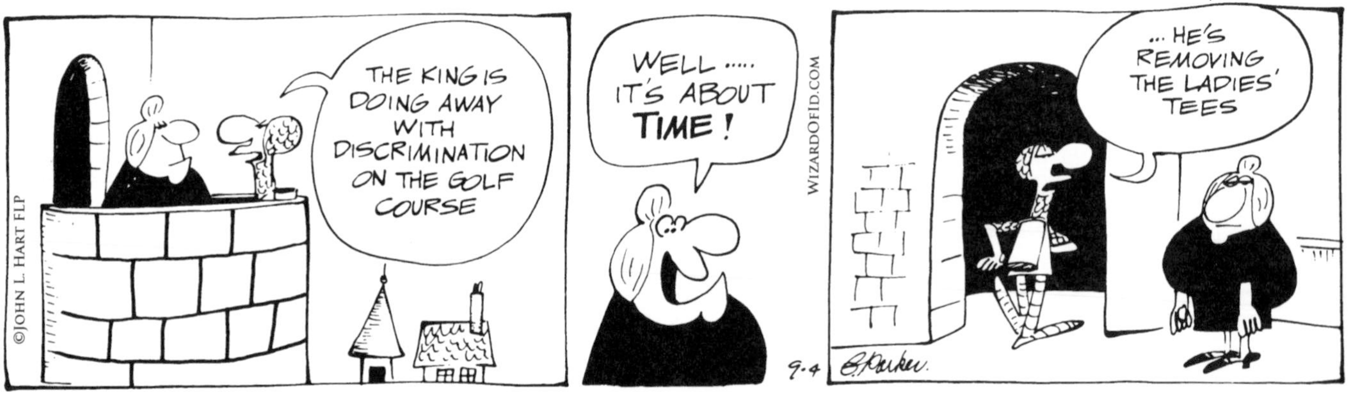
THE KING IS DOING AWAY WITH DISCRIMINATION ON THE GOLF COURSE
WELL ..... IT'S ABOUT TIME!
... HE'S REMOVING THE LADIES' TEES
©JOHN L. HART FLP
9-4
WIZARDOFID.COM

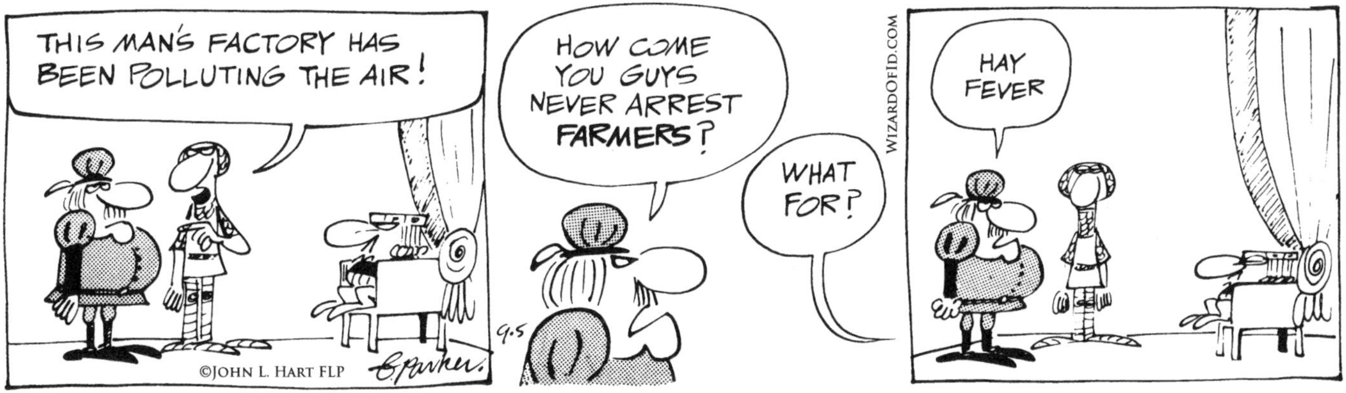
THIS MAN'S FACTORY HAS BEEN POLLUTING THE AIR!
HOW COME YOU GUYS NEVER ARREST FARMERS?
WHAT FOR?
HAY FEVER
©JOHN L. HART FLP
9·5
WIZARDOFID.COM

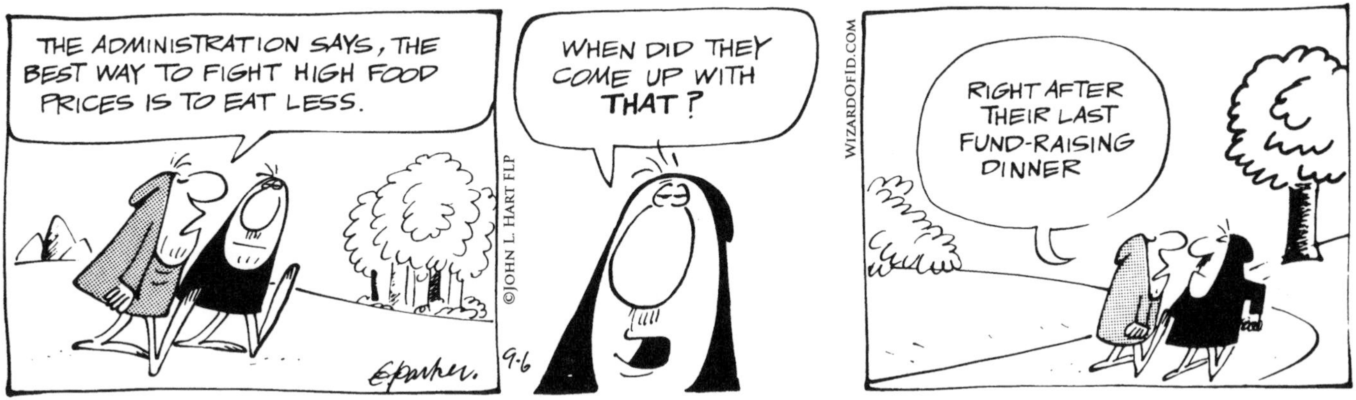
THE ADMINISTRATION SAYS, THE BEST WAY TO FIGHT HIGH FOOD PRICES IS TO EAT LESS.
WHEN DID THEY COME UP WITH THAT?
RIGHT AFTER THEIR LAST FUND-RAISING DINNER
©JOHN L. HART FLP
9·6
WIZARDOFID.COM

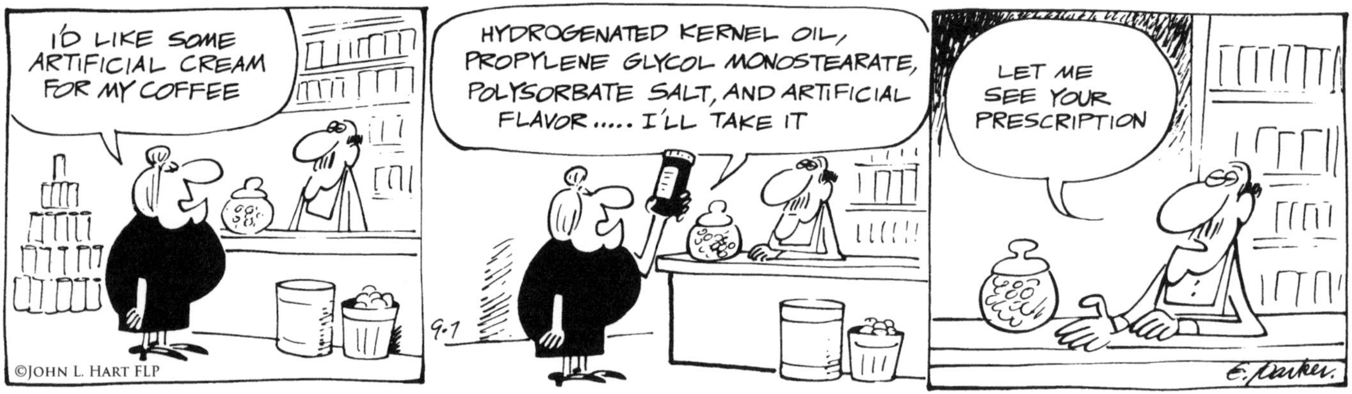
I'D LIKE SOME ARTIFICIAL CREAM FOR MY COFFEE
HYDROGENATED KERNEL OIL, PROPYLENE GLYCOL MONOSTEARATE, POLYSORBATE SALT, AND ARTIFICIAL FLAVOR..... I'LL TAKE IT
LET ME SEE YOUR PRESCRIPTION
9·7
©JOHN L. HART FLP
E. Parker.

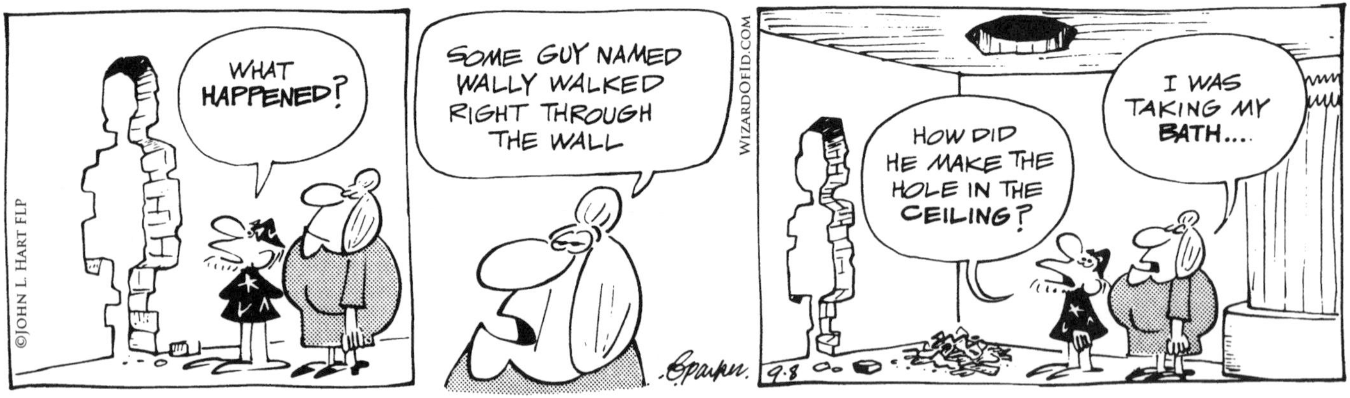
WHAT HAPPENED?
SOME GUY NAMED WALLY WALKED RIGHT THROUGH THE WALL
HOW DID HE MAKE THE HOLE IN THE CEILING?
I WAS TAKING MY BATH....
©JOHN L. HART FLP
WIZARDOFID.COM
9·8
E. Parker.

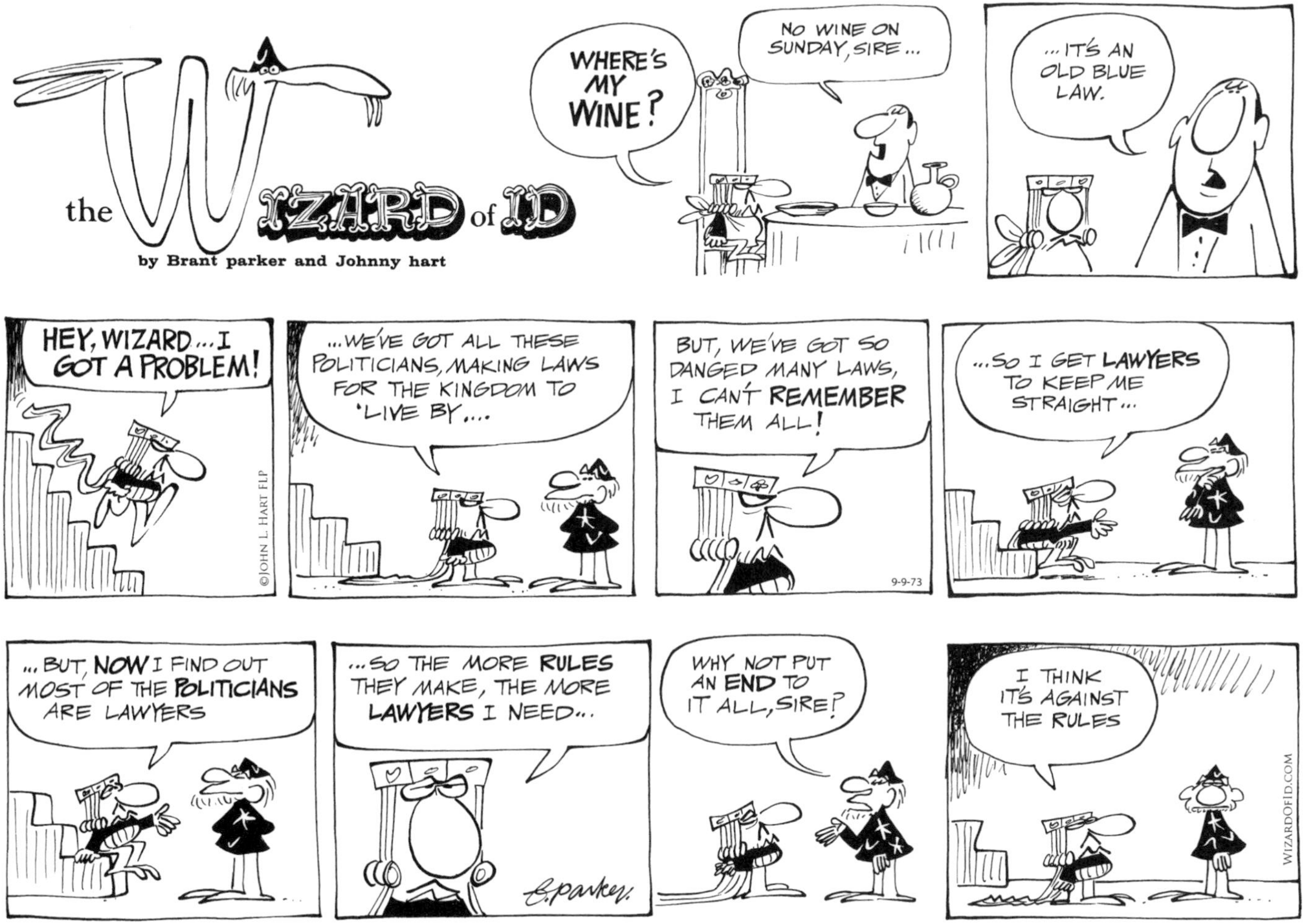

the WIZARD of ID
by Brant parker and Johnny hart
WHERE'S MY WINE?
NO WINE ON SUNDAY, SIRE...
...IT'S AN OLD BLUE LAW.
HEY, WIZARD...I GOT A PROBLEM!
©JOHN L. HART FLP
...WE'VE GOT ALL THESE POLITICIANS, MAKING LAWS FOR THE KINGDOM TO 'LIVE BY....
BUT, WE'VE GOT SO DANGED MANY LAWS, I CAN'T REMEMBER THEM ALL!
9-9-73
...SO I GET LAWYERS TO KEEP ME STRAIGHT...
...BUT, NOW I FIND OUT MOST OF THE POLITICIANS ARE LAWYERS
...SO THE MORE RULES THEY MAKE, THE MORE LAWYERS I NEED...
B. parker.
WHY NOT PUT AN END TO IT ALL, SIRE?
I THINK IT'S AGAINST THE RULES
WIZARDOFID.COM

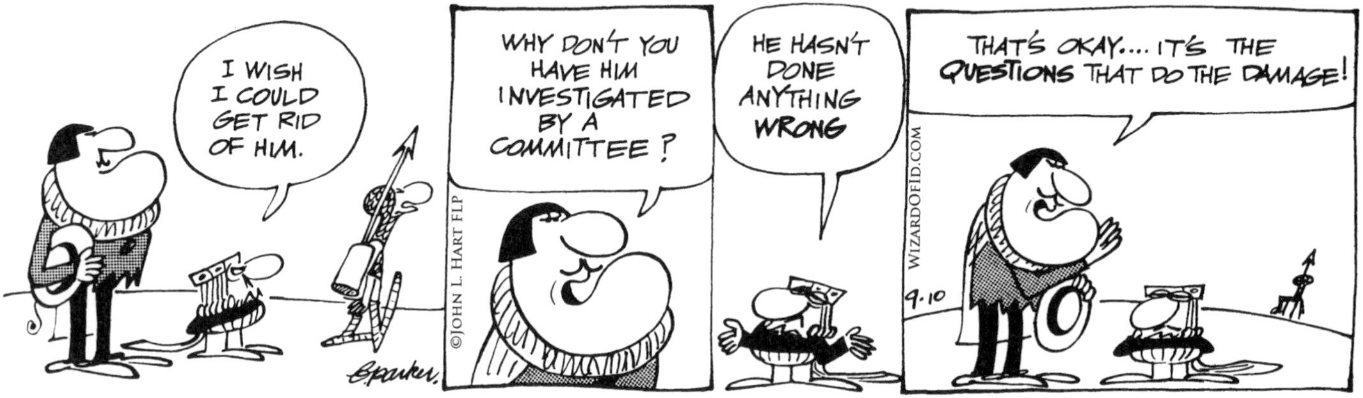
I WISH I COULD GET RID OF HIM.
WHY DON'T YOU HAVE HIM INVESTIGATED BY A COMMITTEE?
HE HASN'T DONE ANYTHING WRONG
THAT'S OKAY.... IT'S THE QUESTIONS THAT DO THE DAMAGE!
©JOHN L. HART FLP
WIZARDOFID.COM
9-10

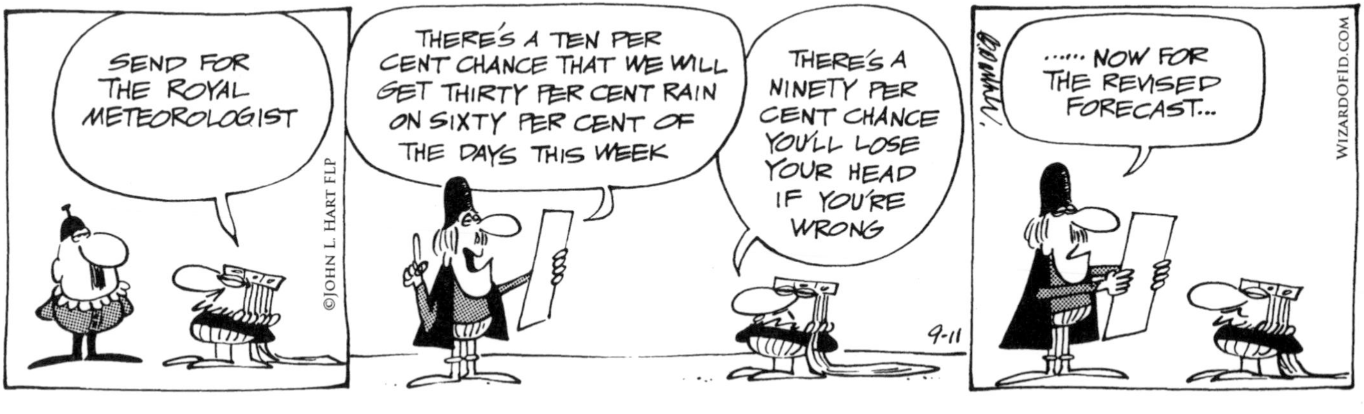
SEND FOR THE ROYAL METEOROLOGIST
THERE'S A TEN PER CENT CHANCE THAT WE WILL GET THIRTY PER CENT RAIN ON SIXTY PER CENT OF THE DAYS THIS WEEK
THERE'S A NINETY PER CENT CHANCE YOU'LL LOSE YOUR HEAD IF YOU'RE WRONG
...... NOW FOR THE REVISED FORECAST...
©JOHN L. HART FLP
WIZARDOFID.COM
9-11

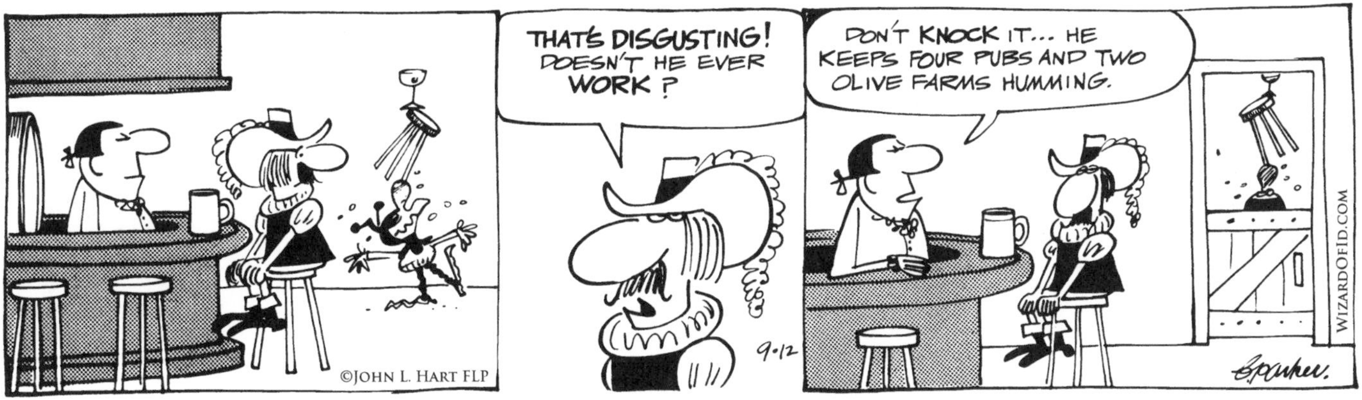
THAT'S DISGUSTING! DOESN'T HE EVER WORK?
DON'T KNOCK IT... HE KEEPS FOUR PUBS AND TWO OLIVE FARMS HUMMING.
©JOHN L. HART FLP
9-12
WIZARDOFID.COM

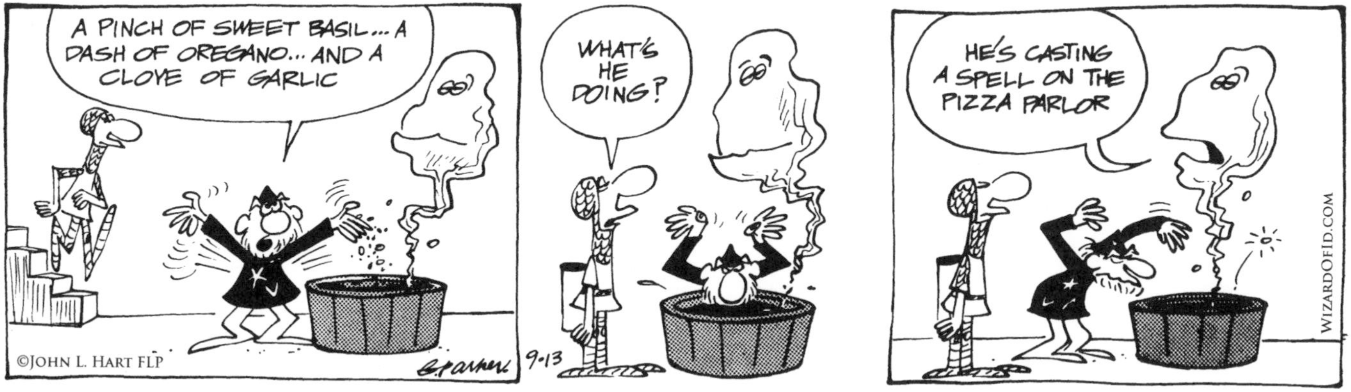
A PINCH OF SWEET BASIL... A DASH OF OREGANO... AND A CLOVE OF GARLIC
WHAT'S HE DOING?
HE'S CASTING A SPELL ON THE PIZZA PARLOR
©JOHN L. HART FLP
9-13
WIZARDOFID.COM

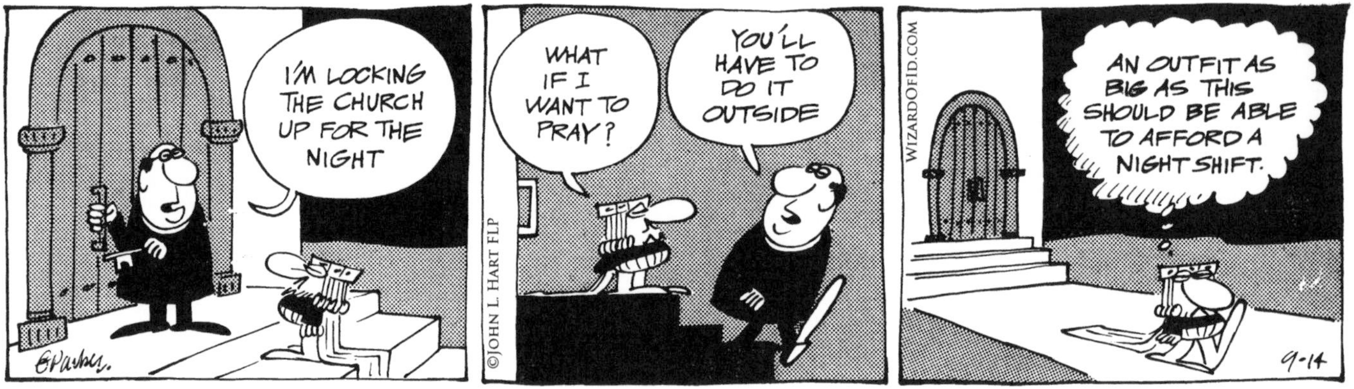
I'M LOCKING THE CHURCH UP FOR THE NIGHT
©JOHN L. HART FLP
WHAT IF I WANT TO PRAY?
YOU'LL HAVE TO DO IT OUTSIDE
WIZARDOFID.COM
AN OUTFIT AS BIG AS THIS SHOULD BE ABLE TO AFFORD A NIGHT SHIFT.
9-14

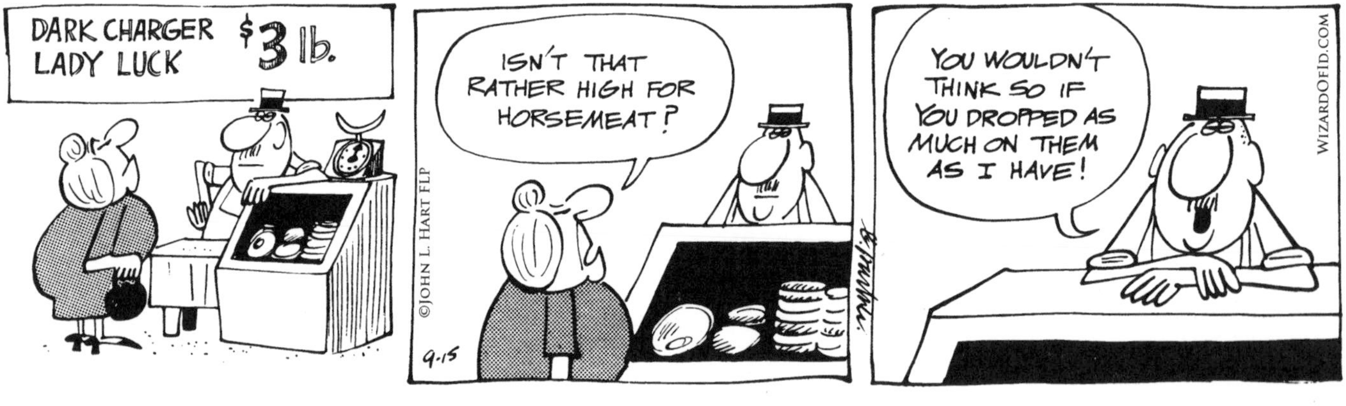
DARK CHARGER
LADY LUCK
$3 lb.
©JOHN L. HART FLP
ISN'T THAT RATHER HIGH FOR HORSEMEAT?
9-15
YOU WOULDN'T THINK SO IF YOU DROPPED AS MUCH ON THEM AS I HAVE!
WIZARDOFID.COM

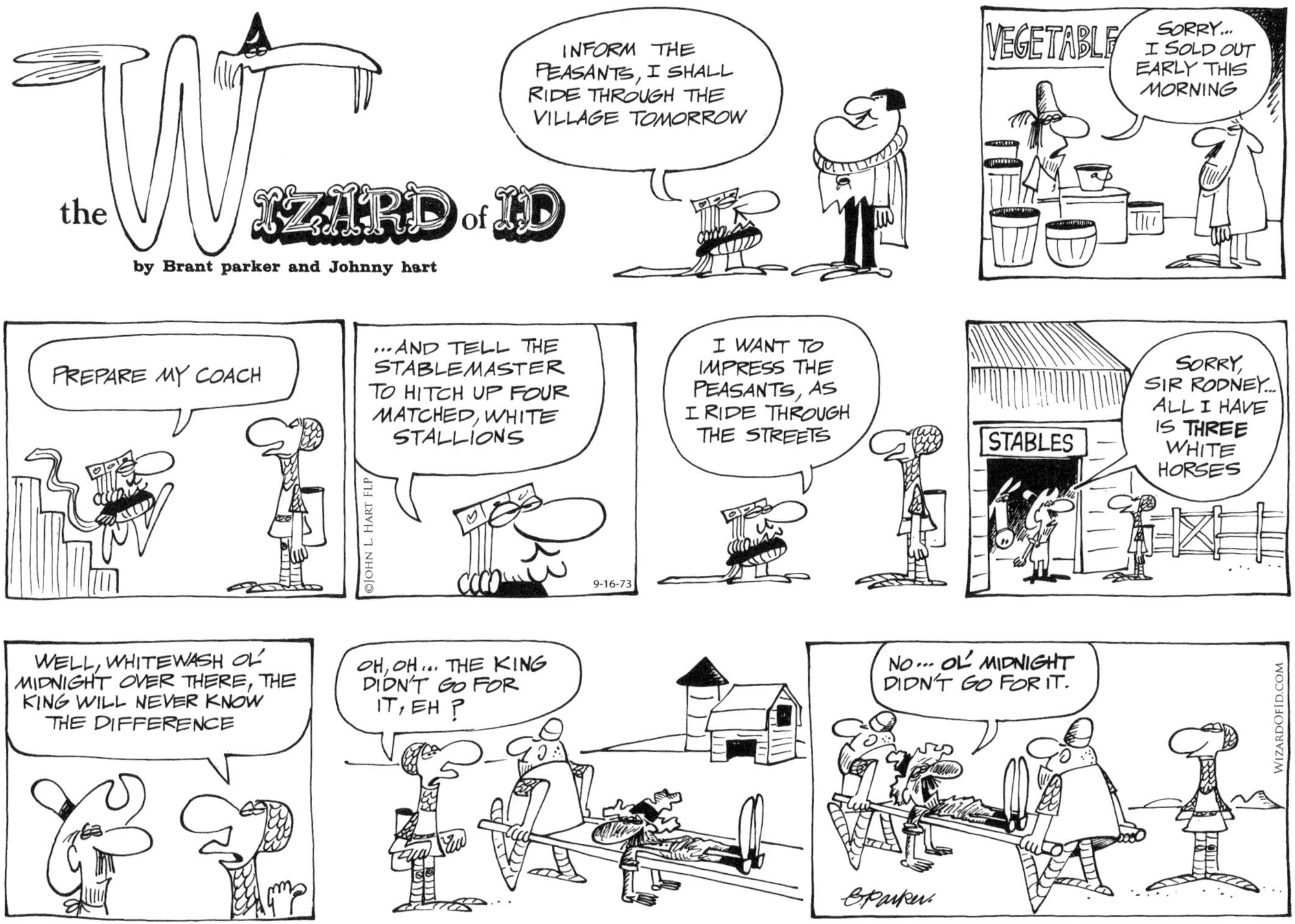
the WIZARD of ID
by Brant parker and Johnny hart
INFORM THE PEASANTS, I SHALL RIDE THROUGH THE VILLAGE TOMORROW
VEGETABLE
SORRY... I SOLD OUT EARLY THIS MORNING
PREPARE MY COACH
...AND TELL THE STABLEMASTER TO HITCH UP FOUR MATCHED, WHITE STALLIONS
©JOHN L. HART FLP
9-16-73
I WANT TO IMPRESS THE PEASANTS, AS I RIDE THROUGH THE STREETS
STABLES
SORRY, SIR RODNEY... ALL I HAVE IS THREE WHITE HORSES
WELL, WHITEWASH OL' MIDNIGHT OVER THERE, THE KING WILL NEVER KNOW THE DIFFERENCE
OH, OH... THE KING DIDN'T GO FOR IT, EH ?
NO... OL' MIDNIGHT DIDN'T GO FOR IT.
B PARKER
WIZARDOFID.COM

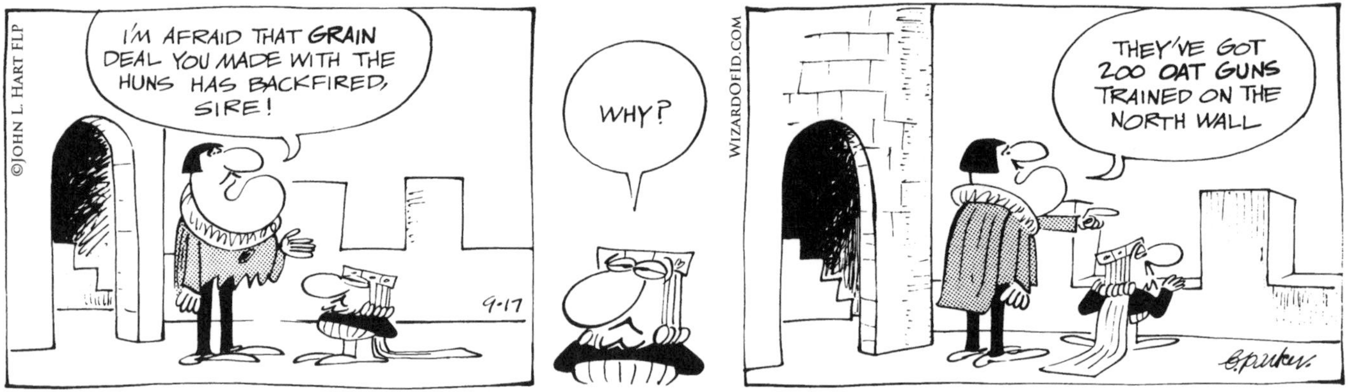
©JOHN L. HART FLP
I'M AFRAID THAT GRAIN DEAL YOU MADE WITH THE HUNS HAS BACKFIRED, SIRE!
9-17
WHY?
WIZARDOFID.COM
THEY'VE GOT 200 OAT GUNS TRAINED ON THE NORTH WALL

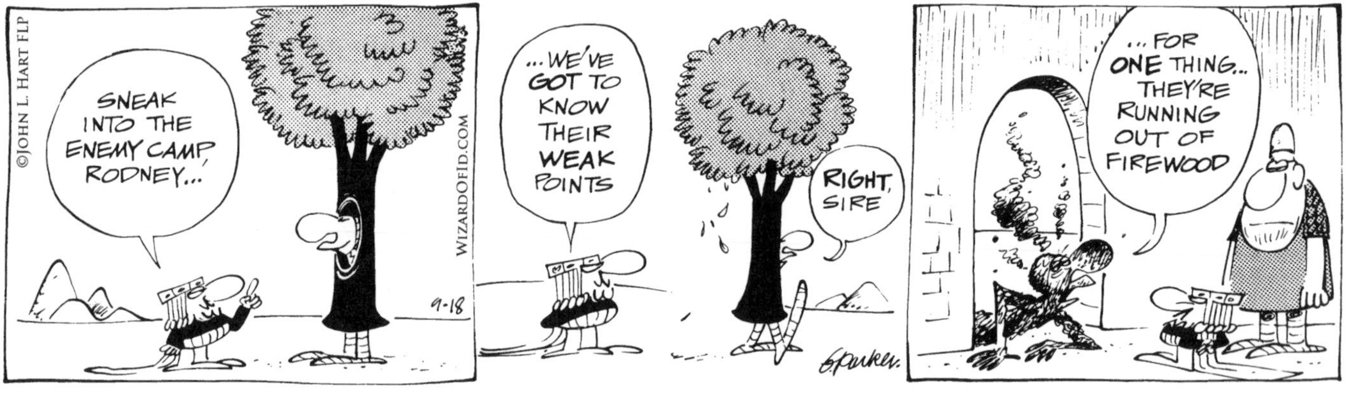
©JOHN L. HART FLP
SNEAK INTO THE ENEMY CAMP, RODNEY...
WIZARDOFID.COM
9-18
...WE'VE GOT TO KNOW THEIR WEAK POINTS
RIGHT, SIRE
...FOR ONE THING... THEY'RE RUNNING OUT OF FIREWOOD

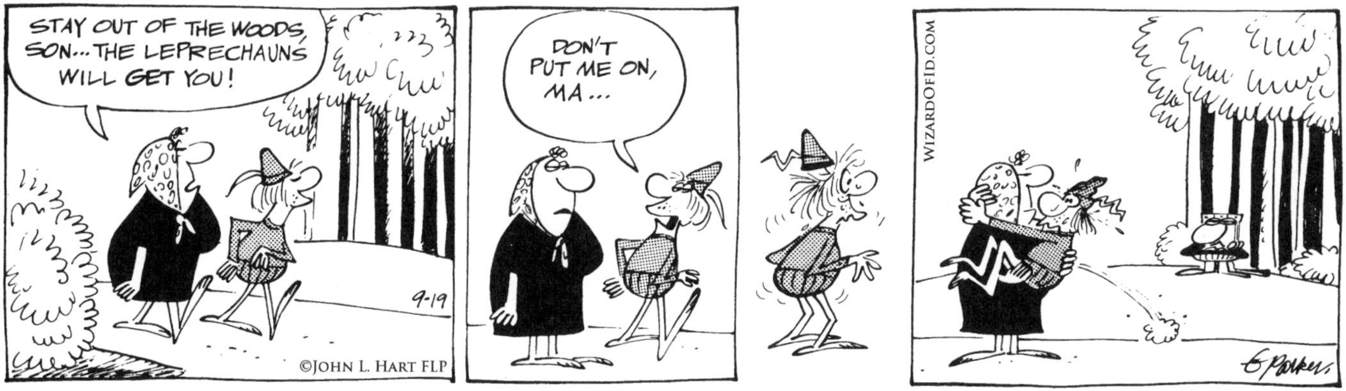
STAY OUT OF THE WOODS, SON... THE LEPRECHAUNS WILL GET YOU!
9-19
©JOHN L. HART FLP
DON'T PUT ME ON, MA...
WIZARDOFID.COM
G Parker

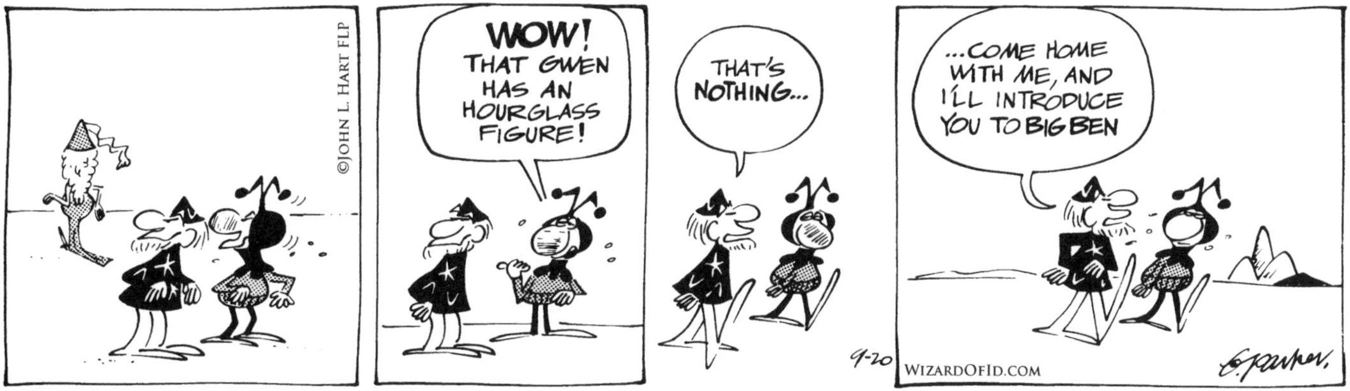
©JOHN L. HART FLP
WOW! THAT GWEN HAS AN HOURGLASS FIGURE!
THAT'S NOTHING...
9-20
...COME HOME WITH ME, AND I'LL INTRODUCE YOU TO BIG BEN
WIZARDOFID.COM
G Parker

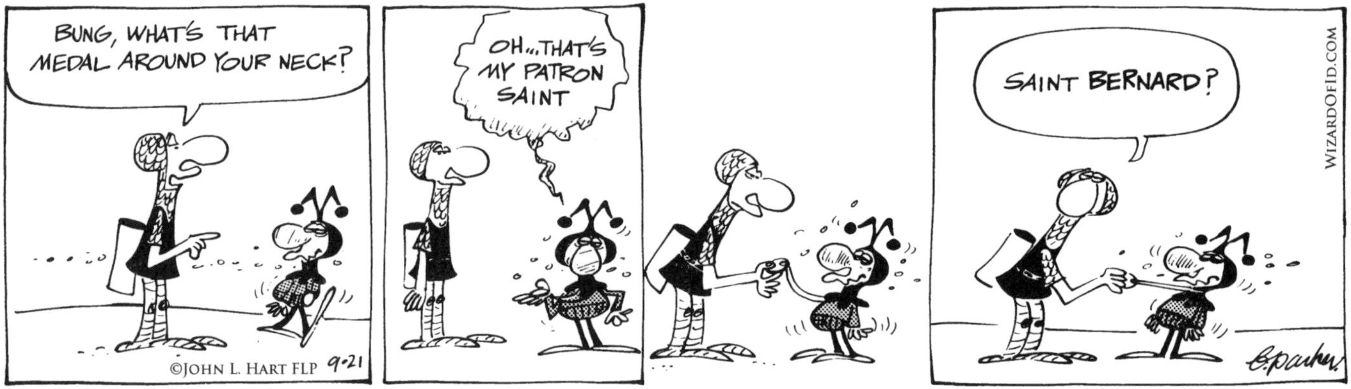
BUNG, WHAT'S THAT MEDAL AROUND YOUR NECK?
OH...THAT'S MY PATRON SAINT
SAINT BERNARD?
©JOHN L. HART FLP
9-21
WIZARDOFID.COM

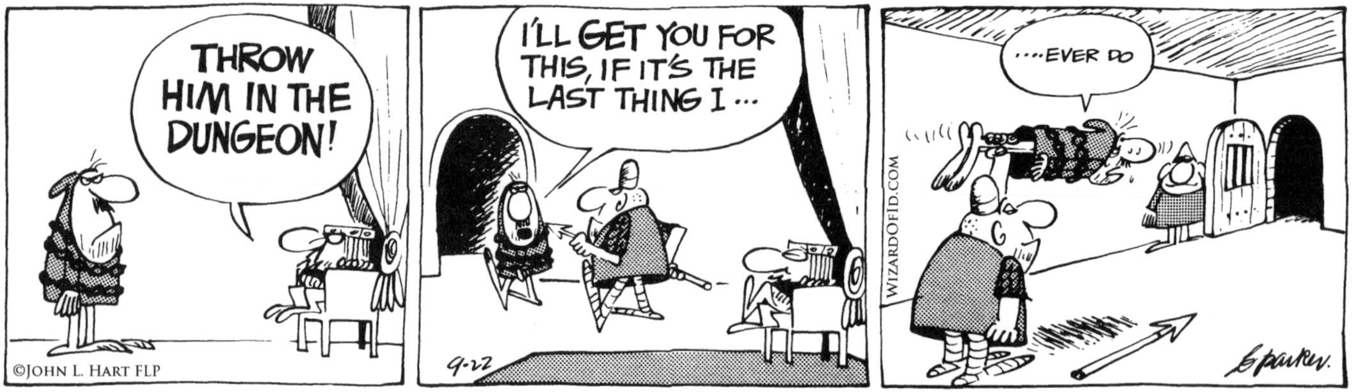
THROW HIM IN THE DUNGEON!
I'LL GET YOU FOR THIS, IF IT'S THE LAST THING I...
....EVER DO
©JOHN L. HART FLP
9-22
WIZARDOFID.COM

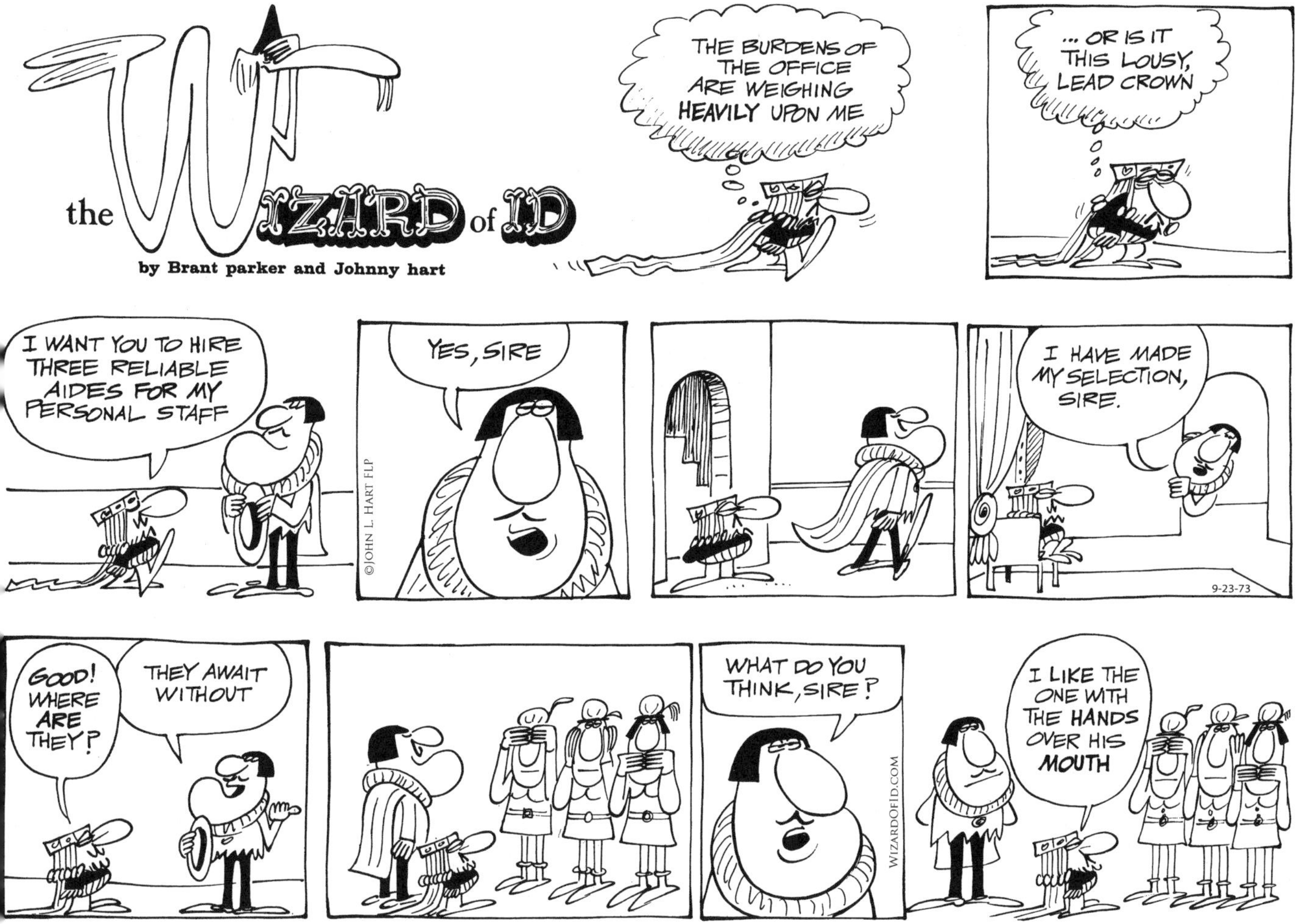
the WIZARD of ID
by Brant parker and Johnny hart
THE BURDENS OF THE OFFICE ARE WEIGHING HEAVILY UPON ME
... OR IS IT THIS LOUSY, LEAD CROWN
I WANT YOU TO HIRE THREE RELIABLE AIDES FOR MY PERSONAL STAFF
YES, SIRE
©JOHN L. HART FLP
I HAVE MADE MY SELECTION, SIRE.
9-23-73
GOOD! WHERE ARE THEY?
THEY AWAIT WITHOUT
WHAT DO YOU THINK, SIRE?
WIZARDOFID.COM
I LIKE THE ONE WITH THE HANDS OVER HIS MOUTH

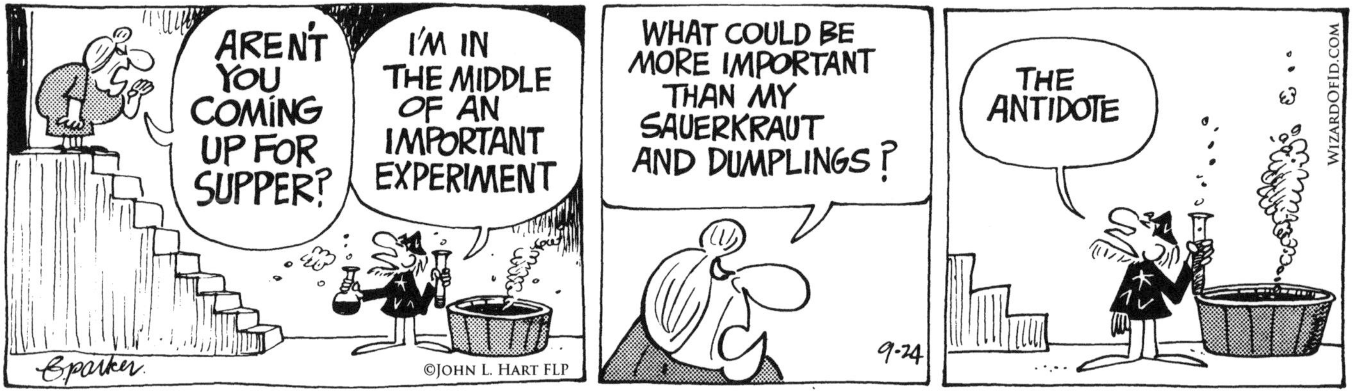
AREN'T YOU COMING UP FOR SUPPER?
I'M IN THE MIDDLE OF AN IMPORTANT EXPERIMENT
©JOHN L. HART FLP
WHAT COULD BE MORE IMPORTANT THAN MY SAUERKRAUT AND DUMPLINGS?
9-24
THE ANTIDOTE
WIZARDOFID.COM

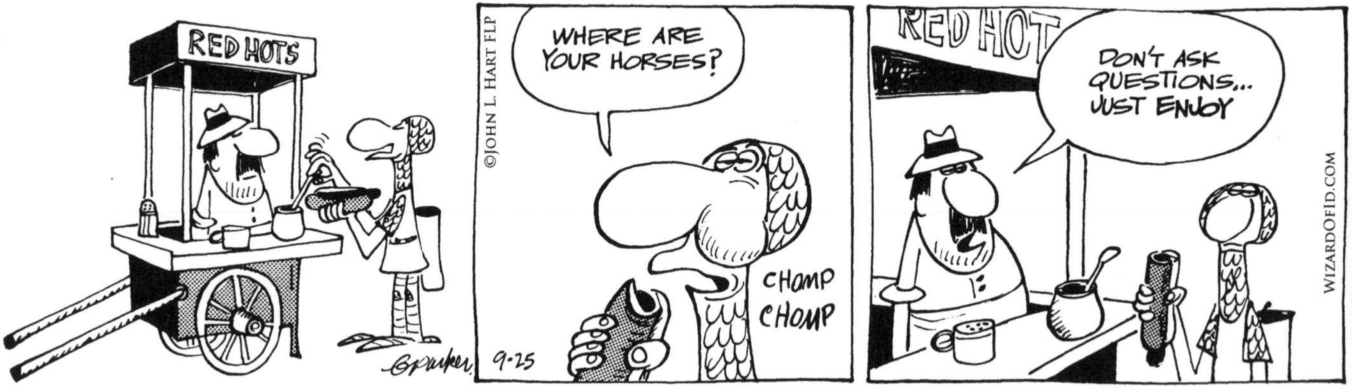
RED HOTS
©JOHN L. HART FLP
WHERE ARE YOUR HORSES?
CHOMP
CHOMP
9-25
RED HOT
DON'T ASK QUESTIONS... JUST ENJOY
WIZARDOFID.COM

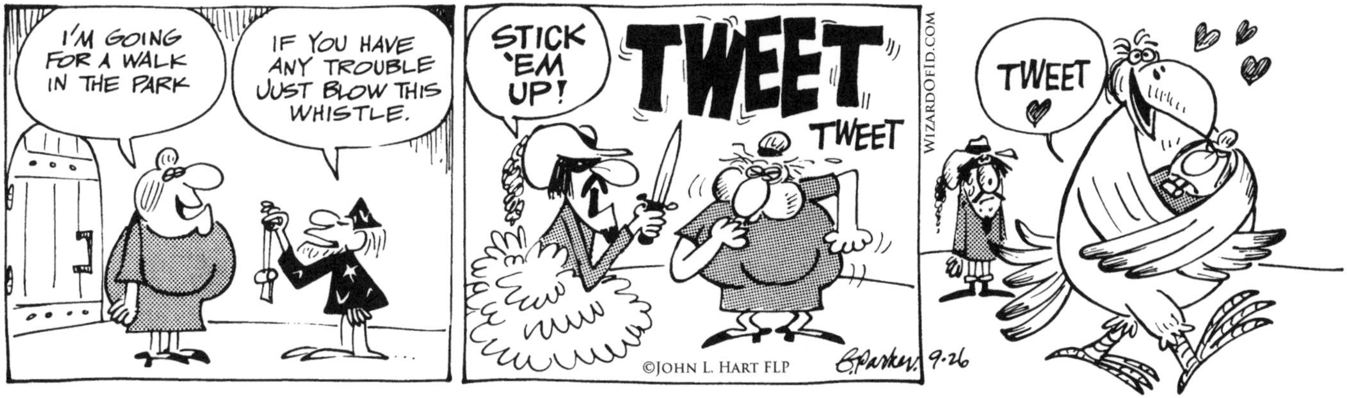
I'M GOING FOR A WALK IN THE PARK
IF YOU HAVE ANY TROUBLE JUST BLOW THIS WHISTLE.
STICK 'EM UP!
TWEET
TWEET
TWEET
©JOHN L. HART FLP
9-26
WIZARDOFID.COM

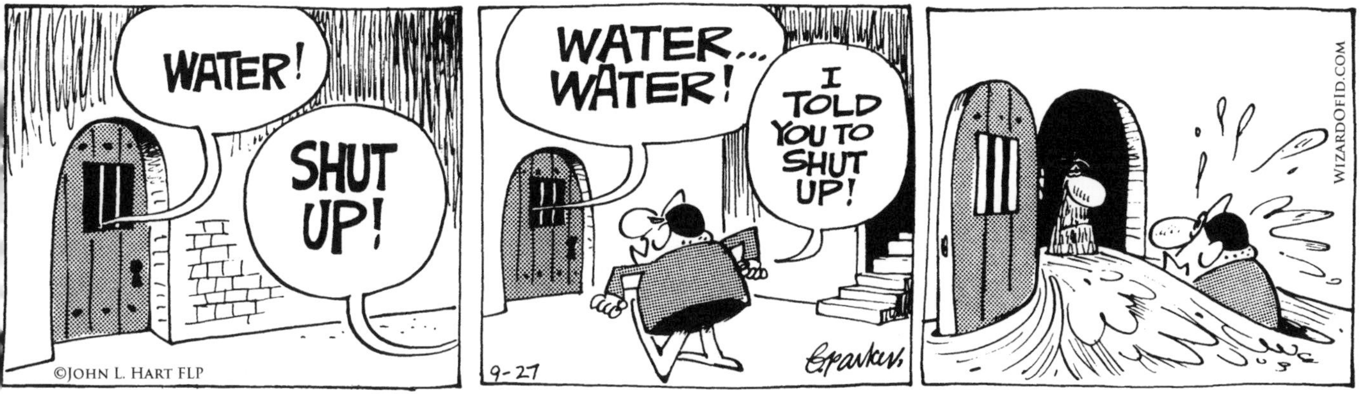
WATER!
SHUT UP!
WATER... WATER!
I TOLD YOU TO SHUT UP!
©JOHN L. HART FLP
9-27
WIZARDOFID.COM

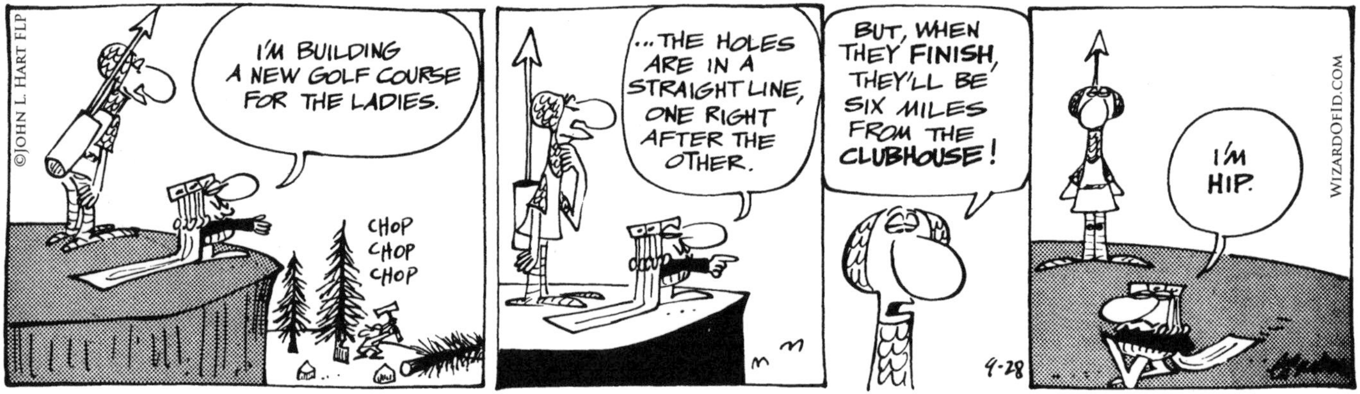
©JOHN L. HART FLP
I'M BUILDING A NEW GOLF COURSE FOR THE LADIES.
CHOP CHOP CHOP
...THE HOLES ARE IN A STRAIGHT LINE, ONE RIGHT AFTER THE OTHER.
BUT, WHEN THEY FINISH, THEY'LL BE SIX MILES FROM THE CLUBHOUSE!
4-28
I'M HIP.
WIZARDOFID.COM

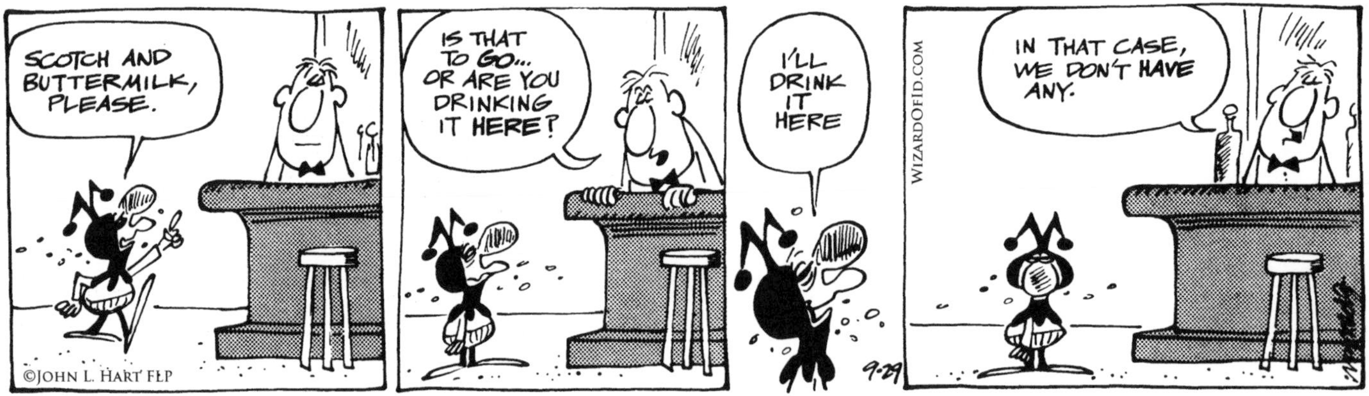
SCOTCH AND BUTTERMILK, PLEASE.
©JOHN L. HART FLP
IS THAT TO GO... OR ARE YOU DRINKING IT HERE?
I'LL DRINK IT HERE
9-29
WIZARDOFID.COM
IN THAT CASE, WE DON'T HAVE ANY.

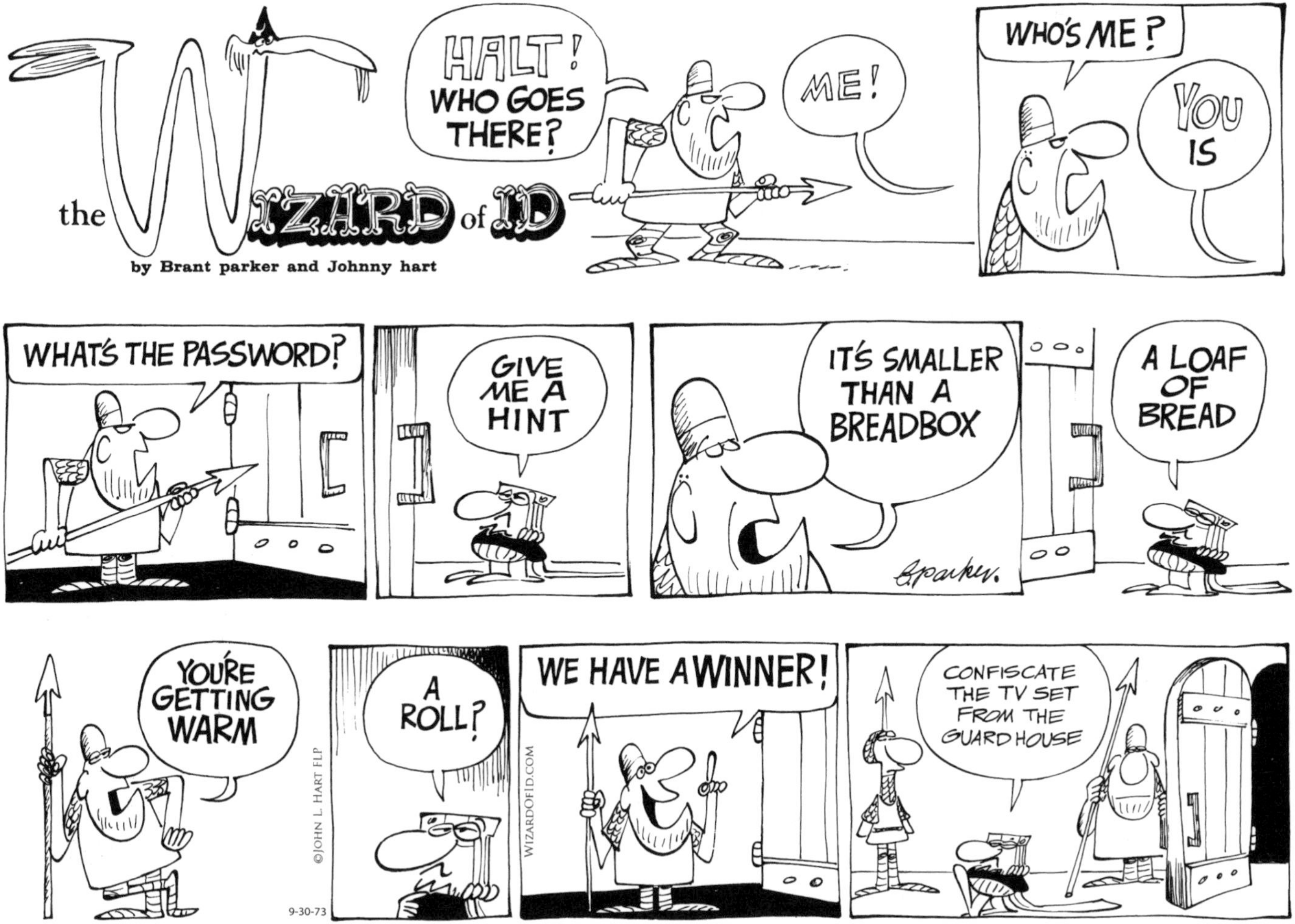
the WIZARD of ID
by Brant parker and Johnny hart
HALT! WHO GOES THERE?
ME!
WHO'S ME?
YOU IS
WHAT'S THE PASSWORD?
GIVE ME A HINT
IT'S SMALLER THAN A BREADBOX
A LOAF OF BREAD
YOU'RE GETTING WARM
A ROLL?
WE HAVE A WINNER!
CONFISCATE THE TV SET FROM THE GUARD HOUSE
©JOHN L. HART FLP
9-30-73
WIZARDOFID.COM

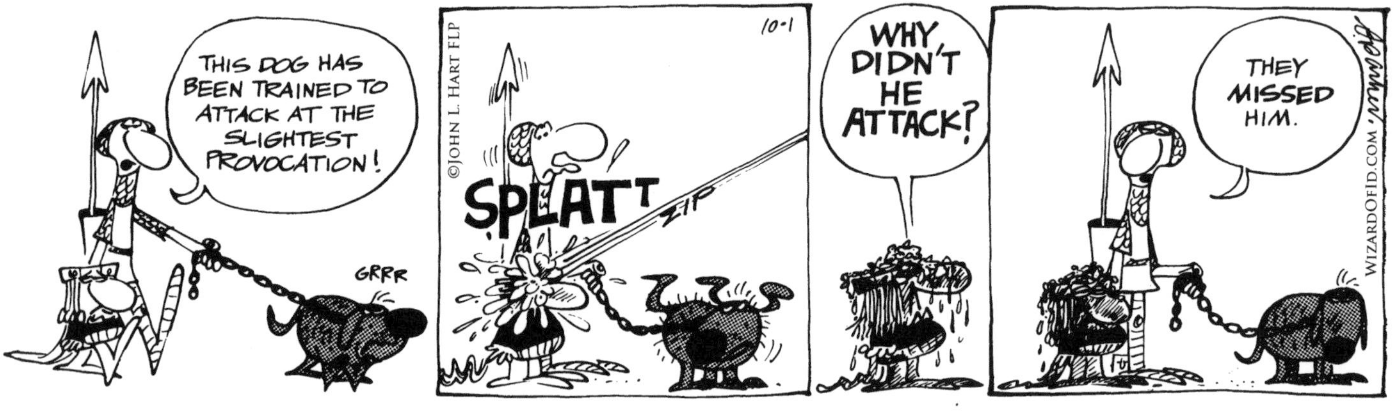
THIS DOG HAS BEEN TRAINED TO ATTACK AT THE SLIGHTEST PROVOCATION!
GRRR
©JOHN L. HART FLP
10-1
SPLATT
ZIP
WHY DIDN'T HE ATTACK?
THEY MISSED HIM.
WIZARDOFID.COM

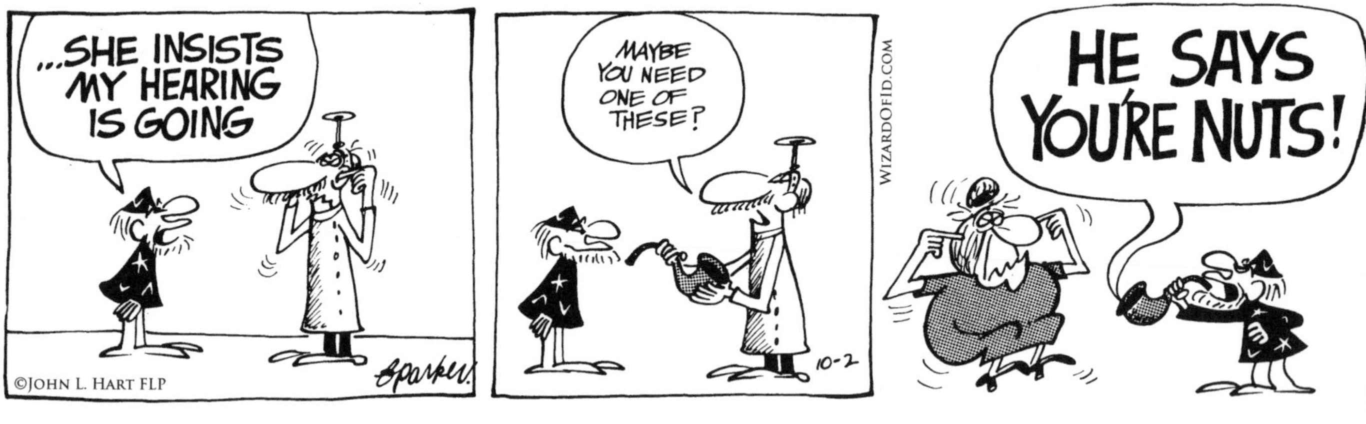
...SHE INSISTS MY HEARING IS GOING
©JOHN L. HART FLP
MAYBE YOU NEED ONE OF THESE?
WIZARDOFID.COM
10-2
HE SAYS YOU'RE NUTS!

ARE YOU A LEG-MAN, SIRE?
I HAVE NO CHOICE
10·3
WIZARDOFID.COM
©JOHN L. HART FLP

WE CAUGHT THIS PEEPING-TOM IN THE ACT!
WHAT HAVE YOU GOT TO SAY FOR YOURSELF?
HI, GUY!
10-4
WIZARDOFID.COM
©JOHN L. HART FLP

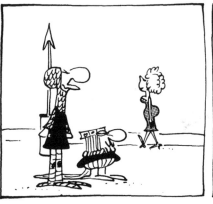

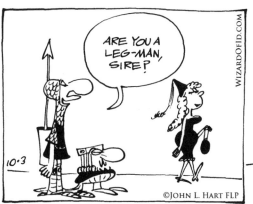

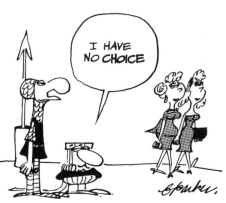

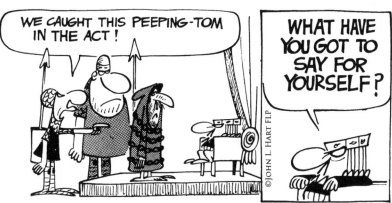

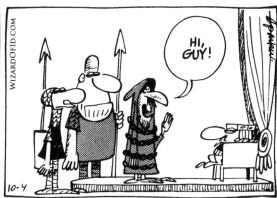

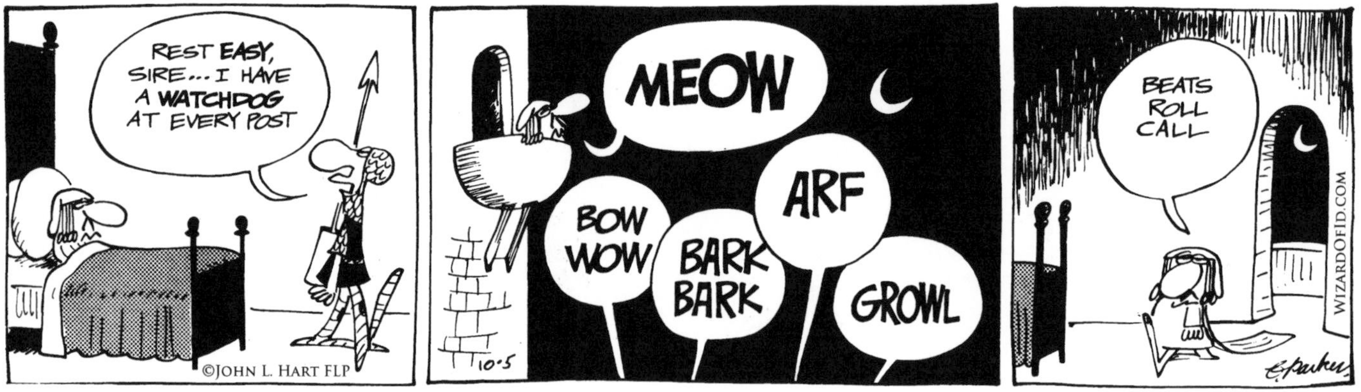

REST EASY, SIRE... I HAVE A WATCHDOG AT EVERY POST
©JOHN L. HART FLP
MEOW
BOW WOW
BARK BARK
ARF
GROWL
10-5
BEATS ROLL CALL
WIZARDOFID.COM

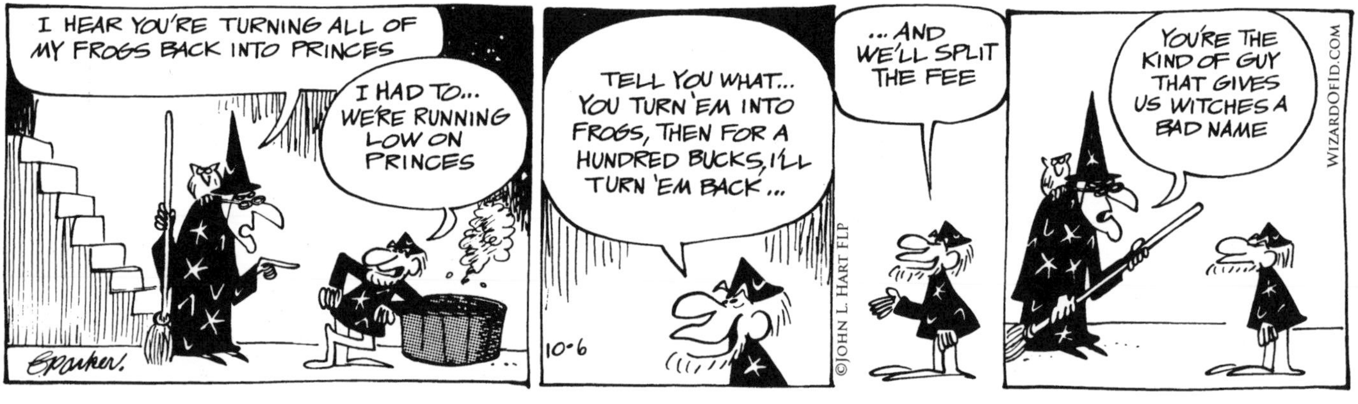

I HEAR YOU'RE TURNING ALL OF MY FROGS BACK INTO PRINCES
I HAD TO... WE'RE RUNNING LOW ON PRINCES
TELL YOU WHAT... YOU TURN 'EM INTO FROGS, THEN FOR A HUNDRED BUCKS, I'LL TURN 'EM BACK...
10-6
©JOHN L. HART FLP
... AND WE'LL SPLIT THE FEE
YOU'RE THE KIND OF GUY THAT GIVES US WITCHES A BAD NAME
WIZARDOFID.COM

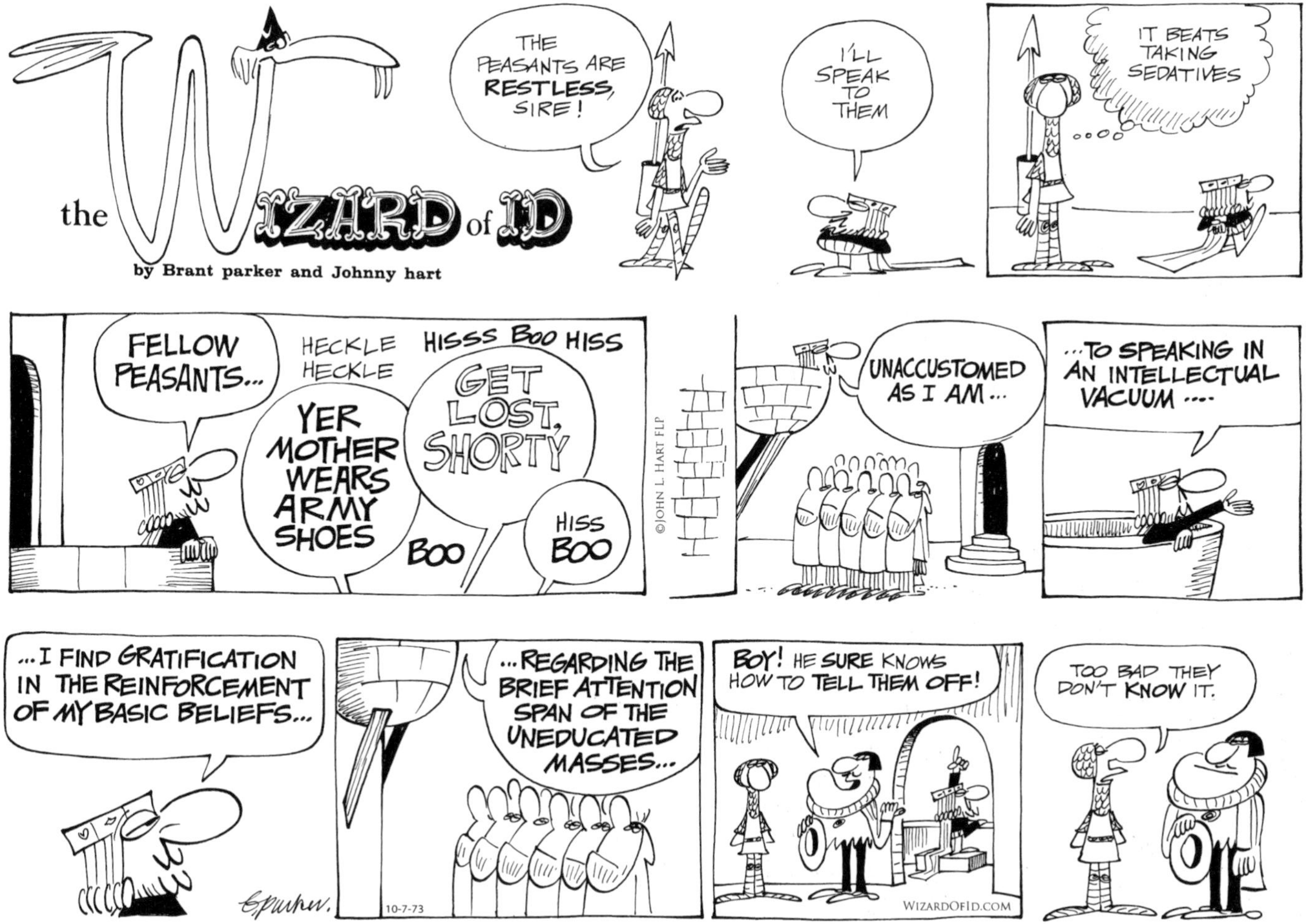
the WIZARD of ID
by Brant parker and Johnny hart
THE PEASANTS ARE RESTLESS, SIRE!
I'LL SPEAK TO THEM
IT BEATS TAKING SEDATIVES
FELLOW PEASANTS...
HECKLE HECKLE
HISSS BOO HISS
YER MOTHER WEARS ARMY SHOES
GET LOST, SHORTY
BOO
HISS BOO
©JOHN L. HART FLP
UNACCUSTOMED AS I AM...
...TO SPEAKING IN AN INTELLECTUAL VACUUM....
...I FIND GRATIFICATION IN THE REINFORCEMENT OF MY BASIC BELIEFS...
B parker.
...REGARDING THE BRIEF ATTENTION SPAN OF THE UNEDUCATED MASSES...
10-7-73
BOY! HE SURE KNOWS HOW TO TELL THEM OFF!
WIZARDOFID.COM
TOO BAD THEY DON'T KNOW IT.

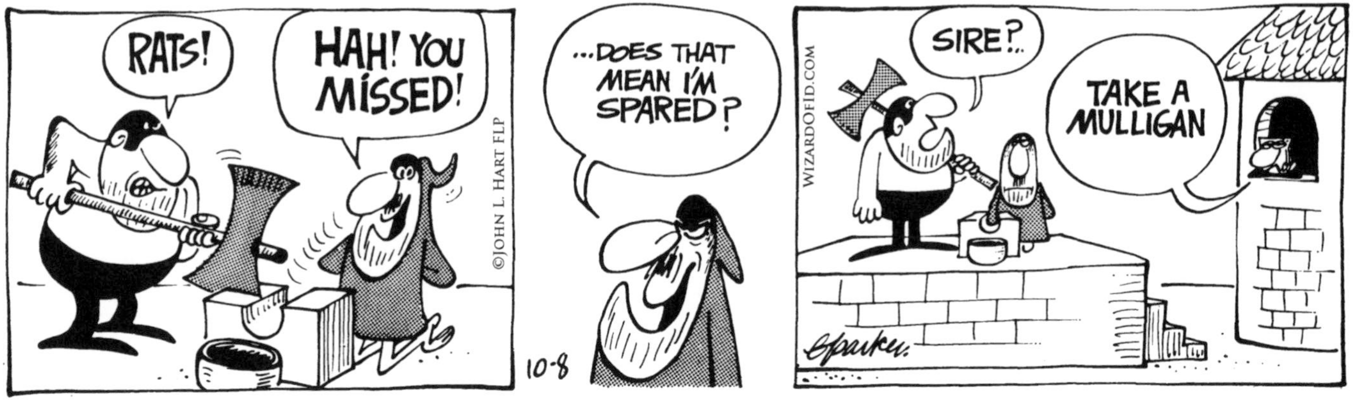
RATS!
HAH! YOU MISSED!
©JOHN L. HART FLP
10-8
...DOES THAT MEAN I'M SPARED?
WIZARDOFID.COM
SIRE?..
TAKE A MULLIGAN

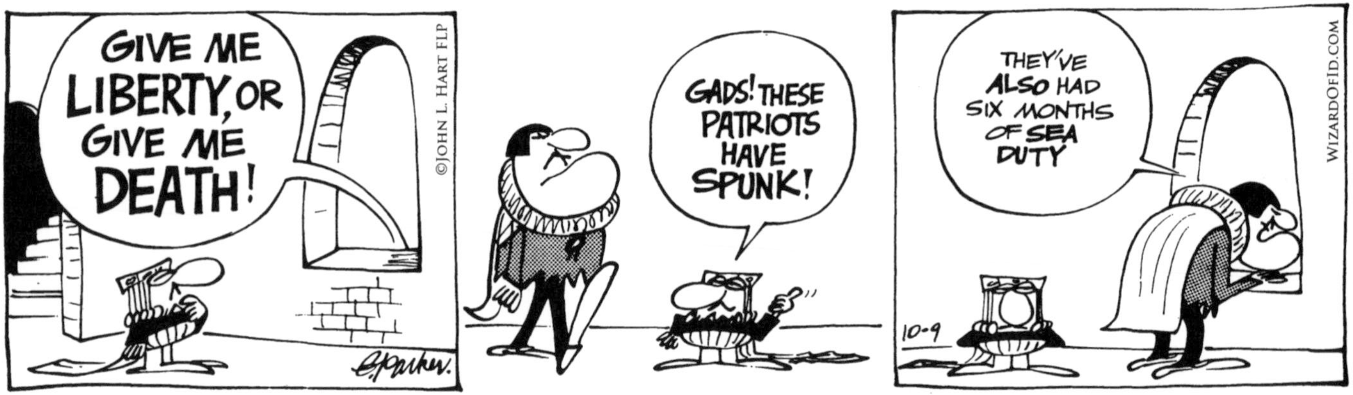
GIVE ME LIBERTY, OR GIVE ME DEATH!
©JOHN L. HART FLP
GADS! THESE PATRIOTS HAVE SPUNK!
THEY'VE ALSO HAD SIX MONTHS OF SEA DUTY
10-9
WIZARDOFID.COM

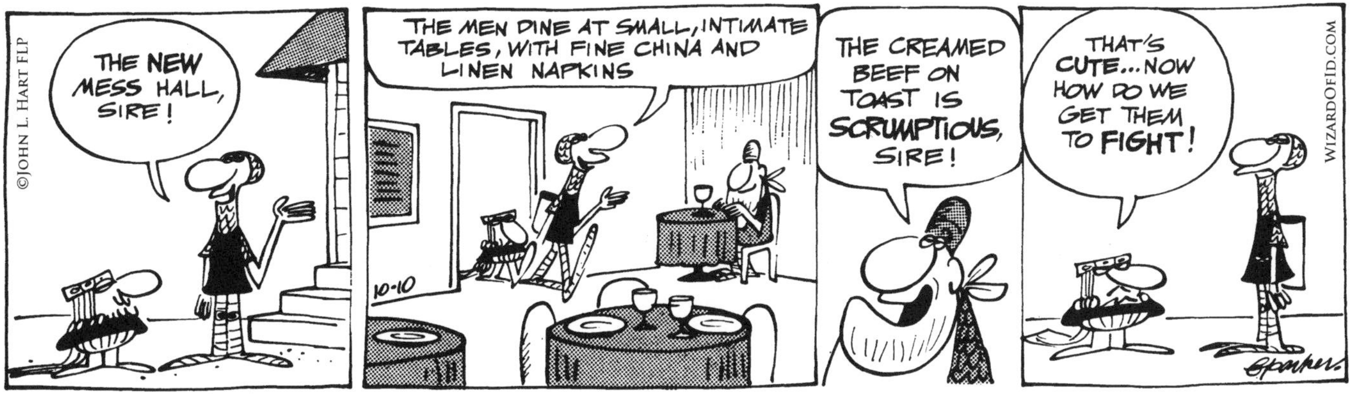

©JOHN L. HART FLP
THE NEW MESS HALL, SIRE!
THE MEN DINE AT SMALL, INTIMATE TABLES, WITH FINE CHINA AND LINEN NAPKINS
10-10
THE CREAMED BEEF ON TOAST IS SCRUMPTIOUS, SIRE!
THAT'S CUTE...NOW HOW DO WE GET THEM TO FIGHT!
WIZARDOFID.COM

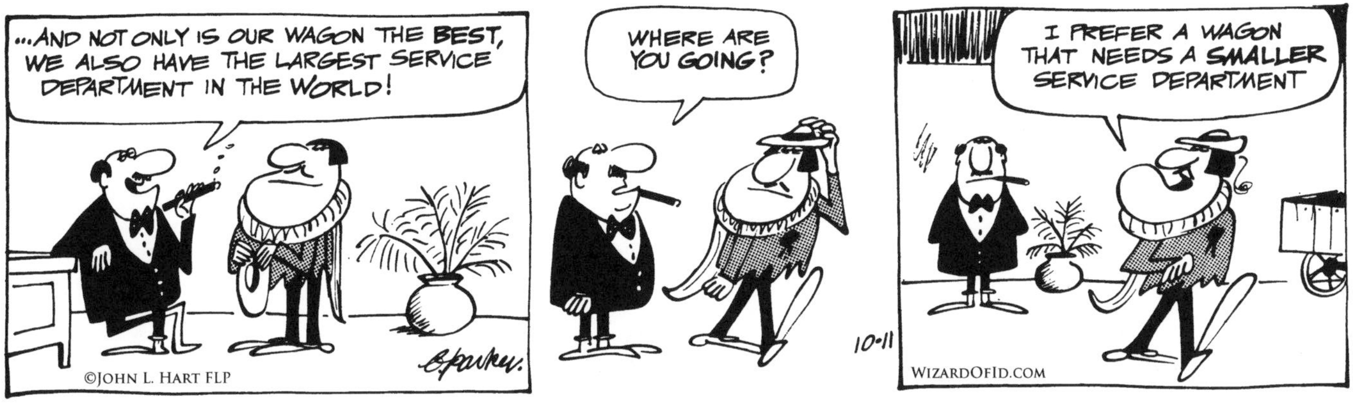

...AND NOT ONLY IS OUR WAGON THE BEST, WE ALSO HAVE THE LARGEST SERVICE DEPARTMENT IN THE WORLD!
©JOHN L. HART FLP
WHERE ARE YOU GOING?
10-11
I PREFER A WAGON THAT NEEDS A SMALLER SERVICE DEPARTMENT
WIZARDOFID.COM

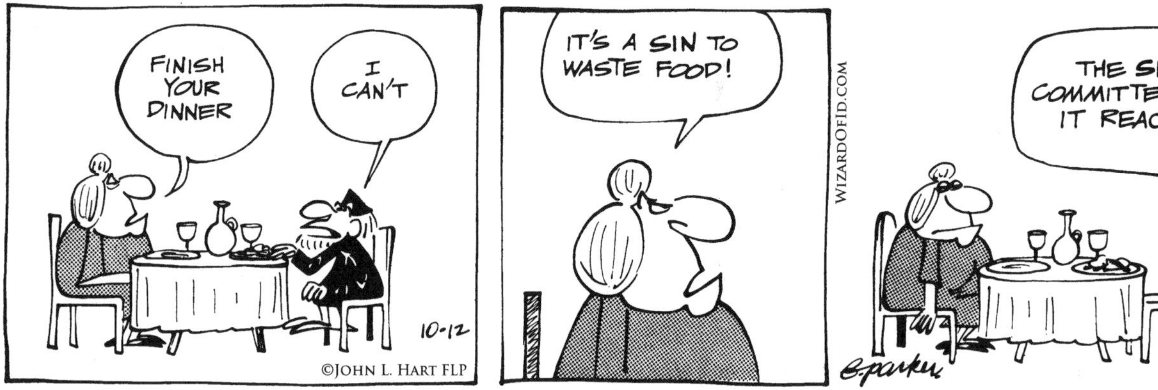
FINISH YOUR DINNER
I CAN'T
10-12
©JOHN L. HART FLP
IT'S A SIN TO WASTE FOOD!
WIZARDOFID.COM
THE SIN WAS COMMITTED BEFORE IT REACHED ME

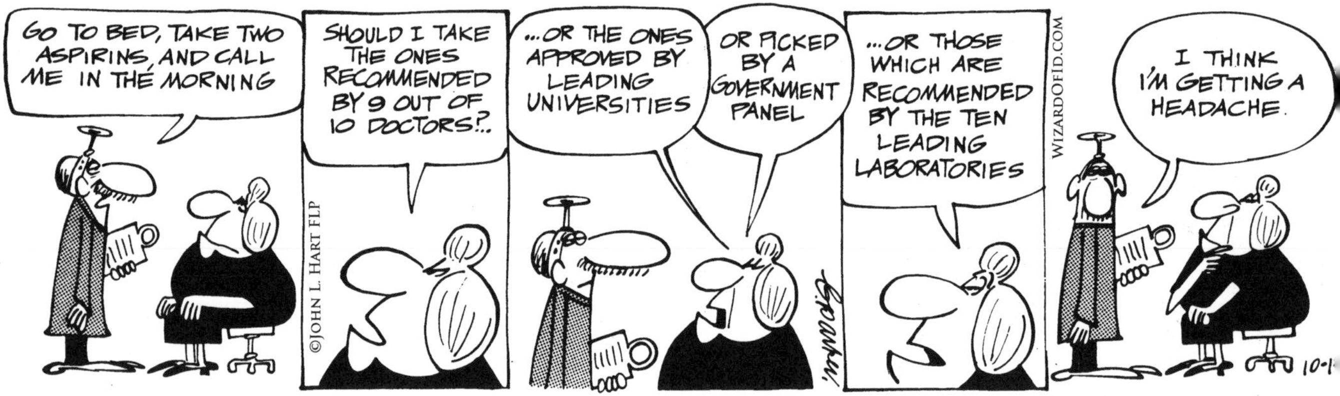
GO TO BED, TAKE TWO ASPIRINS, AND CALL ME IN THE MORNING
SHOULD I TAKE THE ONES RECOMMENDED BY 9 OUT OF 10 DOCTORS?..
©JOHN L. HART FLP
...OR THE ONES APPROVED BY LEADING UNIVERSITIES
OR PICKED BY A GOVERNMENT PANEL
...OR THOSE WHICH ARE RECOMMENDED BY THE TEN LEADING LABORATORIES
WIZARDOFID.COM
I THINK I'M GETTING A HEADACHE.

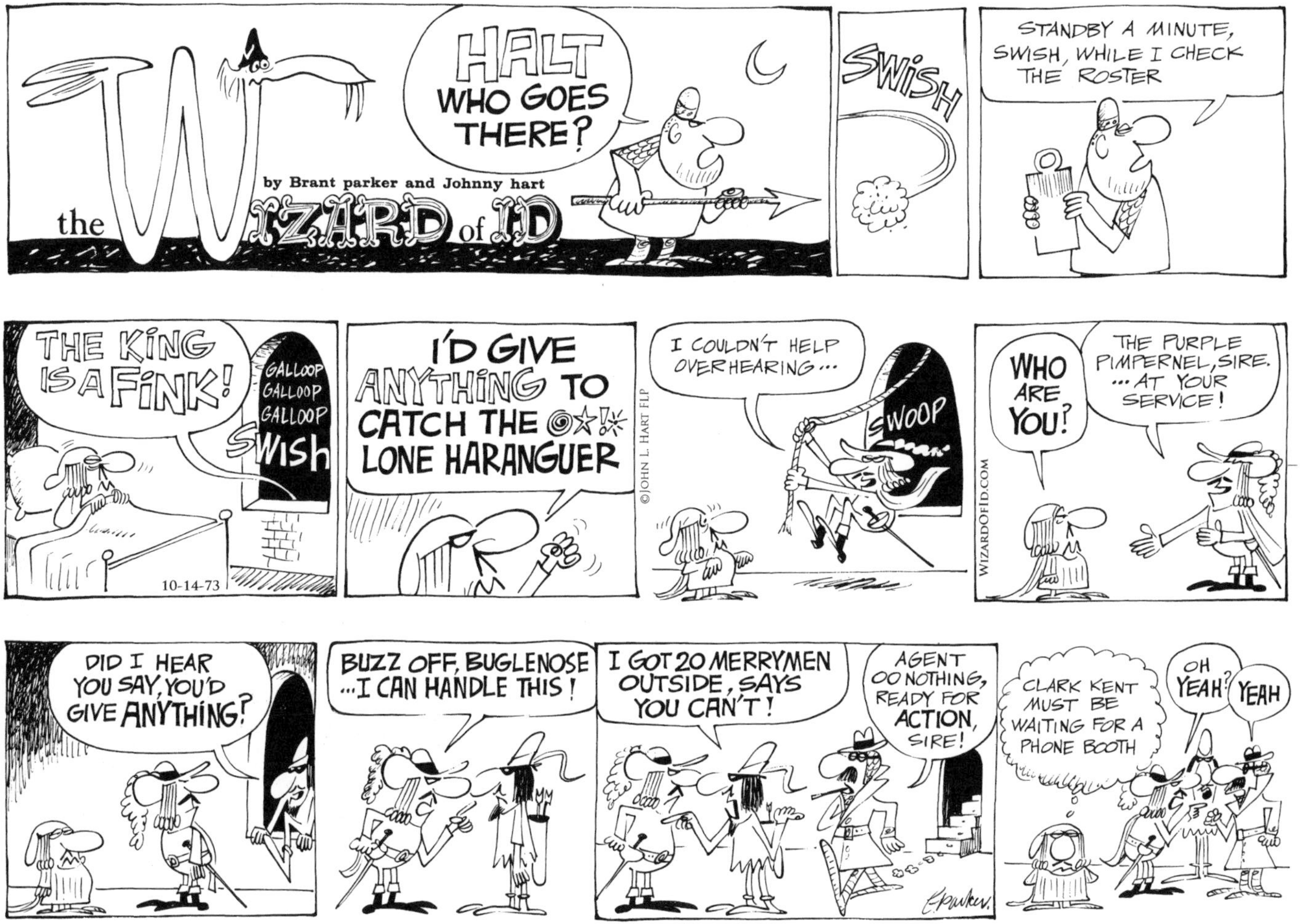
the WIZARD of ID
by Brant parker and Johnny hart
HALT WHO GOES THERE?
SWISH
STANDBY A MINUTE, SWISH, WHILE I CHECK THE ROSTER
THE KING IS A FINK!
GALLOOP GALLOOP GALLOOP
SWISH
10-14-73
I'D GIVE ANYTHING TO CATCH THE @☆!* LONE HARANGUER
©JOHN L. HART FLP
I COULDN'T HELP OVERHEARING...
SWOOP
WHO ARE YOU?
THE PURPLE PIMPERNEL, SIRE. ...AT YOUR SERVICE!
WIZARDOFID.COM
DID I HEAR YOU SAY, YOU'D GIVE ANYTHING?
BUZZ OFF, BUGLENOSE ...I CAN HANDLE THIS!
I GOT 20 MERRYMEN OUTSIDE, SAYS YOU CAN'T!
AGENT OO NOTHING, READY FOR ACTION, SIRE!
CLARK KENT MUST BE WAITING FOR A PHONE BOOTH
OH YEAH?
YEAH

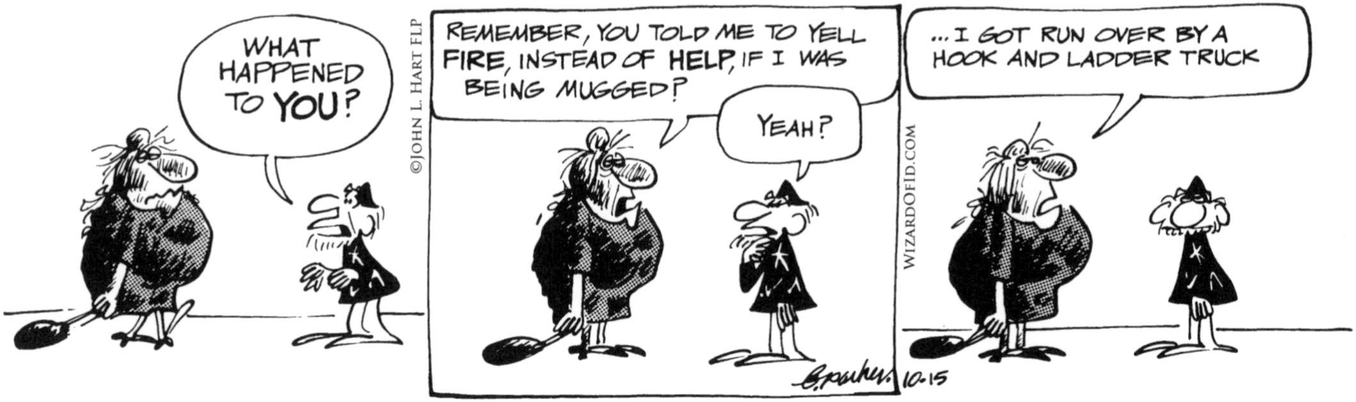
WHAT HAPPENED TO YOU?
©JOHN L. HART FLP
REMEMBER, YOU TOLD ME TO YELL FIRE, INSTEAD OF HELP, IF I WAS BEING MUGGED?
YEAH?
10-15
WIZARDOFID.COM
...I GOT RUN OVER BY A HOOK AND LADDER TRUCK

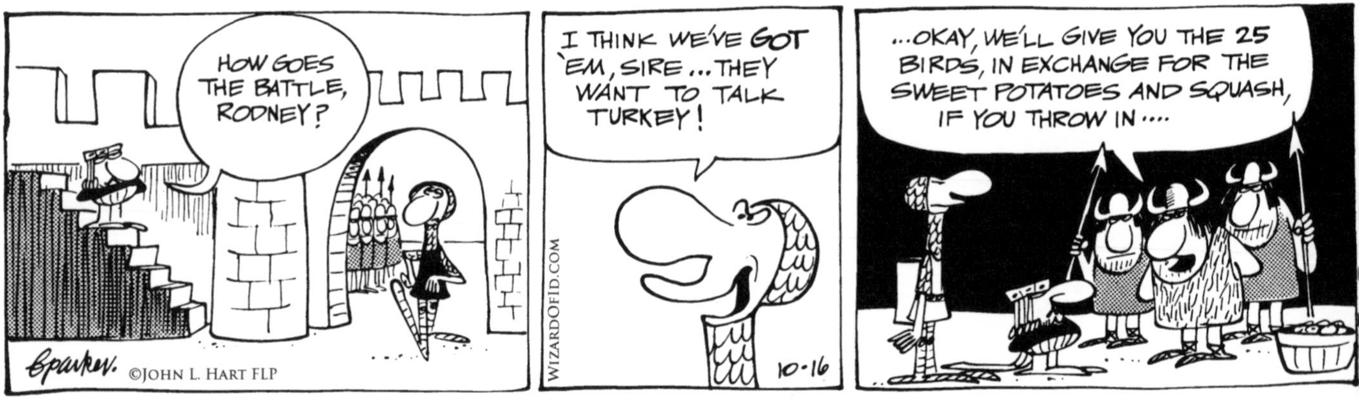
HOW GOES THE BATTLE, RODNEY?
©JOHN L. HART FLP
WIZARDOFID.COM
I THINK WE'VE GOT 'EM, SIRE ... THEY WANT TO TALK TURKEY!
10-16
...OKAY, WE'LL GIVE YOU THE 25 BIRDS, IN EXCHANGE FOR THE SWEET POTATOES AND SQUASH, IF YOU THROW IN....

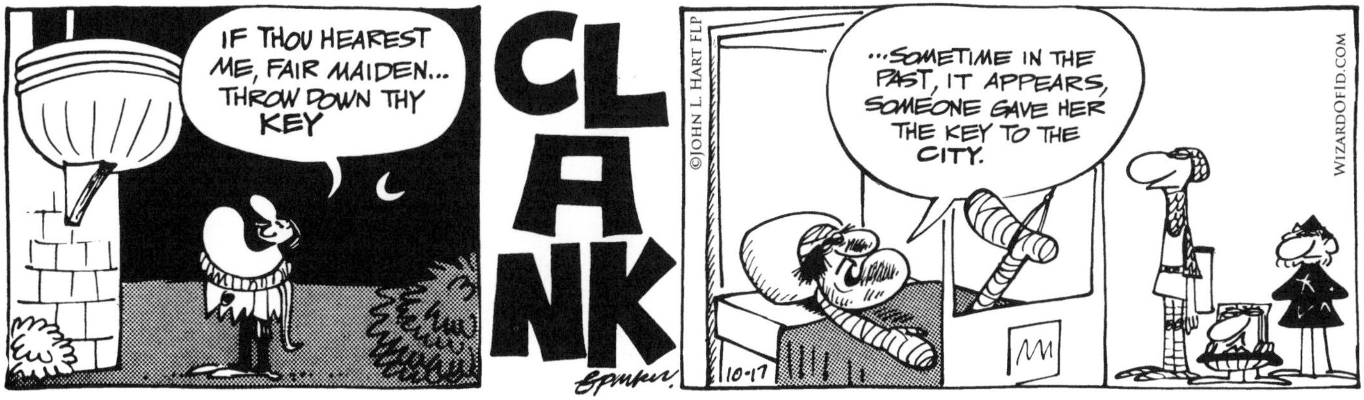
IF THOU HEAREST ME, FAIR MAIDEN... THROW DOWN THY KEY
CLANK
©JOHN L. HART FLP
10-17
...SOMETIME IN THE PAST, IT APPEARS, SOMEONE GAVE HER THE KEY TO THE CITY.
WIZARDOFID.COM

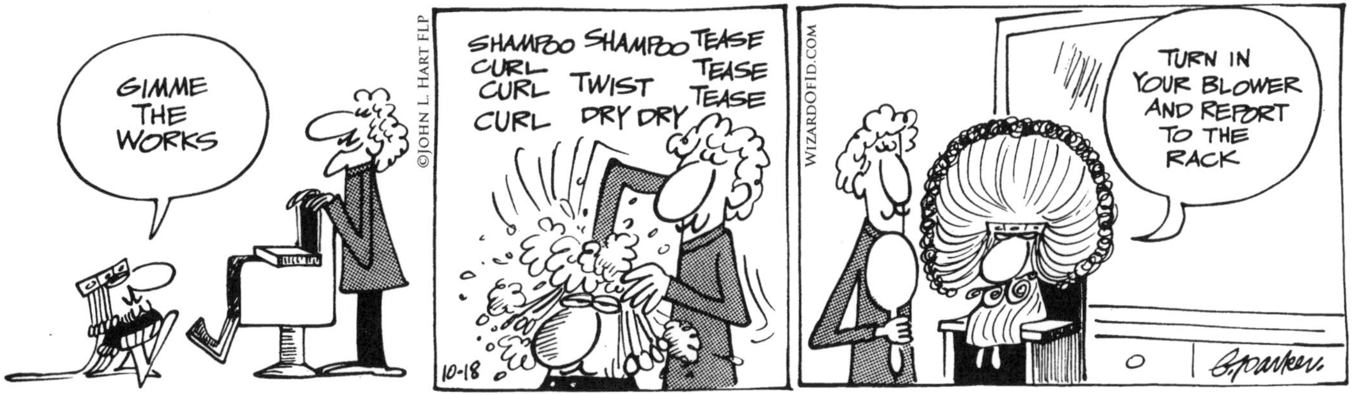
GIMME THE WORKS
©JOHN L. HART FLP
SHAMPOO SHAMPOO TEASE
CURL
CURL TWIST TEASE
TEASE
CURL DRY DRY
10-18
WIZARDOFID.COM
TURN IN YOUR BLOWER AND REPORT TO THE RACK

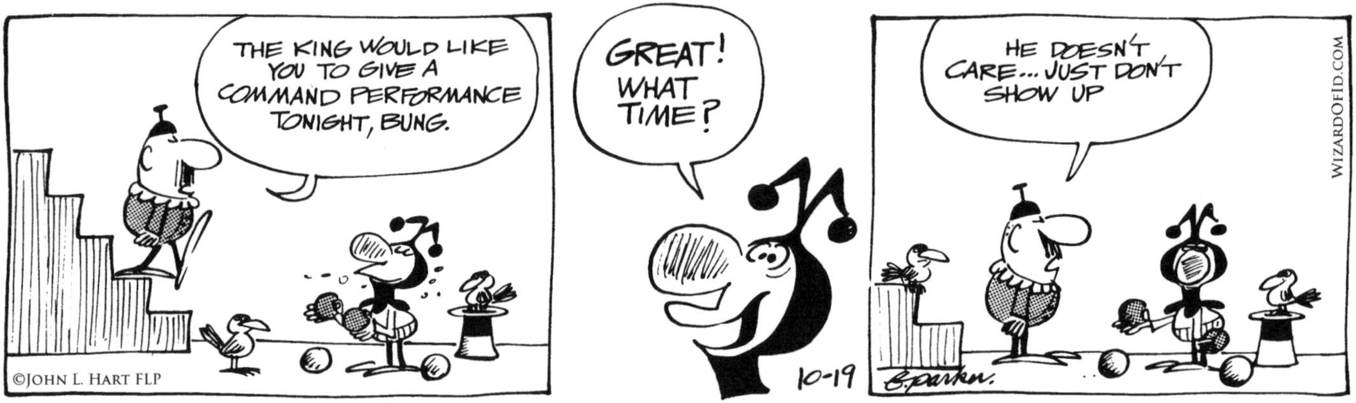
THE KING WOULD LIKE YOU TO GIVE A COMMAND PERFORMANCE TONIGHT, BUNG.
GREAT! WHAT TIME?
HE DOESN'T CARE... JUST DON'T SHOW UP
©JOHN L. HART FLP
10-19
WIZARDOFID.COM

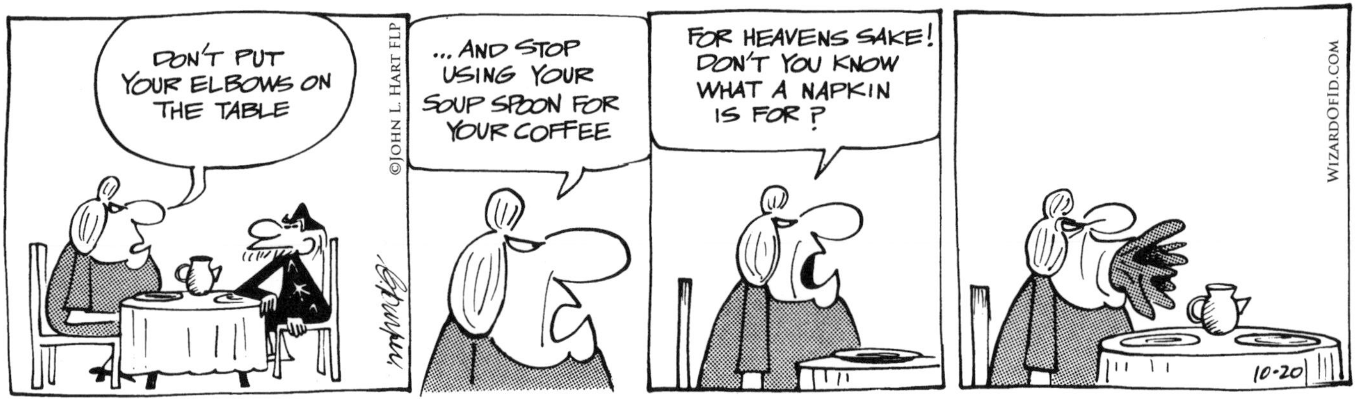
DON'T PUT YOUR ELBOWS ON THE TABLE
©JOHN L. HART FLP
...AND STOP USING YOUR SOUP SPOON FOR YOUR COFFEE
FOR HEAVENS SAKE! DON'T YOU KNOW WHAT A NAPKIN IS FOR?
10-20
WIZARDOFID.COM

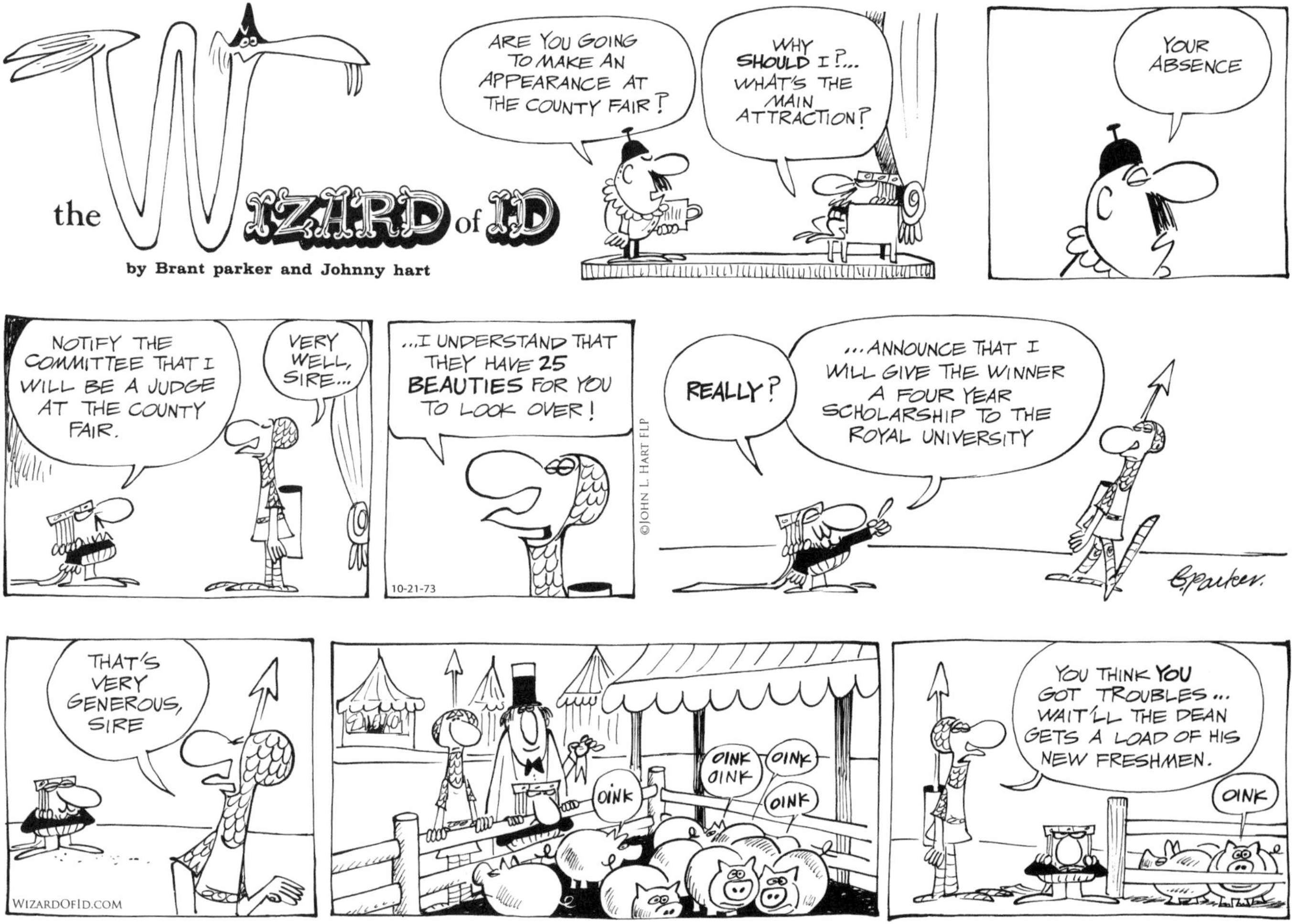

the WIZARD of ID
by Brant parker and Johnny hart
ARE YOU GOING TO MAKE AN APPEARANCE AT THE COUNTY FAIR?
WHY SHOULD I?... WHAT'S THE MAIN ATTRACTION?
YOUR ABSENCE
NOTIFY THE COMMITTEE THAT I WILL BE A JUDGE AT THE COUNTY FAIR.
VERY WELL, SIRE...
...I UNDERSTAND THAT THEY HAVE 25 BEAUTIES FOR YOU TO LOOK OVER!
10-21-73
©JOHN L. HART FLP
REALLY?
...ANNOUNCE THAT I WILL GIVE THE WINNER A FOUR YEAR SCHOLARSHIP TO THE ROYAL UNIVERSITY
B.parker.
THAT'S VERY GENEROUS, SIRE
WIZARDOFID.COM
OINK
OINK OINK
OINK
OINK
YOU THINK YOU GOT TROUBLES... WAIT'LL THE DEAN GETS A LOAD OF HIS NEW FRESHMEN.
OINK

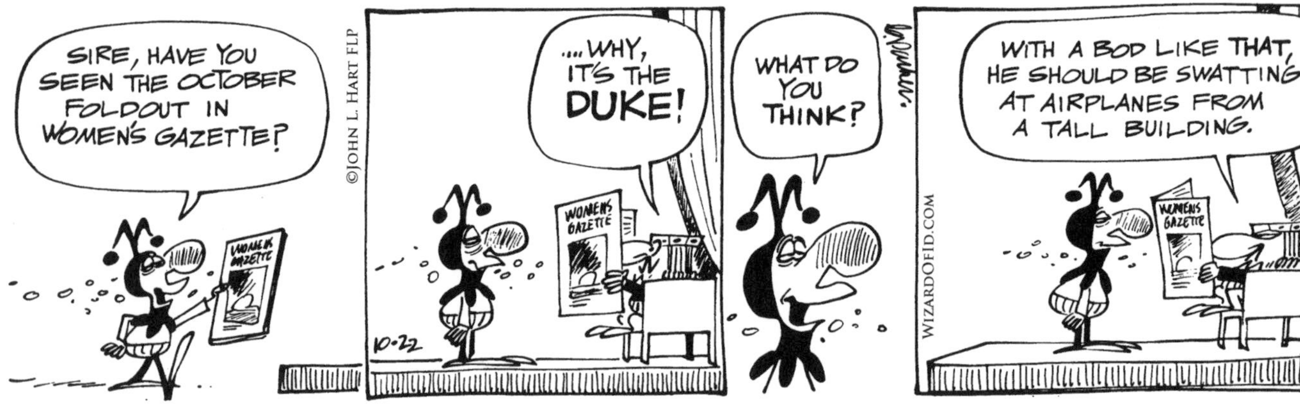
SIRE, HAVE YOU SEEN THE OCTOBER FOLDOUT IN WOMEN'S GAZETTE?
WOMEN'S GAZETTE
©JOHN L. HART FLP
...WHY, IT'S THE DUKE!
WOMENS GAZETTE
10-22
WHAT DO YOU THINK?
WITH A BOD LIKE THAT, HE SHOULD BE SWATTING AT AIRPLANES FROM A TALL BUILDING.
WOMENS GAZETTE
WIZARDOFID.COM

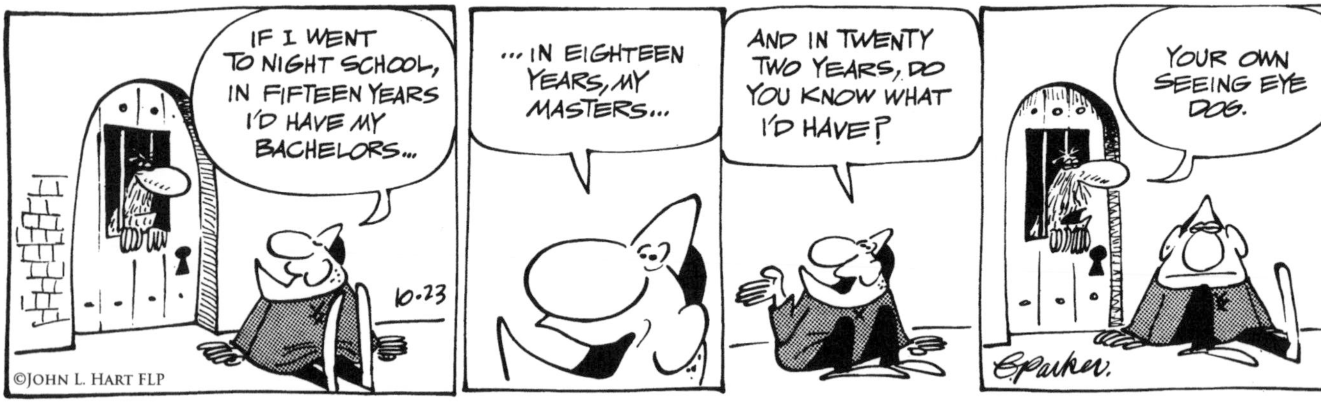
IF I WENT TO NIGHT SCHOOL, IN FIFTEEN YEARS I'D HAVE MY BACHELORS...
10-23
©JOHN L. HART FLP
...IN EIGHTEEN YEARS, MY MASTERS...
AND IN TWENTY TWO YEARS, DO YOU KNOW WHAT I'D HAVE?
YOUR OWN SEEING EYE DOG.
B.Parker.
WIZARDOFID.COM

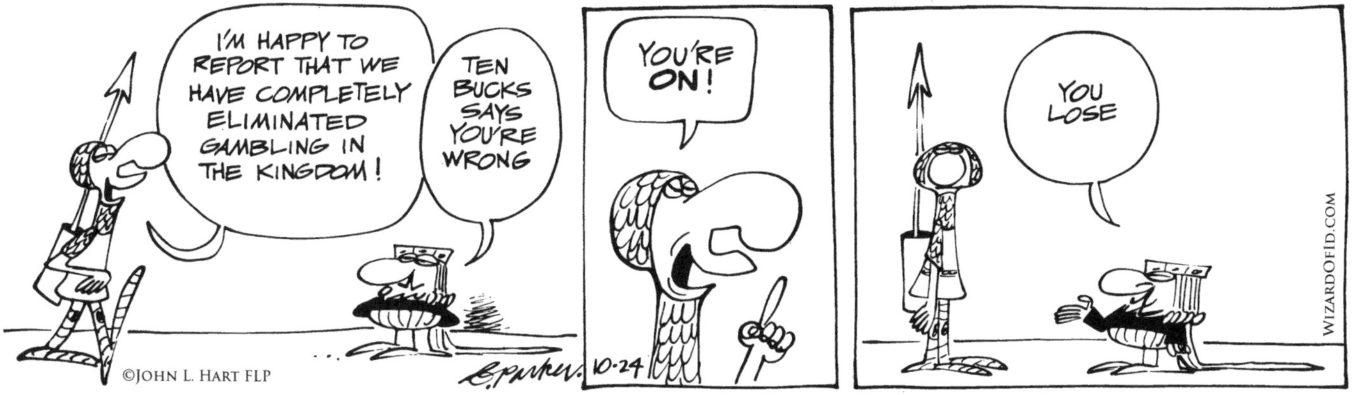
I'M HAPPY TO REPORT THAT WE HAVE COMPLETELY ELIMINATED GAMBLING IN THE KINGDOM!
TEN BUCKS SAYS YOU'RE WRONG
YOU'RE ON!
YOU LOSE
©JOHN L. HART FLP
WIZARDOFID.COM
10-24

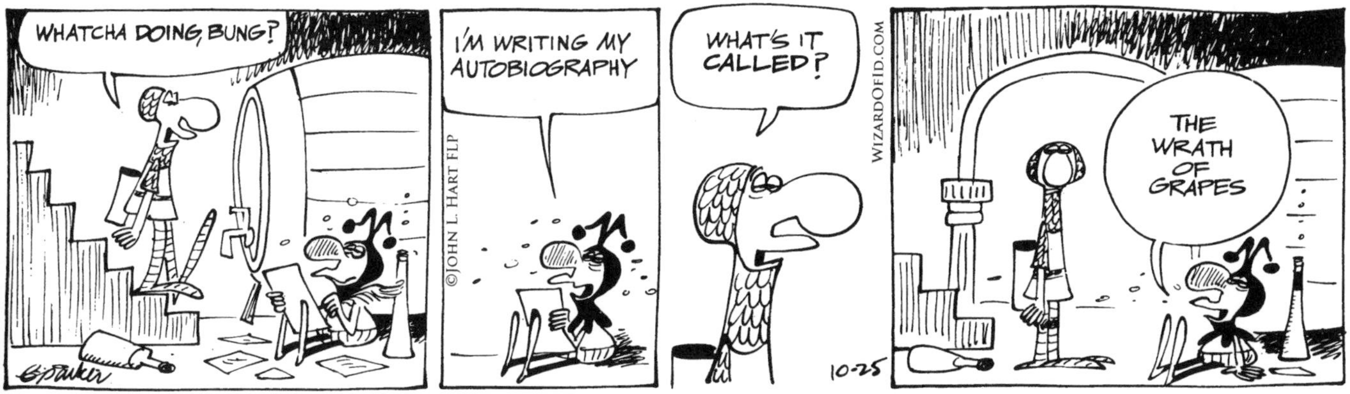
WHATCHA DOING, BUNG?
I'M WRITING MY AUTOBIOGRAPHY
WHAT'S IT CALLED?
THE WRATH OF GRAPES
©JOHN L. HART FLP
WIZARDOFID.COM
10-25

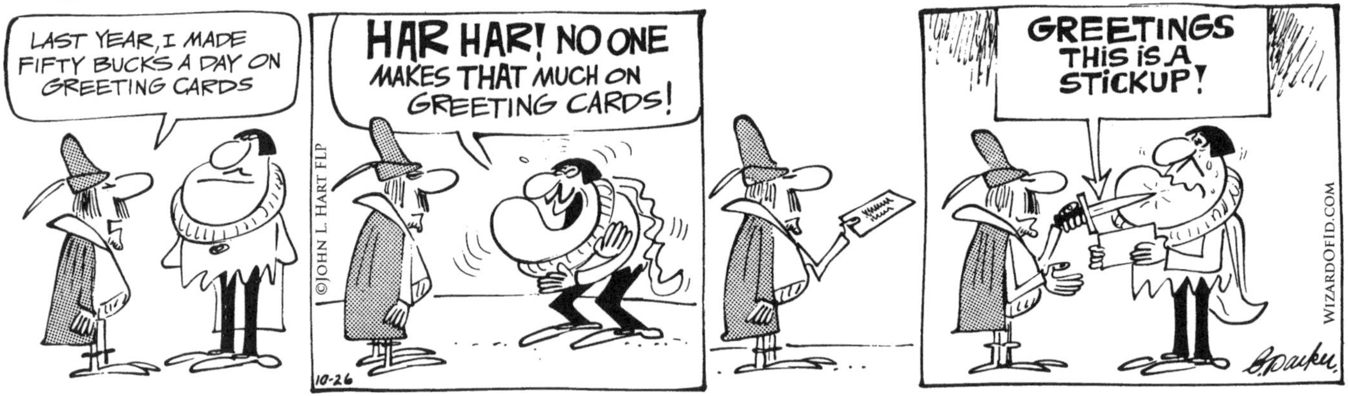
LAST YEAR, I MADE FIFTY BUCKS A DAY ON GREETING CARDS
HAR HAR! NO ONE MAKES THAT MUCH ON GREETING CARDS!
GREETINGS THIS IS A STICKUP!
©JOHN L. HART FLP
10-26
WIZARDOFID.COM

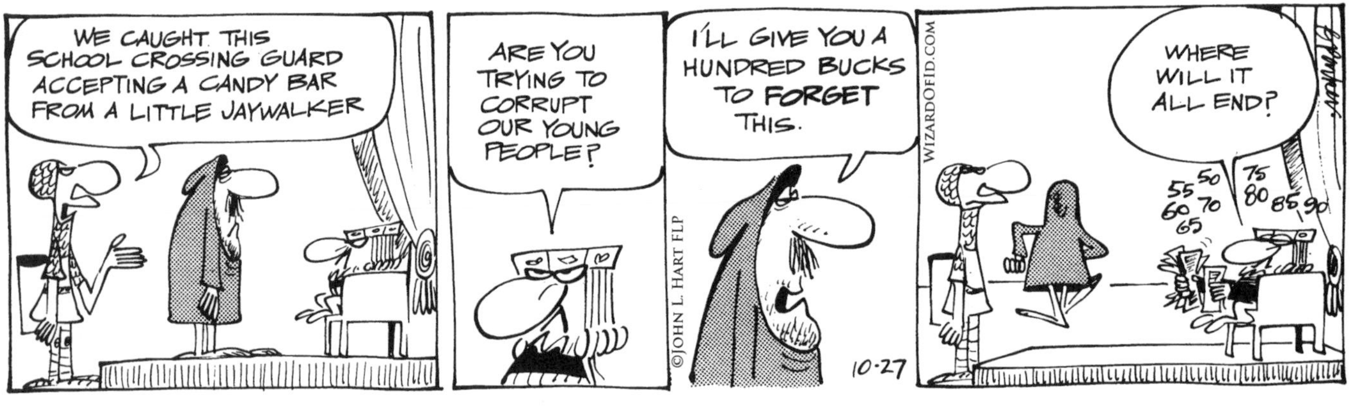
WE CAUGHT THIS SCHOOL CROSSING GUARD ACCEPTING A CANDY BAR FROM A LITTLE JAYWALKER
ARE YOU TRYING TO CORRUPT OUR YOUNG PEOPLE?
I'LL GIVE YOU A HUNDRED BUCKS TO FORGET THIS.
©JOHN L. HART FLP
10-27
WIZARDOFID.COM
WHERE WILL IT ALL END?
50 55 60 65 70 75 80 85 90

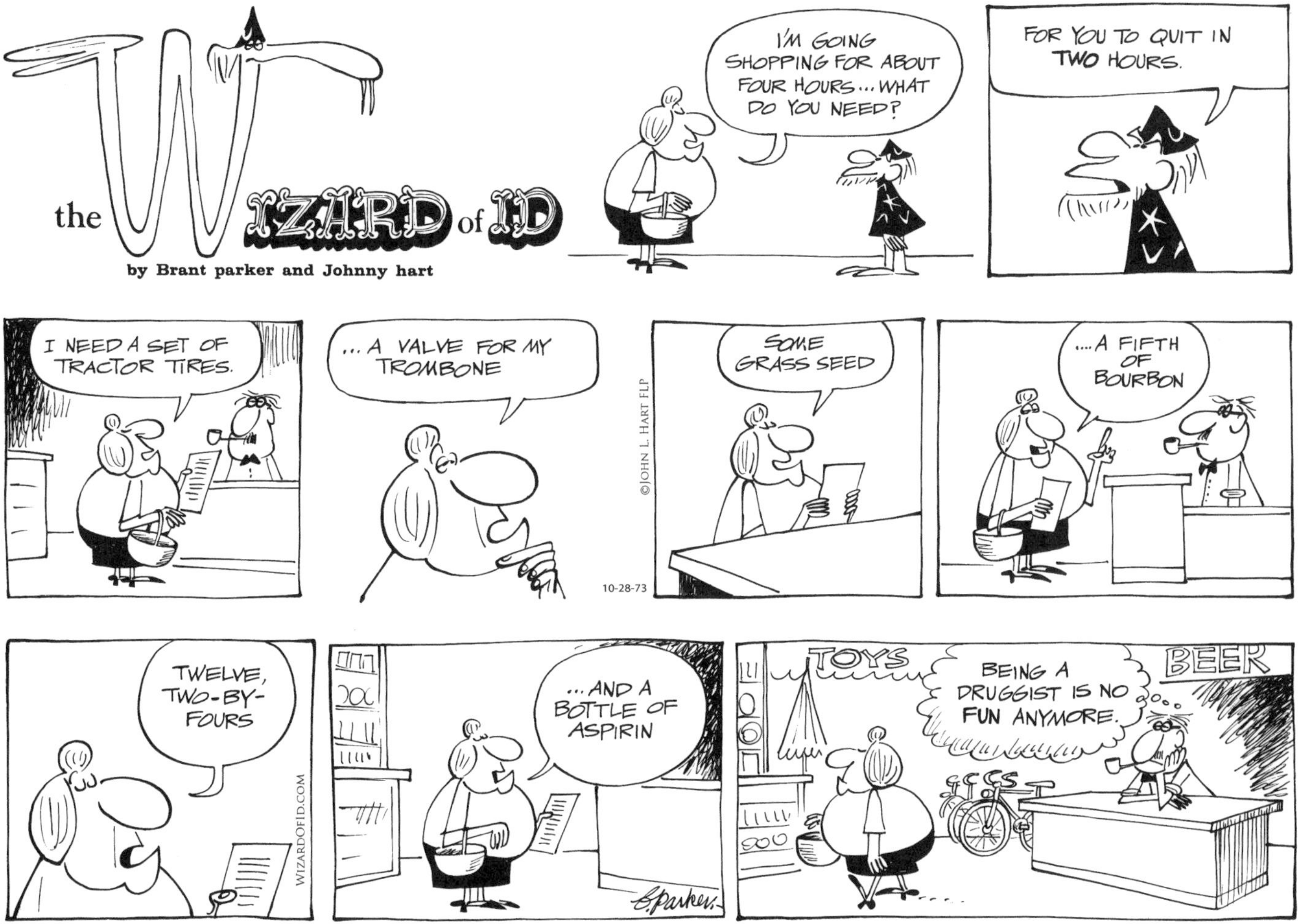
the WIZARD of ID
by Brant parker and Johnny hart
I'M GOING SHOPPING FOR ABOUT FOUR HOURS... WHAT DO YOU NEED?
FOR YOU TO QUIT IN TWO HOURS.
I NEED A SET OF TRACTOR TIRES.
... A VALVE FOR MY TROMBONE
©JOHN L. HART FLP
10-28-73
SOME GRASS SEED
....A FIFTH OF BOURBON
TWELVE, TWO-BY-FOURS
WIZARDOFID.COM
...AND A BOTTLE OF ASPIRIN
B.Parker
TOYS
BEER
BEING A DRUGGIST IS NO FUN ANYMORE.

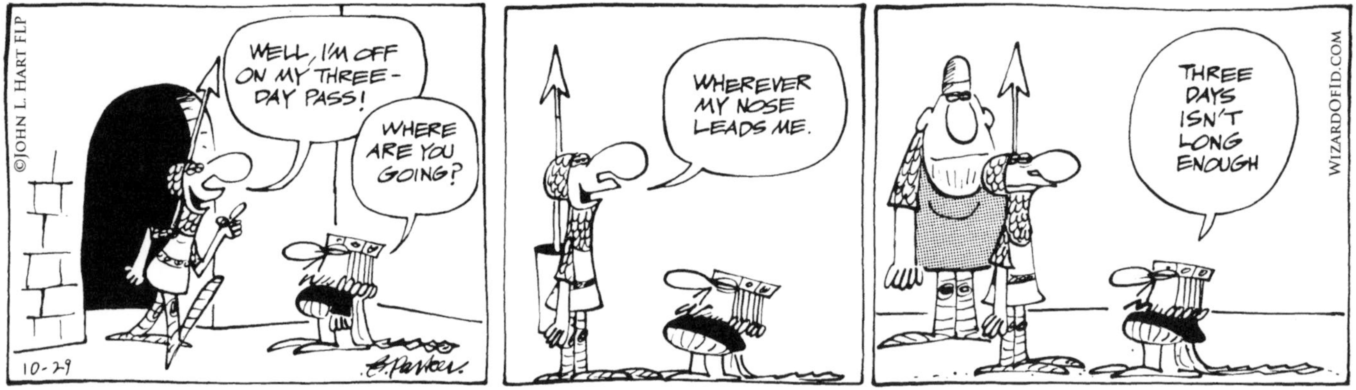
©JOHN L. HART FLP
WELL, I'M OFF ON MY THREE-DAY PASS!
WHERE ARE YOU GOING?
WHEREVER MY NOSE LEADS ME.
THREE DAYS ISN'T LONG ENOUGH
WIZARDOFID.COM
10-29

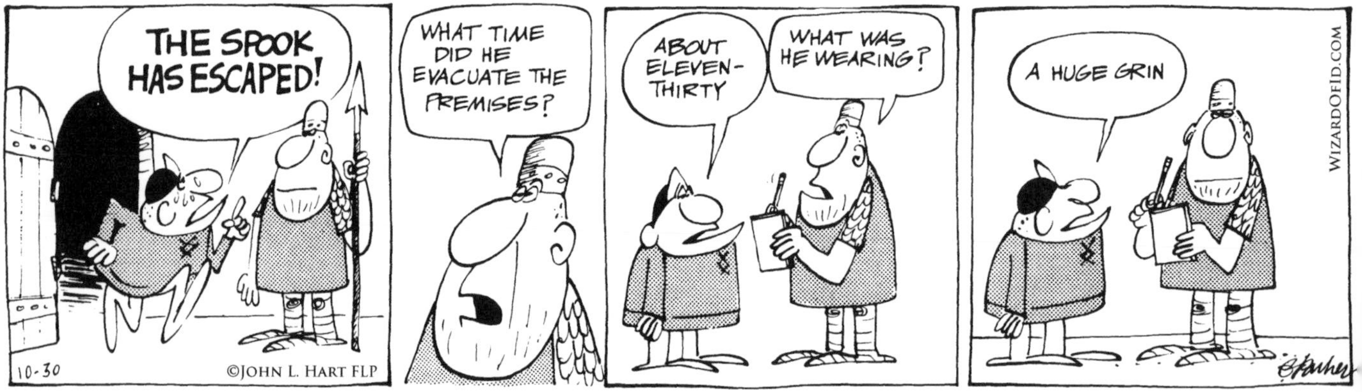
THE SPOOK HAS ESCAPED!
10-30
©JOHN L. HART FLP
WHAT TIME DID HE EVACUATE THE PREMISES?
ABOUT ELEVEN-THIRTY
WHAT WAS HE WEARING?
A HUGE GRIN
WIZARDOFID.COM

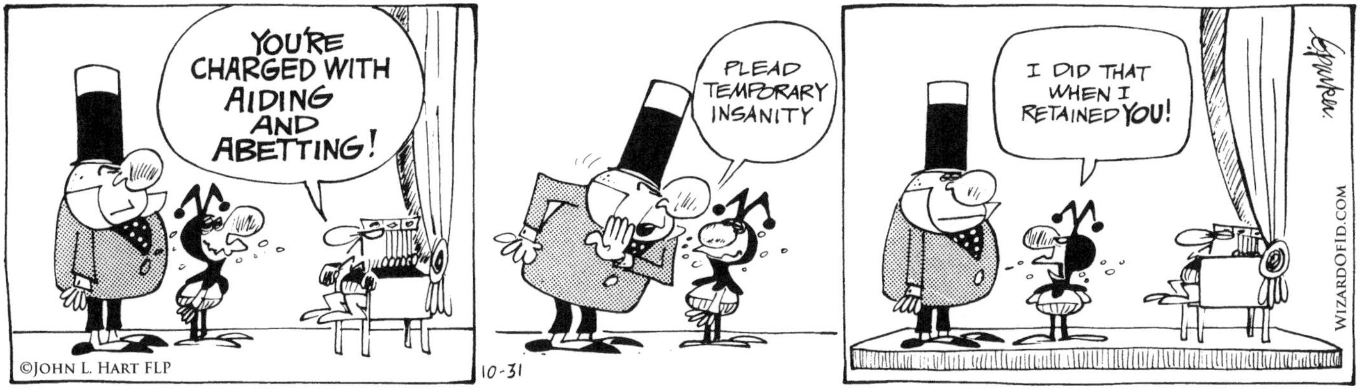
YOU'RE CHARGED WITH AIDING AND ABETTING!
©JOHN L. HART FLP
PLEAD TEMPORARY INSANITY
10-31
I DID THAT WHEN I RETAINED YOU!
WIZARDOFID.COM

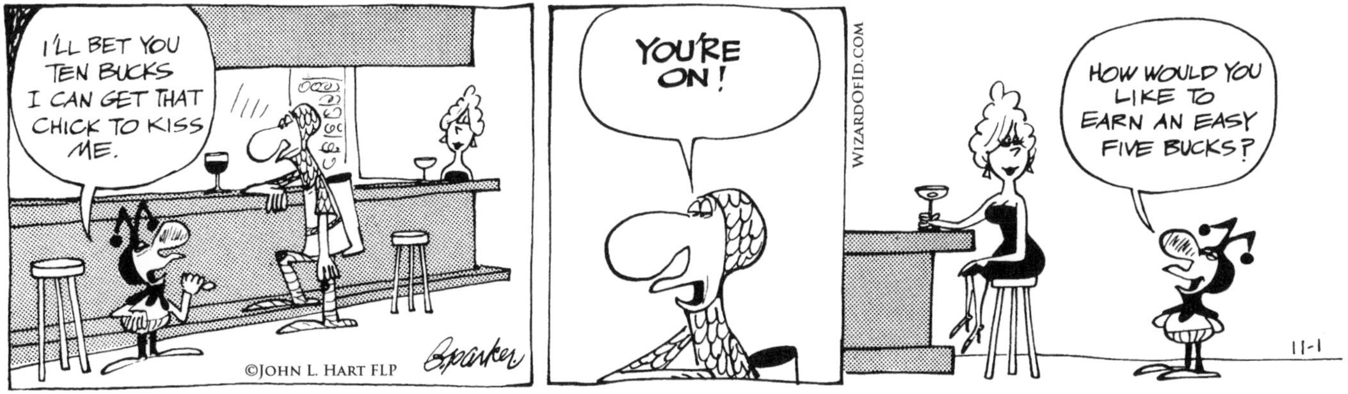
I'LL BET YOU TEN BUCKS I CAN GET THAT CHICK TO KISS ME.
©JOHN L. HART FLP
YOU'RE ON!
WIZARDOFID.COM
HOW WOULD YOU LIKE TO EARN AN EASY FIVE BUCKS?
11-1

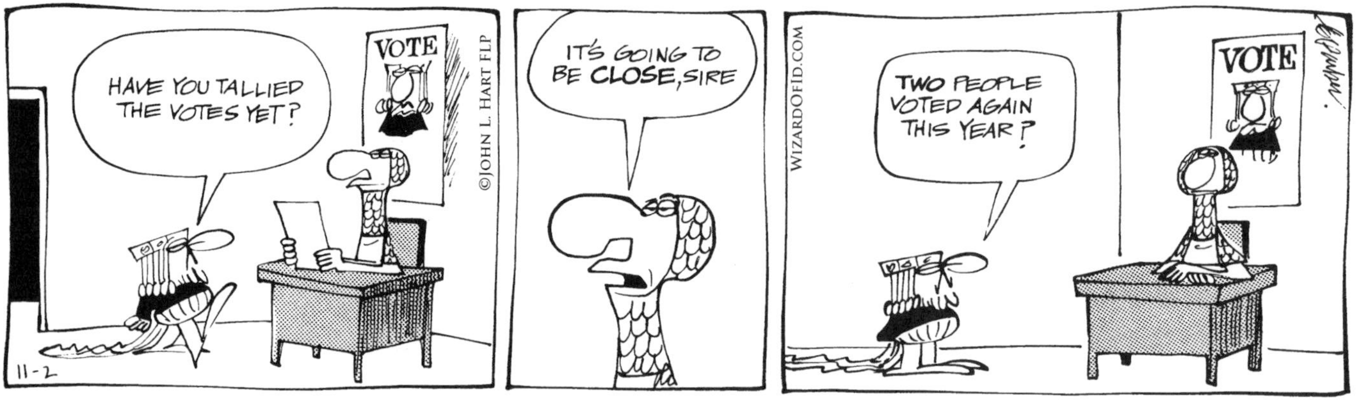
HAVE YOU TALLIED THE VOTES YET?
VOTE
©JOHN L. HART FLP
11-2
IT'S GOING TO BE CLOSE, SIRE
WIZARDOFID.COM
TWO PEOPLE VOTED AGAIN THIS YEAR?
VOTE

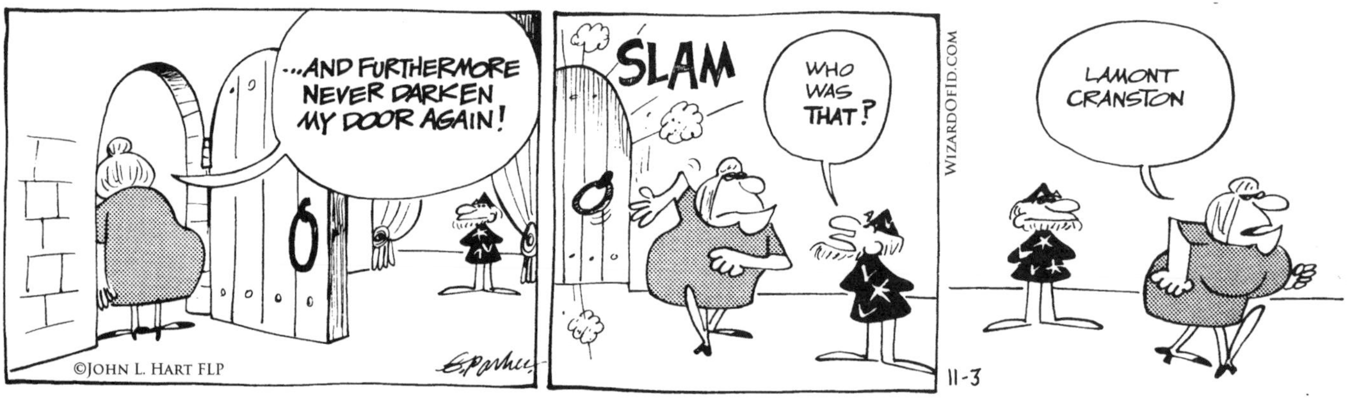
...AND FURTHERMORE NEVER DARKEN MY DOOR AGAIN!
©JOHN L. HART FLP
SLAM
WHO WAS THAT?
WIZARDOFID.COM
11-3
LAMONT CRANSTON

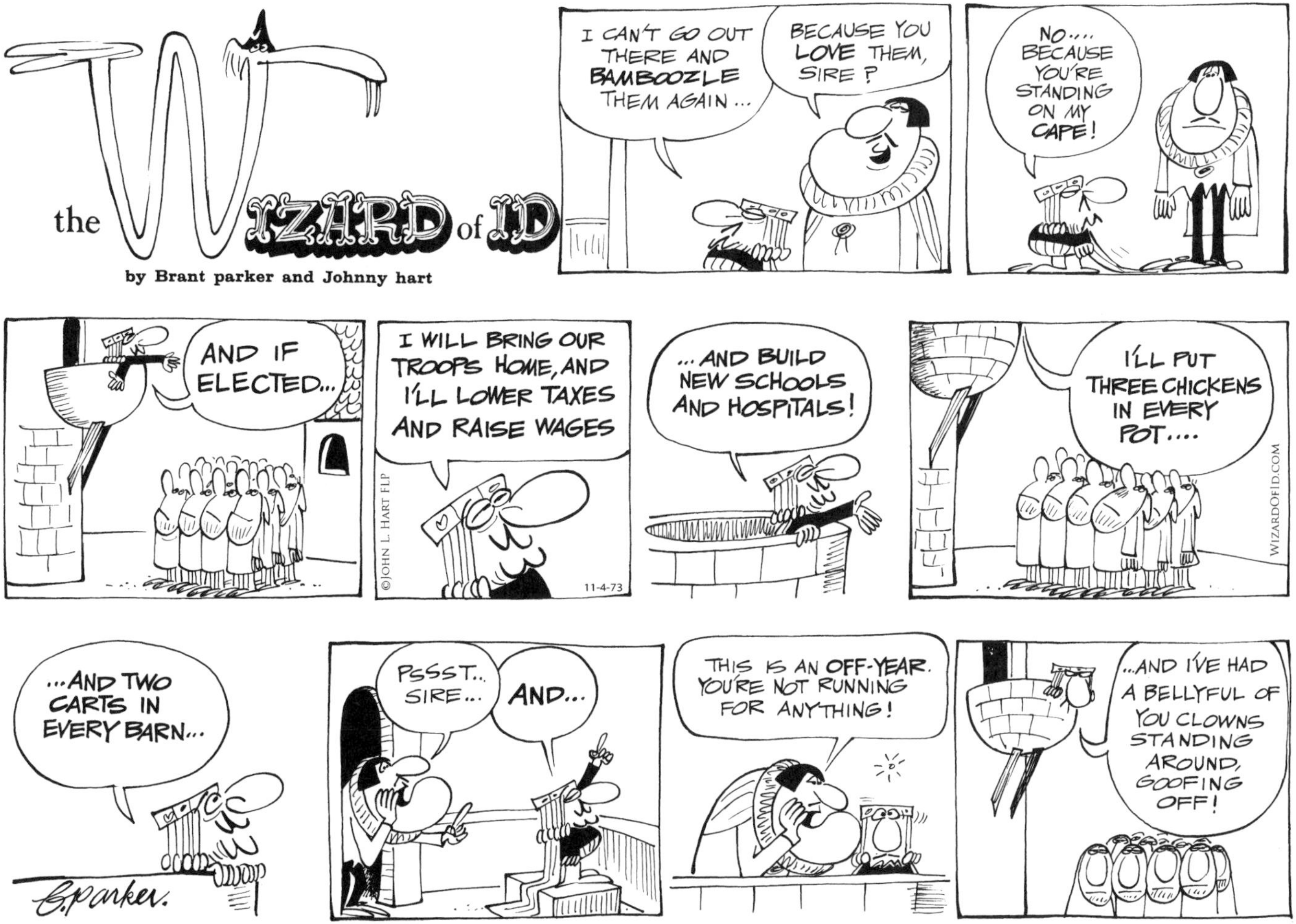
the WIZARD of ID
by Brant parker and Johnny hart
I CAN'T GO OUT THERE AND BAMBOOZLE THEM AGAIN...
BECAUSE YOU LOVE THEM, SIRE?
NO.... BECAUSE YOU'RE STANDING ON MY CAPE!
AND IF ELECTED...
I WILL BRING OUR TROOPS HOME, AND I'LL LOWER TAXES AND RAISE WAGES
©JOHN L. HART FLP
11-4-73
...AND BUILD NEW SCHOOLS AND HOSPITALS!
I'LL PUT THREE CHICKENS IN EVERY POT....
WIZARDOFID.COM
...AND TWO CARTS IN EVERY BARN...
B.parker.
PSSST... SIRE...
AND...
THIS IS AN OFF-YEAR. YOU'RE NOT RUNNING FOR ANYTHING!
...AND I'VE HAD A BELLYFUL OF YOU CLOWNS STANDING AROUND, GOOFING OFF!

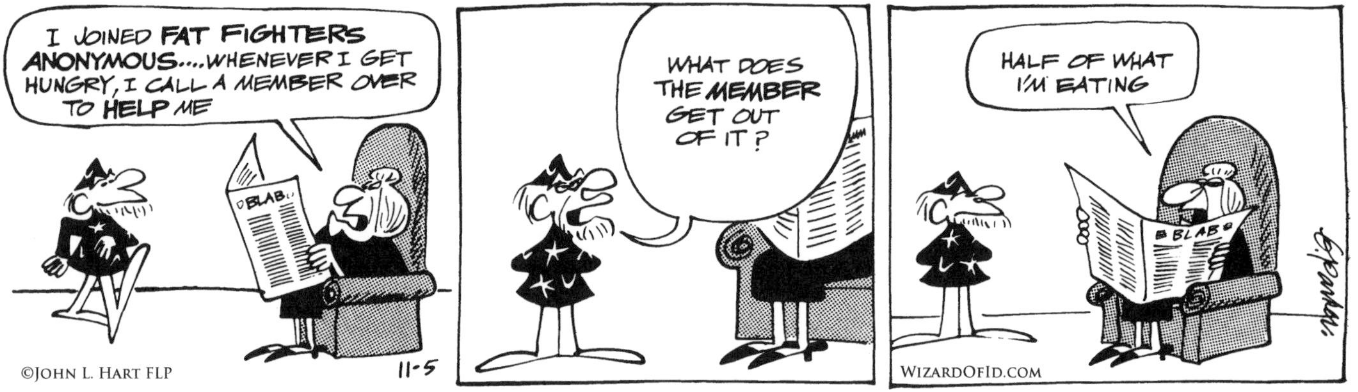
I JOINED FAT FIGHTERS ANONYMOUS....WHENEVER I GET HUNGRY, I CALL A MEMBER OVER TO HELP ME
BLAB
©JOHN L. HART FLP
11-5
WHAT DOES THE MEMBER GET OUT OF IT ?
HALF OF WHAT I'M EATING
BLAB
WIZARDOFID.COM

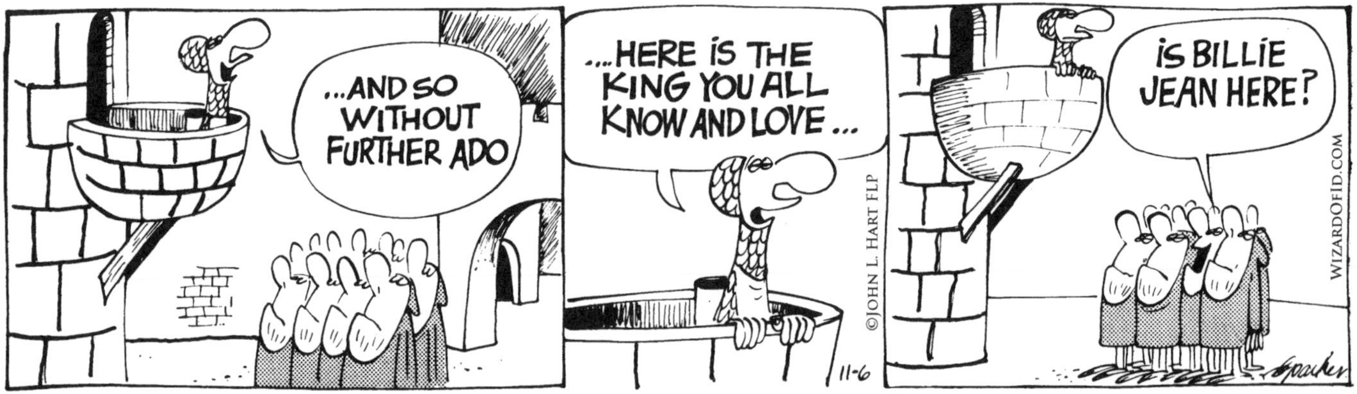
...AND SO WITHOUT FURTHER ADO
...HERE IS THE KING YOU ALL KNOW AND LOVE ...
©JOHN L. HART FLP
11-6
IS BILLIE JEAN HERE?
WIZARDOFID.COM

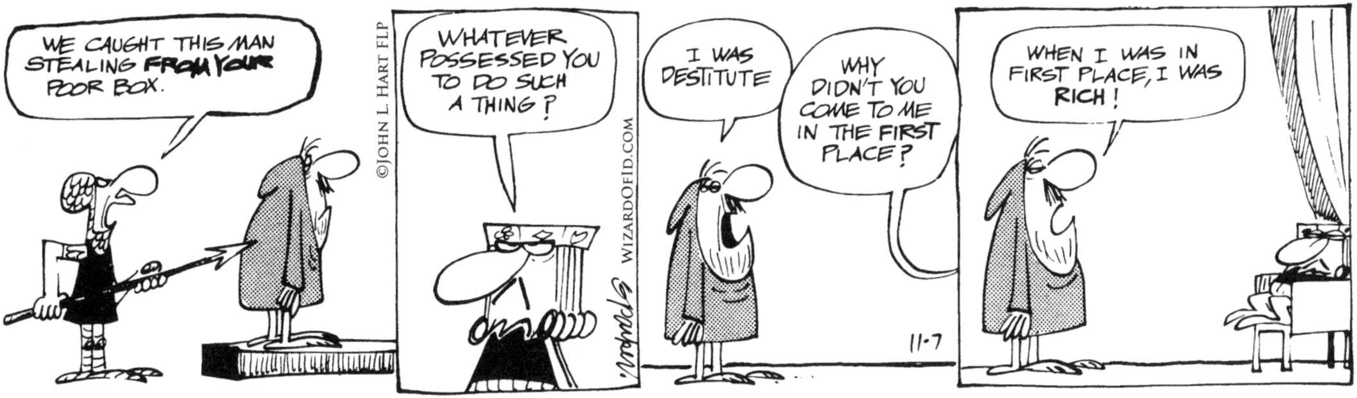
WE CAUGHT THIS MAN STEALING FROM YOUR POOR BOX.
©JOHN L. HART FLP
WHATEVER POSSESSED YOU TO DO SUCH A THING?
WIZARDOFID.COM
I WAS DESTITUTE
WHY DIDN'T YOU COME TO ME IN THE FIRST PLACE?
11-7
WHEN I WAS IN FIRST PLACE, I WAS RICH!

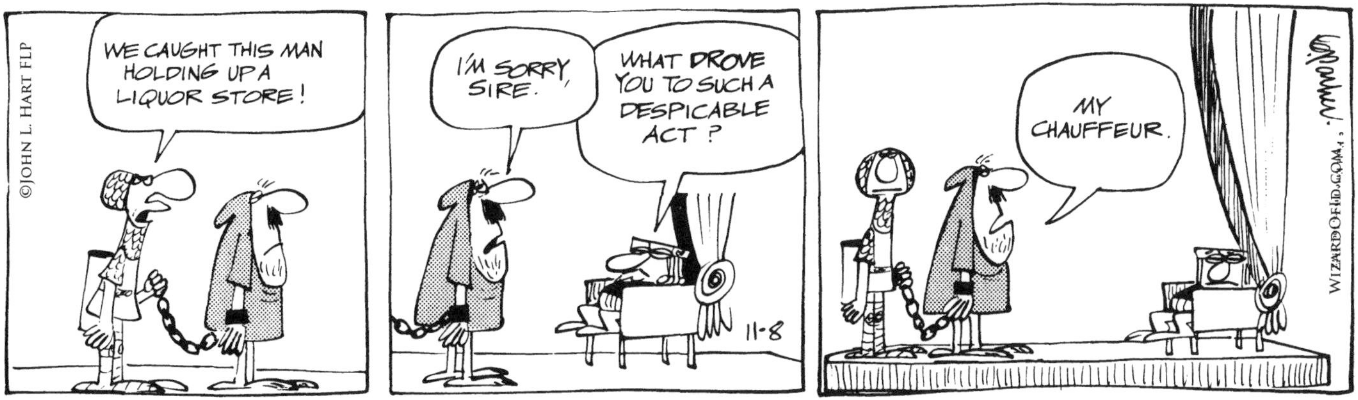
©JOHN L. HART FLP
WE CAUGHT THIS MAN HOLDING UP A LIQUOR STORE!
I'M SORRY, SIRE.
WHAT DROVE YOU TO SUCH A DESPICABLE ACT?
11-8
MY CHAUFFEUR.
WIZARDOFID.COM

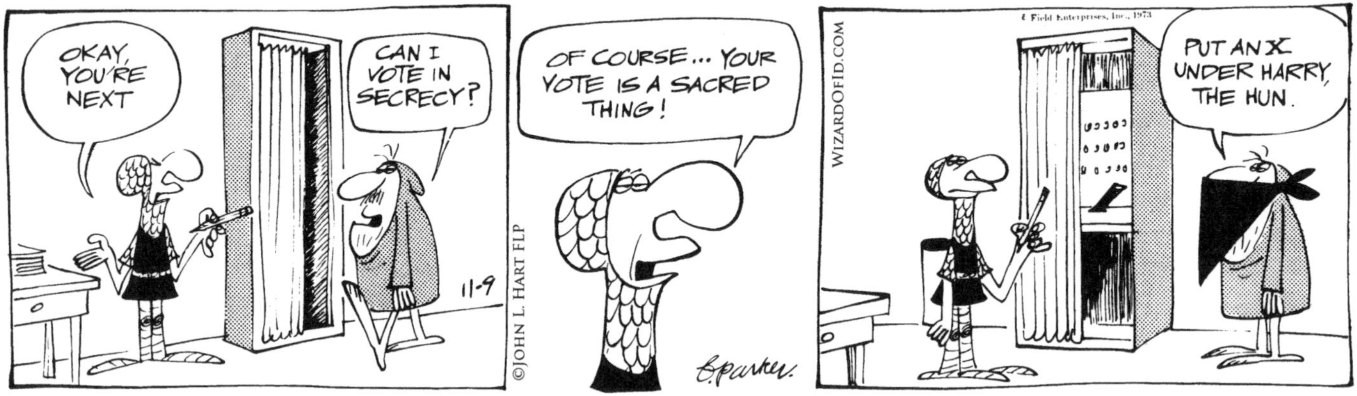
OKAY, YOU'RE NEXT
CAN I VOTE IN SECRECY?
OF COURSE... YOUR VOTE IS A SACRED THING!
PUT AN X UNDER HARRY, THE HUN.
11-9
©JOHN L. HART FLP
© Field Enterprises, Inc., 1973
WIZARDOFID.COM

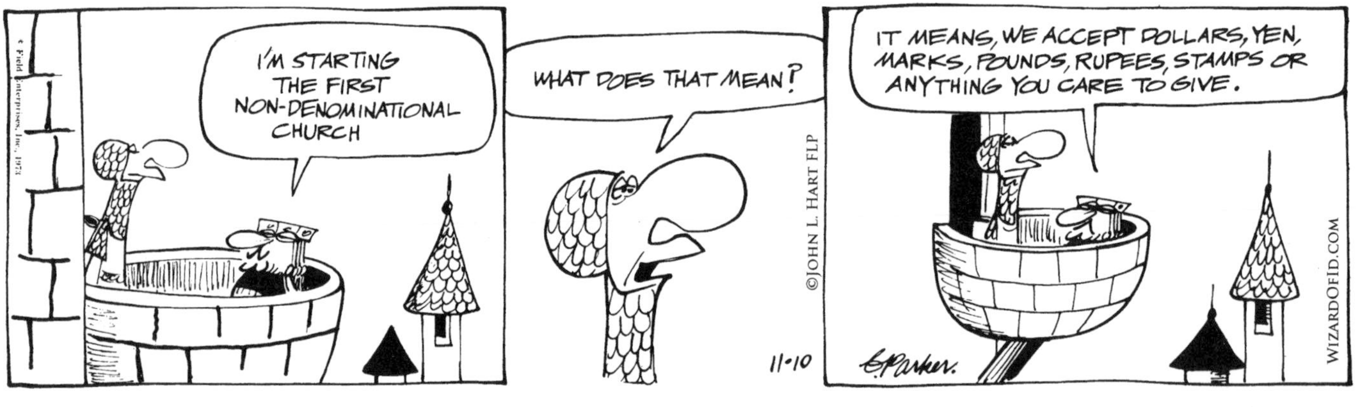
I'M STARTING THE FIRST NON-DENOMINATIONAL CHURCH
WHAT DOES THAT MEAN?
IT MEANS, WE ACCEPT DOLLARS, YEN, MARKS, POUNDS, RUPEES, STAMPS OR ANYTHING YOU CARE TO GIVE.
11-10
© Field Enterprises, Inc., 1973
©JOHN L. HART FLP
WIZARDOFID.COM

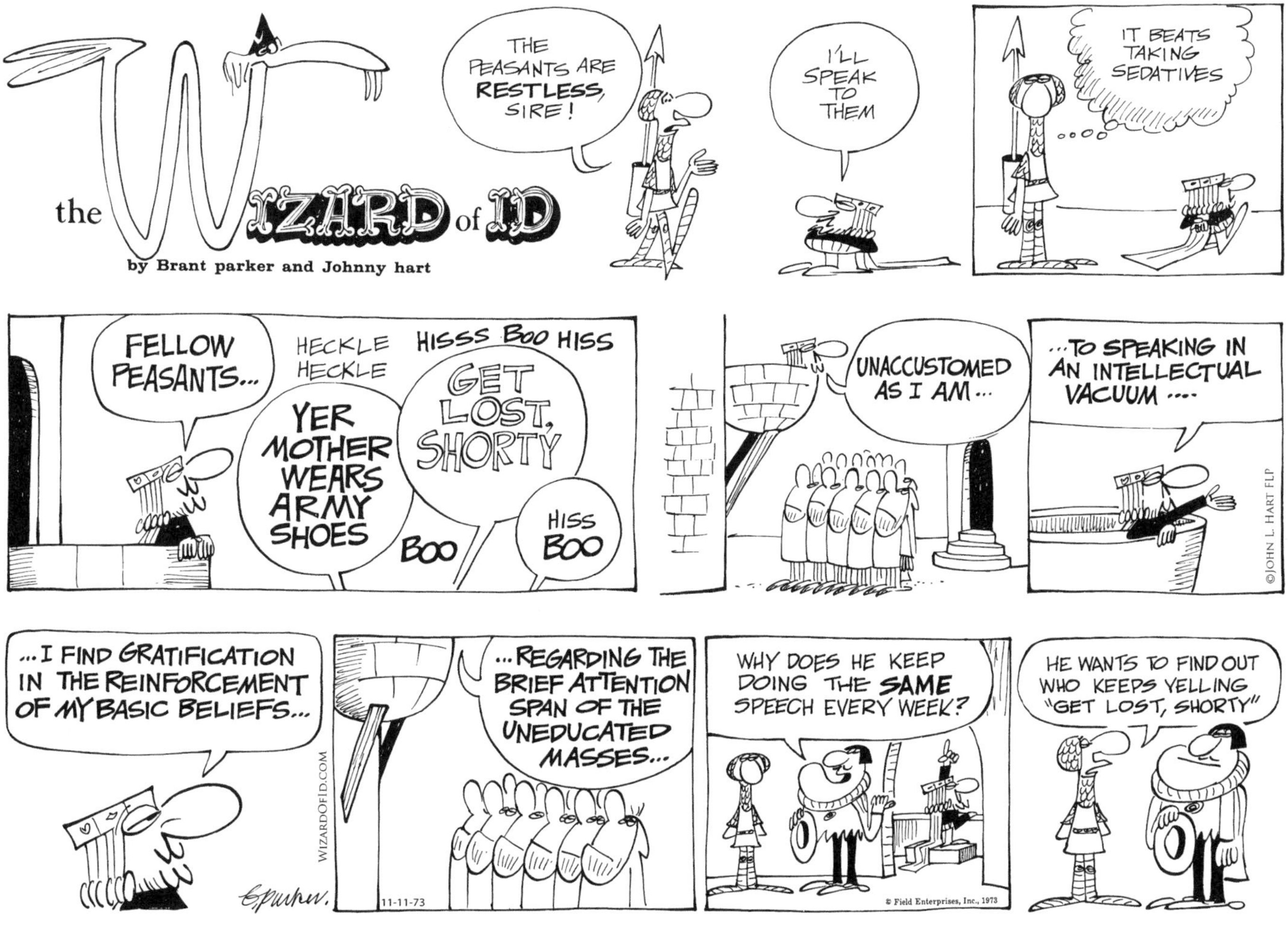
the WIZARD of ID
by Brant parker and Johnny hart
THE PEASANTS ARE RESTLESS, SIRE!
I'LL SPEAK TO THEM
IT BEATS TAKING SEDATIVES
FELLOW PEASANTS...
HECKLE HECKLE
HISSS BOO HISS
YER MOTHER WEARS ARMY SHOES
GET LOST, SHORTY
BOO
HISS BOO
UNACCUSTOMED AS I AM...
...TO SPEAKING IN AN INTELLECTUAL VACUUM ....
©JOHN L. HART FLP
...I FIND GRATIFICATION IN THE REINFORCEMENT OF MY BASIC BELIEFS...
WIZARDOFID.COM
...REGARDING THE BRIEF ATTENTION SPAN OF THE UNEDUCATED MASSES...
11-11-73
WHY DOES HE KEEP DOING THE SAME SPEECH EVERY WEEK?
© Field Enterprises, Inc., 1973
HE WANTS TO FIND OUT WHO KEEPS YELLING "GET LOST, SHORTY"

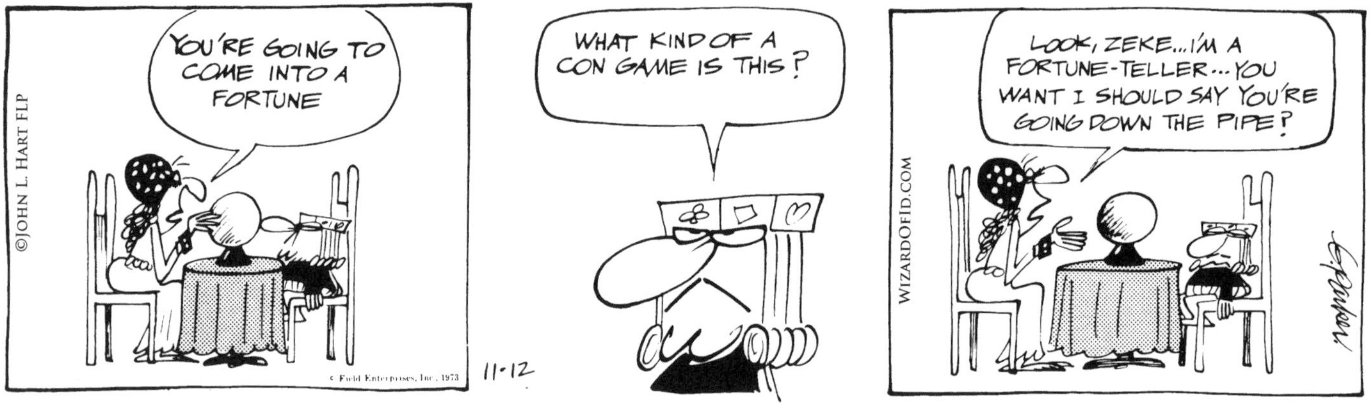
©JOHN L. HART FLP
YOU'RE GOING TO COME INTO A FORTUNE
© Field Enterprises, Inc., 1973
11-12
WHAT KIND OF A CON GAME IS THIS?
WIZARDOFID.COM
LOOK, ZEKE...I'M A FORTUNE-TELLER...YOU WANT I SHOULD SAY YOU'RE GOING DOWN THE PIPE?

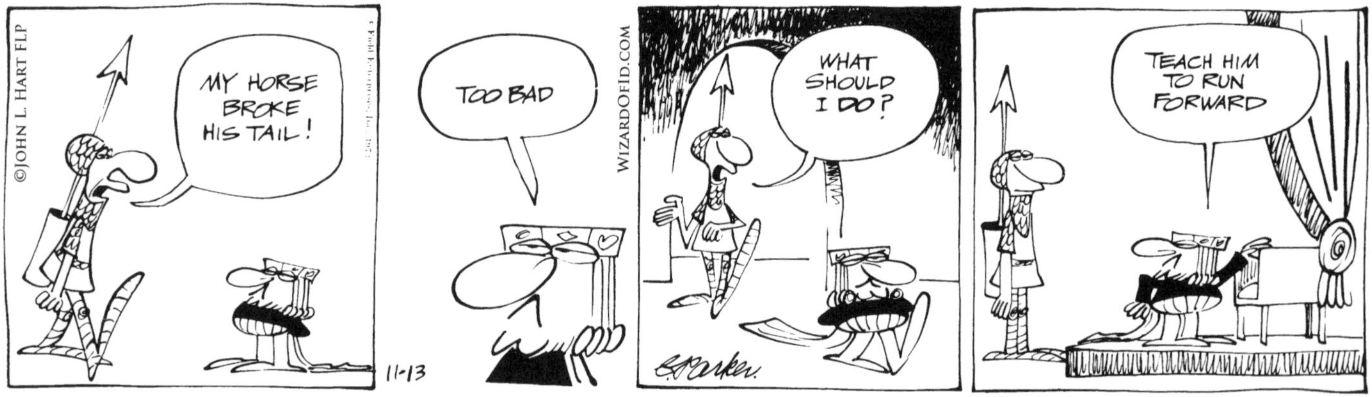
©JOHN L. HART FLP
MY HORSE BROKE HIS TAIL!
11-13
TOO BAD
WIZARDOFID.COM
WHAT SHOULD I DO?
B. Parker
TEACH HIM TO RUN FORWARD

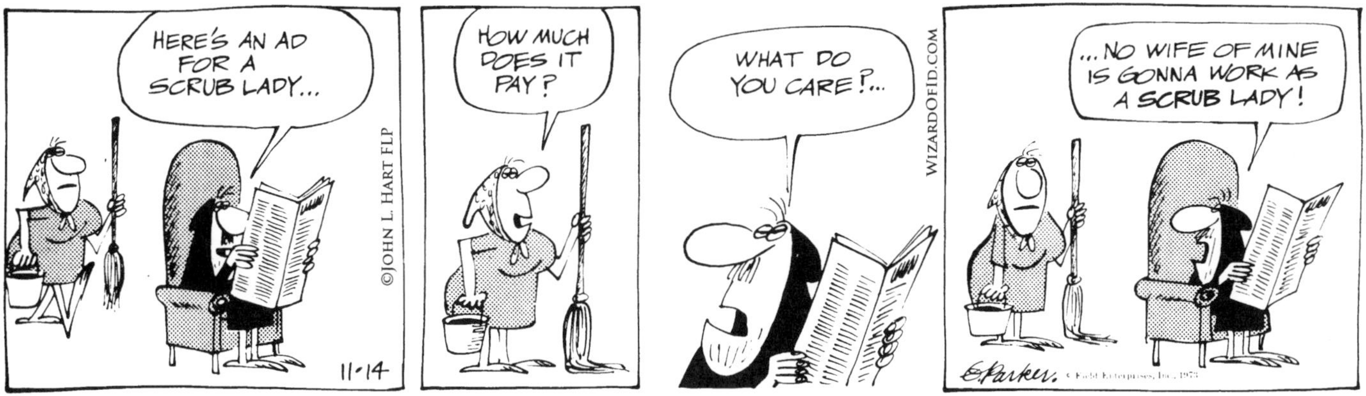

HERE'S AN AD FOR A SCRUB LADY...
HOW MUCH DOES IT PAY?
WHAT DO YOU CARE?!...
...NO WIFE OF MINE IS GONNA WORK AS A **SCRUB** LADY!
11-14
©JOHN L. HART FLP
WIZARDOFID.COM

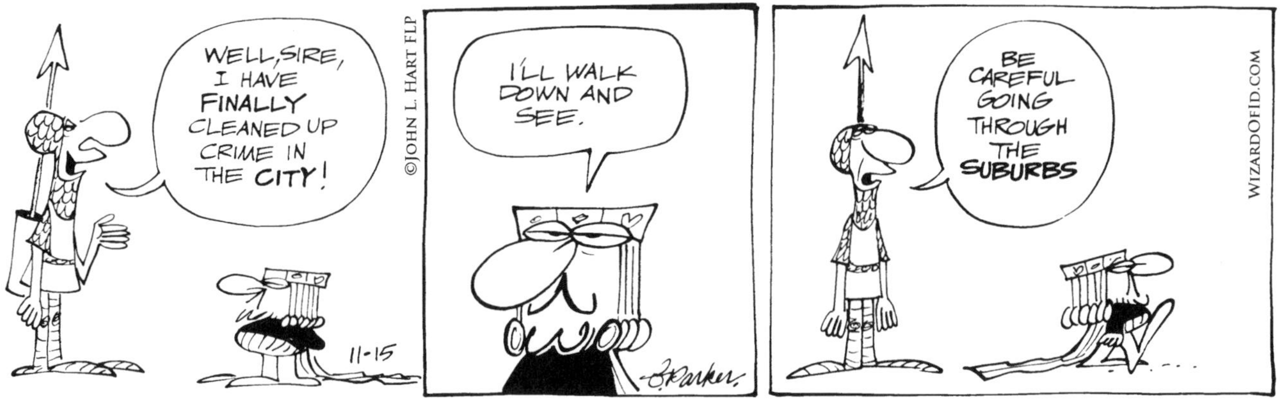

WELL, SIRE, I HAVE **FINALLY** CLEANED UP CRIME IN THE **CITY**!
I'LL WALK DOWN AND SEE.
BE CAREFUL GOING THROUGH THE **SUBURBS**
11-15
©JOHN L. HART FLP
WIZARDOFID.COM

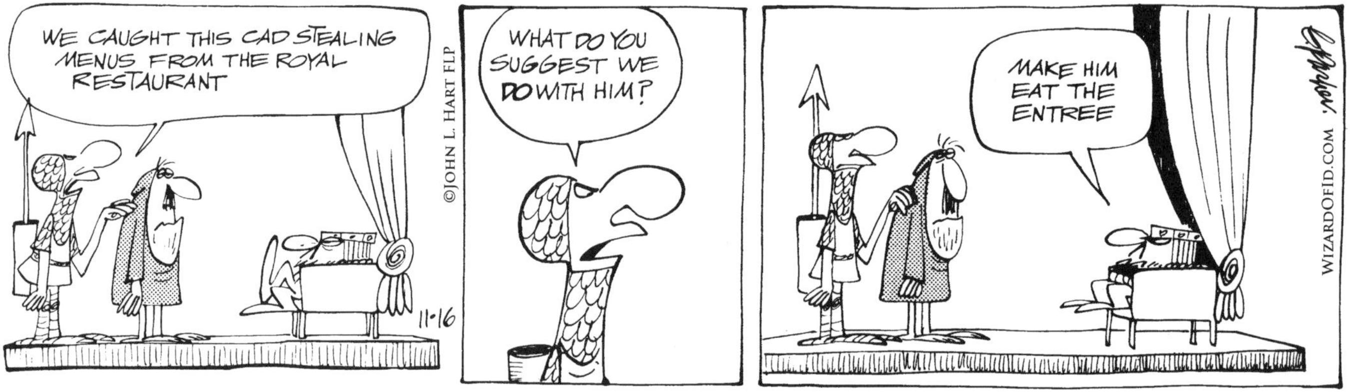

WE CAUGHT THIS CAD STEALING MENUS FROM THE ROYAL RESTAURANT
©JOHN L. HART FLP
11-16
WHAT DO YOU SUGGEST WE DO WITH HIM?
MAKE HIM EAT THE ENTREE
WIZARDOFID.COM

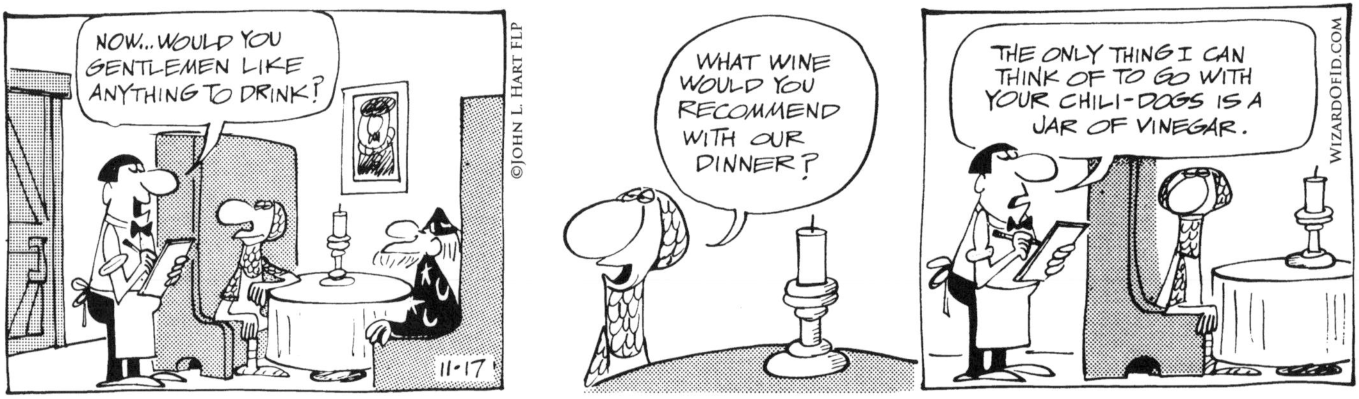

NOW... WOULD YOU GENTLEMEN LIKE ANYTHING TO DRINK?
©JOHN L. HART FLP
11-17
WHAT WINE WOULD YOU RECOMMEND WITH OUR DINNER?
THE ONLY THING I CAN THINK OF TO GO WITH YOUR CHILI-DOGS IS A JAR OF VINEGAR.
WIZARDOFID.COM

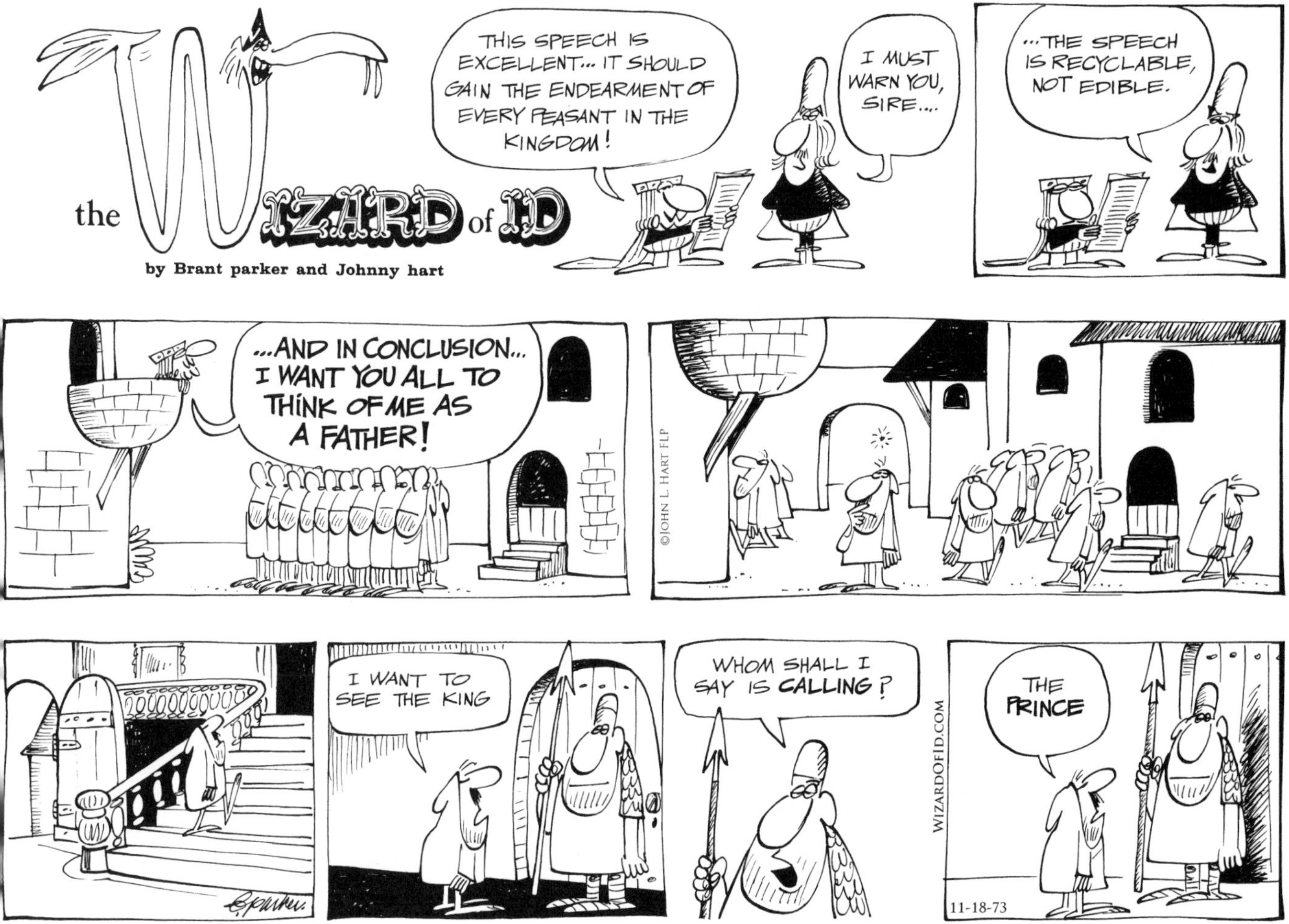
the WIZARD of ID
by Brant parker and Johnny hart
THIS SPEECH IS EXCELLENT... IT SHOULD GAIN THE ENDEARMENT OF EVERY PEASANT IN THE KINGDOM!
I MUST WARN YOU, SIRE....
...THE SPEECH IS RECYCLABLE, NOT EDIBLE.
...AND IN CONCLUSION... I WANT YOU ALL TO THINK OF ME AS A FATHER!
©JOHN L. HART FLP
I WANT TO SEE THE KING
WHOM SHALL I SAY IS CALLING?
WIZARDOFID.COM
THE PRINCE
11-18-73

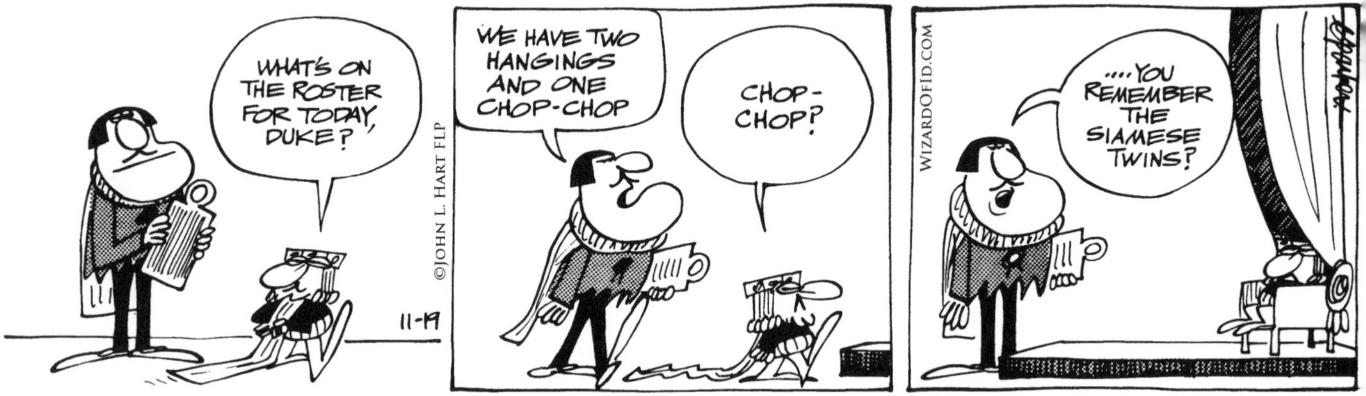
WHAT'S ON THE ROSTER FOR TODAY, DUKE?
©JOHN L. HART FLP
11-19
WE HAVE TWO HANGINGS AND ONE CHOP-CHOP
CHOP-CHOP?
WIZARDOFID.COM
....YOU REMEMBER THE SIAMESE TWINS?

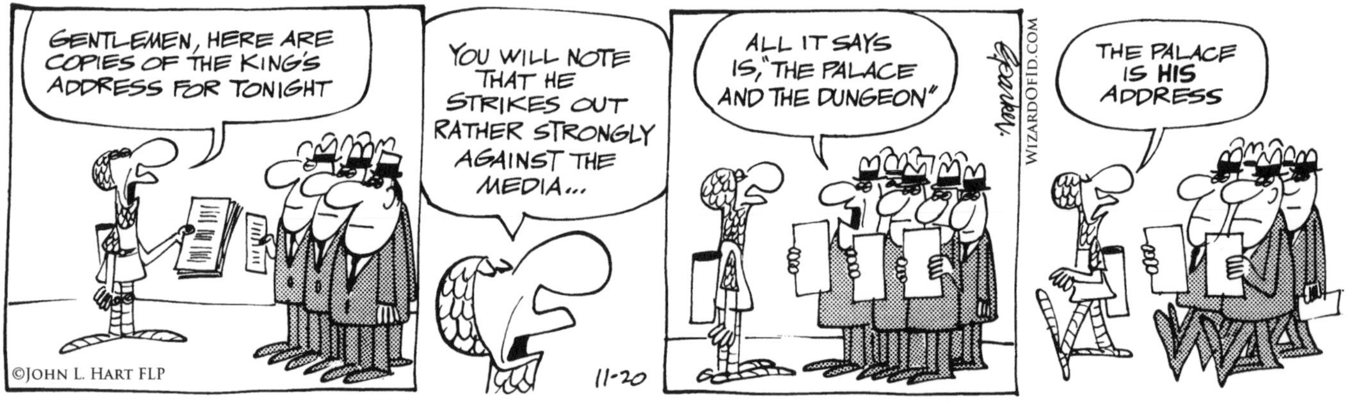
GENTLEMEN, HERE ARE COPIES OF THE KING'S ADDRESS FOR TONIGHT
©JOHN L. HART FLP
YOU WILL NOTE THAT HE STRIKES OUT RATHER STRONGLY AGAINST THE MEDIA...
11-20
ALL IT SAYS IS, "THE PALACE AND THE DUNGEON"
WIZARDOFID.COM
THE PALACE IS HIS ADDRESS

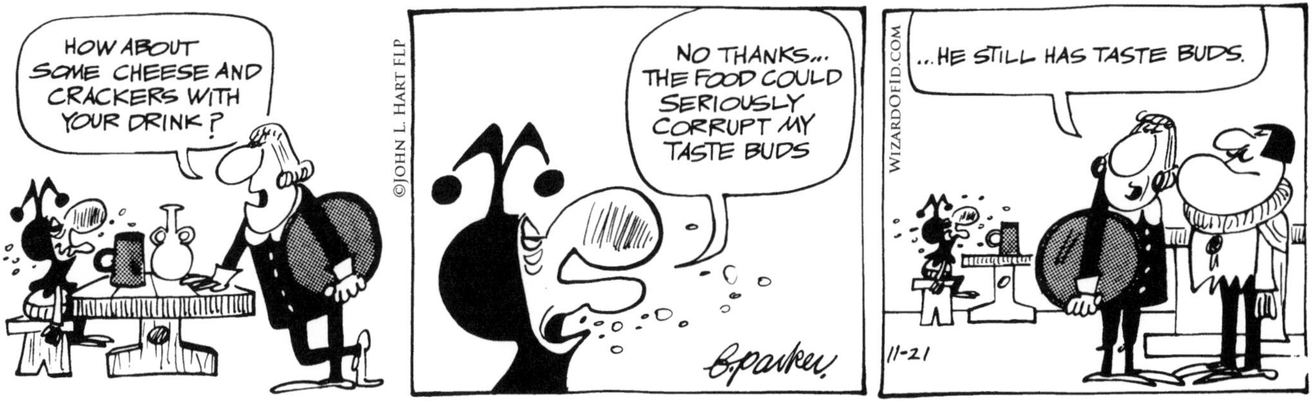
HOW ABOUT SOME CHEESE AND CRACKERS WITH YOUR DRINK?
©JOHN L. HART FLP
NO THANKS... THE FOOD COULD SERIOUSLY CORRUPT MY TASTE BUDS
B. parker
WIZARDOFID.COM
...HE STILL HAS TASTE BUDS.
11-21

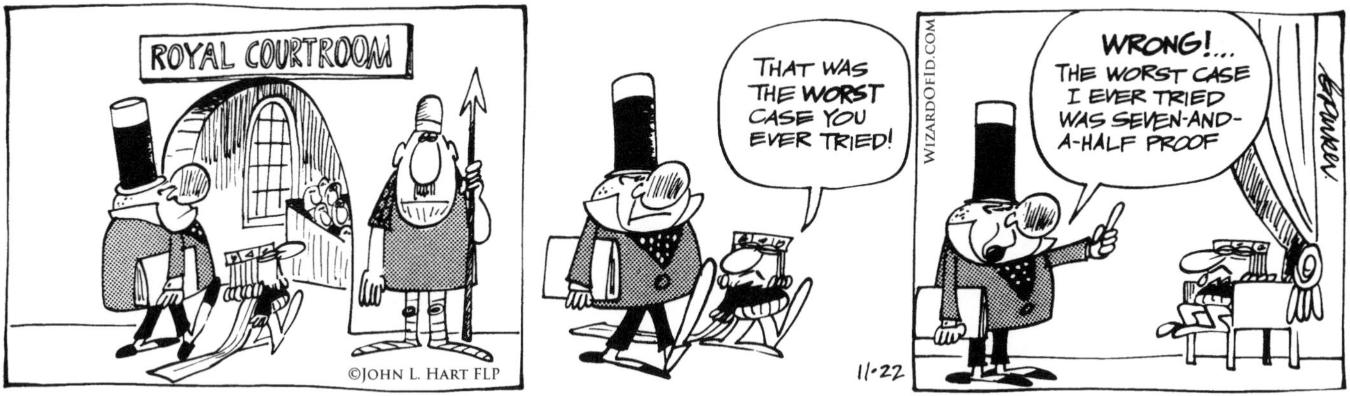
ROYAL COURTROOM
©JOHN L. HART FLP
THAT WAS THE **WORST** CASE YOU EVER TRIED!
11-22
WIZARDOFID.COM
WRONG!... THE WORST CASE I EVER TRIED WAS SEVEN-AND-A-HALF PROOF
parker

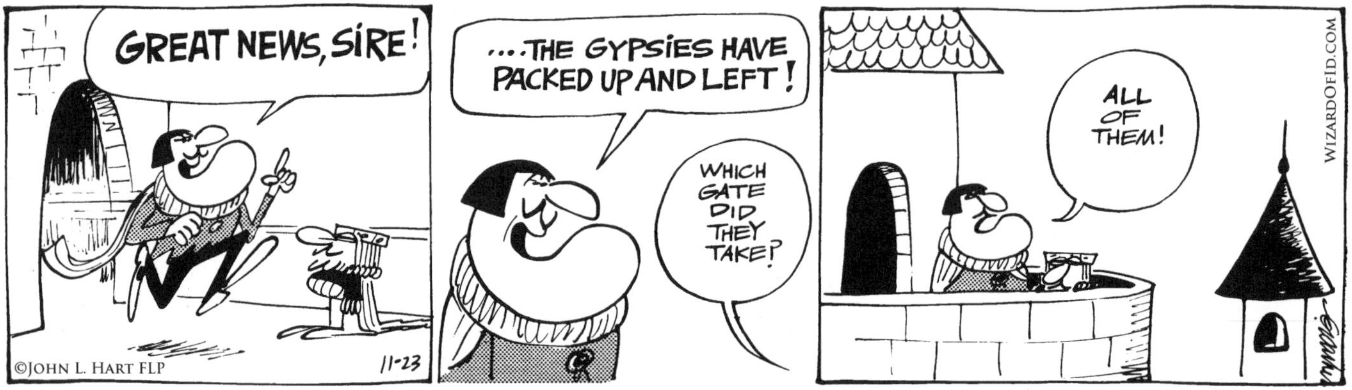
GREAT NEWS, SIRE!
©JOHN L. HART FLP
11-23
....THE GYPSIES HAVE PACKED UP AND LEFT!
WHICH GATE DID THEY TAKE?
ALL OF THEM!
WIZARDOFID.COM

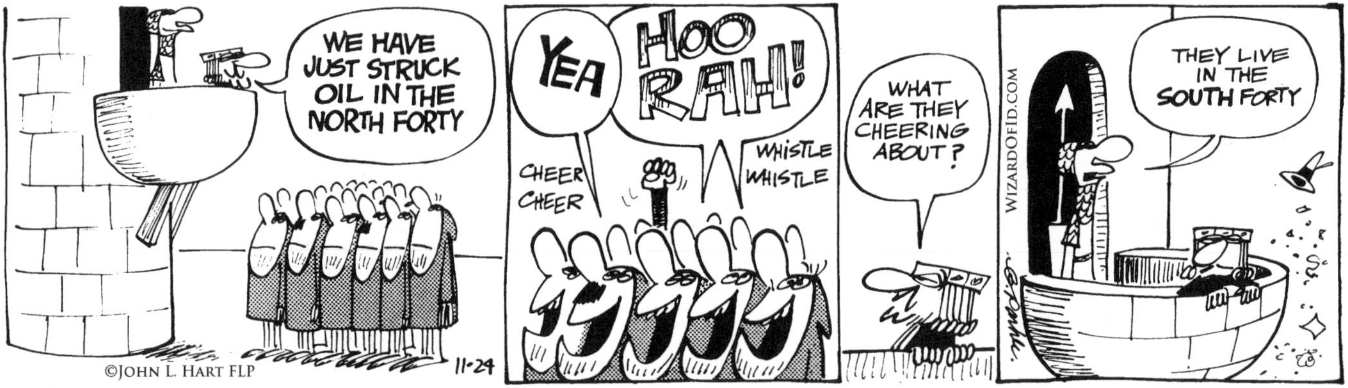
WE HAVE JUST STRUCK OIL IN THE NORTH FORTY
©JOHN L. HART FLP
11-24
YEA
HOO RAH!
CHEER CHEER
WHISTLE WHISTLE
WHAT ARE THEY CHEERING ABOUT?
THEY LIVE IN THE SOUTH FORTY
WIZARDOFID.COM

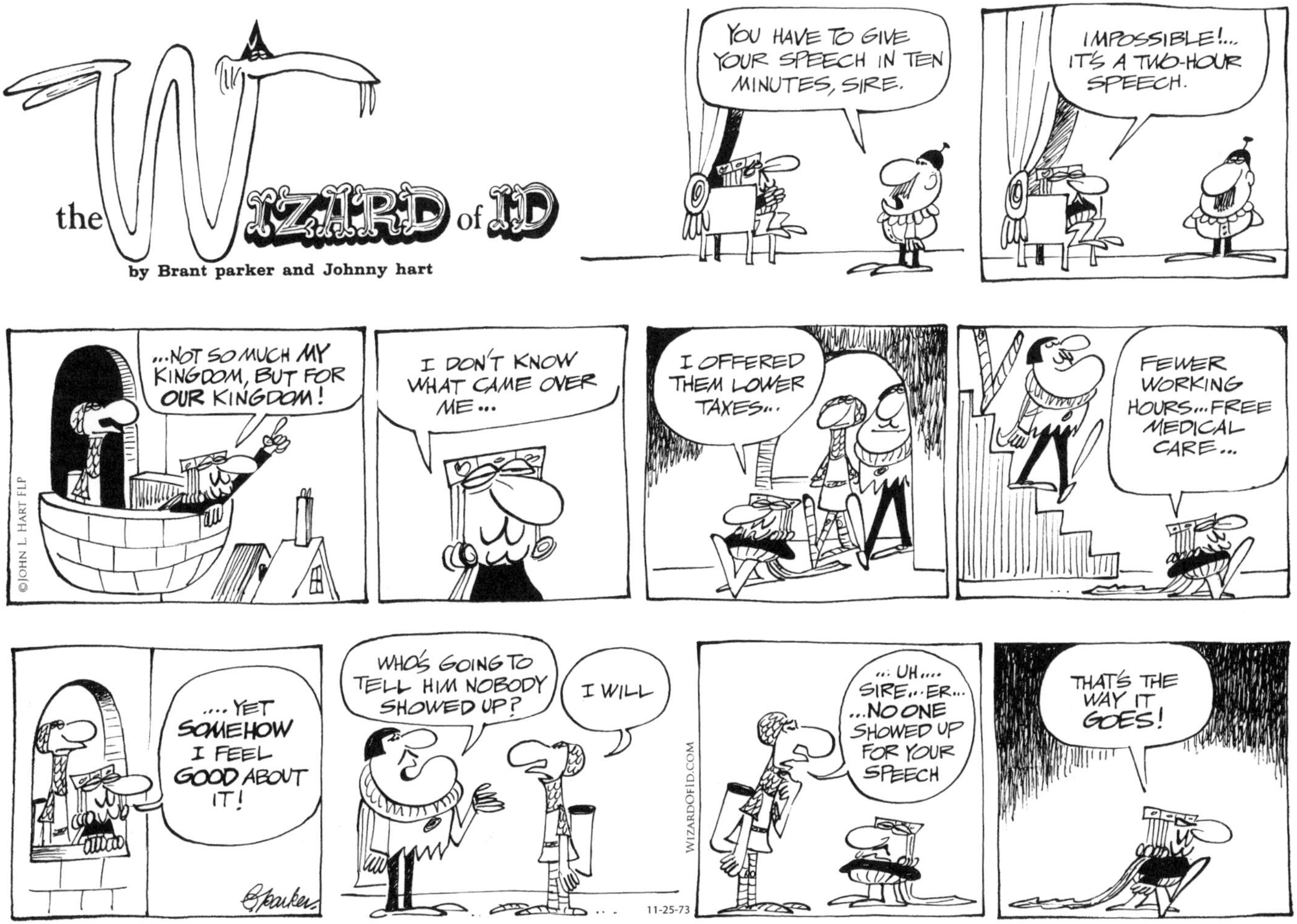
the WIZARD of ID
by Brant parker and Johnny hart
YOU HAVE TO GIVE YOUR SPEECH IN TEN MINUTES, SIRE.
IMPOSSIBLE!... IT'S A TWO-HOUR SPEECH.
...NOT SO MUCH MY KINGDOM, BUT FOR OUR KINGDOM!
I DON'T KNOW WHAT CAME OVER ME...
I OFFERED THEM LOWER TAXES...
FEWER WORKING HOURS...FREE MEDICAL CARE...
.... YET SOMEHOW I FEEL GOOD ABOUT IT!
WHO'S GOING TO TELL HIM NOBODY SHOWED UP?
I WILL
...: UH.... SIRE... ER... ...NO ONE SHOWED UP FOR YOUR SPEECH
THAT'S THE WAY IT GOES!
©JOHN L. HART FLP
WIZARDOFID.COM
11-25-73

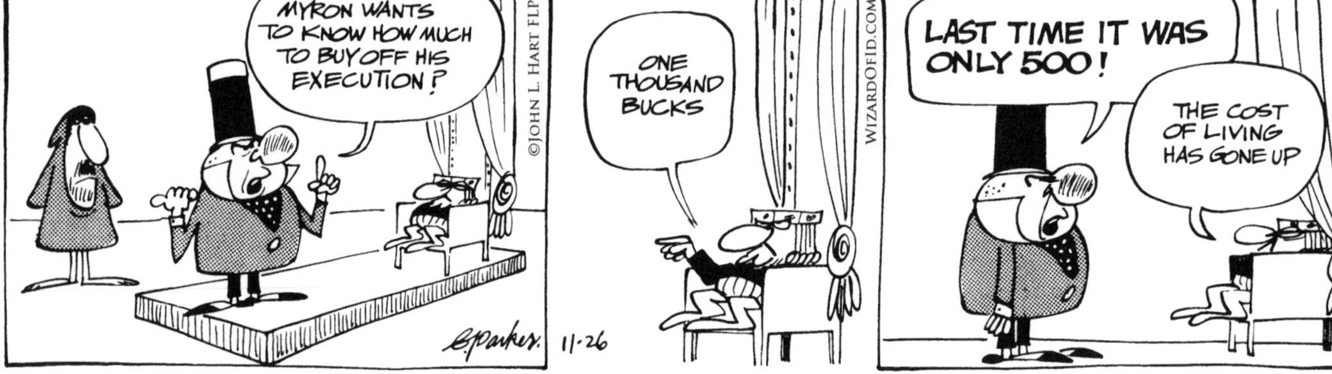
MYRON WANTS TO KNOW HOW MUCH TO BUY OFF HIS EXECUTION?
ONE THOUSAND BUCKS
LAST TIME IT WAS ONLY 500!
THE COST OF LIVING HAS GONE UP
©JOHN L. HART FLP
WIZARDOFID.COM
11-26

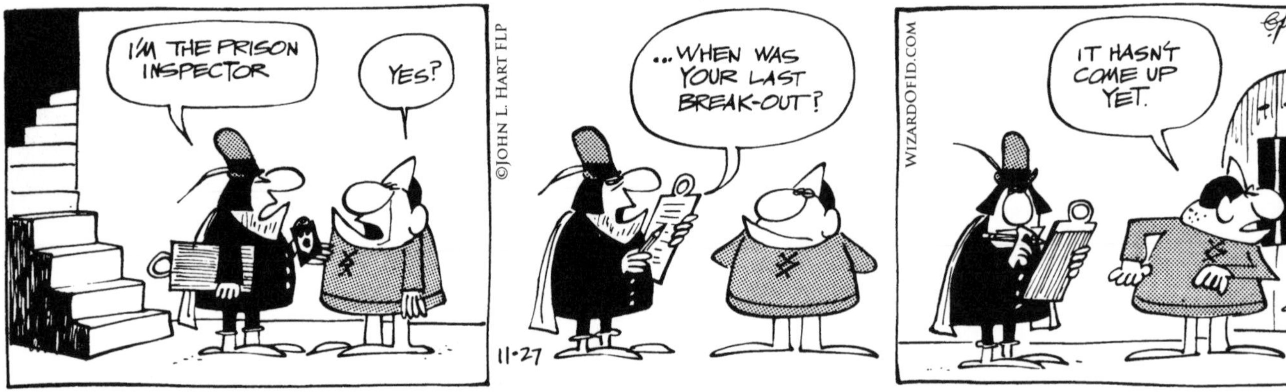
I'M THE PRISON INSPECTOR
YES?
...WHEN WAS YOUR LAST BREAK-OUT?
IT HASN'T COME UP YET.
©JOHN L. HART FLP
WIZARDOFID.COM
11-27

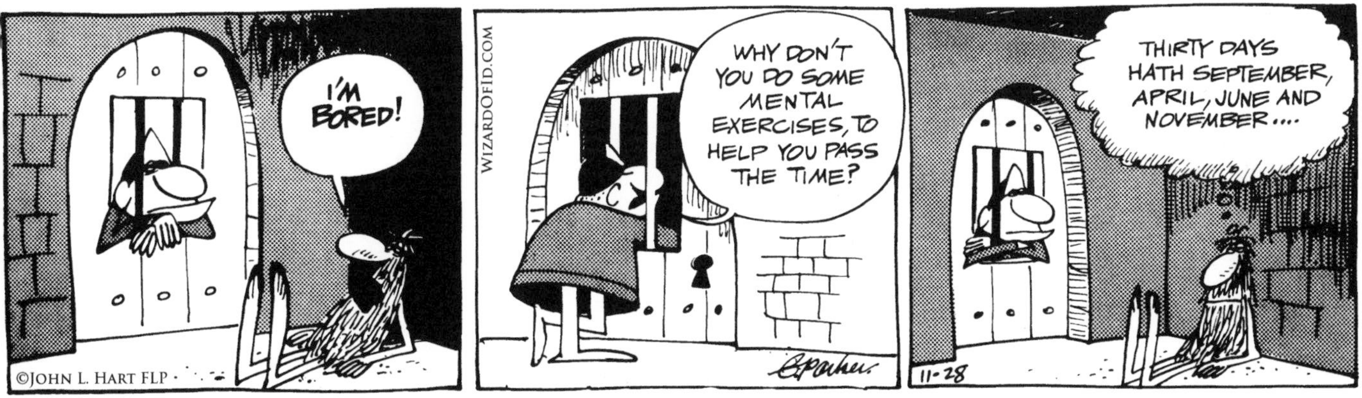
I'M BORED!
WIZARDOFID.COM
WHY DON'T YOU DO SOME MENTAL EXERCISES, TO HELP YOU PASS THE TIME?
THIRTY DAYS HATH SEPTEMBER, APRIL, JUNE AND NOVEMBER....
11-28
©JOHN L. HART FLP

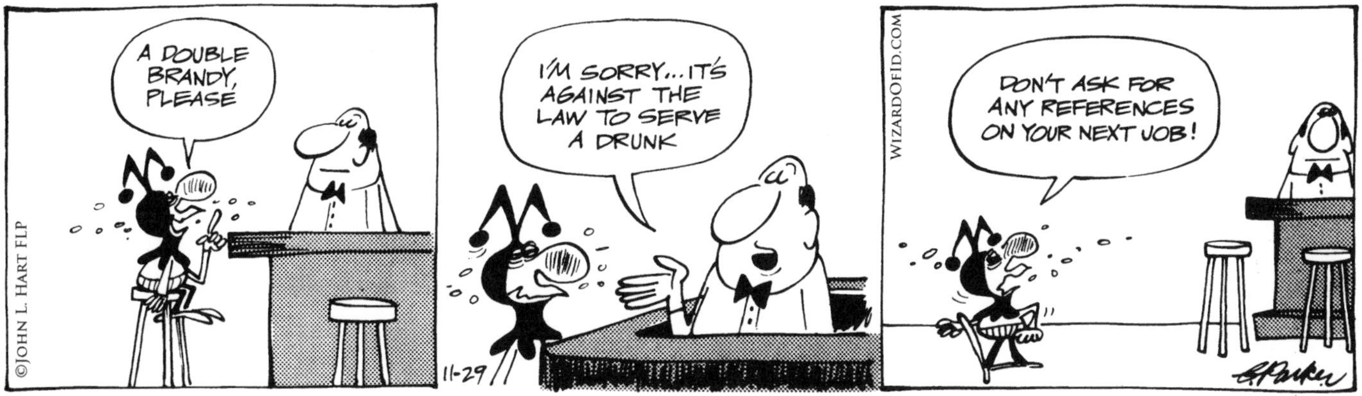
A DOUBLE BRANDY, PLEASE
I'M SORRY...IT'S AGAINST THE LAW TO SERVE A DRUNK
WIZARDOFID.COM
DON'T ASK FOR ANY REFERENCES ON YOUR NEXT JOB!
11-29
©JOHN L. HART FLP

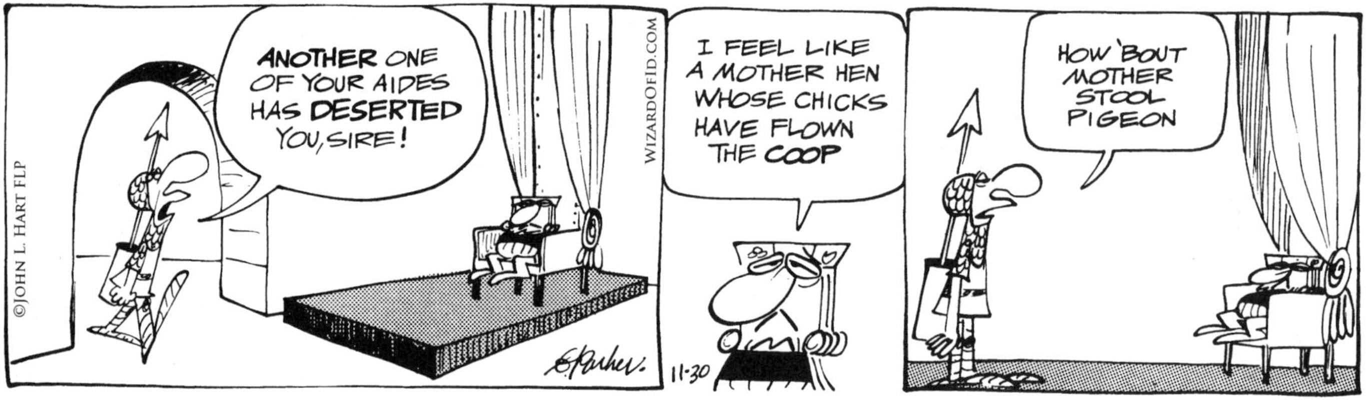
©JOHN L. HART FLP
WIZARDOFID.COM
ANOTHER ONE OF YOUR AIDES HAS DESERTED YOU, SIRE!
I FEEL LIKE A MOTHER HEN WHOSE CHICKS HAVE FLOWN THE COOP
HOW 'BOUT MOTHER STOOL PIGEON
11-30

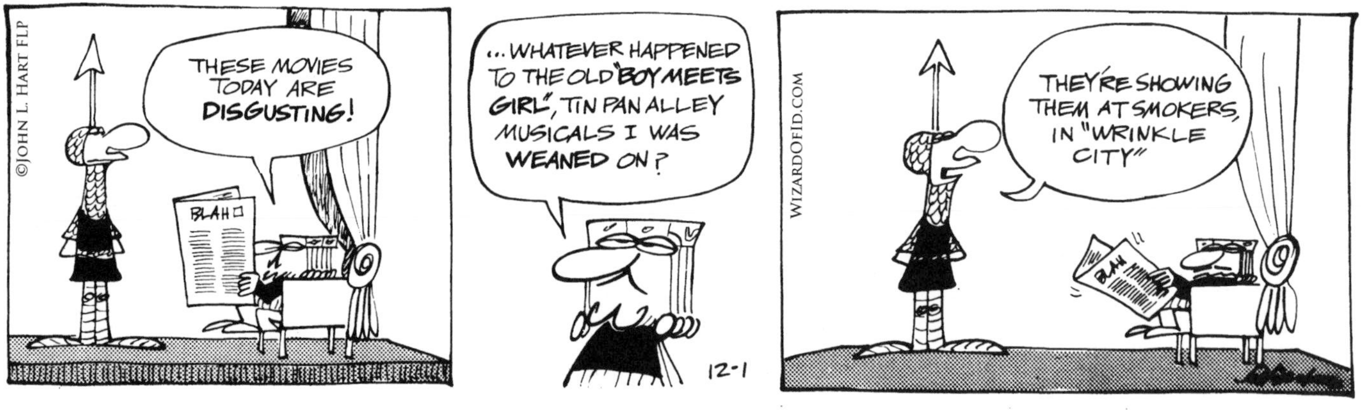
©JOHN L. HART FLP
WIZARDOFID.COM
THESE MOVIES TODAY ARE DISGUSTING!
BLAH
...WHATEVER HAPPENED TO THE OLD "BOY MEETS GIRL", TIN PAN ALLEY MUSICALS I WAS WEANED ON?
THEY'RE SHOWING THEM AT SMOKERS, IN "WRINKLE CITY"
BLAH
12-1

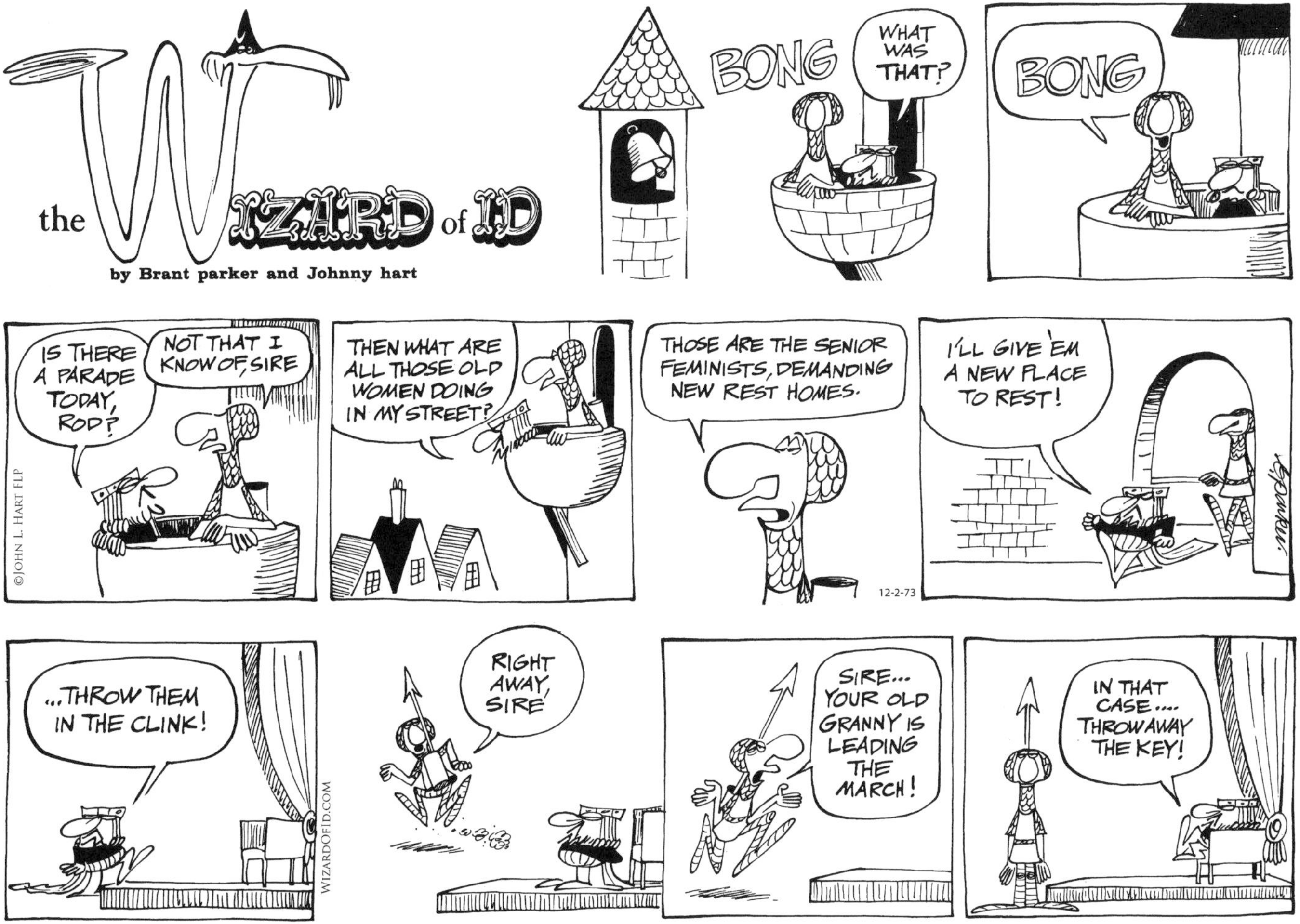
the Wizard of Id
by Brant parker and Johnny hart
BONG
WHAT WAS THAT?
BONG
IS THERE A PARADE TODAY, ROD?
NOT THAT I KNOW OF, SIRE
THEN WHAT ARE ALL THOSE OLD WOMEN DOING IN MY STREET?
THOSE ARE THE SENIOR FEMINISTS, DEMANDING NEW REST HOMES.
12-2-73
I'LL GIVE 'EM A NEW PLACE TO REST!
...THROW THEM IN THE CLINK!
RIGHT AWAY, SIRE
SIRE... YOUR OLD GRANNY IS LEADING THE MARCH!
IN THAT CASE.... THROW AWAY THE KEY!
©JOHN L. HART FLP
WIZARDOFID.COM

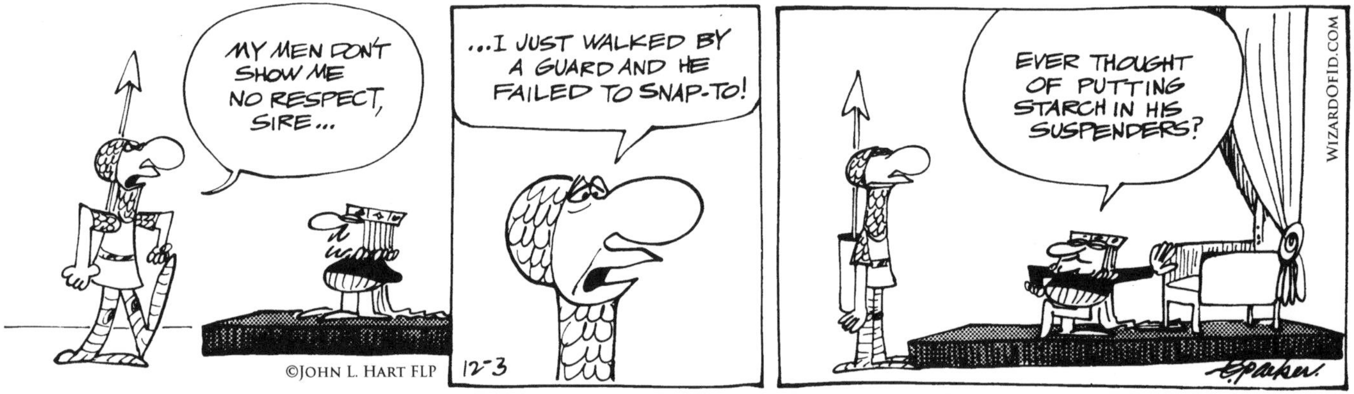
MY MEN DON'T SHOW ME NO RESPECT, SIRE...
©JOHN L. HART FLP
...I JUST WALKED BY A GUARD AND HE FAILED TO SNAP-TO!
12-3
EVER THOUGHT OF PUTTING STARCH IN HIS SUSPENDERS?
WIZARDOFID.COM

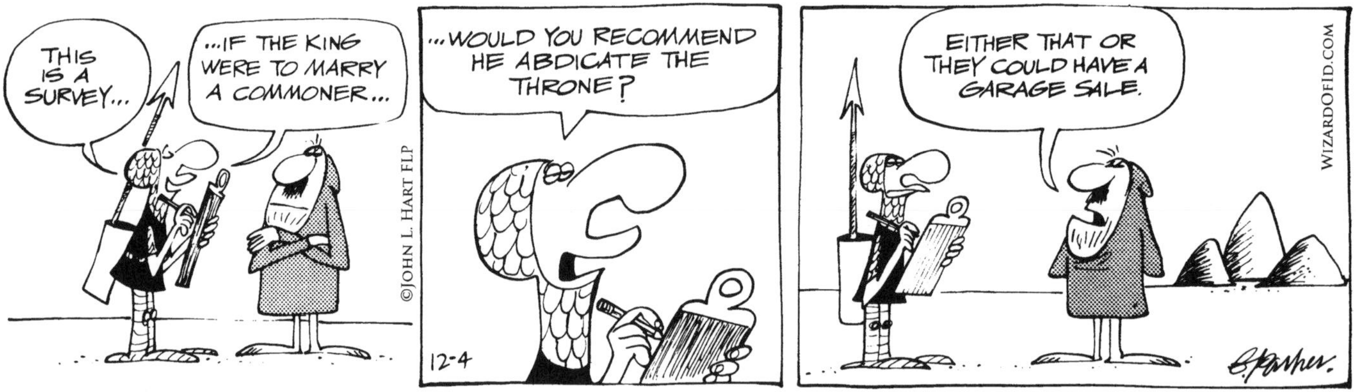
THIS IS A SURVEY...
...IF THE KING WERE TO MARRY A COMMONER...
©JOHN L. HART FLP
...WOULD YOU RECOMMEND HE ABDICATE THE THRONE?
12-4
EITHER THAT OR THEY COULD HAVE A GARAGE SALE.
WIZARDOFID.COM

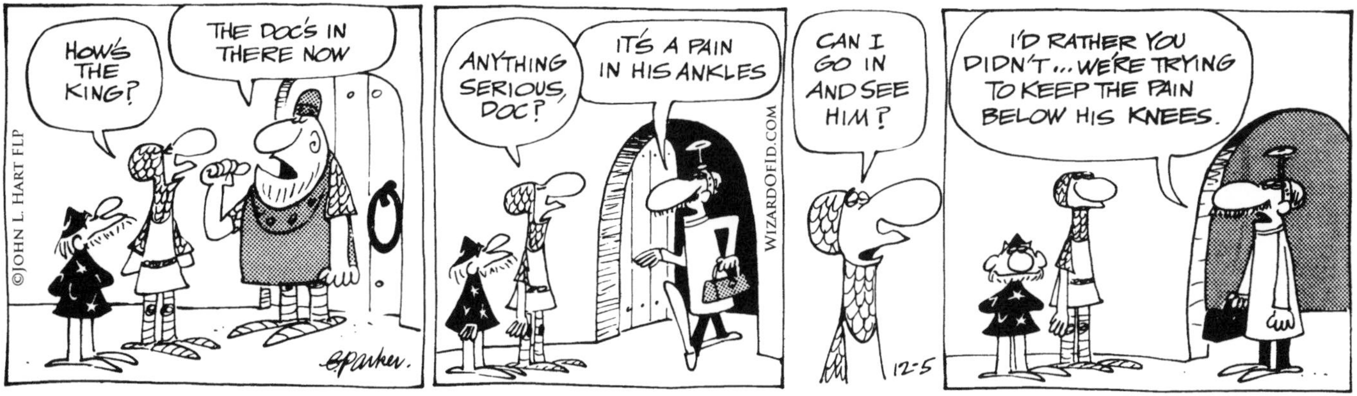

HOW'S THE KING?
THE DOC'S IN THERE NOW
©JOHN L. HART FLP
Parker.
ANYTHING SERIOUS, DOC?
IT'S A PAIN IN HIS ANKLES
WIZARDOFID.COM
CAN I GO IN AND SEE HIM?
12-5
I'D RATHER YOU DIDN'T... WE'RE TRYING TO KEEP THE PAIN BELOW HIS KNEES.

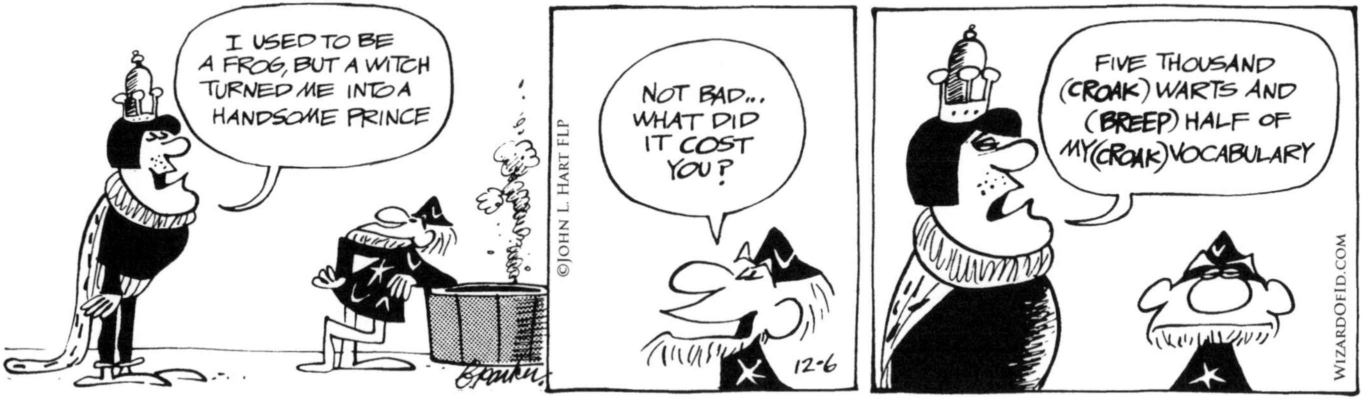

I USED TO BE A FROG, BUT A WITCH TURNED ME INTO A HANDSOME PRINCE
Parker.
©JOHN L. HART FLP
NOT BAD... WHAT DID IT COST YOU?
12-6
FIVE THOUSAND (CROAK) WARTS AND (BREEP) HALF OF MY (CROAK) VOCABULARY
WIZARDOFID.COM

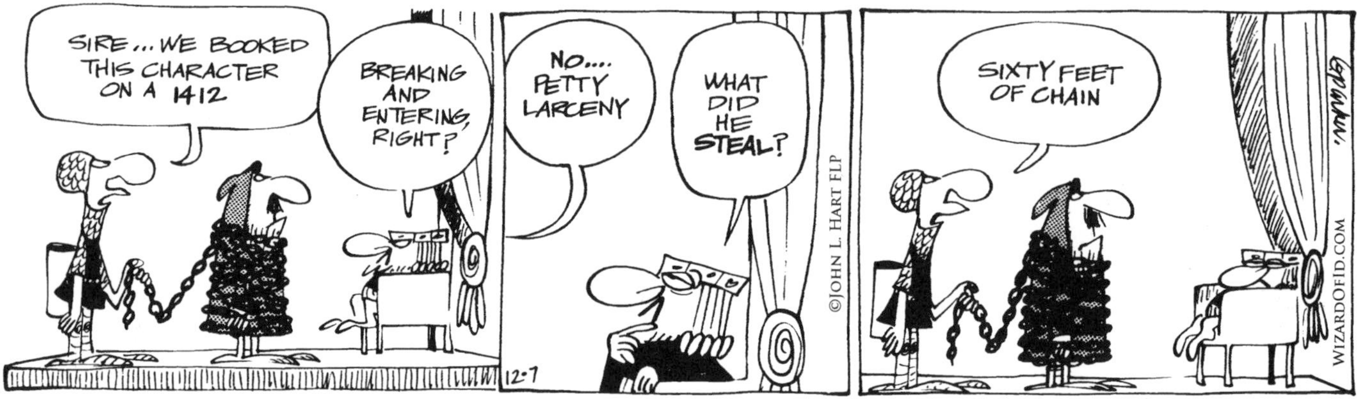
SIRE... WE BOOKED THIS CHARACTER ON A 1412
BREAKING AND ENTERING, RIGHT?
NO.... PETTY LARCENY
WHAT DID HE STEAL?
SIXTY FEET OF CHAIN
12-7
©JOHN L. HART FLP
WIZARDOFID.COM

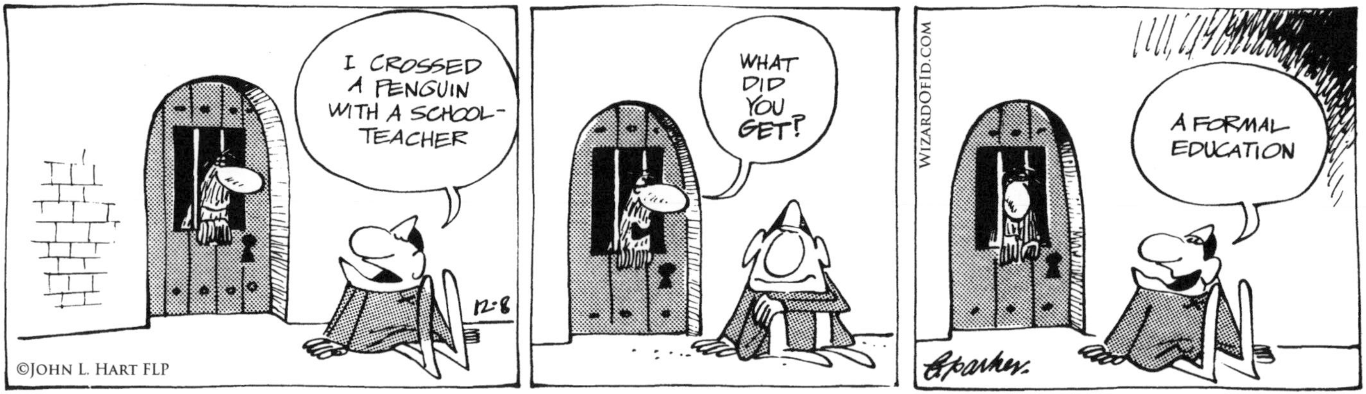
I CROSSED A PENGUIN WITH A SCHOOL-TEACHER
WHAT DID YOU GET?
A FORMAL EDUCATION
12-8
©JOHN L. HART FLP
WIZARDOFID.COM

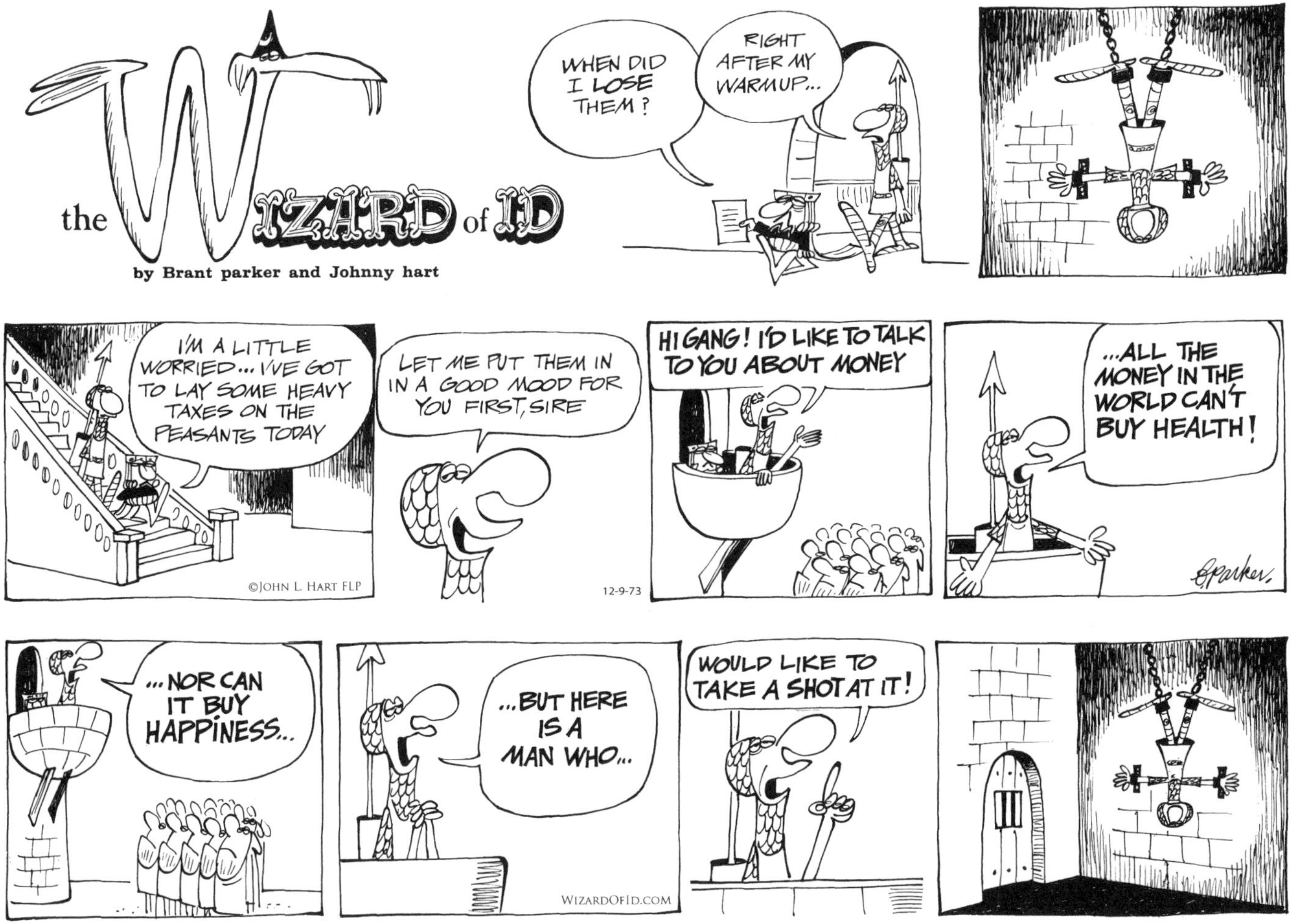
the WIZARD of ID
by Brant parker and Johnny hart
WHEN DID I LOSE THEM?
RIGHT AFTER MY WARMUP...
I'M A LITTLE WORRIED... I'VE GOT TO LAY SOME HEAVY TAXES ON THE PEASANTS TODAY
©JOHN L. HART FLP
LET ME PUT THEM IN IN A GOOD MOOD FOR YOU FIRST, SIRE
12-9-73
HI GANG! I'D LIKE TO TALK TO YOU ABOUT MONEY
...ALL THE MONEY IN THE WORLD CAN'T BUY HEALTH!
Bparker.
...NOR CAN IT BUY HAPPINESS...
...BUT HERE IS A MAN WHO...
WIZARDOFID.COM
WOULD LIKE TO TAKE A SHOT AT IT!

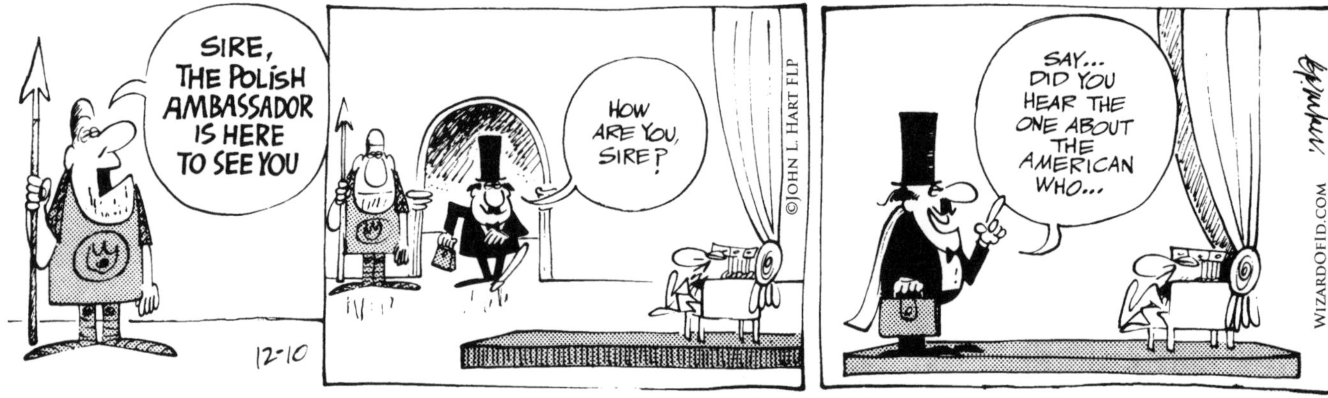
SIRE, THE POLISH AMBASSADOR IS HERE TO SEE YOU
12-10
HOW ARE YOU, SIRE?
©JOHN L. HART FLP
SAY... DID YOU HEAR THE ONE ABOUT THE AMERICAN WHO...
WIZARDOFID.COM

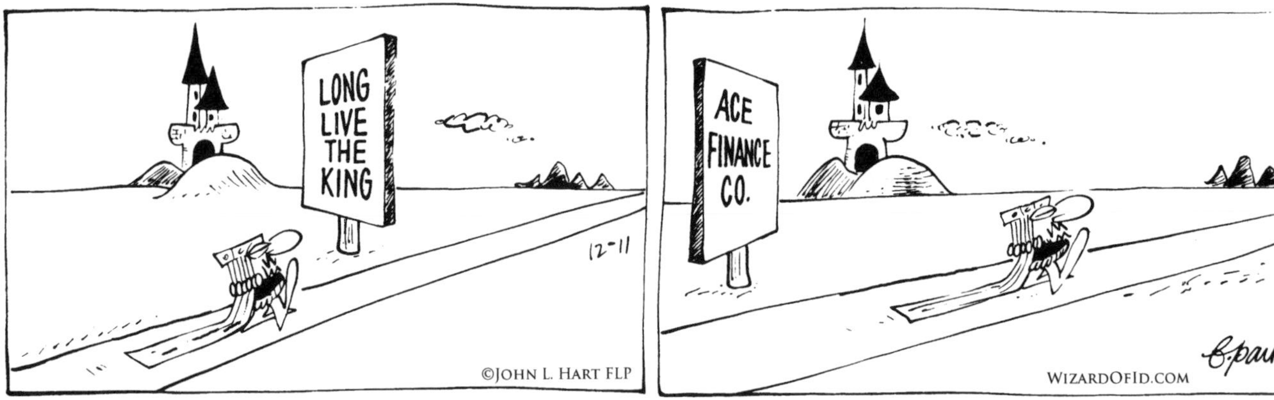
LONG LIVE THE KING
12-11
©JOHN L. HART FLP
ACE FINANCE CO.
WIZARDOFID.COM

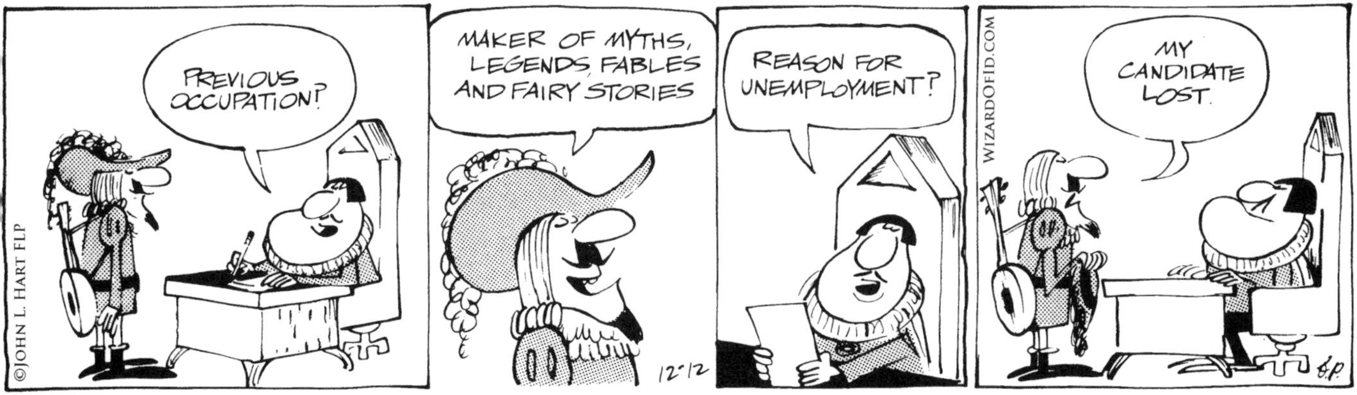
©JOHN L. HART FLP
PREVIOUS OCCUPATION?
MAKER OF MYTHS, LEGENDS, FABLES AND FAIRY STORIES
12-12
REASON FOR UNEMPLOYMENT?
WIZARDOFID.COM
MY CANDIDATE LOST.

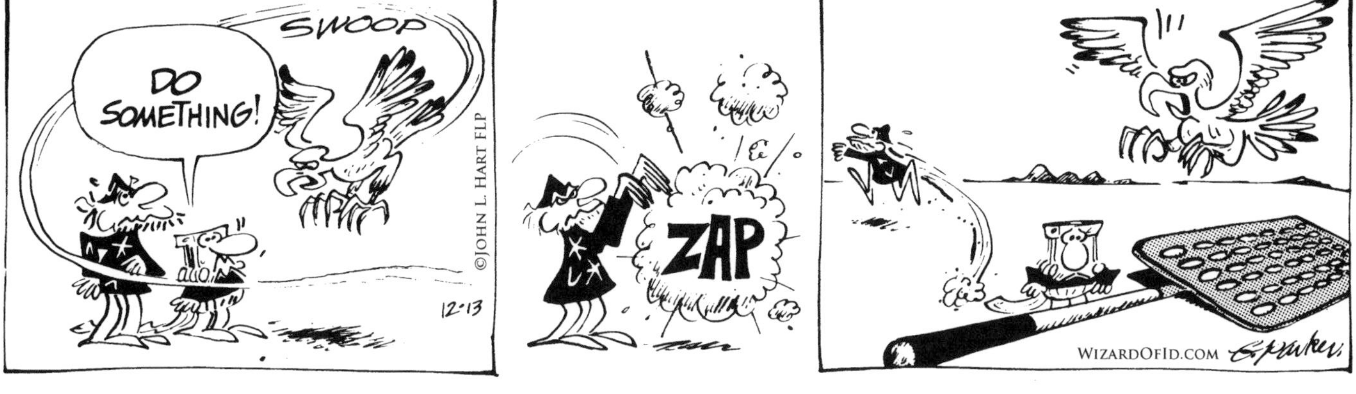
SWOOP
DO SOMETHING!
©JOHN L. HART FLP
12-13
ZAP
WIZARDOFID.COM

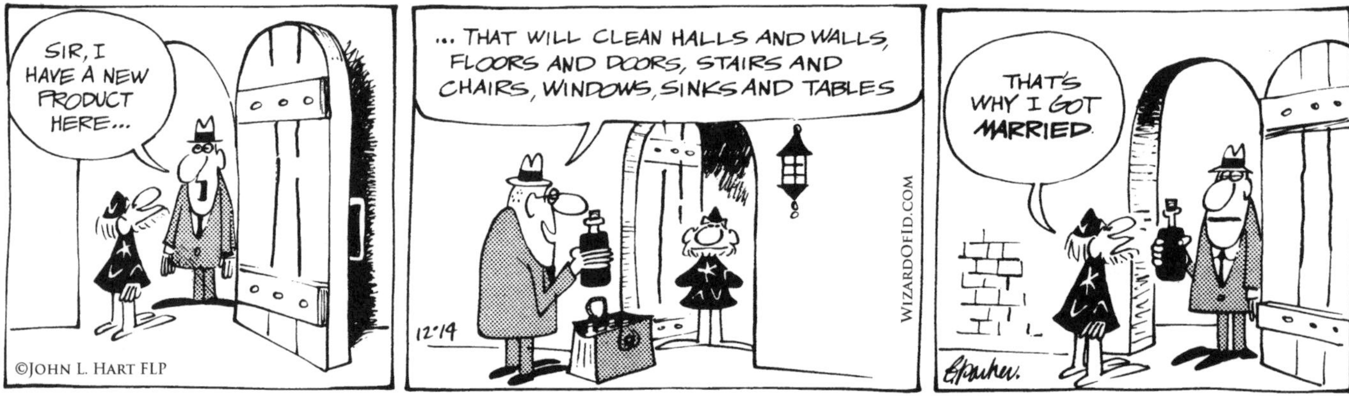
SIR, I HAVE A NEW PRODUCT HERE...
©JOHN L. HART FLP
... THAT WILL CLEAN HALLS AND WALLS, FLOORS AND DOORS, STAIRS AND CHAIRS, WINDOWS, SINKS AND TABLES
12-14
WIZARDOFID.COM
THAT'S WHY I GOT MARRIED.

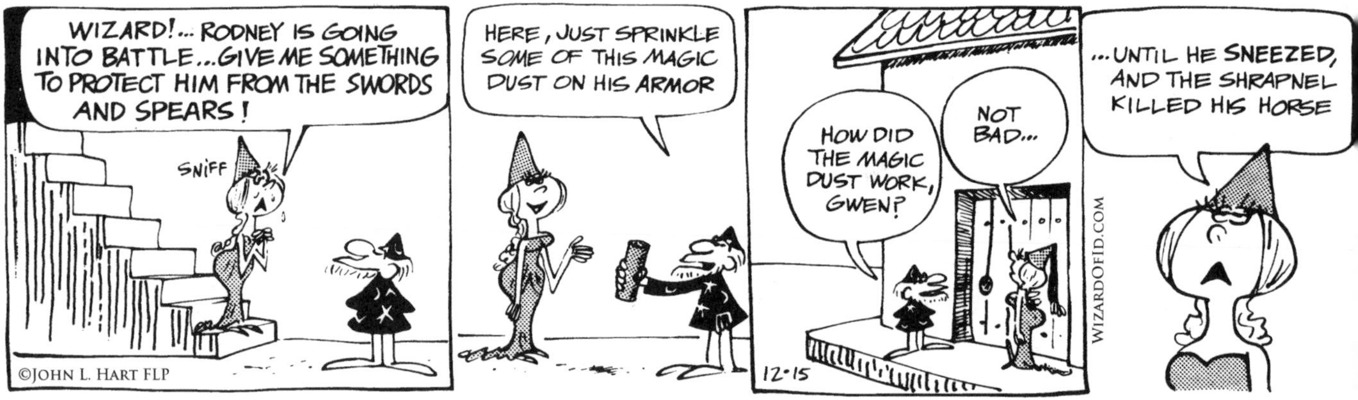
WIZARD!... RODNEY IS GOING INTO BATTLE...GIVE ME SOMETHING TO PROTECT HIM FROM THE SWORDS AND SPEARS!
SNIFF
©JOHN L. HART FLP
HERE, JUST SPRINKLE SOME OF THIS MAGIC DUST ON HIS ARMOR
HOW DID THE MAGIC DUST WORK, GWEN?
NOT BAD...
12-15
WIZARDOFID.COM
...UNTIL HE SNEEZED, AND THE SHRAPNEL KILLED HIS HORSE

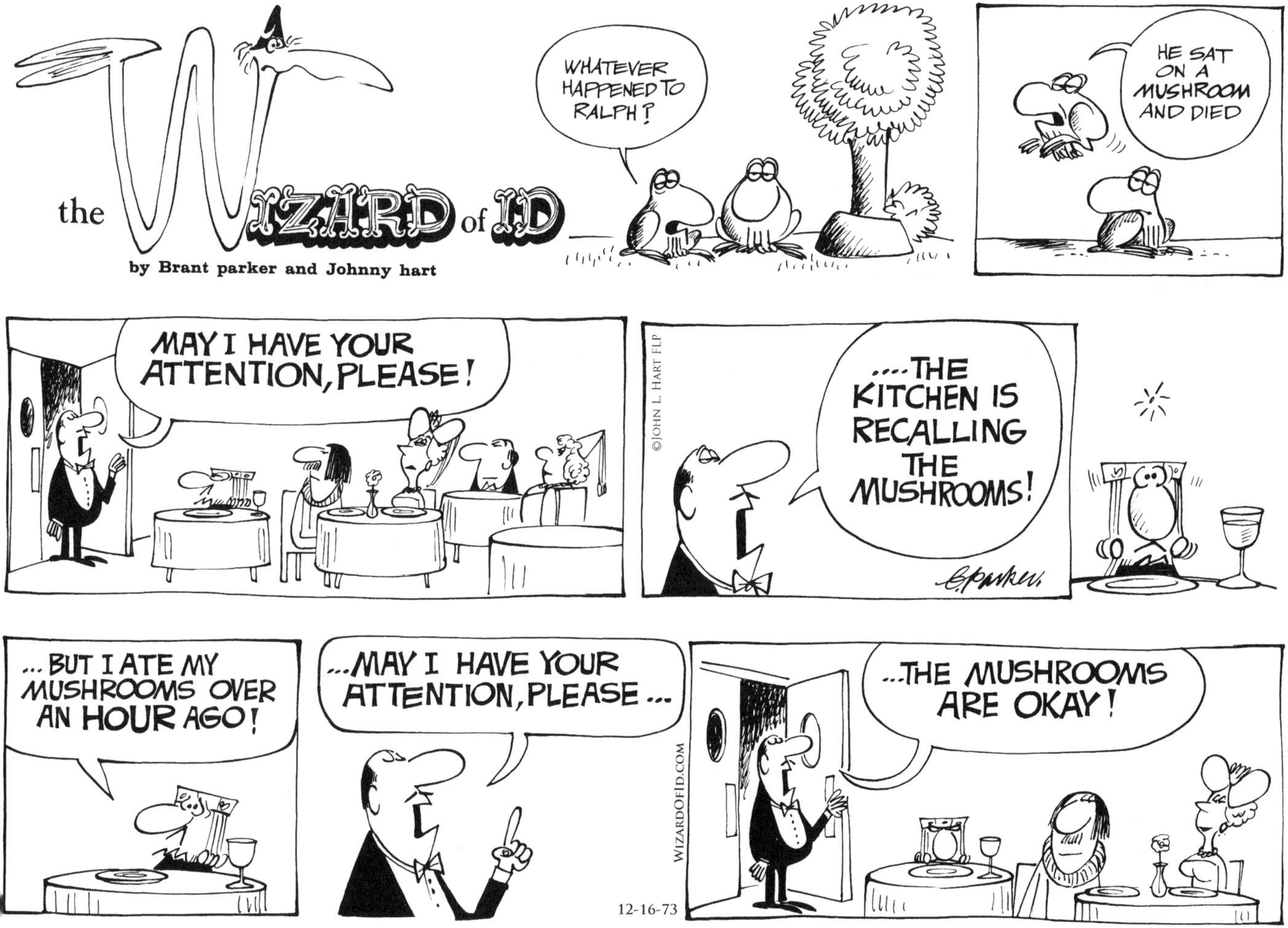
the WIZARD of ID
by Brant parker and Johnny hart
WHATEVER HAPPENED TO RALPH?
HE SAT ON A MUSHROOM AND DIED
MAY I HAVE YOUR ATTENTION, PLEASE!
©JOHN L. HART FLP
....THE KITCHEN IS RECALLING THE MUSHROOMS!
B.parker
...BUT I ATE MY MUSHROOMS OVER AN HOUR AGO!
...MAY I HAVE YOUR ATTENTION, PLEASE...
WIZARDOFID.COM
...THE MUSHROOMS ARE OKAY!
12-16-73

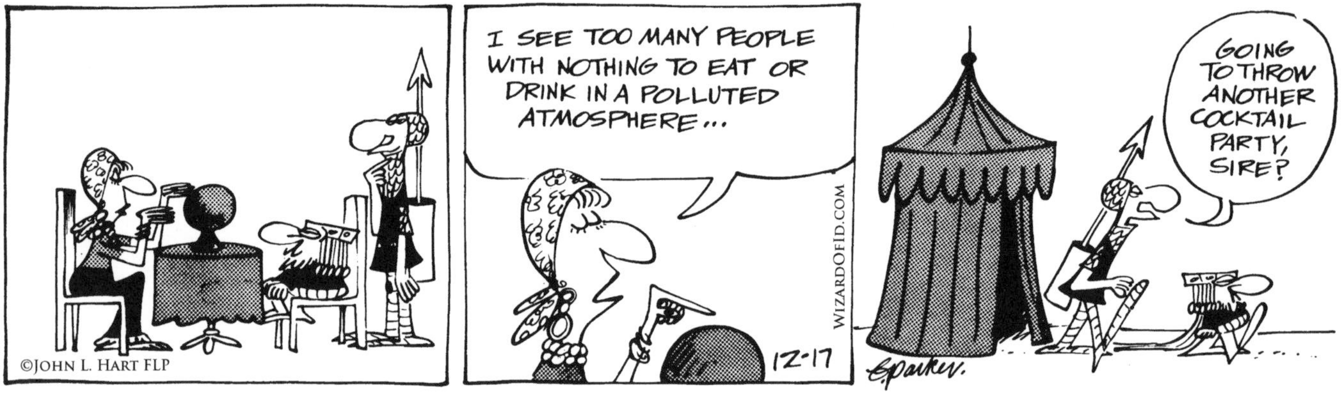
I SEE TOO MANY PEOPLE WITH NOTHING TO EAT OR DRINK IN A POLLUTED ATMOSPHERE...
GOING TO THROW ANOTHER COCKTAIL PARTY, SIRE?
©JOHN L. HART FLP
WIZARDOFID.COM
12-17
B.Parker.

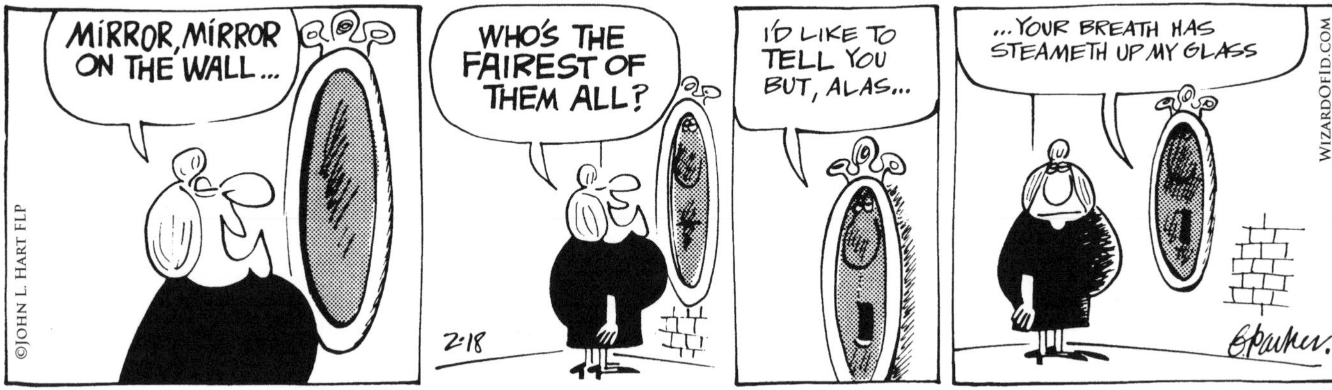
MIRROR, MIRROR ON THE WALL...
WHO'S THE FAIREST OF THEM ALL?
I'D LIKE TO TELL YOU BUT, ALAS...
...YOUR BREATH HAS STEAMETH UP MY GLASS
©JOHN L. HART FLP
WIZARDOFID.COM
2-18
B.Parker.

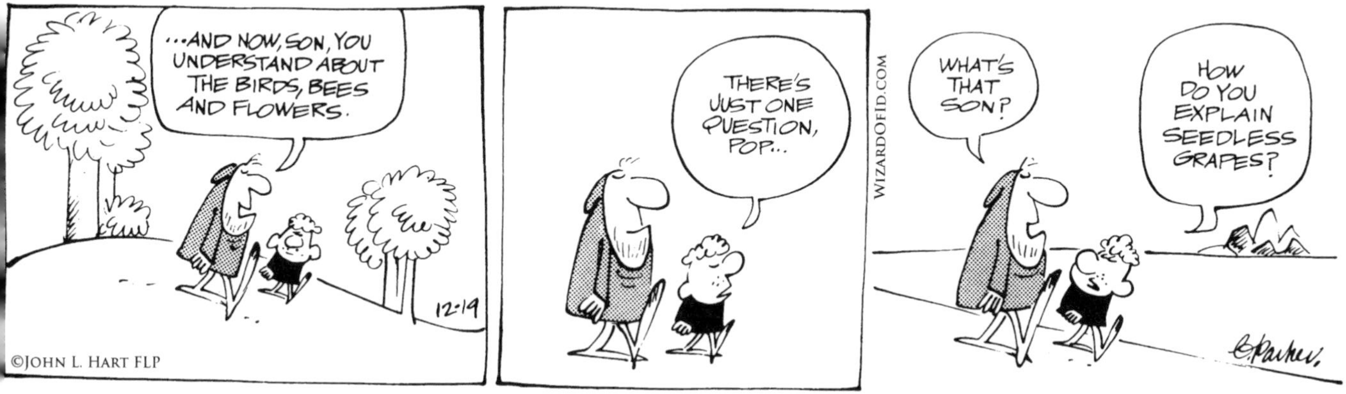
...AND NOW, SON, YOU UNDERSTAND ABOUT THE BIRDS, BEES AND FLOWERS.
12-19
©JOHN L. HART FLP
THERE'S JUST ONE QUESTION, POP...
WIZARDOFID.COM
WHAT'S THAT SON?
HOW DO YOU EXPLAIN SEEDLESS GRAPES?
B. Parker.

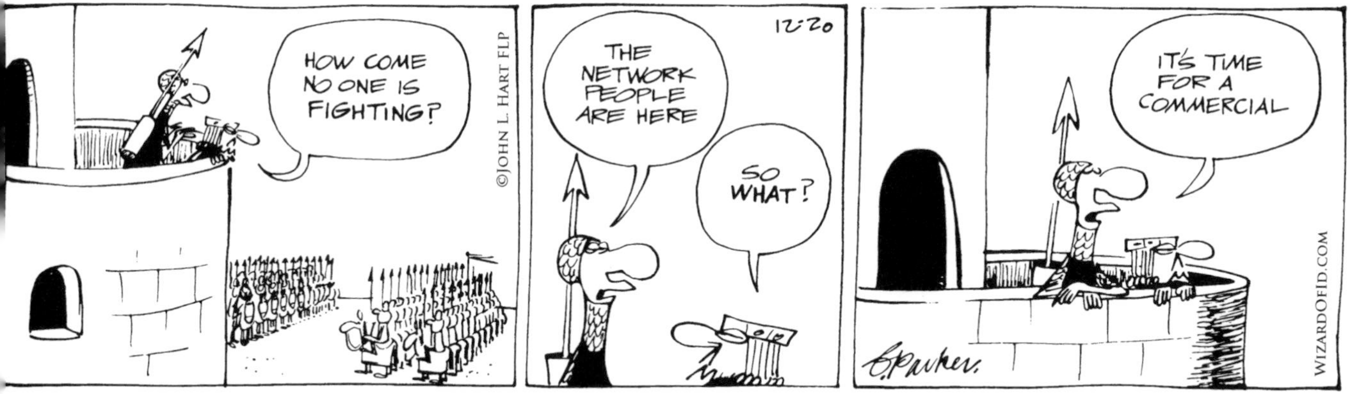
HOW COME NO ONE IS FIGHTING?
©JOHN L. HART FLP
12-20
THE NETWORK PEOPLE ARE HERE
SO WHAT?
IT'S TIME FOR A COMMERCIAL
B. Parker.
WIZARDOFID.COM

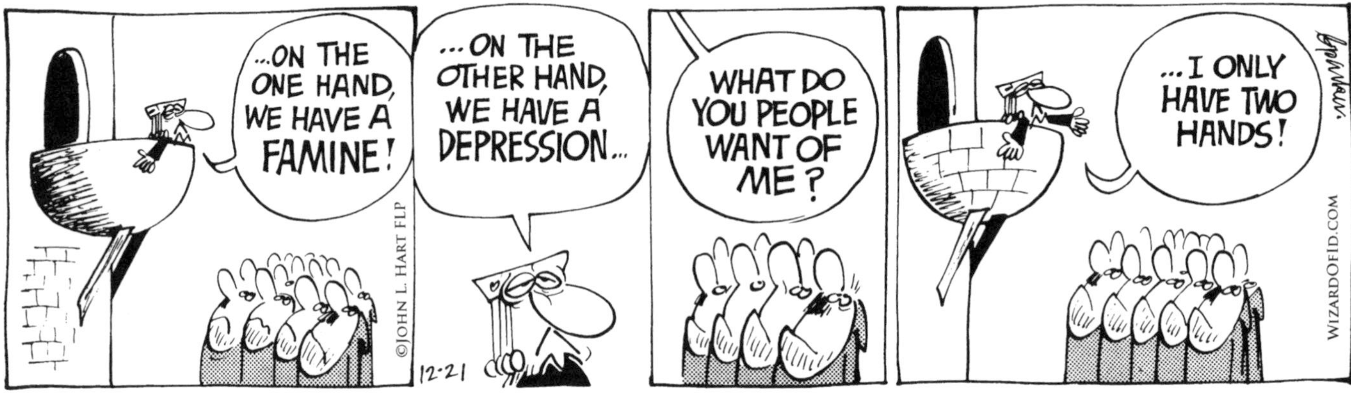

...ON THE ONE HAND, WE HAVE A FAMINE!
...ON THE OTHER HAND, WE HAVE A DEPRESSION...
WHAT DO YOU PEOPLE WANT OF ME?
...I ONLY HAVE TWO HANDS!
©JOHN L. HART FLP
12·21
WIZARDOFID.COM

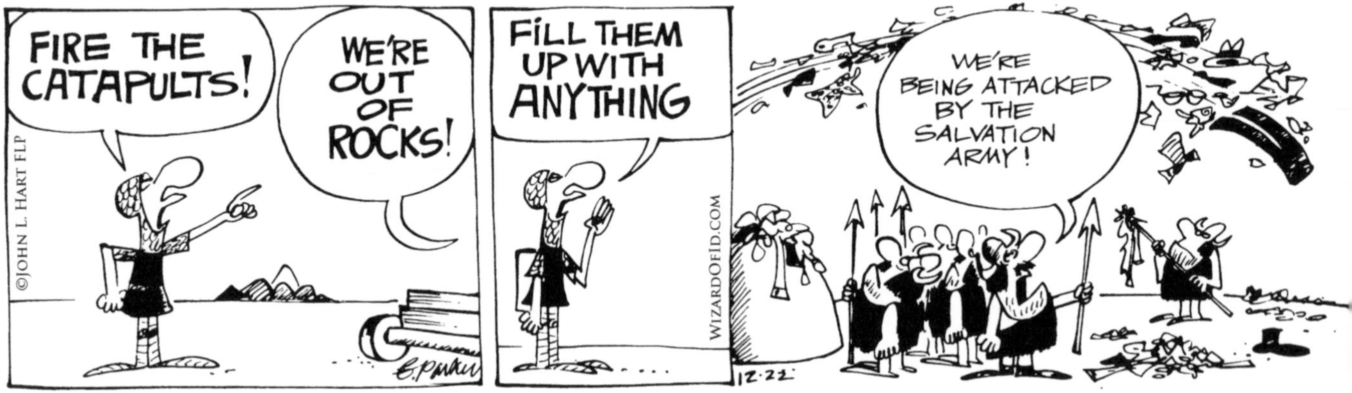

FIRE THE CATAPULTS!
WE'RE OUT OF ROCKS!
FILL THEM UP WITH ANYTHING
WE'RE BEING ATTACKED BY THE SALVATION ARMY!
©JOHN L. HART FLP
WIZARDOFID.COM
12·22

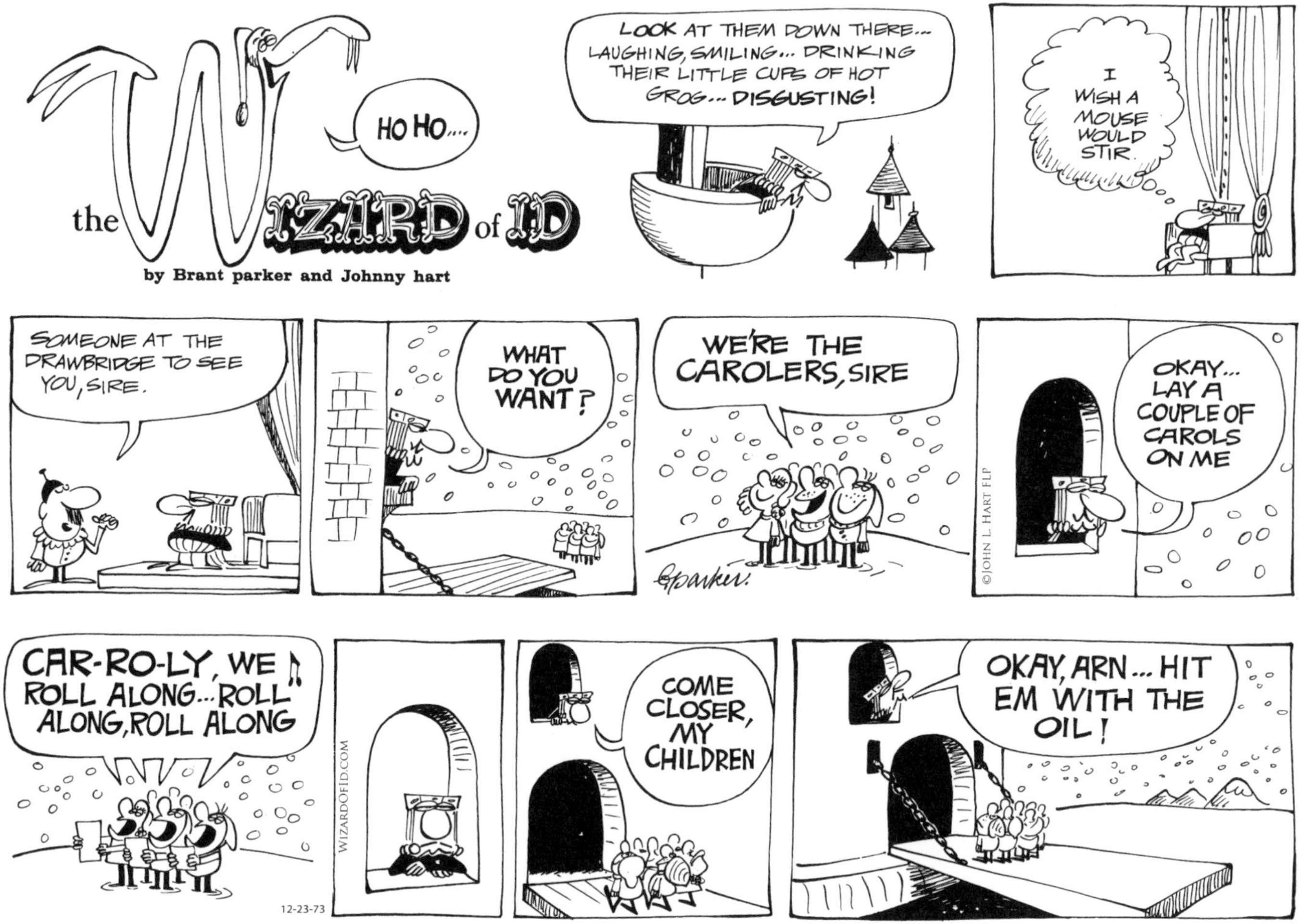
the Wizard of Id
by Brant parker and Johnny hart
HO HO....
LOOK AT THEM DOWN THERE... LAUGHING, SMILING... DRINKING THEIR LITTLE CUPS OF HOT GROG... DISGUSTING!
I WISH A MOUSE WOULD STIR.
SOMEONE AT THE DRAWBRIDGE TO SEE YOU, SIRE.
WHAT DO YOU WANT?
WE'RE THE CAROLERS, SIRE
parker
OKAY... LAY A COUPLE OF CAROLS ON ME
©JOHN L. HART FLP
CAR-RO-LY, WE ROLL ALONG... ROLL ALONG, ROLL ALONG
12-23-73
WIZARDOFID.COM
COME CLOSER, MY CHILDREN
OKAY, ARN... HIT EM WITH THE OIL!

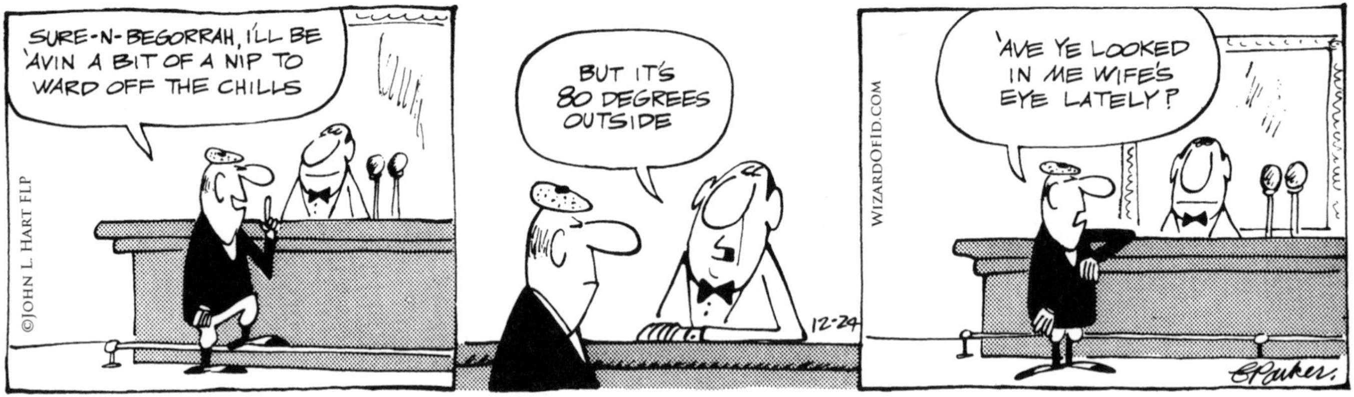
SURE-N-BEGORRAH, I'LL BE 'AVIN A BIT OF A NIP TO WARD OFF THE CHILLS
BUT IT'S 80 DEGREES OUTSIDE
'AVE YE LOOKED IN ME WIFE'S EYE LATELY?
©JOHN L. HART FLP
WIZARDOFID.COM
12-24
B. Parker.

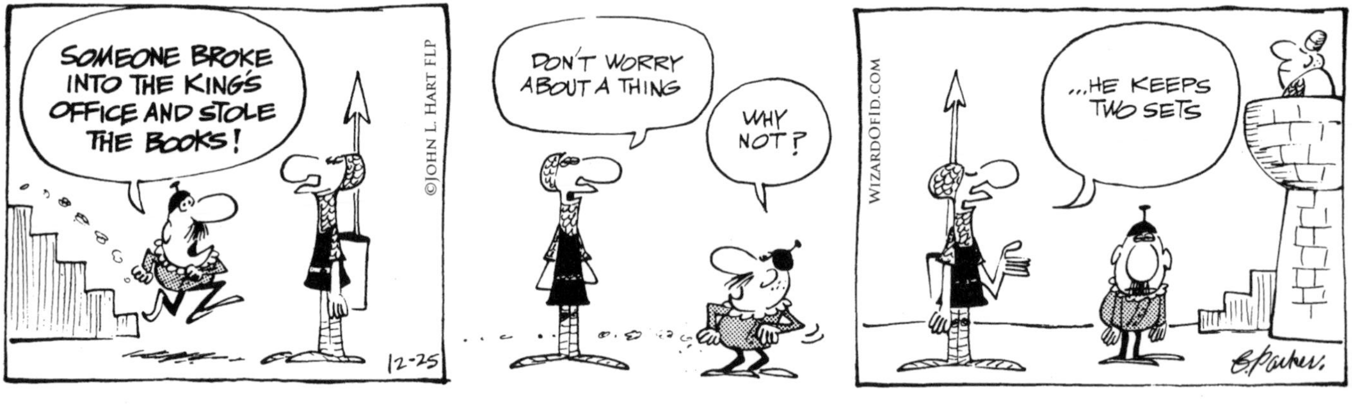
SOMEONE BROKE INTO THE KING'S OFFICE AND STOLE THE BOOKS!
DON'T WORRY ABOUT A THING
WHY NOT?
...HE KEEPS TWO SETS
©JOHN L. HART FLP
WIZARDOFID.COM
12-25
B. Parker.

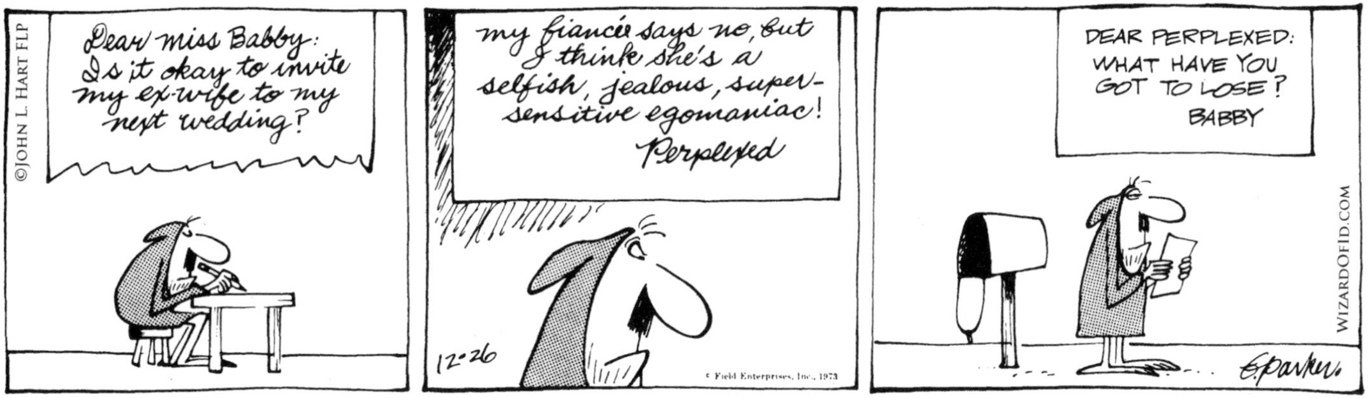
©JOHN L. HART FLP
Dear miss Babby:
Is it okay to invite my ex-wife to my next wedding?
my fiancée says no, but I think she's a selfish, jealous, super-sensitive egomaniac!
Perplexed
12-26
© Field Enterprises, Inc., 1973
DEAR PERPLEXED:
WHAT HAVE YOU GOT TO LOSE?
BABBY
WIZARDOFID.COM
B. Parker

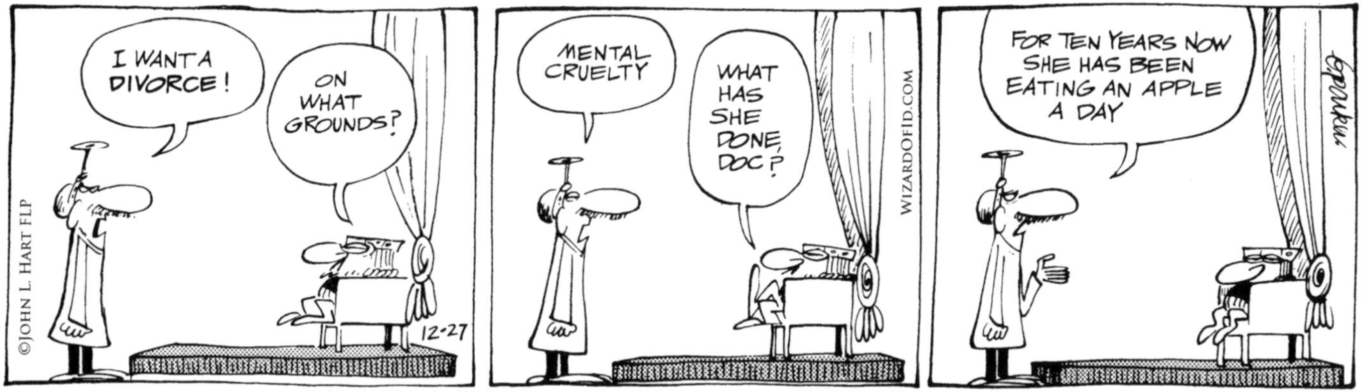
©JOHN L. HART FLP
I WANT A DIVORCE!
ON WHAT GROUNDS?
12-27
MENTAL CRUELTY
WHAT HAS SHE DONE, DOC?
WIZARDOFID.COM
FOR TEN YEARS NOW SHE HAS BEEN EATING AN APPLE A DAY
B. Parker

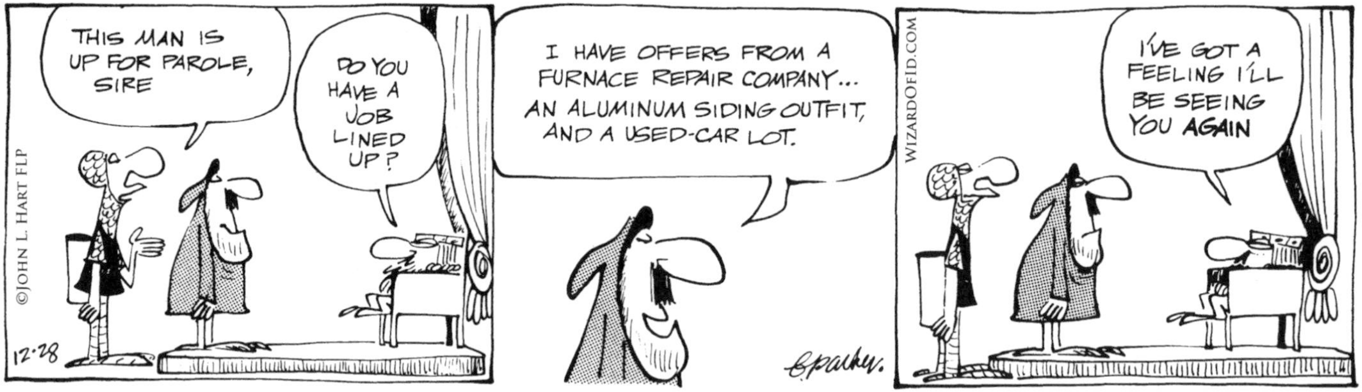
THIS MAN IS UP FOR PAROLE, SIRE
DO YOU HAVE A JOB LINED UP?
©JOHN L. HART FLP
12-28
I HAVE OFFERS FROM A FURNACE REPAIR COMPANY... AN ALUMINUM SIDING OUTFIT, AND A USED-CAR LOT.
WIZARDOFID.COM
I'VE GOT A FEELING I'LL BE SEEING YOU **AGAIN**

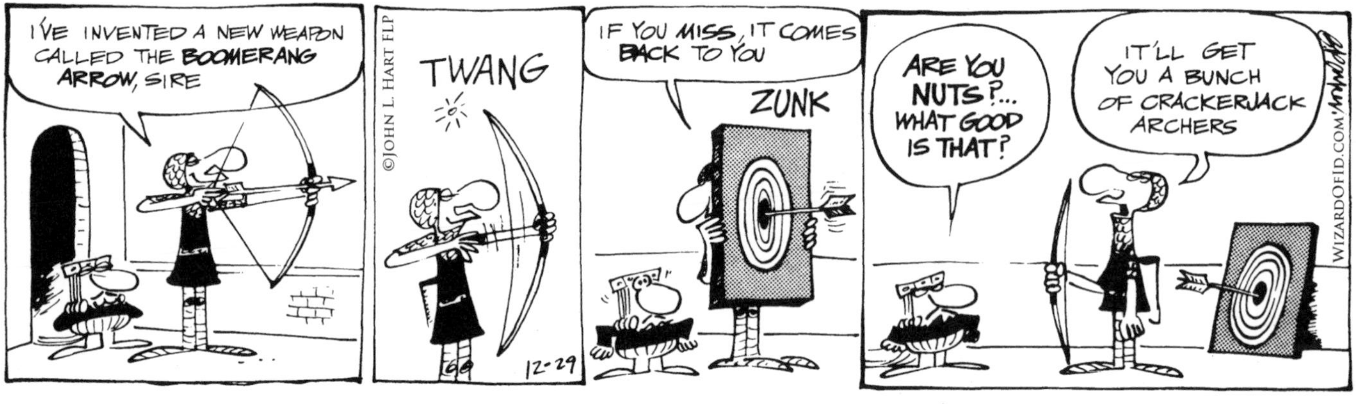
I'VE INVENTED A NEW WEAPON CALLED THE **BOOMERANG ARROW**, SIRE
©JOHN L. HART FLP
TWANG
12-29
IF YOU **MISS**, IT COMES **BACK** TO YOU
ZUNK
ARE YOU NUTS?... WHAT GOOD IS THAT?
IT'LL GET YOU A BUNCH OF CRACKERJACK ARCHERS
WIZARDOFID.COM

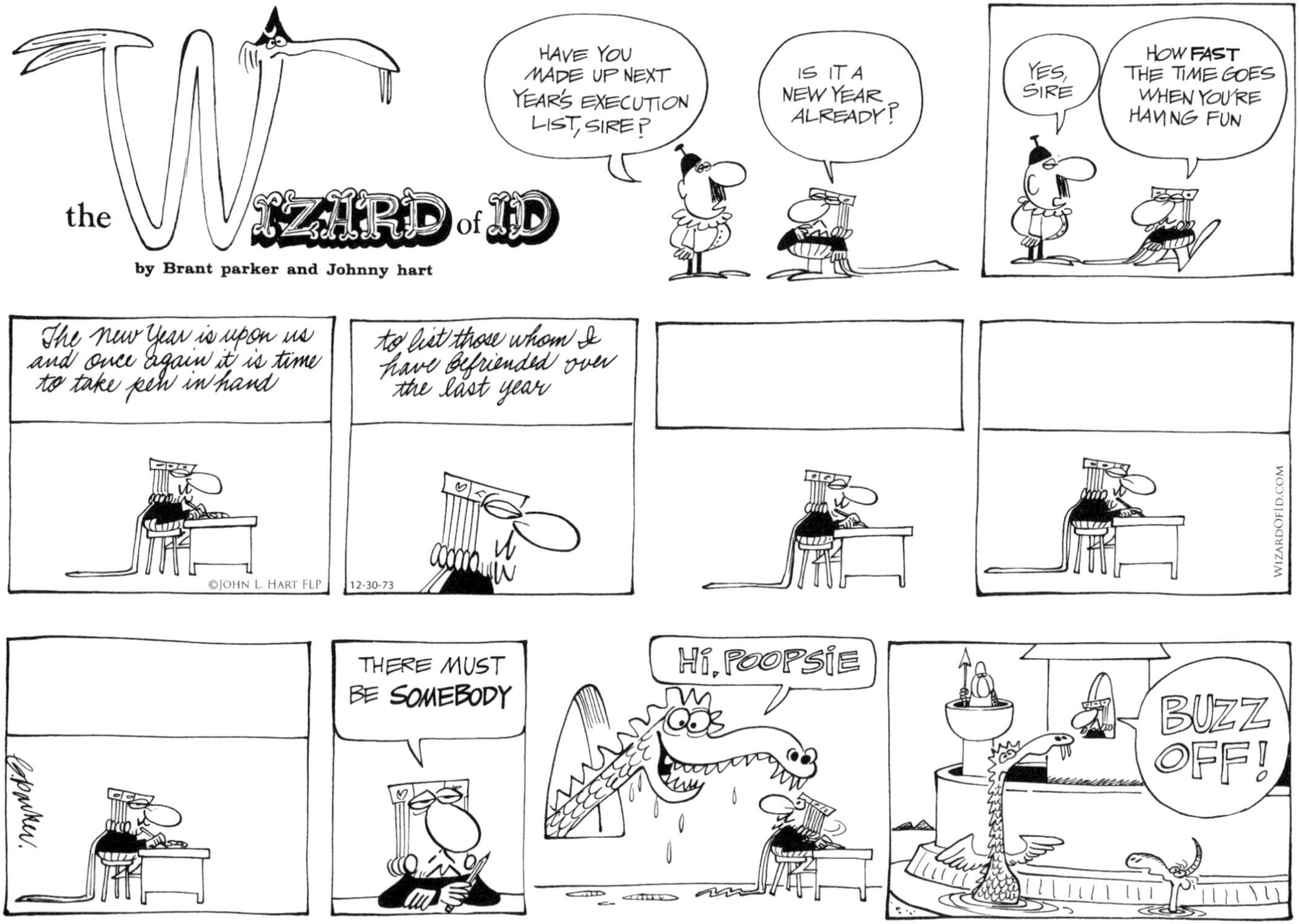

the WIZARD of ID
by Brant parker and Johnny hart
HAVE YOU MADE UP NEXT YEAR'S EXECUTION LIST, SIRE?
IS IT A NEW YEAR ALREADY?
YES, SIRE
HOW FAST THE TIME GOES WHEN YOU'RE HAVING FUN
The new Year is upon us and once again it is time to take pen in hand
©JOHN L. HART FLP
to list those whom I have befriended over the last year
12-30-73
WIZARDOFID.COM
parker.
THERE MUST BE SOMEBODY
HI, POOPSIE
BUZZ OFF!

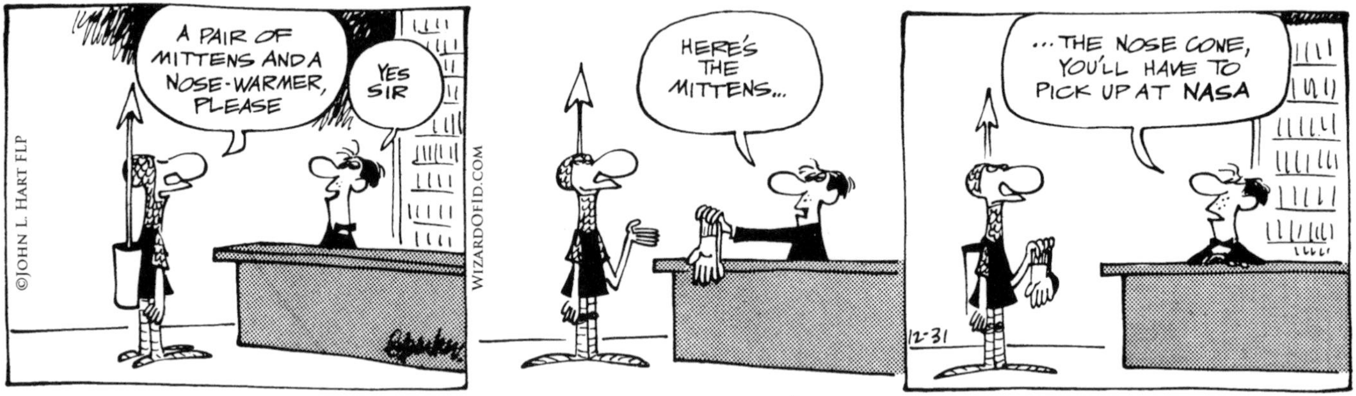
A PAIR OF MITTENS AND A NOSE-WARMER, PLEASE
YES SIR
HERE'S THE MITTENS...
...THE NOSE CONE, YOU'LL HAVE TO PICK UP AT NASA
©JOHN L. HART FLP
WIZARDOFID.COM
12-31

40 YEARS OF MIRTH, MERRIMENT AND MAYHEM
AVAILABLE NOW FROM ALL GOOD BOOKSTORES AND ONLINE RETAILERS

WWW.TITANBOOKS.COM

JOIN BEETLE AND THE CAMP SWAMPY GANG
IN THESE CLASSIC COLLECTIONS!

AVAILABLE NOW FROM ALL GOOD BOOKSTORES AND ONLINE RETAILERS

WWW.TITANBOOKS.COM

THE DAILIES COLLECTION

AVAILABLE NOW

WWW.TITANBOOKS.COM

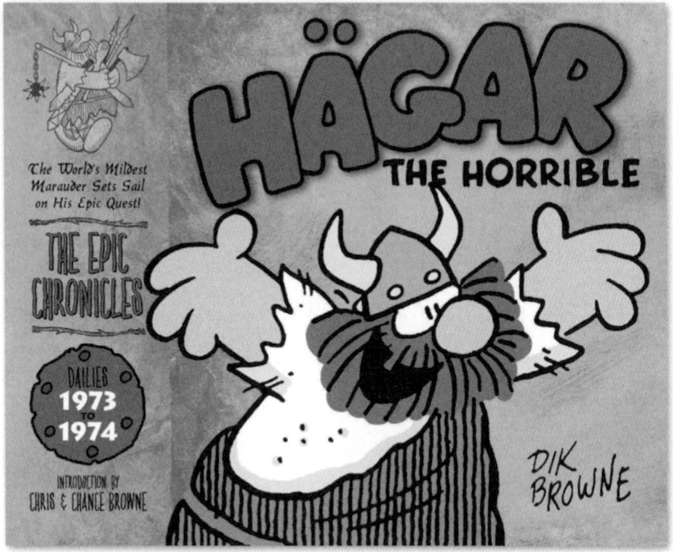
HÄGAR THE HORRIBLE
The World's Mildest Marauder Sets Sail on His Epic Quest!
THE EPIC CHRONICLES
DAILIES 1973 TO 1974
INTRODUCTION BY CHRIS & CHANCE BROWNE
DIK BROWNE

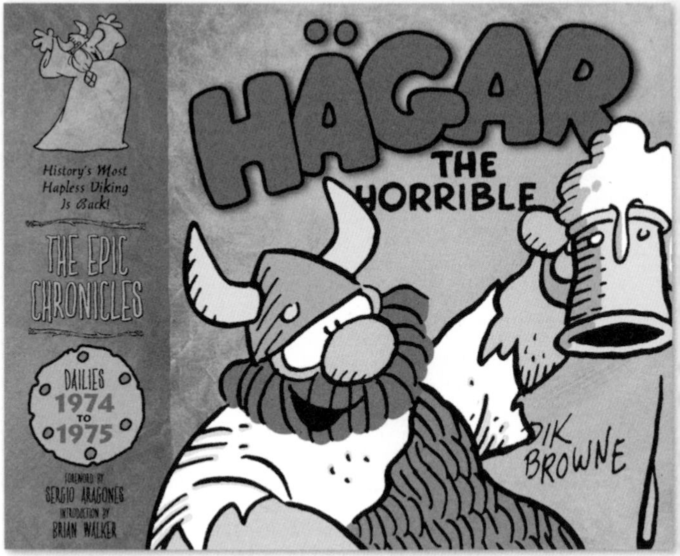
HÄGAR THE HORRIBLE
History's Most Hapless Viking Is Back!
THE EPIC CHRONICLES
DAILIES 1974 TO 1975
FOREWORD BY SERGIO ARAGONES
INTRODUCTION BY BRIAN WALKER
DIK BROWNE